System Design and Behavioral Intelligence

A Modern Guide to Technical Thinking and Behavioral Skills for Senior Engineering Roles

Shalini Goyal
Alok Sharan

<packt>

System Design and Behavioral Intelligence

This book was written by Shalini Goyal and Alok Sharan. Generative AI tools were used only to assist with ideation, phrasing, and diagram drafts, and all technical content and code were created, verified, and tested by the authors and Packt's editorial team. Packt does not accept AI-generated content that replaces expert authorship.

Portfolio Director: Gebin George
Relationship Lead: Sonia Chauhan
Project Manager: Prajakta Naik
Content Engineer: Afzal Shaikh
Technical Editors: Rahul Limbachiya, Sumant Jadhav
Indexer: Tejal Soni
Production Designer: Shantanu Zadage
Growth Lead: Nimisha Dua

First published: September 2026
Production reference: 3211026

Published by Packt Publishing Ltd.
Grosvenor House
11 St Paul's Square
Birmingham
B3 1RB, UK

ISBN 978-1-80834-405-3

packtpub.com

Forewords

I have spent most of my career in technology, from working on satellite and airborne communications as a defense contractor to leading engineering organizations inside Fortune 500 companies. Across all of those environments, one lesson has stayed remarkably consistent: technical expertise matters enormously, but technical expertise alone is never enough.

The further you progress in technology, the more the job changes.

Early in your career, you are often rewarded for knowing the answer. Later, you are expected to know which questions to ask. You have to make decisions when the information is incomplete, weigh competing priorities, explain trade-offs, influence people you do not manage, and make calls that may affect customers, revenue, risk, and entire teams.

That is why *System Design and Behavioral Intelligence* by **Shalini Goyal** and **Alok Sharan** feels so relevant right now.

The authors bring together two subjects that are too often treated separately. The first is system design: understanding how to build systems that can scale, survive failure, meet business requirements, and evolve over time. The second is behavioral intelligence: the ability to communicate your thinking, exercise judgment, work through ambiguity, influence others, navigate conflict, and demonstrate how you operate when the answer is not obvious.

In the real world, those skills are inseparable.

I have worked with incredibly talented engineers who could solve extremely difficult technical problems. But as their careers progressed, something changed. The question was no longer simply, "*Can you solve this?*" It became, "*Can you explain why this is the right problem to solve? Can you evaluate the trade-offs? Can you bring other people with you? Can you make the decision when every option has consequences?*"

Those are very different skills. And they are becoming even more important in the age of AI.

AI can help us write code, generate tests, explore solutions, analyze information, and move faster. I use AI myself, and I believe strongly in its potential. But faster execution does not eliminate the need for engineering judgment. It increases it.

Someone still has to determine what should be built. Someone has to understand the business problem behind the technical request. Someone has to decide what happens when performance, cost, security, reliability, and speed pull in different directions. Someone has to recognize when a technically elegant solution is the wrong solution for the organization.

That is the distinction this book makes so well. System design is not simply drawing architecture diagrams or memorizing patterns. It is learning to make decisions in context and understand the consequences of those decisions. The authors take readers from foundational concepts into real-world design problems, including distributed systems, messaging platforms, social systems, and agentic AI.

Then they tackle something equally important: how your judgment becomes visible to other people.

That matters because many capable technology professionals experience a frustrating gap between what they know and what others can see. They may have years of experience, yet struggle to explain their impact in an interview. They may be technically respected, yet have difficulty influencing a difficult stakeholder. They may know exactly what went wrong with a system, but have never learned how to communicate the decisions they would make differently.

Shalini and Alok give readers practical ways to close that gap. They address conflict, risk, stakeholder management, leadership, behavioral interviews, storytelling, seniority, and the ability to turn experience into evidence of judgment and impact.

That is why this is more than an interview-preparation book. It is a book about becoming the kind of technology professional people trust with larger problems.

Technology will continue to change. The tools will change. AI capabilities will change. Architectures will change. But our ability to think clearly, make good decisions, understand trade-offs, communicate those decisions, and lead other human beings through uncertainty will continue to matter.

Shalini Goyal and Alok Sharan have created a practical guide to developing both sides of that equation.

And that is exactly why this is a book technology professionals need now.

Stephanie Hills, Ph.D.

Executive & Technology Advisor

Former Fortune 500 Technology Executive

When I was asked to write this foreword, I wondered what makes this book different from others already written about system design. The answer became clear with every page: engineering success depends as much on human judgment as on technical knowledge.

A senior engineer is expected to make difficult choices, explain trade-offs clearly, handle disagreement, and earn the trust of others. These skills shape architecture reviews, production incidents, interviews, and everyday teamwork. Yet we rarely learn them together.

Shalini and Alok bring these two sides of engineering into one practical guide. The system design chapters explain the fundamentals through practical examples, including distributed systems and agentic AI. The behavioral chapters help you learn from their experiences and talk about them in a clear and honest way.

I appreciated the focus on reasoning. Throughout the book, you are asked to explain why you made each decision, what was learned, and what might be done differently next time. That habit is valuable in an interview, but it matters even more throughout a career.

This feels especially relevant as AI changes how software is built. Writing code may become faster, but deciding what to build and taking responsibility for the outcome will remain deeply human work.

I hope you read this book actively. Sketch your own designs before studying the examples. Question the assumptions. Write down the experiences that shaped you. The real value will come from connecting the ideas in these pages with your own work.

I believe this book will be useful whether you are preparing for your next engineering role or growing as a technical leader.

Raul Junco

ANDMORE

Contributors

About the authors

Shalini Goyal is Executive Director and Regional Head of Payments Technology for Regulatory Reporting at J.P. Morgan, with 20+ years of experience across Amazon, Publicis Sapient, Optum Health, and others. Her technical leadership has reached billions of customers through large-scale digital transformation, cloud adoption, and AI-driven initiatives.

A global public speaker and mentor, she frequently addresses conferences, podcasts, and YouTube audiences on AI, system design, and career growth. With a following of 130,000+ on LinkedIn and X, she makes complex technical concepts accessible to everyone from engineers to CTOs and CEOs navigating change in tech. A professor at Zigurat University and a TechWomen100 finalist, she is dedicated to helping engineers thrive in an AI-driven future.

Alok Sharan is a technology expert who has spent two decades building software architectures that help enterprises achieve their business objectives through innovative design, development, and engineering. Throughout his career, he has worked across a broad range of technologies, specializing in digital transformation, guiding organizations through on-premises-to-AWS cloud migrations, and delivering robust Identity and Access Management solutions.

Alok is known for his ability to create purpose-built solutions, underpinned by strong problem-solving skills and deep architectural expertise. His experience is further demonstrated by a number of industry-recognized certifications, including TOGAF, AWS Solutions Architect - Professional, and AWS Machine Learning Specialty.

Acknowledgements

This book would not exist without the many remarkable people who carried us through it.

First and foremost, to our children, Samarth and Arnav. Thank you for your patience, your understanding, and a love that never once wavered. So much of this book took shape in long evenings, late nights, and weekends that were rightfully yours, and every one of those hours was your gift to us. We could not have reached the final page without you by our side.

To our dear friend Kajla Piplani (Director, Financial Services), our heartfelt thanks. Your wisdom, candid feedback, and ideas shaped many of the behavioral frameworks, bringing depth and life to ideas we could only have sketched ourselves.

Mayank Kedia (Senior Principal Engineering Manager, Stellantis) and Shri Krishna (Associate Director, Deloitte India), we owe you a special debt. As early reviewers, readers, and contributors, you gave us the honest critiques we needed to hear, and you gave them generously, sharing your time and hard-won expertise in the in-depth conversations woven into these pages.

To Sohin Keshwani (Engineering Manager, Google), thank you for generously sharing your journey and insights on preparing for system design and behavioral interviews at a Big Tech company, such as Google. Your experience has added a valuable and personal perspective to this book.

To Apratim Gupta (Software Architect) and Kartikey Singh (Technical Architect, Victoria's Secret & Co), thank you for reading early, thinking deeply, and offering suggestions we returned to again and again. Your insight left its mark on this book.

And finally, to everyone who lifted this journey in ways large and small, the mentors, colleagues, fellow engineers, and readers who believed we could take on this challenge: this book carries a piece of each of you. It is as much yours as it is ours.

—Shalini Goyal and Alok Sharan

About the reviewers

Manjot Singh is a software engineer based in the San Francisco Bay Area with nearly a decade of experience building large-scale distributed systems, AI-powered products, and cloud infrastructure. He holds a Master's degree in Computer Science and is an AWS Certified Solutions Architect. Throughout his career, he has worked at companies including Meta, Apple, UnitedHealth Group, and Walmart, where he has built products across generative AI, platform engineering, developer tooling, and data infrastructure. He invests significant time in mastering modern AI systems, agentic workflows, and production-grade machine learning with the goal of building impactful AI companies in the future.

Yaseen Mohammad is a Senior Software Engineer with over seven years of experience designing large-scale distributed systems, AI/ML infrastructure, backend platforms, cloud infrastructure, and full-stack applications. He works on AI/ML infrastructure, including embedding platforms, vector processing at scale, retrieval systems, feature-serving pipelines, LLM platform components, evaluation, and observability. His expertise also includes system design, scalability, reliability, performance engineering, event-driven architectures, APIs, microservices, data-intensive systems, and production software development, with a focus on scalable and resilient systems. The views expressed are his own and do not represent any current or former employer.

Table of Contents

Chapter 15: Behind the Big Tech Bar: Core Values and Leadership Principles 417

Chapter 16: Demonstration to Evaluation of Behavioral Intelligence 437

Preface

Modern engineering demands more than knowing how individual technologies work. It requires the ability to design systems that scale, reason through architectural trade-offs, and communicate decisions with clarity. *System Design and Behavioral Intelligence* brings those skills together, building a practical foundation in system design while showing how strong technical thinking translates into real-world problem solving.

The journey begins with the fundamentals of system design and distributed systems, from core algorithms, patterns, building blocks, security, and observability to a structured method for approaching design problems. You will then put these concepts into practice by designing systems inspired by Slack, distributed key-value stores, real-time bidding platforms, Instagram, and agentic AI for investment research.

But technical knowledge tells only part of the story. The later chapters turn to behavioral intelligence—how your experiences, decisions, values, and actions reveal the way you work. You will learn to turn experience into meaningful signals, build a story bank, understand leadership principles and core values, and demonstrate behavioral intelligence effectively. Together, these two dimensions help you become not just a better system designer, but a more thoughtful and effective technology professional.

Who this book is for

This book is for software engineers, backend developers, senior developers, solution architects, engineering managers, executives, and computer science students preparing for technical interviews. It is also valuable for professionals targeting senior engineering roles at product companies and MAANG organizations.

What this book covers

Chapter 1, The Art and Science of System Design, lays the foundation for understanding system design—not just as an interview topic, but as a critical skill for building scalable, reliable systems in the real world.

Chapter 2, Concepts Refresher: Knowledge Bites, covers the essential concepts that appear in almost every system design interview you will face. These concepts will later lead toward more complex building blocks to make system designs even more robust.

Chapter 3, Distributed Systems: Algorithms, Techniques, and Patterns, moves from foundational concepts into the algorithms and patterns that hold distributed systems together, including Raft, circuit breakers, and more. It presents a collection of design techniques, architectural patterns, and supporting algorithms that are used extensively in the industry.

Chapter 4, The Building Blocks of System Design, moves from algorithms into the architectural building blocks that hold large-scale systems together: how data is stored, replicated, and retrieved across distributed environments.

Chapter 5, Cross-Cutting Concerns: Security and Observability, talks about security and observability, the two cross-cutting concerns that span everything that we have learned so far. We will take a deep dive to understand why security and observability should be planned from the beginning rather than at a later stage.

Chapter 6, Elements and the Method to Design a System, provides a walkthrough of the elements of a real system design interview, from gathering requirements all the way through to managing your time under pressure.

Chapter 7, Designing a Slack-like Messaging System, shares a full end-to-end design of a distributed messaging system, so you can see exactly how each element plays out in a real problem.

Chapter 8, Designing a Distributed Key-Value Datastore, helps you design a distributed key-value datastore, one of the most fundamental and frequently tested system design challenges you will face.

Chapter 9, Designing a Real-Time Bidding (RTB) System for Advertising, shifts into a completely different domain: designing a real-time bidding system for advertising, where millisecond latency and massive throughput are not nice-to-haves but hard requirements.

Chapter 10, Designing an Instagram-like Social Media System, walks you through the systematic approach to designing a social media platform like Instagram. By the end of this chapter, you should be able to scope the social media problem correctly.

Chapter 11, Designing an Agentic AI System for Investment Research, designs a system where the content is produced by machines reasoning on your behalf. This chapter forces a new set of design questions: how do agents coordinate, how do we control their cost, and how do we trust an output no human wrote?

Chapter 12, The Signal Beneath the Stories: What Behavioral Intelligence Is, provides a deep understanding of what behavioral intelligence is, the seven dimensions behavioral intelligence is built on, and how the bar rises with seniority.

Chapter 13, The Power of Behavioral Intelligence at Work, moves from definition to practice, into the workplace situations where behavioral intelligence is built and shown long before any interview, talking about conflict, risk, performance, productivity, and influence without authority.

Chapter 14, From Experience to Signal: Frameworks and the Story Bank, turns from the work itself to the interview room: the answer frameworks, from STAR and its Reflection extension to CAR and SOAR, and the story bank that turns your experience into ready evidence.

Chapter 15, Behind the Big Tech Bar: Core Values and Leadership Principles, goes inside Big Tech behavioral interviews, showing how companies like Meta, Amazon, Apple, Netflix, and Google anchor their questions to their values and principles, the questions they actually ask, and how to craft responses that meet each bar.

Chapter 16, Demonstration to Evaluation of Behavioral Intelligence, teaches how to turn every interview, whatever its outcome, into career capital through different strategies and how to sit on the other side of the table once the right opportunity presents itself.

Chapter 17, Appendix, contains solutions to the quizzes from *Part 1* of the book. It also includes interview scenarios to help you prepare for your next interview.

To get the most out of this book

This book is organized into two parts, and you will get the most from it by treating them as two halves of one skill rather than two separate subjects. *Part 1* develops your ability to design systems and reason through architectural trade-offs. *Part 2* develops your ability to communicate that thinking and show the judgment behind it. You can read straight through, or begin with the part that matches your immediate goal and come back to the other, but we encourage you to work through both. The two dimensions reinforce each other, and the engineers who stand out are fluent in both.

We assume you are comfortable with the basics of software development and a working sense of how applications are built and run. You do not need prior system design experience or any particular technology stack. Read with a notebook beside you. In *Part 1*, pause at each design problem and sketch your own solution before you read ours. In *Part 2*, take the self-assessment, build your story bank as you go, and answer the practice questions at the end of each chapter out loud rather than only in your head. This material rewards active practice far more than passive reading.

One practical note is that this book is printed in black and white, but several of the diagrams rely on color to make their point. Where a figure uses color to carry meaning, download the color images PDF described under Download the color images so that you can see it as intended.

Download the color images

We also provide a PDF file that has color images of the screenshots/diagrams used in this book. You can download it here: `https://packt.link/gbp/9781808344053`.

Conventions used

There are a number of text conventions used throughout this book.

`CodeInText`: Indicates code words in text, database table names, folder names, filenames, file extensions, pathnames, dummy URLs, user input, and Twitter handles. For example: "A `get(key)` method for reading and `put<key, value>` method for writing will do the trick."

A block of code or structured data, such as estimates, is presented as follows:

```
{
  "time": "2026-05-14T10:11:42.318Z",
  "level": "INFO",
  "service": "order-service",
  "event": "order_placed",
  "user_id": UID2217,
  "order_id": 11002345,
  "order_value_gbp": 35.10,
  "latency_ms": 156,
  "trace_id": "4bf92f3577b34da6a3ce929d0e0e4736"
  }
```

Bold: Indicates a new term, an important word, or words that you see on the screen. For instance, words in menus or dialog boxes appear in the text like this. For example: "When two or more distinct messages are processed by a hash function but produce the same hash code, it is known as a **hash collision** (or hash clash)."

> **Note**
>
> Warnings or important notes appear like this.

> **Tip**
>
> Tips and tricks appear like this.

Get in touch

Feedback from our readers is always welcome.

General feedback: If you have questions about any aspect of this book or have any general feedback, please email us at `customercare@packt.com` and mention the book's title in the subject of your message.

Errata: Although we have taken every care to ensure the accuracy of our content, mistakes do happen. If you have found a mistake in this book, we would be grateful if you reported this to us. Please visit `http://www.packt.com/submit-errata`, click **Submit Errata**, and fill in the form.

Piracy: If you come across any illegal copies of our works in any form on the internet, we would be grateful if you would provide us with the location address or website name. Please contact us at `copyright@packt.com` with a link to the material.

If you are interested in becoming an author: If there is a topic that you have expertise in and you are interested in either writing or contributing to a book, please visit `http://authors.packt.com/`.

Share your thoughts

Once you've read *System Design and Behavioral Intelligence*, we'd love to hear your thoughts! Scan the QR code below to go straight to the Amazon review page for this book and share your feedback.

`https://packt.link/r/1808344057`

Your review is important to us and the tech community and will help us make sure we're delivering excellent quality content.

Free benefits with your book

This book comes with free benefits to support your learning. Activate them now for instant access (see the "How to unlock" section for instructions).

Here's a quick overview of what you can instantly unlock with your purchase:

How to unlock

Scan the QR code (or go to `packtpub.com/unlock`). Search for this book by name, confirm the edition, and then follow the steps on the page.

UNLOCK NOW

Note: Keep your invoice handy. Purchases made directly from Packt don't require one.

Part 1

System Design

Designing great systems is not about memorizing architectures or drawing boxes and arrows. It is about understanding the fundamentals, asking the right questions, evaluating trade-offs, and making sound decisions as requirements evolve. This part builds that foundation, beginning with the core concepts, algorithms, patterns, and building blocks behind modern distributed systems. It then brings security, observability, and a structured system design methodology into the picture. With that groundwork in place, you will put it to work on a series of real-world case studies, each chosen to stress a different set of challenges: a distributed messaging system in the style of Slack, a distributed key-value datastore, a real-time bidding system for advertising, an Instagram-like social media platform, and an agentic AI system for investment research. Together, they move from classic distributed systems problems to the newer questions raised by AI-driven architectures, leaving you ready to reason through design problems you would love to solve.

This part of the book includes the following chapters:

- *Chapter 9, Designing a Real-Time Bidding (RTB) System for Advertising*
- *Chapter 10, Designing an Instagram-like Social Media System*
- *Chapter 11, Designing an Agentic AI System for Investment Research*

1

The Art and Science of System Design

> *"There are two ways of constructing a software design: one way is to make it so simple that there are obviously no deficiencies, and the other way is to make it so complicated that there are no obvious deficiencies."*
>
> *—C.A.R. (Tony) Hoare, 1980 ACM Turing Award lecture, "The Emperor's Old Clothes"*

In January 2026, Dario Amodei, the CEO of Anthropic, the company behind Claude, made a prediction at the World Economic Forum in Davos that rattled the tech industry. He said AI models could handle *"most, maybe all"* of what software engineers do within six to twelve months.

But buried inside that same statement was something far more revealing than the headline. Describing how his own engineers already work, he said: "*I don't write any code anymore. I just let the model write the code. I edit it. I do the things around it.*"

That last phrase deserves your full attention. **"*The things around it*"** is not an afterthought. It is the real job that matters even more today. It is deciding what needs to be built and why. It is choosing which database fits the access pattern. It is defining how two services will communicate when one of them is slow, or down, or returning nonsense. In other words, it is system design. The CEO of one of the most advanced AI companies in the world was describing a present where **system design** is one of the most sought-after skills that remains entirely human-dominated. The first part of the book is about building that skill.

Every system you admire today handles millions of users without falling over. It recovers from failures nobody notices. It scales up for a flash sale and back down when the traffic disappears.

None of that was true on day one. What you're looking at started as rough boxes and lines on a whiteboard, the same as everything else. The sophistication came later, one hard lesson at a time.

If a system design interview is on your horizon, you'll find that the concepts and structured thinking here will help you walk into that conversation with confidence. But what you build in this book outlasts any single interview. System design is an engineering discipline, and the judgment you develop here is the judgment you'll carry into every architecture decision for the rest of your career.

This part of the book is written for people who want to get better at making those calls. Not by memorizing patterns from a cheat sheet, but by building genuine understanding of how systems behave under immense pressure, how they grow over time, and where they tend to break.

We'll start by grounding ourselves in the basics—what system design actually is, why it matters now more than ever, and the architecture patterns that you'll see used again and again throughout this book.

In a nutshell, we will be covering the following topics in this chapter:

- What is system design, really?
- Why system design matters in the age of AI
- Distributed system fundamentals
- Common architecture patterns
- From real-world challenges to interviews
- Typical domains in system design
- System design interview evaluation criteria

So, what exactly is this skill that Amodei is pointing at? Let's define it properly.

> **Note**
>
> **Download the code bundle and the PDF version of this book**
>
> Your purchase includes a DRM-free PDF copy of this book, the code bundle, and a range of exclusive benefits. To unlock everything, follow the *Free benefits with your book* section in the *Preface*.

What is system design, really?

At its core, system design is about engineering decisions in context—not a neat diagram, but a trail of decisions and trade-offs. Which database do we pick? Do we split this into two services or keep it as one? What happens when this component goes down at 2 AM and nobody's awake? These aren't theoretical questions. They come up on real projects, with real deadlines, and the answers have consequences that stick around for years. The tricky part is that you often have to make these calls when you do not yet understand the full scope of the problem, especially right at the beginning.

This is exactly where system design becomes the bridge between product vision and engineering execution, ensuring that what gets built actually works, scales, and endures. If we were to put it into a single definition, we could say the following:

> **Note**
>
> System design is the discipline of transforming a product idea into a real-world, scalable service that meets user expectations while operating within practical constraints.

It sits at the intersection of **architecture**, **operations**, and **business constraints**, requiring technical acumen as much as contextual judgment. Let's understand each of the three elements:

- **Architecture**: Selecting and assembling the right building blocks (databases, caches, load balancers, queues, etc.) into a coherent system with well-defined data flows and service boundaries.
- **Operations**: Anticipating system behavior under load, setting up observability, planning capacity, and building automated mechanisms for scaling, fault recovery, and deployment.
- **Business constraints**: Navigating trade-offs among reliability, cost, compliance, and speed-to-market. Designing a system is rarely about what's ideal; it's about what's viable, valuable, and sustainable.

For most system designs, solutions begin with a high-level architecture diagram. This serves as a shared mental model, helping you map out the major components, data flows, and boundaries before diving into specifics. You can consider it a starting blueprint. Once this big-picture view is clear, you can progressively refine the design to address specifics.

Figure 1.1 is an example of a high-level template:

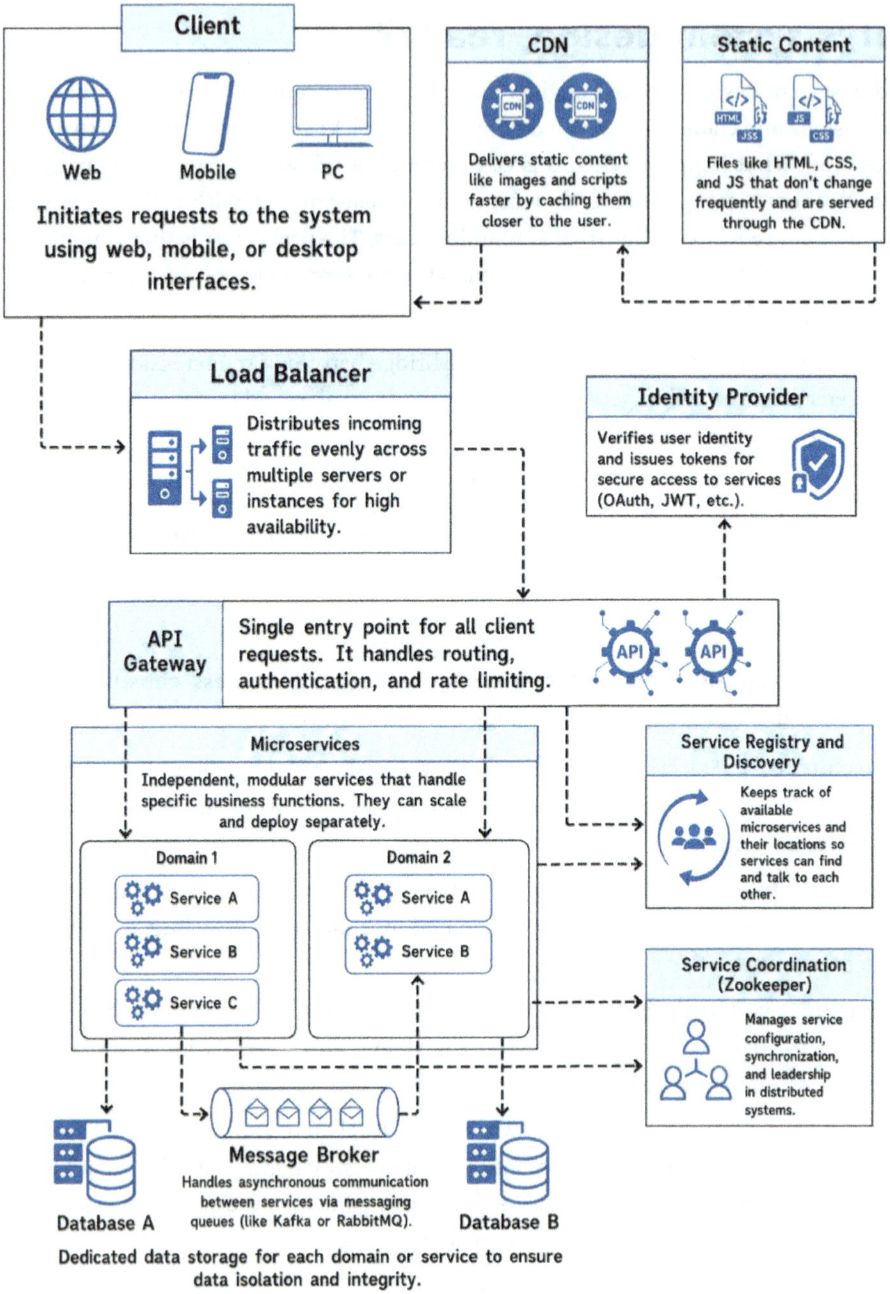

Figure 1.1: High-level overview of microservices architecture

The preceding figure illustrates a typical **microservices architecture**. It shows how client requests flow through components such as the load balancer and API gateway to independently deployable services. It also highlights supporting components for authentication, service discovery, asynchronous communication, coordination, caching, and data storage.

> **Note**
>
> If some of the components shown in the diagram are relatively new to you or you feel less confident about them, they are discussed at length in upcoming chapters.

System design problems are usually framed around a case in a distributed environment, and for good reason. This is because most high-demand systems are built to handle heavy usage with geographically distributed users in mind. Understanding how distributed systems work and the unique challenges they present is fundamental to effective design. In the next section, we will explore what makes these systems different in more detail.

Why system design matters in the age of AI?

In the modern era of AI, there are several skills that are still relevant and crucial. In many conversations, it becomes evident that there are three skills that cannot be fully replaced by AI: one is domain knowledge, the second is system design, and the third is behavioral intelligence.

As AI becomes increasingly capable of generating code and assisting with software development, many engineers and architects wonder which skills will continue to differentiate them. If you listen to conversations across the industry, the message is remarkably consistent: the three skills mentioned earlier remain among the most valuable and enduring skills. These are the capabilities that require context, judgment, experience, and decision-making—qualities that AI can support but cannot replace.

System design is the skill that determines how you approach meaningful technical problems. It's the difference between patching issues as they arise and building systems that hold up under pressure. And it's what separates engineers who simply implement features from those who shape the technical direction of their teams. To explain why it matters in real-world scenarios, here is a story that illustrates exactly that.

Note

A candidate's story

An engineer sat in a meeting room with three colleagues, whiteboard markers in hand, discussing what their new system should look like.

The previous system was ancient, built by people who had since left the organization. Over time, the engineer had developed a strong working knowledge of it and was considered the expert on the system, which had been built to serve niche customers. He had deep domain knowledge of the existing features and understood the technical pain points better than anyone else because of the time he had spent keeping it alive. Those pain points had become so severe that the system was now slated for decommissioning.

The decision had been made, and the team was determined to build something entirely new. This time, they didn't just want to make it work; they wanted it to scale for more users, multiple platforms (such as web and mobile), and future demand.

At that point, however, the engineer had yet to fully appreciate the difference between understanding a system and designing one from the ground up. His expertise with the old system was valuable: he knew what had broken, what had frustrated users, and where the bottlenecks were. However, knowing what went wrong doesn't automatically teach you how to build something that won't break in the first place.

That project changed the way he thought about system design for good. It forced him to think beyond immediate feature requests and consider questions he had never had to answer before: What happens when the system goes from 10,000 users to 100,000? How do we ensure the mobile app doesn't drain batteries while staying in sync with the web platform? What breaks first when traffic spikes unexpectedly? How do we deploy updates without taking the system down?

The system the team eventually built was far from perfect, but the experience taught him something invaluable.

System design isn't just about making things work; it's also about knowing what to do when they don't.

If any of this sounds familiar, you are not alone. Most organizations are dealing with this from both directions at once: legacy systems strain under years of accumulated decisions and demand a redesign, while new systems need to be built from scratch to keep pace with business demands. This is precisely why system design has become the most heavily weighted skill in software engineering.

The need for good system design becomes more pressing in the context of a distributed system. Let's look at what makes distributed systems different and why they add a layer of complexity worth understanding on its own.

Distributed system fundamentals

A distributed system consists of multiple independent nodes (machines) that work together and appear as a single coherent system to the user. These systems coordinate over a network and are designed to handle scale and faults while maintaining availability, often across geographical boundaries. Distributed systems form the foundation of large-scale platforms you use daily, from cloud services like AWS and Google Cloud to distributed databases like Cassandra and global applications like WhatsApp and Netflix.

Distributed systems are both powerful and challenging because of the characteristics they inherently possess. We will discuss these characteristics in more detail in *Chapter 4*. Here is a brief explanation of what they refer to:

- **High Availability**: Through redundancy and replication, the system remains operational even when individual components fail. If one server goes down, others seamlessly take over.
- **Horizontal Scalability**: Instead of upgrading to bigger, more expensive hardware (vertical scaling), you simply add more machines to handle increased load.
- **Global Presence**: The system can deploy across multiple regions, serving users worldwide with reduced latency by keeping data and services geographically closer to users.
- **Fault Isolation**: Failures in one region or node are contained and don't trigger system-wide collapse, minimizing **single points of failure (SPoF)** that could bring down the entire system.

Challenges and trade-offs

While these characteristics make distributed systems powerful, they also introduce inherent complexities:

- **CAP theorem trade-offs**: You must choose between consistency, availability, and partition tolerance, as you can't have all three. We will discuss this in *Chapter 4*.
- **Coordination complexity**: Keeping nodes in sync (e.g., through distributed consensus) is technically challenging and impacts performance.

- **Network latency**: Cross-region communication adds unpredictable delays that can degrade the user experience.
- **Debugging difficulty**: Issues often span multiple machines, logs, and time zones, making root cause analysis significantly more complex.

Common architectural patterns for distributed systems

Understanding distributed systems is only the first step. The real challenge lies in choosing how to structure them. In modern software architecture, there's no one-size-fits-all solution or universal approach. The key is selecting the right architectural pattern for your specific requirements and constraints.

As software systems have grown more complex, especially with the rise of cloud computing and globally distributed users, some architectural patterns have proven particularly effective. Among these, two patterns stand out as foundational in modern, cloud-scale, globally distributed systems: **microservices and event-driven architecture (EDA).** Each pattern brings its own distinct strengths, trade-offs, and use cases. Before we dive into specific system design problems, let's explore these architectural styles at a high level. Understanding them now will help you make informed design choices throughout the rest of this book.

Microservices

Microservices, used here as a singular pattern name, is an architectural pattern that structures an application as a collection of small, independent, and loosely coupled services. Each service is designed to handle a specific business capability, such as user authentication, payment processing, or notification delivery, and operates independently, promoting agility, resilience, and scalability.

Indicators that microservices can be a good choice during design:

- Your system has multiple well-defined business domains
- Features require different tech stacks or databases
- Some components need to scale independently (e.g., search and billing)
- You need fault isolation between modules

You're building a modular system with long-term complexity in mind.

EDA

In an EDA, services communicate primarily by emitting and reacting to events. Instead of direct calls between components, each service produces events when something happens, and other services subscribe to them and act on those events asynchronously. This decouples producers/publishers from consumers/subscribers, enabling greater flexibility, responsiveness, and scalability in complex systems.

Indicators that EDA can be a good choice during design:

- Components need to react asynchronously
- Loose coupling between services is required
- High scalability and responsiveness are required
- Real-time (stream) processing is your use case
- You're using microservices and need a way for them to communicate

Beyond these leading approaches, there are several other architectural patterns (e.g., monolith, micro-kernel, and service-oriented architecture (SOA)). A general awareness of them will help you recognize the right solution for a given problem. However, they appear far less frequently in system design interviews and modern distributed system discussions, so we will not be covering them in detail in this book. Where relevant, we will reference them in passing so you know when to explore them further on your own.

At this point, you have a solid grounding in what system design is, why it matters, and an understanding of distributed system fundamentals and the architectural patterns that show up again and again in real-world systems. But there is a practical question worth addressing: how does all of this show up in a system design interview? Let's explore that in the next section.

From real-world challenges to interviews

System design interviews have become one of the most important stages in the hiring process, especially for engineering roles at major tech companies. Unlike coding interviews, which test your ability to solve algorithmic problems, these interviews evaluate something harder to measure: your ability to drive a conversation, make design decisions with incomplete or ambiguous information, and arrive at a credible blueprint for a working system.

This is exactly why companies weight this round so heavily. It is the closest they can get to watching you do the actual job, navigating the kind of ambiguous, high-stakes problems that define senior engineering work. The questions are not hypothetical. They come from the same challenges that real engineering teams face: systems that must scale under growing demand, maintain consistency during failures, and meet performance constraints that often conflict with each other. The difference is that in an interview, you need to compress it all into a single conversation.

In the next two sections, we will walk through the most common problem domains you are likely to encounter, so you can recognize the underlying patterns when a question lands in front of you. Then we will break down how interviewers typically evaluate your response, because knowing how you are being assessed changes how you structure your thinking, and that alone can shift the outcome.

Typical domains in system design

There are far too many system design problems out there. Can you be prepared for every possible design problem? Can you memorize the use cases and know exactly which components will fit together for each scenario? Can you know every problem domain and gain deep expertise across all of them?

The answer to all these questions is obviously "no". And you don't need to.

> **Note**
>
> A story from the field
>
> During a system design interview for a Software Engineering Manager role at Amazon, an engineer was fully prepared to discuss e-commerce systems, payments at scale, and architectures built to serve billions of users globally. Instead, he was asked to design a recommendation engine for Netflix, assuming the core platform infrastructure was already in place.
>
> The problem had almost nothing to do with what he had prepared for. That was entirely the point—*interviews rarely test you on the exact domain you know best.*
>
> What carried him through was years of building systems across different domains, but this time, he had 45 minutes instead of several weeks to work through the same concerns.

Most interview questions, and most real-world architecture decisions, fall into a small number of recurring domains. The specific product changes from one question to the next, but the underlying challenges repeat. A recommendation engine and a news feed look like entirely different problems until you realize they both deal with personalization, ranking, and delivering content at scale.

What follows is a map of the ten domains you are most likely to encounter. We are not going deep into any of them here. The goal right now is recognition. When a question lands in front of you, you should be able to place it within a domain and immediately know which architectural concerns are in play. *Figure 1.2* illustrates these ten domains.

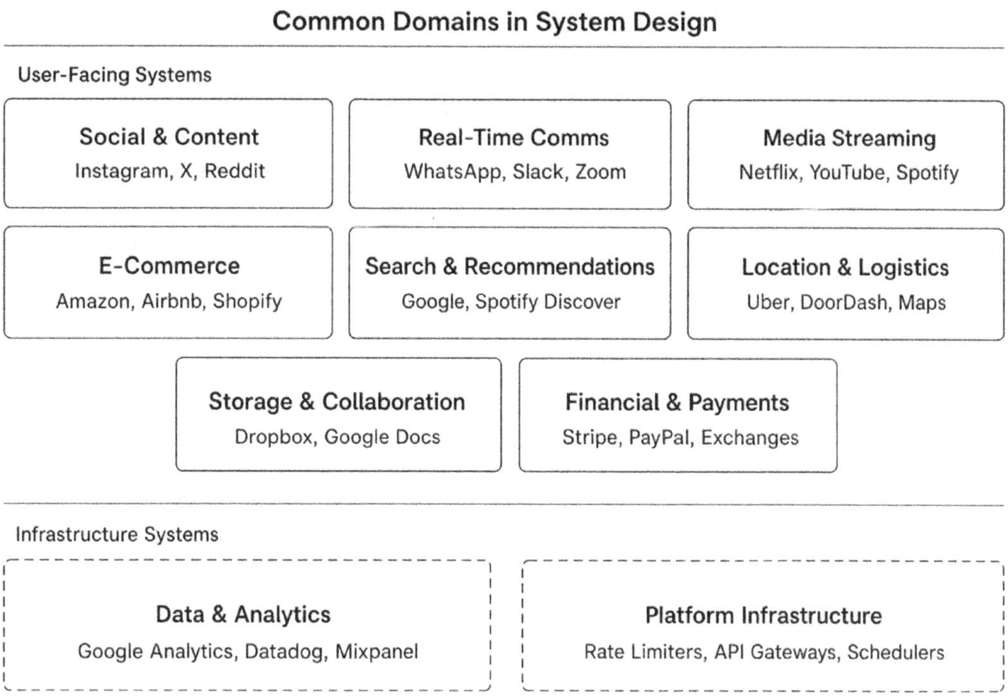

Figure 1.2: Common domains in system design

Let's give a quick walkthrough of each of these:

- **Social and content platforms.** Feeds, timelines, user-generated content, and engagement at scale. Systems like Instagram, X/Twitter, Reddit, and LinkedIn live here.
- **Real-time communication.** Messaging, presence, group conversations, and voice or video calling. Systems like WhatsApp, Slack, Zoom, and Discord live here.
- **Media streaming and delivery.** On-demand and live video or audio, content encoding, and distribution. Systems like Netflix, YouTube, Spotify, and Twitch live here.
- **E-commerce and marketplaces.** Product catalogs, inventory management, checkout flows, and multi-sided platforms. Systems like Amazon, Shopify, Airbnb, and Uber live here.
- **Search, ranking, and recommendations.** Indexing, relevance scoring, and personalization engines. Systems like Google Search, Netflix recommendations, and Spotify Discover live here.
- **Location and logistics.** Ride-sharing, delivery, routing, and geospatial services. Systems like Uber, DoorDash, and Google Maps live here.

- **Storage and collaboration.** Cloud file storage, syncing, and real-time document collaboration. Systems like Dropbox, Google Drive, and Google Docs live here.
- **Financial and payment systems.** Payment processing, digital wallets, trading platforms, and ledgers. Systems like Stripe, PayPal, and stock exchanges live here.
- **Data and analytics infrastructure.** Event pipelines, logging, monitoring, and metrics at scale. The systems behind your app's crash reports, the dashboards your ops team watches at 2 AM, or the pipelines that move millions of click events from your application into a data warehouse every hour. Systems like Google Analytics, Datadog, and Mixpanel live here.
- **Platform infrastructure.** Rate limiters, API gateways, notification services, and task schedulers. These are not user-facing products but appear frequently in interviews because they test distributed systems thinking directly.

Each of these domains carries its own set of dominant trade-offs, and we will explore them as the book progresses. For now, the important thing is to see the landscape. The more domains you can recognize, the less any single interview question can catch you off guard.

System design interview evaluation criteria

Imagine being asked to design a system that can serve millions of users worldwide in real time, for a platform such as LinkedIn or Instagram. How do you ensure it does what the business needs, scales easily, works reliably, and performs well, even under heavy load? And how do you articulate all of these ideas under immense pressure and within a limited time window?

That's precisely what system design interviews evaluate: your ability to understand business problems and develop solution approaches that address both the functional requirements and non-functional requirements (such as scalability, reliability, and performance) while remaining flexible enough to adapt to future changes.

Designing systems is not only about coming up with the "right" solution; rather, it is about demonstrating your thought process, problem-solving skills, and ability to address different constraints. Interviewers typically evaluate several key dimensions. In the following sections, we will dissect each skill involved in system design.

Figure 1.3 highlights what the interviewers really assess during a system design round:

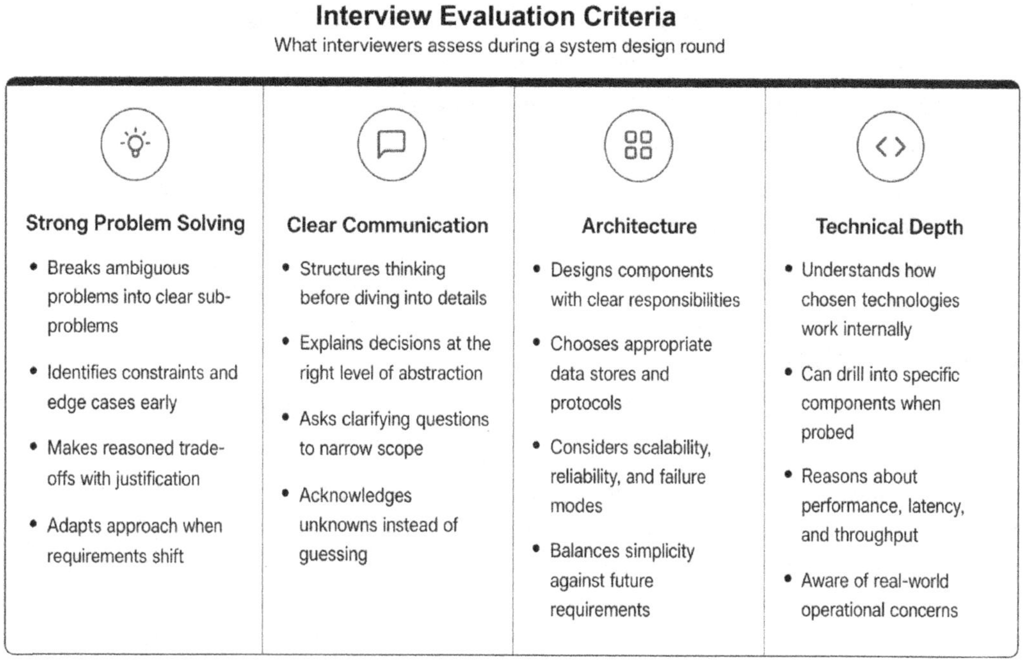

Figure 1.3: Interview evaluation criteria

In the following sections, we will explore each criterion in more detail.

Problem-solving approach

Interviewers want to see if you understand the problem clearly and how you break it down into manageable pieces. Are you asking relevant clarifying questions about vague requirements before jumping to solutions? Do you understand the users of the system, the expected traffic, and the main features the system must support? Are you considering edge cases and special scenarios that could affect the design? Strong candidates ask thoughtful questions that reveal constraints, edge cases, and potential challenges early in the conversation.

Sample clarifying questions:

1. Who will be the users of this system, and what activities will they perform? What is the expected user scale—thousands, millions, or billions?
2. Should we build it as a highly available system or a fault-tolerant one? Do we need 99.9% uptime, or is occasional downtime acceptable?
3. What's the expected data retention policy? Should we keep data indefinitely or archive/ delete it after a certain period?
4. What are the performance expectations? Are we optimizing for speed, cost, or consistency?

Communication

"*Any organization that designs a system will produce a design whose structure is a copy of the organization's communication structure.*"— Melvin Conway, 1968 (Conway's Law).

Effective communication matters in any system design discussion, whether you're in a design review at work or an interview. You should be able to clearly express your thought process, collaborate on design ideas, and receive feedback constructively. These discussions demand structured thinking—how you break down a complex problem into smaller pieces and explain your approach step by step. This includes asking clarifying questions upfront, confirming requirements as you go, and ensuring your solution addresses the system's actual needs.

Example**:** When designing a chat system, start by clarifying the scope: Is this for authenticated users only, or is it open to anyone? Should it support one-to-one messaging, group chats, or channel-based conversations? Are we building text-only messaging, or should it handle audio and video calls as well? Once the scope is clear, walk through your approach systematically. Explain how you'll handle functional requirements—user authentication, message storage, delivery confirmation, offline message queuing—while also addressing non-functional concerns like scalability, latency, and availability. Pause periodically to ask, "Does this align with what you're looking for?" or "Should I dive deeper into this component or move on?"

Strong and clear communication demonstrates that you can not only design systems but also collaborate effectively in team settings.

The key is simple: **think out loud.** Don't go silent while you're working through a problem. Narrate your reasoning, share your assumptions, and invite the interviewer into your thought process. This turns the whole process into a conversation rather than an interrogation.

Architecture: design and component breakdown

The stakeholders are interested in seeing how you break the system into smaller, manageable components. This includes identifying the key building blocks of the system, such as web servers, databases, caches, load balancers, and message queues.

For example, while designing a social media feed, you might break down the system into the following components:

- Client Layer: Where the user interacts with the system (e.g., web or mobile application)
- Authentication Layer: Where users and the clients they use (e.g., web or mobile) are authenticated
- API Gateway: An intermediary between the client and backend services
- Backend Services: Microservices that handle user data, posts, and timelines
- Database: Stores user profiles, posts, and relationships (followers and following)
- Cache: Frequently accessed data, like user timelines, is cached to reduce database load

Technical depth

This is where you demonstrate the breadth and depth of your technical expertise. Here, the evaluation is based on the depth of knowledge you demonstrate when selecting components to solve the business problem. It includes your ability to make informed decisions and explain trade-offs between different approaches, as well as knowing when to use certain tools or architectures, like relational databases versus NoSQL, or monolith versus microservices. Your design should address scalability, reliability, security, and performance, while showing an awareness of constraints such as cost and complexity.

For instance, if you are asked to design a URL shortener, you might explain the trade-offs between using a relational database for strict consistency versus a NoSQL database for scalability. You could also discuss how caching mechanisms and load balancers reduce latency under heavy usage. The key is to demonstrate that you can weigh the pros and cons of each component.

Summary

In this chapter, we laid the foundation for understanding system design—not just as an interview topic, but as a critical skill for building scalable, reliable systems in the real world. We began with the fundamentals: what system design actually means and why it matters beyond landing a job. Through the story we shared from work experience, we explored the difference between writing code and designing systems and how that shift in thinking shapes your entire engineering career.

We then examined distributed systems—the backbone of modern applications—and their key characteristics: high availability, horizontal scalability, global presence, and fault isolation. We also acknowledged the inherent challenges they introduce: CAP theorem constraints, coordination complexity, network latency, and debugging difficulty.

To prepare you for the types of problems you'll encounter, we explored common system design interview domains, as each one represents a distinct set of technical challenges and trade-offs you'll need to navigate.

Finally, we discussed what interviewers actually evaluate during system design interviews: your problem-solving approach, communication skills, and technical depth. Success isn't about memorizing solutions; it's about demonstrating structured thinking and the ability to make informed trade-offs.

Now that you understand what system design is and why it matters, it's time to build your technical vocabulary. The next chapter covers the essential concepts that come up time and again in system design interviews and real-world architecture discussions—from network models and DNS to hashing, encryption, and beyond. Think of it as sharpening your tools before building something significant.

Before you move on to the next chapter, take a few minutes to complete the quiz at the end of this chapter. You'll find similar quizzes throughout the book, and they're designed to help you understand whether you've truly grasped the concepts.

Some questions will test your understanding of key ideas, while others will challenge you to think through trade-offs and make decisions, just as you would in a real system design interview. If you get a question wrong, don't worry; that's actually part of the learning process. It highlights the areas where you need a little more practice or understanding of the topics covered in the current chapter.

Quiz

Q1: Why is system design important in large-scale applications?

A) To make code syntax easier

B) To ensure scalability, reliability, and performance

C) To reduce UI complexity

D) To improve only database queries

Q2. Which of the following is NOT a key goal of system design?

A) Scalability

B) Maintainability

C) Debugging syntax errors

D) Reliability

Q3. Which system design type focuses on independent services communicating via APIs?

A) Monolithic

B) Microservices

C) Layered architecture

D) Client-server

Q4. What is the primary goal of a distributed system?

A) To simplify single-threaded execution

B) To centralize all computing in one location

C) To reduce the number of users accessing a system

D) To allow multiple independent machines to work together as one system

Q5. Which of the following is an example of a distributed system?

A) A single desktop application

B) A cluster of web servers behind a load balancer

C) A standalone relational database on one machine

D) A local word processor

Q6. What best describes an event-driven architecture?

A) A system where components communicate only through direct API calls

B) A system where components react to events and communicate via message passing

C) A system where events are logged but never acted upon

D) A system limited to synchronous operations

Q7. Which of the following is a benefit of event-driven systems?

A) Tighter coupling between services

B) Reduced scalability due to dependencies

C) A high degree of decoupling and real-time responsiveness

D) Requires manual polling for updates

References

Distributed-systems foundations

[1] Van Steen, M., & Tanenbaum, A. S. (2017). Distributed Systems (3rd ed.). Maarten van Steen. (Freely available at `https://www.distributed-systems.net/`)

[2] Kleppmann, M. (2017). Designing Data-Intensive Applications. O'Reilly Media.

Architectural patterns

[3] Lewis, J., & Fowler, M. (2014). "Microservices." `https://martinfowler.com/articles/microservices.html`

[4] Newman, S. (2021). Building Microservices: Designing Fine-Grained Systems (2nd ed.). O'Reilly Media.

[5] Fowler, M. (2015). "MonolithFirst." `https://martinfowler.com/bliki/MonolithFirst.html`

[6] Richardson, C. "Pattern: Microservice Architecture." `https://microservices.io/patterns/microservices.html`

[7] Confluent. "Event-Driven Architecture." `https://www.confluent.io/learn/event-driven-architecture/`

Reliability and the interview context

[8] Nygard, M. T. (2018). Release It! Design and Deploy Production-Ready Software (2nd ed.). Pragmatic Bookshelf.

[9] Brewer, E. (2012). "CAP Twelve Years Later: How the 'Rules' Have Changed." IEEE Computer, 45(2). `https://doi.org/10.1109/MC.2012.37`

[10] Donne Martin. "The System Design Primer." `https://github.com/donnemartin/system-design-primer`

2

Concepts Refresher: Knowledge Bites

Every modern system design problem in an interview, or in production, is built on a handful of fundamental concepts. These concepts form the roots from which all other design decisions grow and shape how systems evolve over time.

This chapter brings together some of these concepts that will later lead toward more complex building blocks to make system designs even more robust. The material is deliberately organized as a refresher rather than a first exposure. Each topic is presented in plain language and then progresses to underlying technical details wherever applicable. Some topics cover only foundational concepts here, as these concepts are discussed at length in forthcoming chapters. We begin with the most fundamental network models and protocols that underpin almost all technical discussions, directly or indirectly. We then highlight some core properties associated with a system that you must understand before moving into system design mode.

The chapter closes by addressing data security and integrity, one of the most important considerations when designing a system. We have added some security-focused concepts as well that should help support your thinking during the design exercise. Also, because a well-designed system is only as good as your ability to measure it, a careful look at the confusion matrix will reveal what raw accuracy hides.

By reinforcing these basics, you will be better equipped to reason about trade-offs, anticipate bottlenecks, and design solutions that stand the test of scale and time. Every subsequent chapter in this book—from distributed algorithms and caching strategies to the end-to-end system design walk-throughs of multiple use cases—might not explicitly expand on the concepts mentioned here, but these concepts remain foundational to the work.

In this chapter, we will cover the following:

- Network models and protocols: Here, we talk about network models (TCP/IP and OSI), the **domain name system** (**DNS**), QUIC and head-of-line blocking, and the working fundamentals of FTPS and SFTP
- System properties and scale: Here, we introduce the ideas of stateful vs. stateless services, vertical vs. horizontal scaling, failover, and throughput vs. latency
- Information security and integrity: Here, we discuss symmetric and asymmetric encryption, hashing and hash functions, checksums, and tokenization for sensitive data
- The confusion matrix: Here, we discuss measuring accuracy and evaluating how well the system's decisions hold up

Network models and protocols

Every system you will ever design is, at some level, two machines trying to have a conversation across a piece of wire they do not control. Network models and protocols help answer the question of how such independent systems can agree on a common language to enable the conversation. A network model is an abstraction that divides the problem into layers such that each layer is responsible for a narrow, defined task. On the other hand, a protocol is the contract that lives within each layer. It specifies and standardizes message formats, sequencing, retries, timeouts, error conditions, and other aspects of communication between systems. Protocols solve specific problems, such as name resolution, encrypted transport, and asynchronous messaging.

This section first walks you through the two main network models and then highlights some protocols. The protocols covered are from the top of the stack, as this is where applications live and design decisions are made explicitly.

Network models

Transmission Control Protocol/Internet Protocol (**TCP/IP**) is the standard model for modern internet communication, designed to streamline data exchange over networks. While the **Open Systems Interconnection** (**OSI**) model was also developed to address similar use cases, the simplicity and practicality of the TCP/IP model led to its early adoption, making it the foundation of today's internet communication.[1]

The OSI model remains a valuable reference for understanding networks due to its clearly defined layer-wise responsibilities. Regardless of the networking model in use, terms like Layer 4 (Transport) and Layer 7 (Application) are commonly used as per the OSI model—even though the TCP/IP model comprises fewer layers. TCP/IP layers are categorized by the network functions they perform, guided by associated standards and protocols.

Figure 2.1 illustrates the TCP/IP and OSI reference models, and highlights how the layers in the two models correspond:

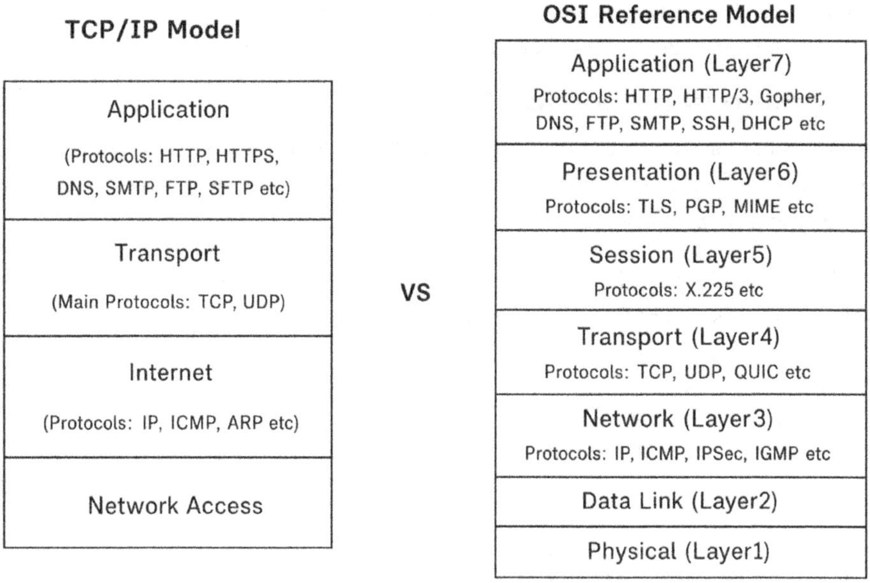

Figure 2.1: TCP/IP vs. OSI reference model

In this discussion, we'll focus on the top three layers of the TCP/IP model. [2]:

- **Application layer**: (Layer-7 equivalent of OSI model) It provides services to the application software. The application layer does not define the application itself, but it defines services that applications need. For example, the HTTP application protocol defines how web browsers can pull the contents of a web page from a web server. Some of the most common protocols here are HTTP, HTTPS, DNS, SMTP, FTP, etc.
- **Transport layer**: (Layer-4 equivalent of OSI model) The two most commonly used transport layer protocols are the **Transmission Control Protocol (TCP)** and the **User Datagram Protocol (UDP)**. These protocols are responsible for facilitating end-to-end communication for applications and devices. The protocol used at this layer determines whether the communication is connection-oriented or connectionless. This layer provides many services, including ordered data packet delivery, connection management, error handling, and data transmission rate control.

- **Internet layer**: The internet layer in this model includes a small number of protocols, but only one major protocol: the **Internet Protocol** (**IP**). In fact, the name TCP/IP simply combines the names of the two most common protocols (TCP and IP) separated by a slash (/). IP provides several features, most importantly, addressing and routing.[3]

DNS (domain name system)

DNS is responsible for translating or resolving host names (the ones you type in a browser) to their associated IP addresses for resource access, e.g., `www.google.com [hostname] = 172.217.14.106 [IP Address]`.[4]

Figure 2.2 illustrates the high-level journey of a DNS query, from the client request through the DNS resolution process to the final IP address:

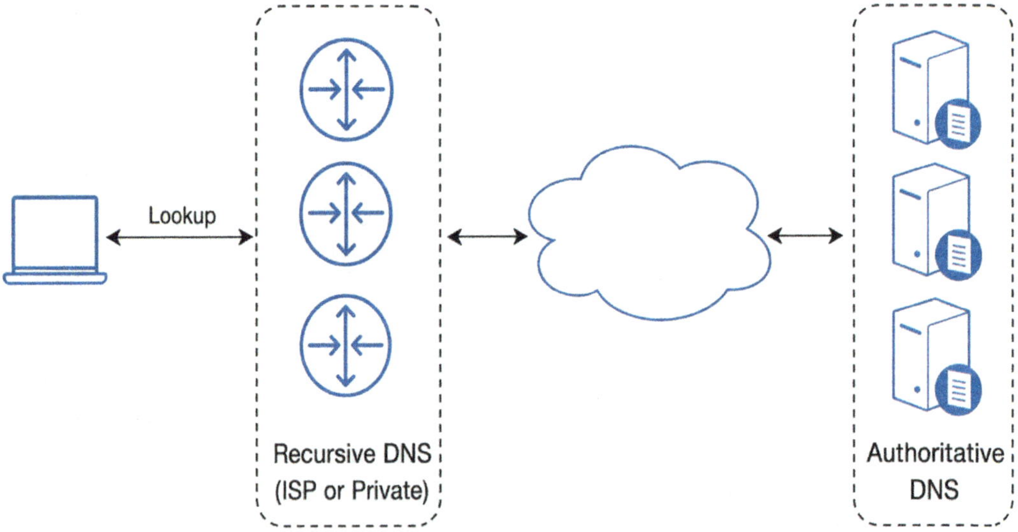

Figure 2.2: A high-level DNS journey

It consists of two main server spaces:

- **Recursive DNS server or DNS resolver**: Its implementation is facilitated by an **Internet Service Provider** (**ISP**), e.g., BT, Comcast, or Airtel, or a corporate private setup.
- **Authoritative DNS server**: Domain owners need to register their desired domain via a domain registrar. Note that *Root* and *Top-level Domain (TLD) servers* are special cases of authoritative DNS servers.

Figure 2.3 provides a view of the main components involved in an end-to-end DNS journey.

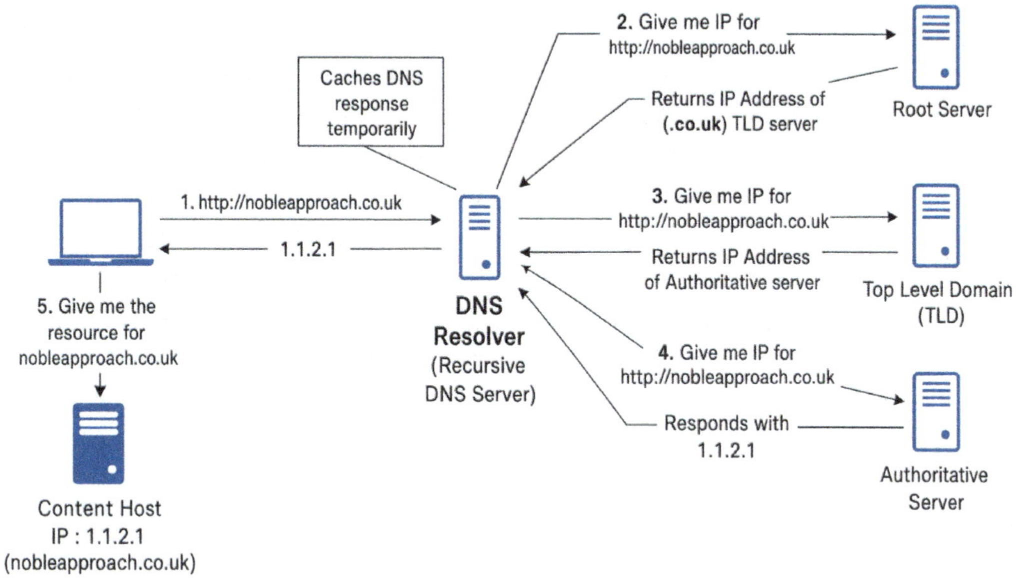

Figure 2.3: Detailed DNS journey

As you can see in the preceding figure, the architecture consists of a request initiator – the client, a DNS resolver, a suite of authoritative servers, and the content host. The content host holds the actual content the client is interested in. All the intermediary steps between the client and the content host are there for the client to discover the content host.

When you search for a web resource, your browser (acting as a client) communicates with the DNS resolver. The action is commonly called *domain lookup or DNS lookup.* If the answer is not found locally, the resolver will interact with authoritative DNS servers to get an answer.

The resolver makes more than one call to get a final answer; hence, DNS resolvers are also called recursive resolvers. Let's understand the journey with the help of an example:

1. A user types a URL in a browser (the client), e.g., `http://www.nobleapproach.co.uk`
2. The request goes to the DNS resolver where it performs a lookup in its local cache. If information is found in the cache, then the response will be returned immediately; otherwise, the lookup journey continues.

3. All ISPs are preconfigured with the native root server IP address. There are a total of 13 Root servers labeled from `A` to `M`. A lookup will be performed by the DNS resolver to the root server for the requested URL. A Root server (also sometimes denoted as a dot`[.]` domain) does not hold the website's IP information, but it does hold the IP address of the **top-level domain** (**TLD**) server. In other words, it holds the TLD server IP for `.co.uk`, `.com`, `.org`, etc. as per your URL. In response to the request, the root server returns the TLD name server IP to the DNS resolver.[5]
4. The resolver then forwards the query to the TLD server, which checks its directory for the domain's authoritative `name server` information. These authoritative details are registered through the NS records configured via the domain registrar. Common authoritative DNS providers include AWS Route 53, Google Cloud DNS, and Cloudflare. These authoritative name servers store the actual DNS records, such as `A` and `CNAME` records, that map a domain to its physical resources, i.e., the content host. If the TLD server locates the relevant authoritative server, it responds to the resolver with its IP address.
5. The DNS resolver then forwards the query to the authoritative server to perform a lookup. The authoritative server will return one or more IP addresses, as configured, for the physical/host server where your site is hosted. When a response is received, the DNS resolver will add the information to its local cache before returning the target machine's IP to the calling client. The caching is performed to avoid expensive DNS lookups for a certain period, usually guided by **time-to-live** (**TTL**) configuration.
6. The client then interacts with the host server, i.e., the content host, and the desired content is rendered.

Note

Role of a domain registrar: Domain registrars are authorized entities accredited by TLD authorities to facilitate domain name management, including registration, within the DNS hierarchy. They provide an interface through which users can verify the availability of domain names and register (or purchase) those that are unclaimed.

Upon registration, the registrar transmits the relevant ownership and registration details to the corresponding TLD server, which maintains the authoritative records for that domain space. Although the registrar may retain a copy of this information for administrative purposes, it does not directly participate in the DNS resolution process.

In most cases, when a domain is initially registered, no authoritative **name server (NS)** records are associated with it at the TLD level. Once a content hosting environment and/ or DNS service is selected, the user, i.e., the domain owner, must update the NS records through the registrar's management interface. The registrar then communicates these updates to the appropriate TLD servers, thereby completing the domain's DNS configuration.

In summary, while the domain registrar does not play an active role during DNS resolution, it serves a crucial administrative function in the coordination and management of domain registration and configuration within the broader DNS infrastructure.

HTTP/3 and QUIC

QUIC (initially used as an acronym for 'Quick UDP Internet Connections' by the creators, but now it is known as QUIC, i.e., no longer an acronym) is the latest addition to transport protocols, initially developed by Google with the aim of providing robust encryption and reducing packet loss and connection and transport latency compared with TCP. It is based on UDP. It also includes built-in TLS support. HTTP mapping over QUIC is now a standard, known as HTTP/3. HTTP mapping over TCP is called HTTP/2. The TLS layer is added separately to HTTP/2 to achieve security.[6][7]

Benefits of QUIC include the following:

- **Faster initial connection**: QUIC's transport and TLS handshake are combined, so a new connection completes in a single round trip (called 1-RTT or one round-trip time). HTTP/2 with TLS 1.2 requires three round trips (*Figure 2.4*) whereas TLS 1.3 requires just two round trips to establish the handshake because of reduced overhead during TLS connection. But regardless of the TLS layer, HTTP/2 suffers from TCP head-of-line blocking. *Figure 2.4* compares the connection establishment process for HTTP/2 over TLS and HTTP/3 over QUIC, highlighting the differences in their handshake flows:

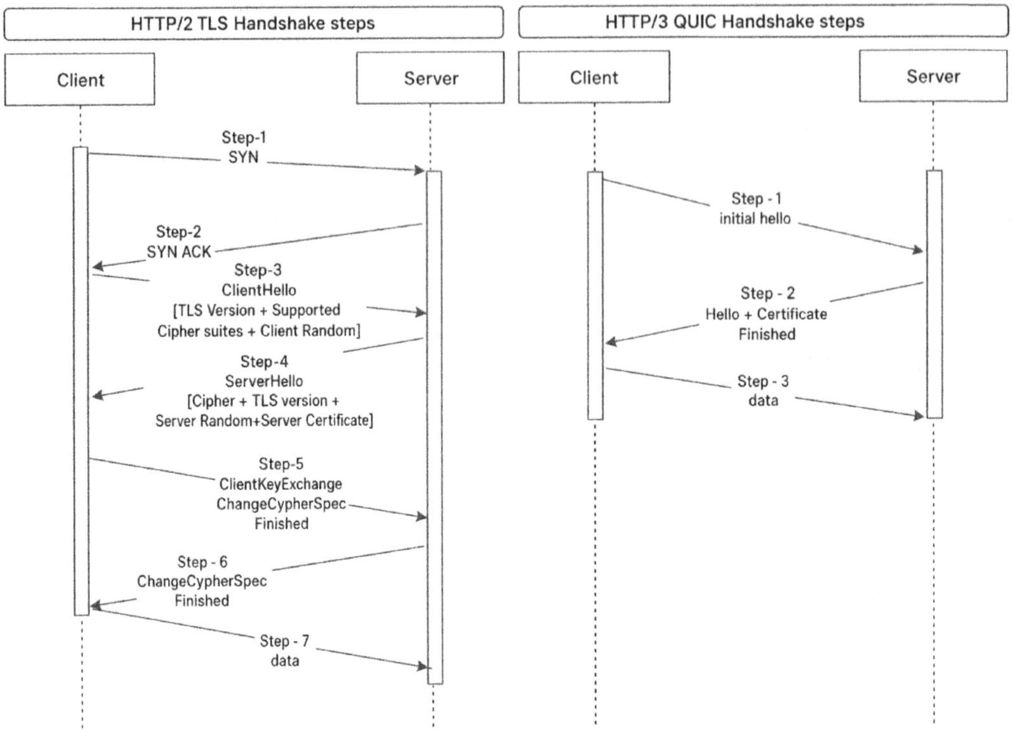

Figure 2.4: `HTTP/2 TLS vs. HTTP/3 QUIC handshake`

- **Multiplexing**: Multiplexing enables multiple requests over a single network connection and is supported by both HTTP/2 and HTTP/3. However, HTTP/2 suffers from head-of-line blocking due to its reliance on the TCP transport protocol. HTTP/3 avoids this issue by using QUIC instead.

Tip

Head-of-line (HoL) blocking occurs when a packet goes missing from the overall stream. With TCP, all subsequent packets across all streams are blocked until the missing packet is retransmitted. With QUIC, only the affected stream is blocked while other streams continue processing normally, resulting in improved reliability and performance [8].

`HTTP/3 real-world` use cases include microservices, blockchain-related use cases, Internet of Things (IoT), web-based multimedia (e.g., designing a YouTube site), virtual reality, video calls, and many more.

FTPS and SFTP for secure file transfer

Conceptual familiarity with these two terms is essential during file transfer operations.

FTPS (File Transfer Protocol Secure), also known as FTP-TLS/SSL or FTP Secure, is based on FTP (File Transfer Protocol) and employs the SSL/TLS protocol for secure authentication and channel encryption.

It involves two communication channels for file transfer: a control channel (not secure) and a data channel (secure).

The client and server use the control channel to send commands that control the communication. The data channel is used to send the actual data file(s).

At a high level, using the control channel, the client presents a signed certificate to authenticate with the server. Upon successful authentication, the server allocates a port (or port range) for secure content transfer. The client then transfers files through the data channel using the designated port(s).

Figure 2.5 illustrates the separate control and data connections used in FTPS, and how they work together during a typical exchange:

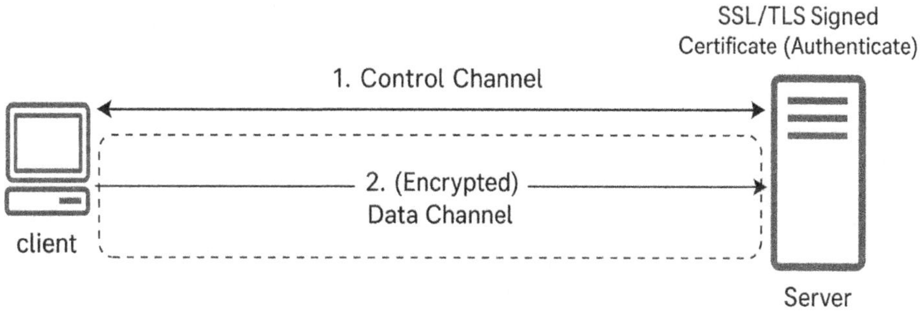

Figure 2.5: FTPS control and data exchange journey

It is not categorized as highly secure because of the use of unsecured control channel communication. But it is still used widely across the industry because of its simplicity of implementation and speed. It is considered efficient for sharing files with external partner systems and trusted business entities.

SFTP (Secure Shell File Transfer Protocol) is an extension of the Secure Shell (SSH) protocol that enables file transfer and management between remote hosts over an SSH connection. Unlike FTPS, SFTP does not use FTP at all. It operates over a single communication channel with end-to-end encryption.

This single-channel approach makes SFTP preferable for companies with strict firewall policies, as they only need to manage one communication channel. Authentication can be performed using username and password credentials or SSH keys, with SSH keys being the more secure option. Additionally, SSH keys do not require signing by a trusted third party.

Figure 2.6 illustrates how SFTP securely transfers files over an SSH connection, from establishing the session to exchanging file data:

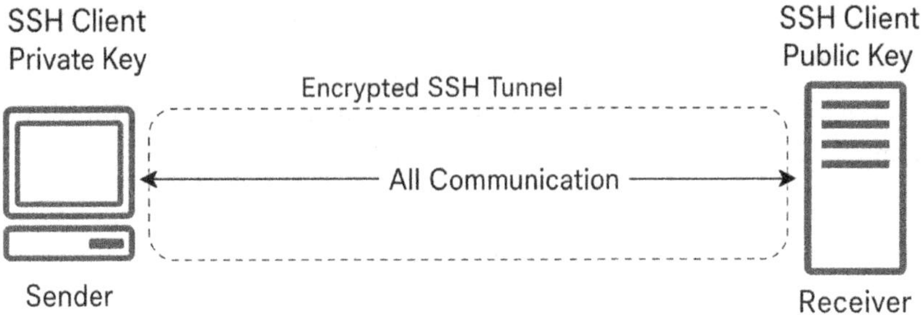

Figure 2.6: SFTP communication

The following table summarizes the main differences between the two protocols:

	FTPS	SFTP
Encryption	SSL/TLS	SSH
Communicating ports	Multiple	One
Transfer speed	Relatively fast	Relatively slow
File management	File Transfer, List, and Delete	File Transfer, List, Delete, Manage permission, Rename, etc.
Authentication	Signed SSL/TLS cert	User/Password or SSH Key. Signing not needed.

Table 2.1: FTPS vs. SFTP

System properties and scale

For every system, there are some basic questions to answer up front: What type of system is it? How will the system scale when it is live? How resilient and reliable is it? And, of course, how will it perform? These are just a few examples. This section introduces some of these concepts. Here, the basics of these concepts are explained before we look at them in more detail in *Chapter 4*, where their technical implementation, trade-offs, use cases, etc., are covered at length.

Stateful vs. stateless

A **state**, as per the dictionary, is *the particular condition that someone or something is in at a specific time*. In a software system, a state (at a given point in time in an application context) can include session state, data state, UI state, or any combination of these.

Stateful means remembering the past state information, which might contribute to deciding the target or changed state. It implies that you can always refer back to the previous state for reference until it is changed or modified. Once modified, the change becomes your current state. It depends on your use case whether you want to maintain the change history or ignore the lineage and continue with the updated information. Stateful systems inherently come with state management overhead, especially when we consider a distributed environment.

Stateless, on the other hand, means no state tracking. This means it does not remember any previous information, and hence, each interaction starts anew. It reduces state management overhead and can also scale well in a distributed system.[9]

We will take a deep dive into this topic in *Chapter 4*. Database records are an example of stateful data. A record in a table reflects the state of that record. All readers of the table will get the same record value, regardless of how many times that record is read. But once updated, the changed information becomes the new state of that record, and hence, any read of the record will return the updated value. Similarly, an example of stateless behavior is an API in which each request contains its own authentication token. Authentication checks performed by the server during any previous call of the same API are not maintained.

Vertical and horizontal scaling

Vertical scaling (or scaling up in general) means increasing the resources (e.g., memory, processing power) of a single machine instance, either by upgrading the machine in place or by migrating to a larger instance.

This is achieved by upgrading an existing system with more powerful hardware (memory, storage, or processing capacity as needed), depending on availability. This method is effective when used in the right scenario. For example, if your ecosystem runs a basic legacy web server and experiences a slight but consistent increase in traffic, upgrading the web server alone may suffice.

Scaling up is relatively easy to incorporate. Some downtime might be needed, but a simple lift-and-shift of existing modules is usually enough to get it up and running. There is no fundamental need for any architectural change in this case. The main limitation of this approach, however, is the finite scalability of a single physical machine. Even with the highest configuration, a machine has limits in terms of memory, processing power, and storage. If further capacity is required, this method becomes impractical, potentially causing performance degradation and reliability issues over time. Furthermore, if the demand decreases in the future, resources are wasted, and the only way to reduce that waste is to replace the larger system with a smaller one (scaling down), which can be inefficient. Also, a single-machine setup introduces a **single point of failure** (**SPoF**).

Vertical scaling can be a good option under the following scenarios:

- You have a monolithic application that isn't designed for distributed systems
- Your system experiences a low-to-moderate persistent traffic increase
- In the context of a transactional system, you need to maintain strong consistency
- You are firefighting for a quick solution to performance bottlenecks without re-architecting your system

In modern cloud-native infrastructure like AWS, Azure, and Google Cloud, vertical scaling can be done quickly by upgrading to a more powerful instance. For example, on AWS, you can start with a `t2.medium` EC2 instance and later upgrade to a `t3.2xlarge` instance if your traffic increases. This flexibility makes vertical scaling more accessible for small-to-medium-sized systems.

Horizontal scaling (or scaling out in general) represents adding more discrete resources, such as servers, to meet increasing system demand. With this approach, you change the number of machines or instances in the group.

That is, rather than replacing/upgrading the existing instance with a higher-capacity one, you add more relatively small instances to the existing setup. For example, imagine you are working with a single application server with a configuration such as C1. When scaling out, you can bring more servers of configuration C1 and then wire them up with the existing server to share the overall responsibility. In theory, it can lead to infinite growth. Also, if your system's demand goes down, you can easily remove one or more instances from the cluster (scaling in).

This approach is preferred for a distributed environment where growth can be substantial in a short span of time. In summary, advantages of this approach include extensive growth potential, improved fault tolerance, better cost efficiency (return on investment), and improved load distribution. *Figure 2.7* shows the impact on resources for the different scaling techniques discussed here.

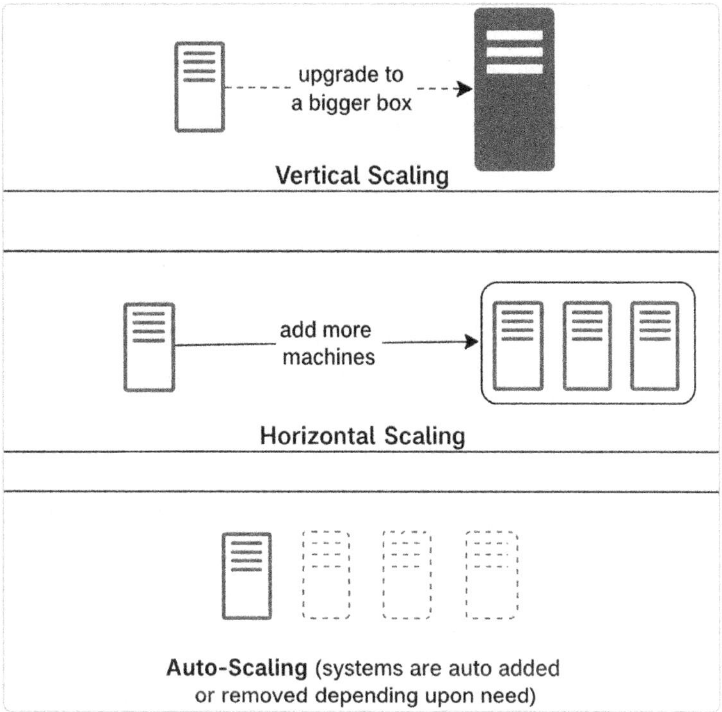

Figure 2.7: Vertical, horizontal, and auto-scaling

Although this type of scaling practice offers substantial flexibility, there are a few trade-offs as well. It can lead to higher operational costs, may require advanced expertise for debugging and monitoring, is usually more complex to set up, involves a consistency trade-off (discussed in the *Database scaling* section of *Chapter 4*), and can introduce network latency, especially in the case of multi-region environments.

Horizontal scaling is ideal under the following scenarios:

- You need to handle large-scale traffic or data volumes that might exceed the capacity of a single server
- You're working with a distributed system or microservices architecture
- Your application requires high availability or needs to continue functioning even if some servers fail
- You are building a multi-region, high-throughput, low-latency platform

Cloud environments like AWS, Azure, and Google Cloud make horizontal scaling easier with services like auto-scaling groups. Auto-scaling automatically adds or removes servers based on demand, ensuring that your system scales dynamically without manual intervention.

Auto-scaling evolved and became more practical with cloud technology and virtualization. Within a cloud environment, horizontal scaling techniques automatically add or remove virtual instances of a predefined configuration from a group of systems in near real time to match the overall demand, typically based on compute requirements. The automatic addition and/or removal of resources is performed based on the criteria configured by the administrator of the platform. This capability is also called *elasticity*. For example, in modern container-based systems, Kubernetes provides built-in auto-scaling using the Horizontal Pod Autoscaler (HPA). HPA automatically increases or decreases the number of application pods based on real-time metrics such as CPU usage, memory usage, or other custom metrics. This allows applications to scale horizontally based on actual demand.

Disaster recovery (failover)

The definition of failover is as follows: *In computing and related technologies such as networking, failover is the process of switching to a redundant or standby computer server, system, hardware component, or network upon the failure or abnormal termination of the previously active application.*

Failover is a mechanism that ensures business continuity by building resilience against unforeseen failures. It works by eliminating **Single Point of Failure** (**SPOF**). In a distributed environment, the health of an operating node is evaluated periodically to identify any issues in overall functioning at different layers of a system. This helps identify an ailing node and take appropriate remedial action, such as switching to a redundant instance in the event of a failure or potential failure.

Failover implementation can be triggered by several conditions in a live system, including:

- **Hardware failure**: For example, a web server may crash or become unavailable.
- **Software failure**: The operating system or deployed application code may fail or stop processing requests correctly.
- **External service failure**: A dependent API may become unavailable. In this case, the application can fail over gracefully by switching to an alternative API or a local service.

A surge in genuine traffic leads to an increase in load on underlying systems. If the traffic exceeds a threshold, the system can stop responding completely or crash.

To implement failover, redundant infrastructure is created for mission-critical systems or system nodes. To mitigate the effects of unforeseen events, e.g., a power outage or cyclone in an area, it is also a common practice to create the redundant infrastructure in a different location or data center altogether. The switchover from your main, i.e., primary infrastructure to the redundant infrastructure can be automated or handled manually, as needed.

Let's look at the two main techniques involved in building hardware-based redundancy:

- **Active-active**: In this approach, the redundant system remains available all the time. In principle, both parallel infrastructures are responsible for serving requests such that in case of any issues in one leg of the setup, the requests can continue to be served automatically by the other active leg. It comes with a higher operating cost overall.
- **Active-passive or active-standby**: In this setup, the redundant or secondary setup does not participate actively in request handling. The secondary continuously monitors the primary and, if issues arise, takes over automatically or is manually promoted to become the new primary. Upon restoration, the original primary can either resume its role, re-establishing the original setup, or become the new secondary.

The use of reverse proxies, load balancers, etc., enables easy implementation and configuration of the desired failover technique. With the maturity of the software industry and cloud-based infrastructure, a few more techniques have evolved, e.g., DNS failover, cold standby, and hot standby. AWS offers four different **disaster recovery (DR)** strategies to implement regional failover to match the cost and RTO/RPO needs of any business: backup and restore, pilot light, warm standby, and multi-site active/active.

Note

DNS failover is a technique that redirects traffic from unreachable or failed servers in one location to other operational servers in a different location or data center.

Failover is vital for a resilient environment, and its significance grows exponentially in the context of distributed systems. It plays a key role in supporting various foundational aspects of software systems, including scalability, high availability, fault tolerance, and overall system reliability.

Throughput vs. latency

Throughput measures the average volume of data successfully transmitted through a network within a given timeframe. This metric indicates the number of data packets that arrive at their intended destinations.

Latency is the delay in network communication, measuring the time data takes to transfer across a network. High latency indicates longer delays, while low latency indicates faster response times. In essence, latency determines the delay users experience when sending or receiving data.

Another concept related to throughput and latency is **bandwidth**. It indicates the maximum amount of data that can be transmitted over a network, that is, the physical or hard limit, e.g., think of a water pipe or an electrical cable. A water pipe imposes a hard limit on how much water it can allow to flow. In this example, bandwidth is the inner hollow circumference that allows water flow. Throughput is how much actual water is being received at the 'out' end or flowing through it (remember, water might not be flowing at 100% capacity), and latency measures how long it takes for water to flow from the entry point to the exit point.

Figure 2.8 depicts the relationship between throughput, latency, and bandwidth:

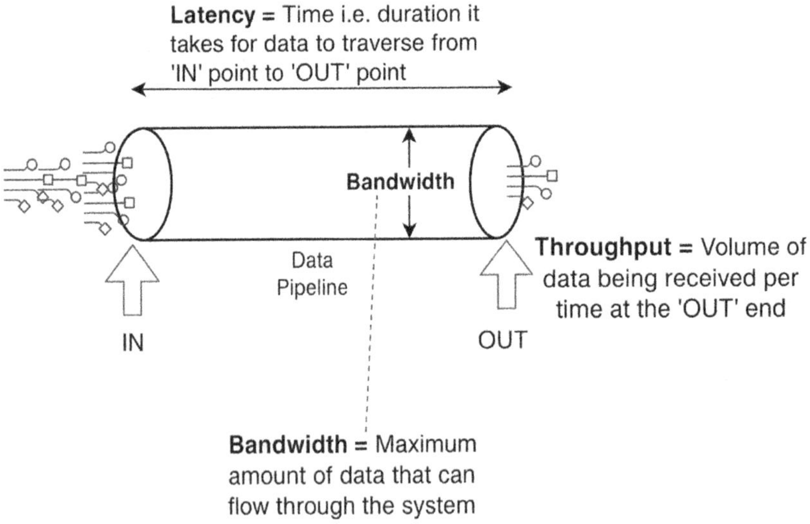

Figure 2.8: Latency, throughput, and bandwidth

To summarize, here are the key differentiations:

	Throughput	Latency
What does it measure?	Throughput measures the volume of data that passes through a network in a given period.	Latency measures the time delay when sending data over the network.
How to measure?	Manually calculate throughput by sending a file or using network testing tools.	Calculate latency using ping times.
Measurement units	Megabits per second (Mbps). [1 byte = 8 bits]	Milliseconds (ms).
Impacting factors	Bandwidth, network processing power, packet loss, and network topology.	Geographical distances, network congestion, transport protocol, and network infrastructure.

Table 2.2: Comparison of throughput and latency

Information security and integrity

This section refreshes your understanding of fundamental techniques used to protect data, verify its integrity, and reduce the exposure of sensitive information. It also highlights how these techniques are applied in different security contexts and the problems they are designed to solve.

Symmetric and asymmetric encryption

Both symmetric and asymmetric encryption are mechanisms for providing information security in the current digital era. They are fundamental building blocks for ensuring security and integrity during data exchange between systems.

Symmetric encryption uses a single key to both encrypt and decrypt the data. In this case, the interacting systems will have the same key at both ends of the communication. The sender will use the key to encrypt data packets, ensuring security in transit, and the receiver will use the same key to decrypt the message at the receiving end. It is a very commonly used approach. An example of this mechanism is **AES (Advanced Encryption Standard)**.[10]

The advantages of this approach include ease of implementation and simple key management. It is also fast, as it requires low computational overhead during the process and is efficient for large data sets.

The trade-offs are that every time a new system joins the communication network, it will have access to the symmetric key, meaning all the systems in such a network can theoretically see each other's messages. This might not be desirable. Also, if the key is compromised, the entire network will become vulnerable.

Typical use cases for symmetric encryption include encrypting data at rest, backups, files, and disks.

Asymmetric encryption uses a public-private key pair. A public key is used by one or more participating systems in the communication channel to interact with the main system. A message encrypted using the public key can only be decrypted using the private key of the pair. Meaning, if the public key is compromised, it will leave no impact on the other participating systems. An example of this technique in use is RSA.[11]

This approach is quite secure as compared to the symmetric technique. It comes with the additional cost of key-pair management, but it is simple to implement as well.

The trade-offs are that it is relatively slow, as more sophisticated computation is needed to decrypt data using a private key when it is encrypted using another key. Moreover, it is not a suitable choice for large volumes of data as it can slow down the process.

Typical use cases for this technique include SSL/TLS-based communication, secure emails, blockchain, and digital signatures.

Hashing and hash functions

Hashing is a process or technique that transforms a string of characters (a message) of variable length into a (generally) shorter fixed-length string also known as a hash, hash code, hash value, digest, etc. We will mostly use the terms hash or hash code interchangeably throughout the book. Once a message is hashed, there is no way to get the same message back from the hash, i.e., it is a one-way process, and hence, usually a hash code and the actual message are both kept for a use case in the form of a key-value pair (e.g., HashTable implementation in Java).

A **hash function** is an implementation approach selected or created to achieve hashing. The function is responsible for generating a hash code for each message, making it ideal for search-like features to find a string in the best case of O(1) time complexity. A hash function should also be deterministic, which means that the same input to the same function should generate the same hash code.

Figure 2.9 illustrates how a hash function transforms input data into a fixed-length hash value, demonstrating the effect of hashing:

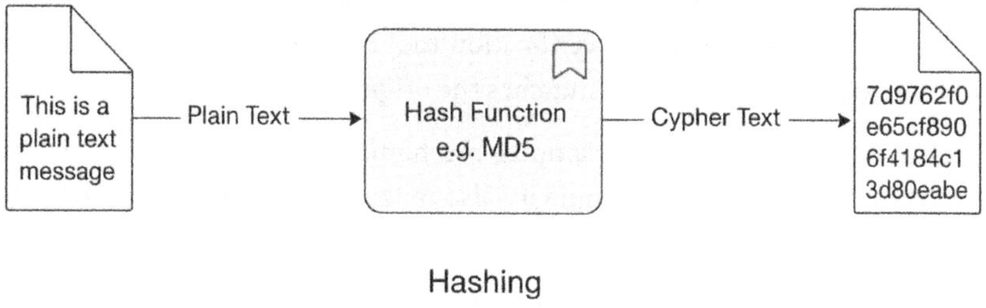

Figure 2.9: The effect of a hash function

When two or more distinct messages are processed by a hash function but produce the same hash code, it is known as a hash collision (or hash clash). While collisions cannot be completely eliminated, there are well-established techniques to reduce their likelihood. Also, there are strategies to manage collisions effectively when they occur, e.g., the use of strong hash functions and salting.

To summarize, some key characteristics of a good hash function are as follows:

- **Deterministic**: Produces the same hash value for the same input
- **Irreversible**: Prevents the original input from being retrieved from the hash value
- **Non-heuristic**: Prevents input bits from being reliably inferred from the generated hash
- **Avalanche property**: Produces an entirely different hash when even a single input bit changes
- **Collision resistance**: Prevents two different inputs from producing the same hash
- **Fixed-length output**: Produces a hash of a fixed length regardless of the input size; for example, SHA-256 always produces a 256-bit hash

The concept of hashing is of particular importance in security-related implementations. Some common names are MD5, SHA-1, SHA-2 (e.g., SHA-256), and SHA-3, which you may be familiar with. MD5 is broken and hence should never be used for security-related work. SHA-1 was deprecated around 2017 after it was demonstrated that two different files could produce the same hash, compromising security posture (famously known as the SHAttered collision attack).[13][14][15]

Checksum

A checksum (or hash sum) is conceptually similar to hashing but is designed for a different set of use cases. It is used as a data integrity verification tool during data transmission between two systems, ensuring that the received data matches the original.

Historically, checksums have relied on simpler mechanisms than hashing, which makes their computation very fast. However, this simplicity also makes checksum values more susceptible to collisions.

For an implementation, a checksum is calculated at the sender's side and appended to the original message. At the receiver's side, the checksum value is recomputed using the entire message (excluding the appended checksum). If the recomputed value matches the original checksum, then the message is considered correct and hence accepted; otherwise, it is rejected. [16]

Figure 2.10 shows how a checksum is generated and used to verify the integrity of data during transmission:

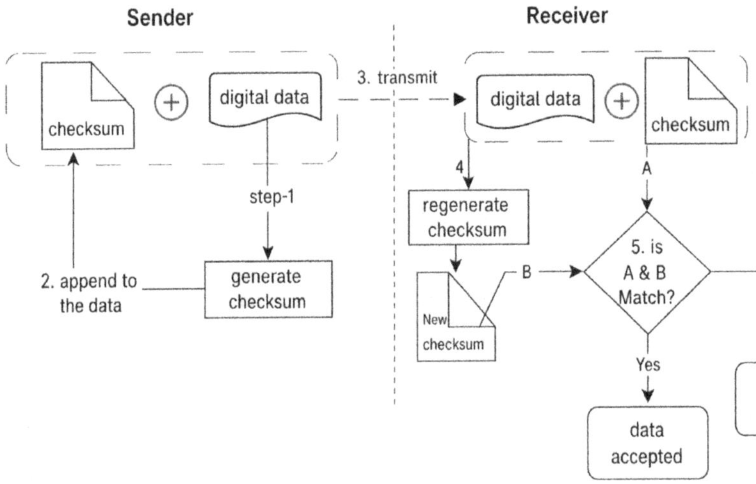

Figure 2.10: Checksum journey

To implement checksums, many algorithms and related implementations exist within the industry. These include the **cyclic redundancy check** (**CRC**) algorithm, Distributed Checksum Clearinghouse, and parity bit.[17]

Use cases for checksums include integrity checks during data transfer (e.g., during migration), file downloads (e.g., for software distribution), and storage implementation (e.g., deduplication).

Tokenization (for data security)

Tokenization in the field of data security refers to the process of substituting sensitive information with any non-sensitive equivalent to enforce data protection. These non-sensitive equivalents are called tokens. The token itself carries no meaning unless it is mapped back to the real/original value for a consuming application. Usually, a third-party secure system is used to perform tokenization, which maintains its own vault/secure-token-data store to keep sensitive data as well as surrogate-value (token) mapping. The mechanism used to generate a token is randomized, but the generated token carries the same length and format as the original data. One of the most popular use cases is tokenizing a credit card number before saving it in merchant storage. Examples of popular tokenization service providers are Stripe, CyberSource, and Braintree.[18]

Tokenization is widely adopted, especially in the financial, insurance, healthcare, and related domains. Organizations in these domains implement tokenization to securely store users' personally identifiable information (PII), e.g., credit card information, permanent account number, and social security number.

Let's understand tokenization with the help of an example. A user uses her credit card to buy a health insurance product online. The user enters her card number, let's say 1234-5678-9012-3456, card expiration date, and other details on the site. The insurance company will have to keep track of the card details used during the payment for future purposes, e.g., issuing a refund, auto-renewal, or some other business use. But under the **PCI-DSS (Payment Card Industry Data Security Standard** - A global security standard designed to protect handling of sensitive data, debit/credit cards, payment information) standards, they are not allowed to store such information. To comply with the standard, they can use an approved third-party data tokenization tool and send the card details to it. Such a tool stores the card information in its secure vault and return a unique token, e.g., TOKN-9876-0000-0001. The insurance company can store this token to maintain its record. Whenever needed, the token can be presented to the same third-party tool in exchange for the actual card details.

Multiple methods exist for implementing tokenization and token generation mechanisms. While this topic is beyond our current scope, additional research is recommended for those interested.

Data obfuscation is a similar concept, but in this case the data elements are obfuscated; e.g., the email address `nobleapproachbooks@gmail.com` can be obfuscated to `n***********$***s@g****.com` or encoded using a mechanism (e.g., base64). The approach is not intended to secure the data itself but is suitable for masking sensitive information in, say, testing environments or for logging.

> **Note**
>
> Tokenization should not be confused with hashing or checksums. While hashing transforms data irreversibly, tokenization preserves the ability to retrieve original values from a token store using valid tokens.

The confusion matrix

While this concept lives primarily in the machine learning and AI world, it is worth covering here for the understanding alone. You will find it relevant when working through system design use cases later.

A confusion matrix is a tabular representation summarizing predicted results for a classification problem (a problem where the outcome belongs to a finite set).

The following table captures four different quadrants:

	Actual result		
		True	**False**
Prediction	**True (i.e., positive)**	**True Positive** (**TP**) Meaning, Predicted = True Actual = True	**False Positive** (**FP**), also known as *Type-I* error Meaning, Predicted = True Actual = False
	False (i.e., negative)	**False Negative** (**FN**), also known as *Type-II* error Meaning, Predicted = False Actual = True	**True Negative** (**TN**) Meaning, Predicted = False Actual = False

Table 2.3: Confusion matrix and classification outcomes

Here is how to understand the table:

- The prefix "True" in a quadrant means a correct prediction, e.g., True Negative.
- The prefix "False" in a quadrant reflects an error in prediction or a mismatch in prediction vs. actual. In case there is a mismatch with the prediction as True, i.e., positive, the quadrant is **False Positive** (**FP**). If the original prediction is False, i.e., negative, and a mismatch occurs, then the quadrant is **False Negative** (**FN**).

Let us add some real-world scenarios and see what kind of information we can retrieve using the confusion matrix above.

Use case 1

Functional: Ensure a username entered by a user is unique on each keypress while registering on a site.

Non-functional: Minimize database interactions to support the expected registration volume at go-live.

There can be several ways to implement this requirement. Suppose we decide to implement custom logic and deploy it on an application server. A confusion matrix can be used to evaluate how accurately this logic predicts the actual availability of a username in the database.

Table 2.4 shows how the confusion matrix evaluates predictions about whether a username is available or already in use:

	Username in database (Actual)		
		Available	**Taken**
Business logic outcome for username (Prediction)	**Available (True)**	TP [No problem]	FP [As per application logic, the username is available. If the application attempts to save it, the database will return a constraint violation, e.g., a unique-key violation]
	Taken (i.e., Available = False)	FN [The application logic incorrectly identifies an available username as taken and therefore prevents the user from proceeding with it.]	TN [No problem]

Table 2.4: Confusion matrix for username availability prediction

Let's analyze *Table 2.4*. A **True Positive (TP)**, i.e., our application logic predicted available and the database agrees, is a happy path. A **True Negative (TN)**, i.e., our application logic predicted taken and the database agrees, is also a happy path. In the case of TN, the user will pick a different username.

The key issue arises when there is a mismatch. A mismatch can occur in one of two ways:

- Your application business logic indicates that the username is available, but the database shows that it is not (False Positive). This mismatch is identified at the database layer and violates the system's non-functional requirement to minimize backend interactions.
- Your application business logic says the username is taken, but it is actually available according to the database record (False Negative). This results in a missed opportunity for the user to select that username.

The design trade-off in this case is to accept some FNs in exchange for never showing the user a FP that survives to the registration step. The next chapter covers the Bloom filter, which follows the same logic.

Use case 2

Send an alert if a fraudulent transaction is detected within a bank.

Say you want to build some custom logic for the alerting system. Such logic will only give you a predicted value, i.e., *Prediction*. The actual fraud is something that you will determine after a more thorough analysis of the user's transactions, patterns, etc. Let's call an actual fraudulent transaction *Actual* and then plot it on the matrix.

The key point is that if the system generates an alert but there is no actual fraudulent transaction (FP), then the bank is safe, although not too happy. But if there is no alert for an actual fraud transaction (FN), then there can be consequences. So while building such a system, ensure that the business logic avoids FN scenarios.

Do it yourself: Try to plot the table for the above example and analyze it.

Summary

Before you can design systems that scale, you need a shared language and an understanding of the concepts used to discuss them. This chapter built that foundation by covering the essential concepts that appear in almost every system design interview you will face.

We began at the network layer, showing how the TCP/IP and OSI reference models give us a shared way to reason about where things break, and traced a request from the browser through DNS to the machine that actually serves it. We then examined the transport-layer step change that HTTP/3 and QUIC represent, and separated the two performance dimensions that interviewers most often conflate. We also discussed state and the underlying behavior of stateless and stateful systems.

We also talked about how to make any system grow, i.e., by making one machine bigger or by adding many smaller ones. Failover, the discipline of surviving a component death without users noticing, completes the reliability set. We ended that section with throughput (how much work per unit time) and latency (how long any single request has to wait).

The chapter also concentrated on the security concepts that quietly holds real systems together. Hashing turns arbitrary inputs into fixed-length identifiers that we use everywhere, from routing keys in a load balancer to fingerprints in a security audit, and we saw both what makes a hash function good and why MD5 and SHA-1 no longer belong in security-sensitive code. Checksums do a narrower job of catching corruption on the wire.

Tokenization replaces sensitive data with meaningless placeholders so that only the systems that truly need the original ever see it. Along the way, we introduced the confusion matrix that lets us judge how well any classifier (a fraud detector or a spam filter) is actually performing under load.

Taken together, these concepts form a fluency test. None of them is difficult in isolation, but the actual value lies in composing an answer under pressure. Examples include picking horizontal scaling because your service is stateless, choosing a symmetric key for bulk data because asymmetric encryption is too slow, and spotting that a latency problem is not a throughput problem in disguise.

Keep this chapter close as a lookup when the later chapters lean on any of the ideas above, and use the references at the end of the chapter to go deeper on any concept where the treatment here felt too compact for your comfort.

The next chapter takes things further, moving from foundational concepts into the algorithms and patterns that hold distributed systems together, including Raft, circuit breakers, and more.

Quiz

Q1. What is the main transport protocol underlying HTTP/3?

A) TCP

B) QUIC

C) FTP

D) ICMP

Q2. What problem does QUIC solve compared to TCP?

A) Increases packet loss

B) Faster connection establishment and reduced latency

C) Incompatible with encryption

D) Works only for emails

Q3. Which feature is unique to QUIC compared to TCP?

A) Multiplexed streams without head-of-line blocking

B) No encryption support

C) Relies on 3-way handshake

D) Requires IP addresses to be static

Q4. Throughput is measured in

A) Seconds per operation

B) Operations or bits per second

C) Time to first byte

D) Packets dropped

Q5. Vertical scaling typically involves which of the following?

A) Adding more servers to handle load

B) Increasing CPU/RAM of a single machine

C) Distributing data across multiple machines

D) Using a CDN for faster access

Q6. Latency is best described as

A) The number of requests served per second

B) The total number of concurrent users

C) The delay before a response is received

D) The total server uptime

Q7. If a system has high throughput but also high latency, what does it indicate?

A) The system is fast for individual requests

B) The system handles many requests, but each takes longer

C) The system is optimized for single-user cases

D) The system is not scalable

Q8. What does "failover" mean in system design?

A) A planned shutdown of servers for maintenance

B) Automatic switching to a standby system when the primary system fails

C) Manual reboot of a crashed server

D) Reducing throughput to handle load

Q9. An interviewer asks: "Your system is experiencing high latency despite adding more servers. What should you check first?"

A) If you are using HTTP/1.0

B) If the servers have complex dashboard presentation

C) If the DNS records are alphabetically sorted

D) Whether the load balancer is evenly distributing requests

Q10. Your monitoring dashboards show your system is handling 50k requests per second with CPU, memory, and disk I/O well within limits. Yet, users across multiple regions report slow page loads and API responses. What's the most likely root cause?

A) Suboptimal TCP/QUIC configuration, causing head-of-line blocking or packet retransmissions

B) Inefficient caching strategy, causing repeated recomputation of dynamic content

C) Network latency due to geographical distance between clients and servers

D) Load balancer stickiness, directing some users to overloaded backend instances

Q11. Which of the following best describes a stateless system?

A) Each request carries all the information needed for processing

B) The server maintains client session data between requests

C) The server stores past responses to optimize future queries

D) The system requires sticky sessions to work correctly

References

Network models

[1] RFC 1122, "Requirements for Internet Hosts – Communication Layers," IETF, 1989 (TCP/IP layering model). `https://www.rfc-editor.org/rfc/rfc1122`

[2] ISO/IEC 7498-1, "Information technology – Open Systems Interconnection – Basic Reference Model: The Basic Model," ISO. `https://www.iso.org/standard/20269.html`

[3] Core internet protocols: RFC 9293 (TCP), RFC 768 (UDP), and RFC 791 (IP), IETF. `https://datatracker.ietf.org/doc/html/rfc9293`

DNS

[4] RFC 1034 and RFC 1035, "Domain Names – Concepts and Facilities / Implementation and Specification," IETF, 1987. `https://datatracker.ietf.org/doc/html/rfc1035`

[5] Root Server Technical Operations Association – the 13 named DNS root servers (A–M). `https://root-servers.org/`

HTTP/3 and QUIC

[6] RFC 9000, "QUIC: A UDP-Based Multiplexed and Secure Transport," IETF, 2021. https://www.rfc-editor.org/info/rfc9000/

[7] RFC 9114, "HTTP/3," IETF, 2022. https://www.rfc-editor.org/rfc/rfc9114.html

[8] A. Langley et al., "The QUIC Transport Protocol: Design and Internet-Scale Deployment," ACM SIGCOMM, 2017 (multiplexing and head-of-line blocking). https://dl.acm.org/doi/10.1145/3098822.3098842

Stateful vs. stateless and scaling

[9] R. T. Fielding, "Architectural Styles and the Design of Network-based Software Architectures," Ch. 5: Representational State Transfer (REST) – the stateless constraint, 2000. https://ics.uci.edu/~fielding/pubs/dissertation/rest_arch_style.htm

Symmetric and asymmetric encryption

[10] NIST FIPS 197, "Advanced Encryption Standard (AES)," 2001 (updated 2023). https://csrc.nist.gov/pubs/fips/197/final

[11] R. L. Rivest, A. Shamir, L. Adleman, "A Method for Obtaining Digital Signatures and Public-Key Cryptosystems," Communications of the ACM, 1978 (RSA). https://people.csail.mit.edu/rivest/Rsapaper.pdf

Hashing and hash functions

[12] NIST FIPS 180-4, "Secure Hash Standard (SHS)" – SHA-1 and the SHA-2 family (e.g., SHA-256). https://doi.org/10.6028/NIST.FIPS.180-4

[13] NIST FIPS 202, "SHA-3 Standard: Permutation-Based Hash and Extendable-Output Functions," 2015. https://csrc.nist.gov/pubs/fips/202/final

[14] RFC 6151, "Updated Security Considerations for the MD5 Message-Digest and HMAC-MD5 Algorithms," IETF, 2011. https://datatracker.ietf.org/doc/html/rfc6151

[15] M. Stevens et al., "The first collision for full SHA-1" (SHAttered), CWI Amsterdam and Google, 2017.https://shattered.io/

Checksums and error detection

[16] RFC 1071, "Computing the Internet Checksum," IETF, 1988. `https://datatracker.ietf.org/doc/html/rfc1071`

[17] W. W. Peterson and D. T. Brown, "Cyclic Codes for Error Detection," Proceedings of the IRE, 1961 (CRC). `https://ieeexplore.ieee.org/document/4066263`

Tokenization and data security

[18] PCI Security Standards Council, "PCI DSS Tokenization Guidelines" (Information Supplement). `https://www.pcisecuritystandards.org/documents/Tokenization_Guidelines_Info_Supplement.pdf`

3

Distributed Systems: Algorithms, Techniques, and Patterns

A distributed system is a composition of multiple loosely coupled independent components that work in tandem to achieve a specific goal. Such a system is expected to serve millions or billions of requests per day, remain available despite partial failures, remain secure, and scale seamlessly to match the demand. A thorough understanding of the design techniques and patterns matters. So does familiarity with the algorithms that implement them. Together, they justify every choice made during system design [30].

The chapter presents a collection of design techniques, architectural patterns, and supporting algorithms that are used extensively in the industry. You will also find them referenced in the book while working through system design problems.

In this chapter, we will cover the following topics:

- Algorithms to generate unique global identifier e.g. Snowflake ID
- Techniques for Data distribution across clusters - Consistent hashing, vNode and Highest random weight
- Distributed consensus algorithm – Raft
- Technique to perform efficient data lookup - Bloom filter
- A proactive technique for data reconciliation – read repair
- A passive, replica convergence strategy – Anti-entropy
- Technique to detect difference in data replicas using a hash-based tree – Merkle tree
- Rate limiting and the underlying techniques used to implement it

- Circuit breaker pattern, and
- Scatter-gather pattern

Most of the mechanisms discussed here play a vital role in the design of platforms such as Riak, Amazon DynamoDB, Apache Cassandra, Apache Kafka, and countless other distributed systems. By the end of this chapter, you should be able to confidently answer some of the most common questions people encounter when designing production grade system. Such as:

- How can unique identifiers be generated in a decentralized setting?
- How should data be distributed across clusters where node membership changes dynamically?
- How can consensus be established among nodes in the presence of failures?
- How can expensive lookups be avoided while maintaining high performance?
- How can replicated data remain synchronized across geographically distributed nodes?
- How can systems defend themselves against traffic spikes, cascading failures, and resource exhaustion?
- How can multiple independent services collaborate to provide a unified response?

Note

Download the code bundle and the PDF version of this book

Your purchase includes a DRM-free PDF copy of this book, the code bundle, and a range of exclusive benefits. To unlock everything, follow the *Free benefits with your book* section in the *Preface*.

Generating unique identifiers at scale

Generating a unique identifier may sound like a simple problem when building a small application. A database sequence or an auto-incrementing number is often enough when a single system manages all the data. However, as systems grow and become distributed, generating unique IDs becomes a much harder problem.

Modern systems often run across multiple servers, regions, and services that need to create identifiers independently. For example, an e-commerce platform may process millions of orders across different regions, a social media platform may create billions of posts and interactions, or a payment system may need to generate transaction IDs across multiple services in real time.

The challenge is to create identifiers that are unique, scalable, available, and efficient without creating a bottleneck. A centralized ID generator can become a single point of failure or a performance limitation, while generating IDs independently across multiple machines introduces the risk of collisions.

In this section, we will explore some common mechanisms used to generate unique identifiers at scale and understand where each approach fits.

Approaches for generating unique identifiers

There is no single approach that works for every system. The right identifier generation strategy depends on factors such as scale, performance requirements, ordering needs, and whether identifiers need to be generated independently across multiple services.

At a high level, identifier generation strategies fall into three broad categories:

- Database-generated identifiers, where a central database generates sequential IDs (for example, auto-increment columns).
- Globally unique identifiers, such as **UUIDs** and **KSUIDs**, which allow multiple systems to generate IDs independently without coordination.
- Distributed ID generators, such as Snowflake, which combine timestamps, machine identifiers, and sequence numbers to produce scalable, time-ordered IDs.

The following sections introduce the most commonly used approaches and discuss their strengths, limitations, and typical use cases.

Database ID Generator: Auto-increment primary keys are a familiar feature when creating database tables. While simple to implement, they don't natively support distributed environments. However, they remain the preferred choice for many single-database applications because they are compact, naturally ordered, and highly efficient for indexing. This mechanism serves as the foundation for two prominent distributed ID generation strategies: primary-primary replication and ticket servers.

UUID (Universally Unique Identifier): Early versions of the UUID specification, such as UUIDv1, generated identifiers using a combination of system timestamps and the machine's MAC address. This approach allowed IDs to be generated independently across different machines without requiring a central authority. However, it depended on reliable timestamp synchronization between systems and exposed machine-specific information. Subsequent versions, such as UUIDv4, used randomly generated 128-bit numbers to minimize collision probability. [1]

UUIDs became widely adopted because they are straightforward to implement and allow globally unique identifiers to be generated across distributed systems without coordination. They are commonly used in microservices, distributed databases, and applications where multiple systems need to create IDs independently.

While UUIDs are simple and effective, they have notable drawbacks. The 128-bit size consumes significant storage space, which may be excessive for simpler systems. Additionally, random number generation disrupts natural ordering and can result in slower database inserts compared to sequential or time-ordered identifiers.

KSUID (K-Sortable Unique Identifier): This is similar to UUID but includes an additional 4 bytes for timestamp data, totaling 20 bytes and consuming more storage than UUID's 16 bytes. KSUIDs use the system clock to calculate timestamps with second-level precision. This clock dependency can create challenges in high-volume distributed environments where clock synchronization may be unreliable. This approach presents almost the same trade-offs as UUID. [3]

ULID (Universally Unique Lexicographically Sortable Identifier): ULID was designed to address one of the key limitations of randomly generated UUIDs by producing identifiers that are lexicographically sortable. It combines a timestamp with a random component, allowing IDs to be ordered by creation time while still maintaining a high degree of uniqueness. Because of this property, ULIDs generally perform better for database indexing than random UUIDs and have become increasingly popular in modern distributed systems.

Database-generated IDs, UUIDs, and ULIDs each solve different aspects of the identifier generation problem. However, organizations operating at internet scale often need a solution that combines uniqueness, ordering, compact storage, and high throughput without relying on a central service. Snowflake addresses these requirements and has inspired many modern distributed ID generation algorithms.

Snowflake IDs: Distributed ID generation at scale

Unlike UUIDs, which rely primarily on randomness to ensure uniqueness, Snowflake combines a timestamp, machine identifier, and sequence number to produce compact, time-ordered IDs with minimal coordination. Like ULIDs, it preserves chronological ordering, but it achieves significantly higher throughput by generating IDs using a machine identifier and sequence counter.

Originated by Twitter (now X), Snowflake ID is one of the most popular, widely adopted and efficient ID generation mechanisms for distributed systems. It was designed to generate unique, compact, time-ordered identifiers independently across thousands of distributed machines without relying on a central coordinator. These properties make Snowflake well suited for high-throughput distributed systems where scalability and ordering are important [2]. It is a 64-bits (8-byte) integer composed of 1-bit reserved/sign bit, a 41-bits timestamp from a custom start date (custom epoch), a 10-bits machine identifier, and a 12-bits sequence number.

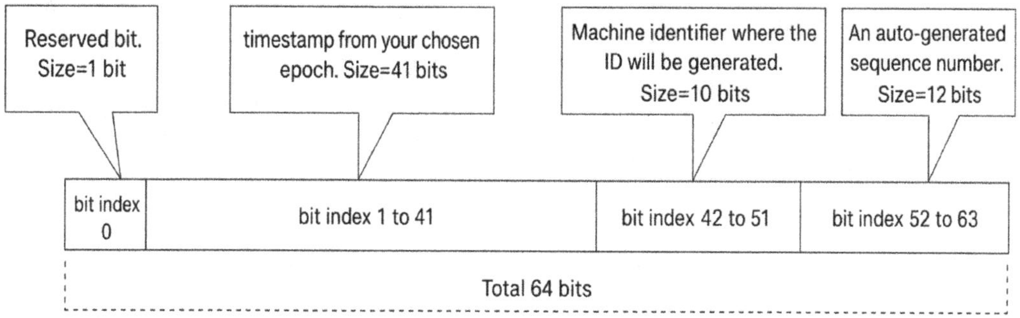

Figure 3.1: The bit layout of a Snowflake ID: timestamp, machine ID, and sequence number

This mechanism can scale rapidly to match a distributed system requirement. Let's take a close look at the formation of this ID in *Table 3.1*:

Bit Index	Purpose	Description
Index=0	Reserved bit	This index is kept reserved (default as 0) to maintain an unsigned number sequence, meaning non-negative numbers. This makes the numbers sortable as well, and the handling of such data becomes easier for many programming languages. If you are creating your own ID generator using the snowflake ID mechanism, you are free to treat this bit as suitable for your use case.
Index=1 to index=41	Timestamp in milliseconds (ms)	Snowflake ID gives you the flexibility to select the epoch that suits your needs. It can be any date of your choice. It does not require to match the traditional UNIX style 01/Jan/1970 00:00:00 UTC epoch These 41 bits are used to store the current time in milliseconds from the epoch you have selected, calculated depending upon your system time. Which means the value stored by these bits will change with every passing millisecond.

Bit Index	Purpose	Description
Index=42 to index=51	Machine identifier	This is the most important factor in achieving ID uniqueness. Each machine is identified using a combination of a uniquely identified data center identifier in conjunction with the physical machine ID, converted into 10 bits. Data center and machine identifier combinations must be carefully created, keeping in mind that new machines and data centers can be added at a later stage.
Index=52 to index=63	Sequence number	These numbers are there to serve multiple requests in a millisecond. It allows you to create up to 2^{12} = 4,096 IDs per millisecond. When the timestamp changes, these bits are reset to 0 (zero), and the sequence restarts.

Table 3.1: The fields of a Snowflake ID and the bits allocated to each

Note

When designing a unique ID generator based on the Snowflake ID, consider these customization opportunities: For example, if your use case doesn't require millisecond-level precision (centisecond precision is enough) but needs to handle more than 4,096 requests in that time, you can reduce timestamp bits (from 41 to 40 total) and assign the extra bit to the sequence counter. A single bit addition in the sequence number will double the number of IDs the system can generate in the given time window. Similarly, the default 10-bit machine ID supports up to 1,024 machines (2^{10}). If your system won't scale to that level per data center, you can reallocate some of those bits to other areas to match your system requirements.

Generating a unique identifier tells us *what* the data is. The next challenge is deciding where that data should live once the system scales across multiple servers. This is where distributed hashing comes in, providing an efficient way to distribute data across nodes.

Distributing data across nodes with hashing

In a distributed environment where scaling horizontally is essential, data distribution is the process of spreading workloads, resources, and data across available systems to optimize utilization and maintain elasticity. To achieve data distribution in such an environment, several distributed hashing techniques are available. Modulo hashing, Rendezvous hashing (pronounced as "ron-day-voo"), also known as Highest Random Weight (HRW), range partitioning, consistent hashing, are a few popular ones in the list. Here we will dive deep into two important distributed hashing techniques in detail.

Consistent hashing

Among the techniques mentioned, consistent hashing is widely adopted for large-scale systems comprising multiple distributed nodes, e.g., distributed databases and distributed file systems. Let us start with an example of a distributed system composed of 10 nodes to store the data where these nodes carry a static identifier, numbered from 1 to 10.To choose a node for storing a data object, you can use a hash function that generates a numeric key for the supplied data object. To find the target data resident node, you would apply a modulo operation (generated numeric key % 10), and the data is stored on the resultant node.

This works well in static environments but breaks down when one or more nodes are added or removed. If a node fails (reducing the total node count from 10 to 9) or a new node joins (increasing the total to 11), the modulo operation (*a mathematical function that finds the remainder after dividing one number by another*) can start producing different results for the same numeric key e.g. for generated numeric key=12 for a data object, 12%10=2 but 12%9=3 and 12%11=1 where 10, 11, and 9 are number of nodes. As a result, locating existing data becomes extremely difficult. Recovery requires rehashing and redistributing the entire dataset to restore correct mappings for the new node counts. As the system scales and nodes are added incrementally, this approach becomes impractical, especially in a medium-to-large-scale environment.

This is where consistent hashing becomes useful. It distributes data evenly across multiple nodes using hash functions while minimizing disruption when nodes join or leave the network. This makes it ideal for large-scale distributed systems. It relies on the fundamentals of a fixed hash function to generate a numeric value in a defined output space for both physical nodes and data objects. For every physical node, a hash computation is performed on a node identifier, such as its IP address. The output of the computation contributes towards creation of a virtual ring structure, often called a hash ring. Each node takes one distinct space on the ring. For understanding, imagine the hash ring as a circular structure like a clock face. There are established algorithms to perform the hashing. The original DynamoDB paper used MD5. It has been replaced by more modern algorithms now a days e.g., MurmurHash family. The same hash function is applied on data objects for storage, lookup etc. operations.

Let us use an example case to understand it further. Say, our chosen hash function generates numeric values in the range 0-24, aligning with our clock face analogy, where positions represent points around the ring. Our distributed system consists of 5 physical nodes available. These nodes will hold actual data objects. Also, consider there are 10 data objects that will be distributed among these 5 physical nodes (as shown in *Figure 3.2*).

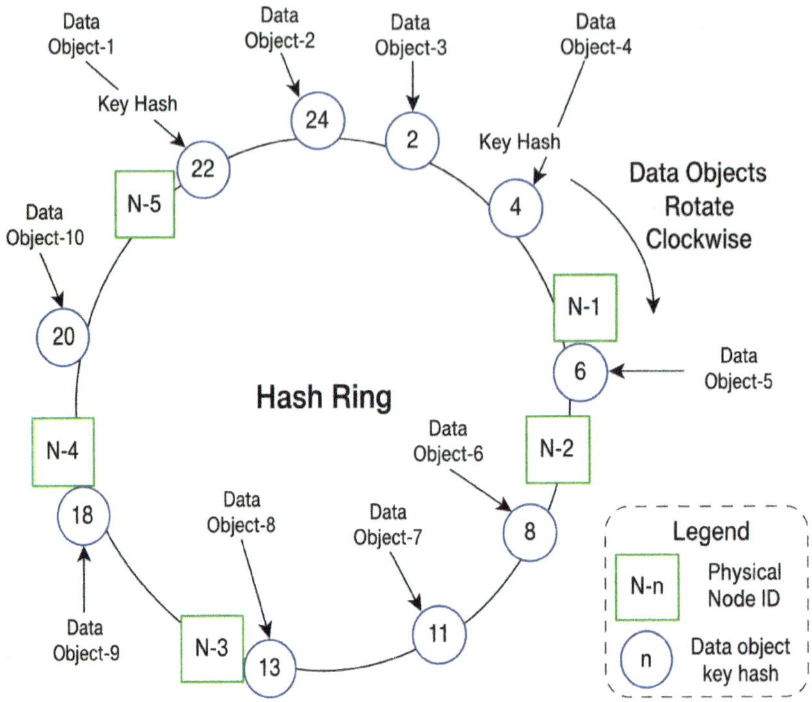

Figure 3.2: A hash ring with data storage nodes and data objects

As per *Figure 3.2* there are two main activities involved:

Nodes placement on the ring - for all five nodes (square shapes), we send their respective IDs to the selected hash function. Assume the hash values of these nodes are: N-1=5, N-2=7, N-3=14, N-4=19, and N-5=21. Each node takes one place on the ring based on their generated node hash.

Data placement on the ring on a node - for each data object, follow the mentioned steps:

1. Calculate the hash using the hash function.
2. Find the location of the data object's hash (small numbered circle in the diagram) on the ring.
3. Start moving clockwise on the ring unless a node is found.
4. Place the data on the first node found.

From the diagram, hash generated for 'Data Object-1' to 'Data Object-4' by the function are 22, 24, 2, and 4. Moving clockwise on the ring gives closest present node as N-1 (with node hash 5). Hence, all the four data objects will be stored on node N-1. Similarly, data object 5 with object hash value 6 will reside on node N-2, and so on.

Handling node addition and removal to the ring

Now say we got another physical node with ID N-6, (*Figure 3.3*) joining the ring. We applied the hash function on the new node, and let's say the hash returns the value 3. In this case, the new node will be added to the ring at location 3. So, does this change the placement of every data object? Let us find out:

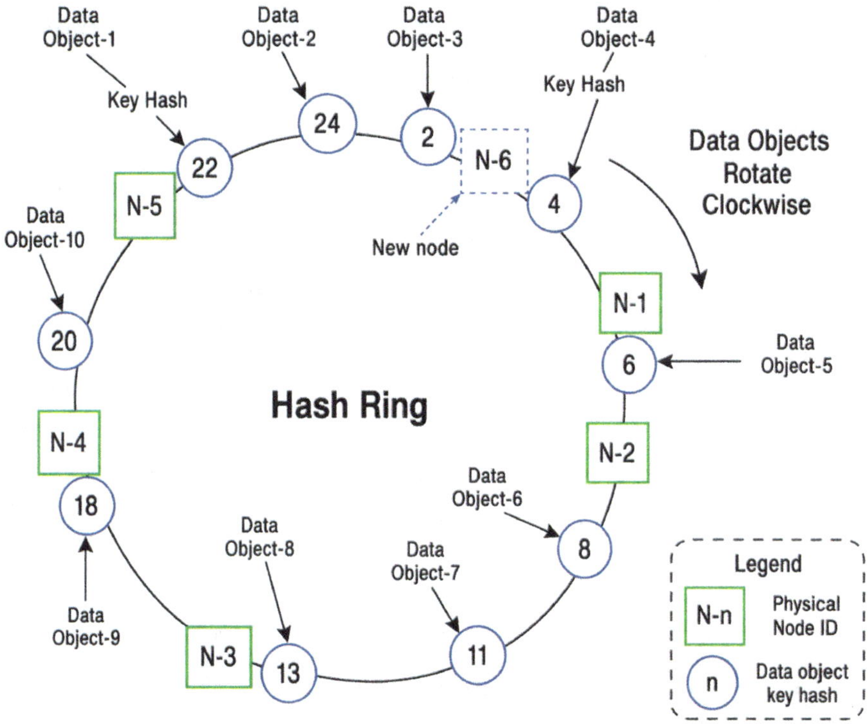

Figure 3.3: Impact of a new node (N-6) joining the hash ring

In the new setup, data object-1, data object-2, and data object-3 will be impacted. This is because their closest node in the clockwise direction on the ring changes from old N-1 to new N-6. But for other data objects, there is no change. Meaning, the overall impact of this new node is limited to a handful of data objects rather than the entire dataset.

Now consider a case where node (N2) becomes faulty and leaves the ring (*Figure-3.4*). Since node N-2 leaves the ring, only the data object, 'Data Object-5' (hash value=6) as per the example, assigned to this node will be impacted. This is because its clockwise neighbor node changes from the previous N-2 to the new N-3. And hence, in this case, 'Data Object-5' will be remapped to the node N-3. All other data objects on the ring will remain agnostic of this change.

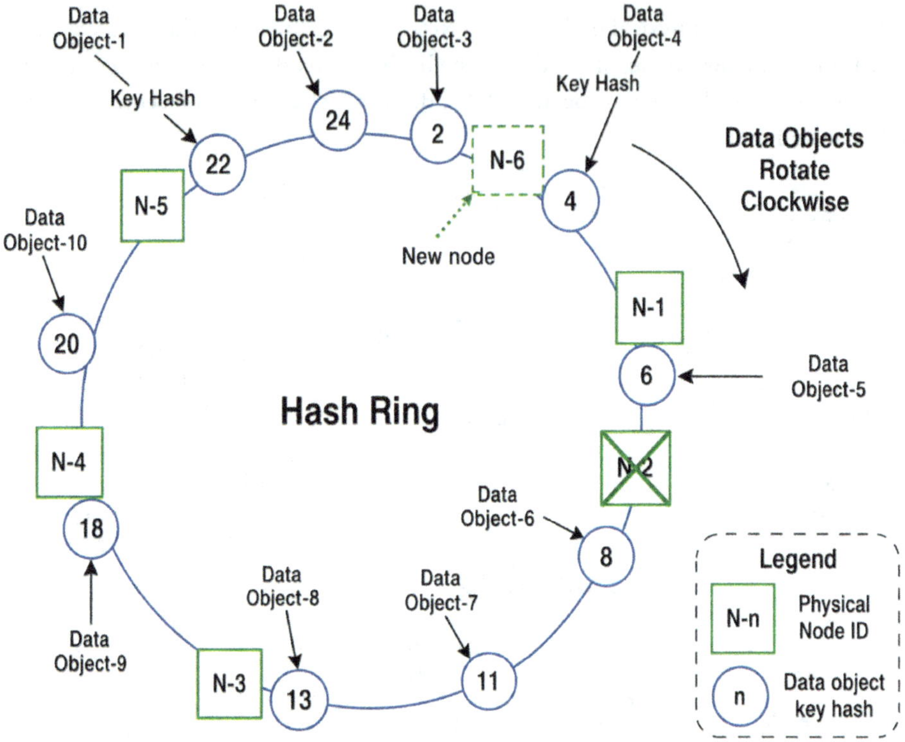

Figure 3.4: Impact of an existing node (N-2) leaving the hash ring

Consistent hashing outlines an easy-to-implement way to distribute data among various available nodes. It also adds a lot of flexibility to add any number of new nodes on demand with minimal impact. The data structure to implement consistent hashing ring formation can be a self-balancing **binary search tree (BST)**. For the selected data structure, the time complexity to identify a node for a CRUD operation is O(log n). Depending upon the use case, some other data structure e.g. sorted array can be used for the hash ring formation.

The main trade-off of using consistent hashing in its basic form is, imbalance in node positioning on the ring that can cause more data objects to be placed on one node, creating further imbalance in request rendering. In *Figure 3.2*, node N-1 keeps more data objects as compared to node N-2. Also, this approach does not deal with the hot-spot (celebrity) problem.

Handling hot spots in data distribution

A hot-spot also known as *celebrity problem* appears when a large number of clients attempt to simultaneously access data from one server (a node in our example). Such a node can become overwhelmed, causing bottlenecks while sending a response. The hot-spot can happen for multiple reasons, such as when data about some latest trend, events, or celebrities is stored on a node that is being requested by multiple clients simultaneously. Ways to handle this problem include application layer caching, replicating data on more nodes, and CDN offloading.

Virtual nodes (vNode)

To minimize the impact of such node imbalance, including hot-spots, an approach is to create a number of virtual replicas for each physical node on the ring. These replicas are called virtual nodes (vNode). The number of replicas, or virtual nodes, for a physical node can differ and is configurable to match the physical server capacity, i.e., not all physical nodes on a ring must have the same number of replicas.

Virtual nodes during consistent hashing can be used to enhance load distribution by creating multiple virtual partitions of a physical server and then spreading those partitions on the hash ring. These virtual nodes are an abstraction to create a logical grouping of data objects that are then mapped to a physical server. The physical servers are the actual data hosts built using hardware such as disk capacity, compute, memory, etc. A virtual node does not have such properties. Let us try to understand this concept using a simplified journey.

As we explained '5-physical servers ring' in our previous example, consider that all the physical servers are of the same capacity, and hence, we decided to create two virtual nodes per physical server. To find the appropriate locations of virtual nodes on the ring, we would require some way to generate different hashes unique to each virtual node. One approach, depending on the number of desired virtual nodes, is to append a sequence, e.g.,`N1_1`, `N1_2` to the physical server identifier (N1) and then use a fixed suitable hash function that will generate different hashes. Place the nodes on the ring in a similar fashion as you have done in the case of vanilla consistent hashing (refer to *Figure 3.5*).

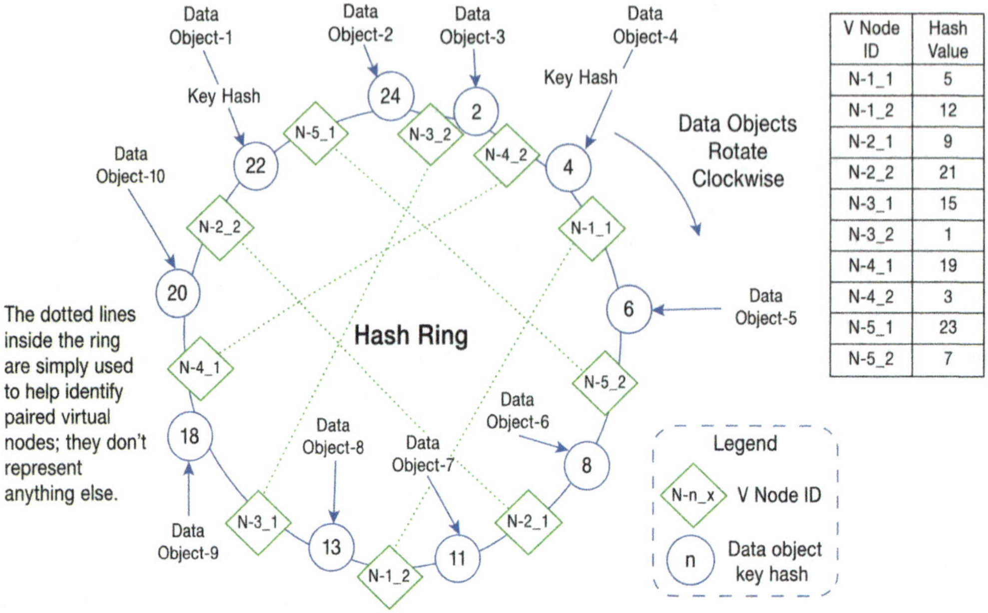

V Node ID	Hash Value
N-1_1	5
N-1_2	12
N-2_1	9
N-2_2	21
N-3_1	15
N-3_2	1
N-4_1	19
N-4_2	3
N-5_1	23
N-5_2	7

Figure 3.5: Distribution Impact of node replicas in case of vNode on the ring

Although *Figure 3.5* uses a very simplified view, the diagram depicts the impact ondata objects' distribution with the increase in the number of virtual nodes. As per some previous testing performed to establish this fact, a significant improvement in request handling can be achieved with the increase in the number of virtual nodes. These virtual nodes will be hosted on their mapped physical servers, but because of better data distribution over multiple physical machines, they create a better request-handling environment. We are assuming here that a virtual node 'N-n_x' is mapped to the physical server 'N-n'. The key to achieving this benefit will be the selection of an efficient hash function that can distribute the virtual nodes homogeneously over the ring.

Replicating data on multiple physical instances should be built to support a physical server failure. Extended adjustments are needed while implementing this approach because when a new physical node joins the ring, then it will have no data. When the virtual nodes for this server are placed on the ring, they can immediately start getting some read requests. To overcome this situation, a replication factor (r) can be configured so that if a server, such as one newly added to the ring, does not have the requested data, it can consult 'r' other physical servers, in the clockwise direction, for this data before responding. Some real-world implementations of this approach are Amazon DynamoDB, Cassandra, and Riak, which uses the vNode approach. [4][7]

Consistent hashing is one of the most common approaches for distributing data across nodes, but it is not the only one. **Highest Random Weight (HRW)** hashing, also known as Rendezvous hashing, achieves the same goal of mapping objects to nodes through a different approach.

Highest random weight hashing (rendezvous hashing)

Highest Random Weight (**HRW**) is another popular distributed hashing technique that ensures assignment of data objects to server node(s). From a paper hosted on Microsoft:

> *"HRW operates as follows: An object name and server address together are used to assign a random 'weight' to each server. The servers are then ordered by weight, and a request is sent to the active server with the highest weight." (Reference:* `https://www.microsoft.com/en-us/research/wp-content/uploads/2017/02/HRW98.pdf`*)*

If servers have unequal capacities, the weights assigned to each server can be scaled by a constant; distributed to clients along with the server's address. This allows servers with higher capacity to receive a proportionately higher portion of the load.

One of the key benefits of HRW is its simpler implementation compared to consistent hashing with virtual nodes. It also has low overhead during node rebalancing because it requires only the server address and object name to determine the assignment. If a server leaves the group, only the data mapped to that server needs to be re-mapped to the remaining servers. Similarly, when a new server is added, recalculation of all object weights can be avoided by storing the previously winning weight.

HRW can also help address the hot-spot problem when combined with an appropriately selected hash function. However, there is still a possibility of a server being overwhelmed because of workload skew. For example, a selective server may attract most requests during a specific event (celebrity problem, latest trend, etc.). Similarly, in a heterogeneous environment (servers of different configurations holding different weights), a server may receive a disproportionate number of active keys.

Since HRW calculates the weight of each object-server combination to determine the highest-weight server, it requires O(N) time complexity to perform CRUD operations, where N represents the number of servers. As a result, it can become relatively slower. However, HRW requires less memory as compared to consistent hashing because it does not require maintaining a virtual ring.

HRW works well for small-to-medium numbers of nodes and objects, but becomes quite expensive as the system scales. This limitation is primarily due to its time complexity [5].

Following are a few use cases:

- Load-balancer implementation
- Caching layer, e.g., Memcached
- Distributed hash tables implementation [6]

Table 3.2 gives a high-level overview and a brief of all the three hashing techniques discussed:

	Modulo Hashing	**Consistent Hashing**	**HRW hashing**
Implementation complexity	Low	Medium	Medium
Time complexity to read	O(1)	O (logN) with BST implementation	O(N)
Node scalability impact	Full rehash	Minimal	Minimal
Hotspot handling	No	using vNode	Partial
Best suited for	Static cluster	Large-scale distributed system	Systems involving a small-medium number of nodes

Table 3.2: Modulo, consistent, and rendezvous (HRW) hashing comparison

Consistent hashing provides an elegant mechanism for distributing data evenly across a dynamic set of nodes while minimizing data movement during topology changes. However, determining where data should reside is only one part of building a reliable distributed system. Once data is replicated across multiple nodes, the system must ensure that every replica agrees on the order and outcome of updates, even in the presence of partial failures. Achieving this agreement is the role of a consensus algorithm. Among the various algorithms, Raft has emerged as one of the most widely adopted due to its emphasis on understandability, fault tolerance, and practical implementation. The following section examines the Raft consensus algorithm in detail.

Reaching agreement across nodes: Consensus

In a distributed environment, to ensure coordination while executing functions such as resource allocation, routing, primary election, etc., an agreement among participating nodes is extremely important. This is needed to achieve data integrity, consistency, reliability, and fault tolerance, to mention a few. Distributed consensus is about guaranteeing that participating nodes can reach a decision despite some failures. This ensures reliable progress even when some nodes are not participating in the given bounded time.

The core of the consensus is to elect a leader, and then all participants follow the instructions of the leader. There are multiple implementations available to achieve consensus in a distributed system, including Paxos (quite complex to fully understand for practical implementation), which is the pioneer in guiding a way in this area. The **Zookeeper atomic broadcast (ZAB)** [11] algorithm designed for the Zookeeper coordination service is an excellent approach to manage leader election but tied to the product. The simplest and the most effective way prevailing in the industry these days is – **Raft**.

> Note
>
> **Byzantine fault tolerant (BFT) vs Crash fault tolerant (CFT) consensus**
>
> BFT represents a category of algorithms that can help attain consensus (agreement on a single value) in a distributed system regardless of whether some components within the system are faulty or malicious. These algorithms are designed to handle the Byzantine Generals' Problem that explicitly acknowledges the presence of malicious actors within the system. Some example algorithms are Practical BFT and HotStuff [12].
>
> CFT, on the other hand, deals with consensus within a distributed system when some nodes are faulty, i.e., it does not consider the malicious aspects. In this approach nodes are either participating nodes or non-participating during the consensus journey. Examples include Paxos and Raft. [9]

Achieving consensus using the Raft algorithm

Raft is a consensus algorithm for managing a replicated log in a distributed system. It was introduced as an alternative to Paxos that offers equivalent safety and fault-tolerance guarantees while remaining much easier to understand and implement. Raft now underpins the coordination layer of systems such as CockroachDB, etcd, HashiCorp Consul and Vault, TiKV, and Kafka's KRaft mode, among others. [10][13]

At a high level, it allows a group of distributed nodes to behave as a single reliable system by ensuring that all nodes agree on the same sequence of changes. To achieve this, Raft divides responsibilities among nodes, elects a leader to coordinate updates, and uses terms to track the progress of the cluster and identify outdated information.

Cluster model and node states

A Raft cluster commonly deployed with an odd number of replicas, conventionally three, five, or seven. This is to maximize fault-tolerance. With 'N' replicas, the cluster can tolerate the failure of up to the [floor value of N/2] nodes while preserving both safety (i.e. no incorrect outcome) and liveness (i.e. eventual progress). Each replica exists in exactly one of three states at a time: **leader**, **follower**, or **candidate**. At any instant there is at most one leader, 'followers' are passive and respond only to incoming requests, 'candidates' are transient and exist only during elections.

Time in Raft is partitioned into 'terms', monotonically increasing integers that function as logical clocks. Each term begins with an election and continues until the next election is triggered. Terms allow nodes to detect and discard stale information from previous leaders.

Leader election

During the initial setup, all the nodes are in 'follower' state. Because only one node can accept writes, Raft must first establish a leader before normal operation begins. A follower expects periodic heartbeats (empty AppendEntries RPCs) from the leader. If no heartbeat arrives within its randomized election timeout (typically 150–300 ms), the follower increments the current term, transitions to candidate, votes for itself, and dispatches RequestVote RPCs to all peers in parallel.

A candidate wins the election when it receives votes from a strict majority of the cluster for the same term. On winning, it transitions to leader and immediately sends heartbeats to assert authority. Three outcomes are possible: the candidate wins; another node has concurrently become leader for the same or a later term, in which case the candidate steps down; or no candidate obtains a majority and the election times out, at which point a new election with an incremented term is initiated. Randomized timeouts make repeated split votes statistically unlikely.

Log replication

Once elected, the leader is the sole authority for client write requests. When a request arrives, the leader appends it as a new entry to its local log and issues AppendEntries RPCs in parallel to all followers. An entry is considered committed once it has been safely replicated on a majority of replicas; only committed entries are applied to the state machine, after which the result can be safely acknowledged to the client.

Each AppendEntries RPC includes the index and term of the entry immediately preceding the new entries. A follower rejects the request if its log does not contain a matching entry, forcing the leader to back up and retry with earlier entries until consistency is restored. This mechanism enforces the log matching property: if two logs contain an entry with the same index and term, the logs are identical in every preceding entry.

Ensuring safety and consistency

While leader election and log replication describe how Raft operates, safety rules ensure that these operations never result in conflicting states across replicas. The election restriction requires that a candidate gather votes only from peers whose log is no more up-to-date than its own, where log freshness is defined by the term of the last entry, with ties broken by index. This guarantees the leader completeness property - any entry committed in a previous term appears in every subsequent leader's log.

Several subtle correctness concerns are addressed by additional rules in the full specification. (1) A leader may not commit an entry from a prior term by counting replicas alone; it must first replicate at least one entry from its own current term. (2) Cluster configuration changes use a joint-consensus protocol in which both the old and the new memberships must form overlapping majorities during the transition. And (3) Client requests carry unique sequence numbers so that retries cannot be applied twice.

Membership changes and log compaction

Cluster membership cannot change atomically. Raft uses joint consensus to ensure that no two disjoint majorities can form during the transition. Log compaction prevents unbounded growth. For this, replicas periodically snapshot the state machine and discard log entries preceding the snapshot, transmitting snapshots to lagging followers via the InstallSnapshot RPC.

Beyond its algorithmic properties, Raft's practical adoption has been driven by its operational simplicity and clear implementation model. Its decomposition into leader election, log replication, and safety has made it a widely adopted consensus protocol in modern infrastructure. etcd, a distributed key-value store commonly used to manage Kubernetes cluster state, uses Raft internally to maintain consistency across replicas. HashiCorp's Raft library provides the consensus implementation used by systems such as Consul and Vault, while CockroachDB uses Raft to replicate individual data ranges. Kafka's KRaft (read as "craft") mode uses a Raft-based approach for metadata management. Comparative analyses of Paxos and Raft show that both provide equivalent safety guarantees, with similar performance characteristics under comparable conditions. Raft's adoption reflects its operational accessibility and ease of implementation rather than a fundamental algorithmic advantage over other consensus protocols [8].

Consensus algorithms ensure that replicated state remains consistent across distributed systems. However, many real-world applications also require maintaining the uniqueness of specific data elements, such as usernames, email addresses, or transaction identifiers. Verifying whether a newly submitted element already exists within a large dataset can become computationally expensive as the dataset grows. Probabilistic data structures, such as the **Bloom filter**, provides an efficient mechanism for performing high-speed membership checks while using minimal memory. The following section examines Bloom filter, its approach, and practical applications in large-scale distributed systems.

Bloom filter

Traditionally, if you have to look for an item in a large dataset, you will have to match the item against each member in the dataset. This is extremely resource and time-consuming. **Bloom filter** solves this problem with desired accuracy using limited resources and speed.

Bloom filter is a space (memory) efficient probabilistic data structure that is used to verify if an element is a member of a set. To perform its tasks, it allows insert (add) and lookup (match) operations within the underlying data structure. Once added, you can not remove an element from the data structure.

Note that the filter itself does not keep any actual data element; rather, it maintains an equivalent calculated marker value denoted in bits. Actual data is stored in its desired storage say cache or database.

How Bloom filter works

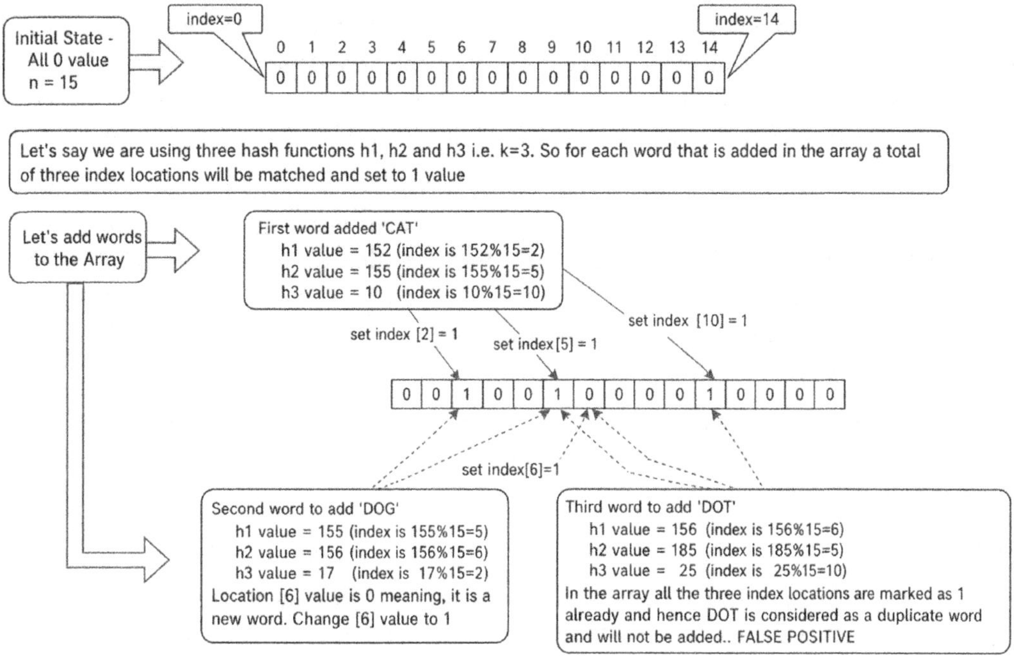

Figure 3.6: A Bloom filter's bit array and its hash functions

Take a bit array (let's call it *master-bit-array*) of size **'n'** with an initial value at all the index locations set to 0 (zero) as default.

To add an element (say a string value) to the filter, apply multiple hash functions on the string. Say there are **'k'** (where k < n) numbers of hash functions, and each hash function will return an integer outcome (R^X where x=1...k) when used with a string. The next step is to apply the 'mod' operation to the integer result (R^X *mod* n = $L^{[x]}$). For each 'k' hash function, this exercise will result in an integer that is less than the value of 'n' i.e., the size of the initial array. For all such returned values of $L^{[x]}$, set the master-bit-array index value to 1 (one). So if the second hash function returns a result=3 (i.e., $L^{[2]}$ =3) then set the bit at index 3 of the array to value 1.

When we need to add another element to the filter, the process above will be repeated, meaning all 'k' number of hash functions will be applied to the new element, and the corresponding 'mod' will be applied to find index locations within the array. If all the index locations for this new element already have a value of '1' in the array, then the new element is considered possibly already present in the dataset. If the value at any of the returned index locations is found to be a 0 (zero), it will be toggled to 1, and the new element will be considered not already available in the dataset.

The approach is pretty effective to guarantee no occurrence of 'false negatives' in a set, but it can return 'false positives' in some scenarios (refer to the section *Confusion Matrix* in *Chapter 2*). Meaning, it is possible that an element is not actually in the set, but the function returns a result saying it is already in it. There will never be a case when an element is in the set but the function says it is not in the set.

The 'master-bit-array' above is the data structure for the bloom filter. Since it uses hash values to perform lookups, for each hash function it demonstrates O(1) time complexity, making it quite fast for the purpose [14].

Use case:

- To look up if an element is already in the cache to reduce unnecessary cache misses, e.g., in the case of a web cache, serving read requests in the case of a distributed data store.
- Distributed databases, e.g., Bigtable and Cassandra, use Bloom filters to minimize unnecessary disk reads while querying data from underlying storage [15].
- Email spam filters use this technique to identify spam emails or blacklisted IPs, reducing time-consuming entire set matches.
- Intrusion detection system

Applications and variations of Bloom filter

Membership testing appears in many other real-world scenarios where it performs far better than a full lookup.

There are algorithms available that allow elements to be deleted from the data structure. These include a Counting Bloom Filter and Cuckoo Filter, to name a couple [16].

Note

How to determine the array size for a Bloom filter

In general, between 4 and 10 hash functions are implemented depending upon the number of elements needed within the filter as well as the desired false positive rate.

To calculate the optimal array size for a filter implementation, the following formula is used:

$m = - (n \times \ln p) / (\ln 2)^2$

Where:

- m = Size of the bit array.
- n = Expected number of elements.
- p = Desired false positive probability.
- ln = Natural logarithm (log base 'e')

So, if you want a filter to handle 1 million elements and you want to maintain a 2% of false positive rate then size of the bit array (m) can be calculated as:

- n = 1,000,000
- p = 2/100 = 0.02
- hence, $\ln p = \ln 0.02 \approx -3.912$
- $(\ln 2)^2 \approx 0.4805$ (approx.)

Putting these values into the preceding formula gives:

m ≈ 8,000,000 bits (rounded figure) ≈ 1 MB of memory

[8 bits = 1 byte; therefore, 8,000,000 bits = 1,000,000 bytes ≈ 1 MB]

Observation: The memory (space requirement) changes inversely as we change the desired false positive probability for the same number of elements.

An ideal number of hash functions for Bloom filter implementation can be calculated as:

$(\ln 2) \times m/n$

Another important area associated with data is data replication and replica handling. Data replication is essential for achieving high availability, fault tolerance, and low-latency access. Yet, replicas inevitably diverge due to network partitions, node failures, delayed updates, or concurrent writes. A distributed system must therefore be capable of detecting inconsistencies between replicas and also repair them efficiently.

In the following sections we examine three widely adopted approaches: read repair, which restores consistency during read operations; Merkle tree, which enables efficient comparison of large datasets; and anti-entropy protocols, which continuously reconcile replicas in the background to ensure eventual convergence.

Proactively reconcile inconsistent data: Read-repair

Read repair is often implemented in systems supporting eventual consistency (BASE) models. It is used to present a consistent data view and enhance the system's reliability while performing a 'read' operation. 'Read repair' comprises many underlying algorithms, e.g., Quorum read, Lazy read, and Immediate read [27].

Cassandra uses read repair to maintain data consistency [26] as per the following example:

Suppose the system consists of a total of 5 nodes with a read consistency level=two.

A client performs a read request. The node that receives a read request from the client can be a 'replica node' or a non-replica node. If the request coordinator is a replica node as well, then one more replica node will be consulted before a response is sent back.

> **Note**
>
> Read consistency level determines how many replica nodes must return a response before the read request is considered successful. For consistency level=2, two replica nodes will be contacted. For level=3, three replica nodes will be contacted before a response to the read request is sent back to the user. With an increase in the number of participating replicas, the read latency can increase.
>
> A replica node is a node in this distributed environment that holds a copy of the data a user has requested. If the node does not contain a copy of the requested data, then it is just a node in the system. Regardless of whether a node is a replica node or not, all nodes can work as a coordinating node, i.e., they can accept requests from users.

To explain the concept, consider that the request coordinator is a non-replica node. In this case, when a read request is received, the nearest replica node for that coordinator will be queried for the full data as per the user's request (let's call it `result-snap-1`). Next, the coordinator will reach out to one more replica node (because consistency level=2), but this time it will only ask for the 'hash' value of the data as per the user's request (let's call it result-digest-2).

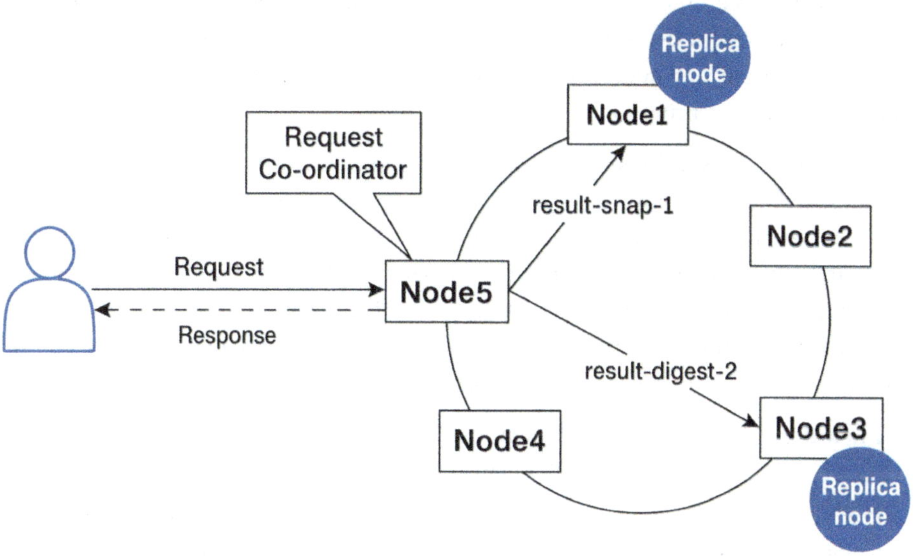

Figure 3.7: The read-repair flow between the coordinator and replica nodes

Once relevant information from both the chosen replica nodes is received, the coordinator will calculate the hash of '`result-snap-1`' and match it against '`result-digest-2`'. If both hashes match, no further action is needed, and the result will be sent back to the user. If there is a mismatch in hash, then the coordinator will ask the second node to send the actual data (let's call it `result-snap-2`) for the request. The coordinator will determine the latest copy between `result-snap-1` and `result-snap-2` (or an amalgamation of data from two result sets). The final copy of the result will be sent back to the user as a response. Also, replica node(s) will be updated with the latest information as sent to the user. This repairs the information on replica node(s) with the most up-to-date information for the next service request.

In the next section we will examine a strategy to perform reconciliation of replicas as a background activity with the help of anti-entropy.

Keeping replicas in sync: Anti-entropy

"Entropy" means "A measure of the disorder or randomness in a closed system" or "A measure of the loss of information in a transmitted message".

Data is often replicated onto multiple nodes in a distributed environment for data availability, reliability, etc. Such replication introduces additional challenges to maintain consistency among these replicas. Anti-entropy guides the way to attain data consistency and integrity in such an environment through eventual convergence.

In its original form it is defined as a background mechanism in which "every site regularly chooses another site at random and by exchanging database content with it resolves any differences between the two" [23]. The mechanism outlines three main properties, i) Each round involves exactly two participants, ii) After the exchange, both participants hold the union of the information they had before exchange (appropriate conflict resolution is accounted for), and iii) if connectivity between the participants are not a constraint, any update on one site will reach to every other participant sites eventually. Let us elaborate the stages involved –

1. **Initiation**: This can be on-demand or can be triggered on a scheduled basis. The interacting participants can follow Push, Pull, and Push-Pull model to request for data.
2. **Data comparison**: This is an important step that require an agreed, deterministic scale between the interacting replicas for data exchange. Below we have highlighted a few ways to achieve this:
    a. **Timestamp based**: The interaction initiator replica can select a timestamp and communicate it with the participating replica during handshake. That means, all data objects (tuples) newer than the supplied timestamp will be shared by the participating replica to the initiator. Worst-case scenario might involve the entire site data movement from the participant to the initiator. For a large-scale replica holding terabytes or petabytes worth of data, it becomes impractical.
    b. **Checksum and recent-update list**: In this approach each replica maintains an update list along with update timestamp. Also, after each create/update operation on a replica a checksum for the entire database is created. During comparison stage, the two participating system first compares the checksum. If there is a match then no further action needed. In case of a mismatch, the participating replicas will exchange their update list. The differentiating data will be shared across.

   c. **Merkle tree**: It is one of the most efficient ways to perform replicas comparison. A detailed overview of this approach is presented in the next section, *Detecting differences between replicas: Merkle trees.* The trade-off of this approach is to keep maintaining the hash tree on updates. This is because every update will change the hash of the tuple as well as all parent nodes in the hierarchy.

3. **Data reconciliation**: Once a mismatch is identified, a corrective technique(e.g. full repair, incremental repair) is implemented to sync the replicas.

Overall, it is quite resource-intensive exercise but it ensures data on each replicated node is in a consistent state regardless of their reads [24]. In real-life use cases, both read-repair and anti-entropy are implemented together. Read-repair ensure that the most up-to-date copy of a data is served to the requester. Anti-entropy, on the other hand, ensures that the entire replica reaches an eventually consistent state.

As explained earlier, we are now going to take detailed look on Merkle trees to understand how it makes make that comparison efficient.

Detecting differences between replicas: Merkle trees

In distributed systems, keeping data consistent across multiple nodes is a common challenge. Systems often need an efficient way to compare large amounts of data, identify differences, and verify data integrity without transferring or comparing the entire dataset. Merkle trees are a powerful data structure that enables this capability and is commonly used as part of distributed system design patterns for data synchronization and efficient verification.

Originally introduced by Ralph Merkle as a mechanism for efficient cryptographic verification, a Merkle tree, also known as a hash tree, is a tree-based data structure where each leaf node represents the hash of an individual object, data block, or record. Each non-leaf node contains the hash generated from the combined hashes of its child nodes. This hierarchical structure creates a single hash value, known as the root hash, which acts as a fingerprint of the entire dataset and enables efficient verification of data changes [25].

Typically, a Merkle tree is a binary tree where each leaf element represents the hash of the object/data/record the leaf corresponds to. Pairing two leaves together, a branch is formed that represents the hash of the concatenated hash of the participating leaves. There is special handling for single/non-pairing leaf records. The process of hash concatenation and hashing on the concatenated hashes continues to formulate more branches until a single remaining top branch is found. This is called the root hash.

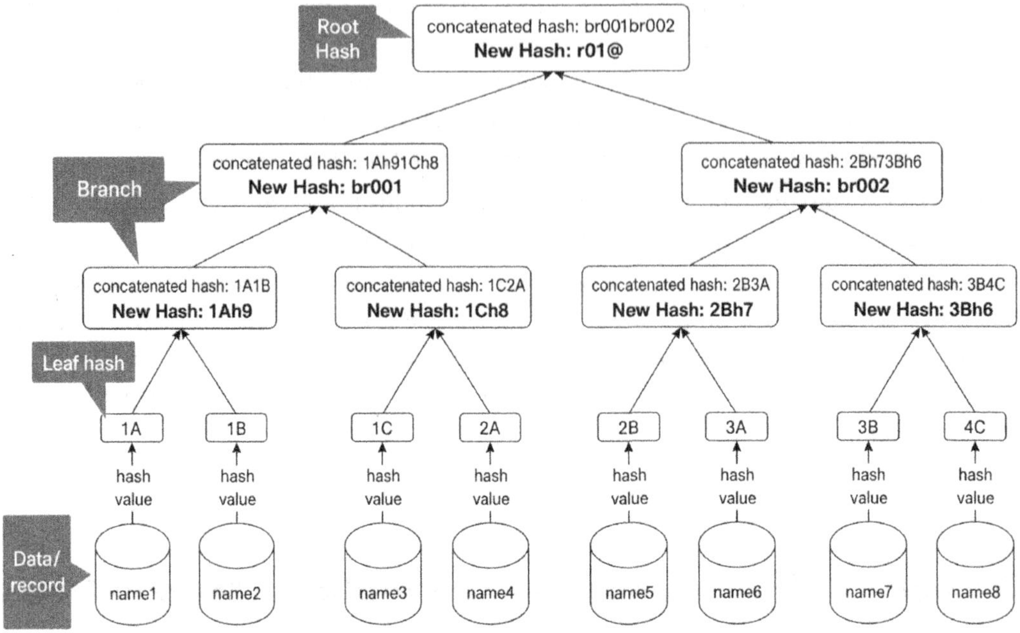

Figure 3.8: A Merkle tree built from data records and their hashes

The root hash acts as a fingerprint of the entire dataset. If any underlying data changes, the corresponding hash values change, causing the root hash to change as well. This allows distributed systems to quickly identify differences between copies of data and synchronize only the changed portions.

In *Figure 3.8*, the actual data items/records are represented as 'name1', 'name2'....'name8'. On each record we have applied the same hash function to get the leaf-level hash. We have then concatenated the leaf hashes in pairs and rehashed them to get a branch-level hash. This operation is repeated until we reach the root.

This approach is particularly useful when you want to compare data spread over multiple nodes in a distributed system to check for consistency. In case of a hash mismatch, you can conclude that some corrective action is needed to attain consistency.

Use case examples: Version control systems, distributed file systems, Certificate Transparency logs, and blockchain networks. In distributed systems such as Amazon Dynamo (as described in its original design paper) and Riak, Merkle trees are used with anti-entropy to efficiently detect differences between replicas and synchronize only the required data in the background. Many of the systems mentioned also use Read repair to proactively fix differences at the moment of a read.

The next few sections focus on some established patterns that are widely used within the industry. We will start with a pattern that is used to protect services from traffic spikes, abusive clients, and other attacks, such as denial-of-service (DoS) attacks. Rate limiting enforces predefined request quotas to preserve system stability and ensure fair resource utilization. We will build an in-depth understanding of rate-limiting with the help of some techniques that can be used to implement it.

Controlling request flow with rate limiting

In computing, rate limiting is a technique used to control traffic flow toward a servicing system. In a web-based system, a server is a servicing system for clients, and hence a rate-limiting technique will be implemented by the server system to limit the number of requests that can be allowed in a defined or agreed interval. [17][19]

There are several benefits to using this technique:

- Enhanced security by reducing **DoS (Denial of service)** attack surface by limiting the rate
- Fair resource usage is achieved by allocating appropriate quotas to consumers. It also enables professional services to offer pricing models
- Improved system health by allowing the system to process a manageable number of requests

A rate limiter can be described as a technique used to determine if some sequence of discrete events conforms to their defined limits. There are multiple approaches available to implement a rate limiter to serve different use cases. We are going to focus on a few of them.

Leaky bucket algorithm

The leaky bucket algorithm is based on the analogy of a water bucket with a hole for the water to flow out gradually. It is primarily used to control the rate at which traffic enters a network or system by allowing a constant transmit rate regardless of the input traffic flow from the external source [18].

Explaining with the analogy: Consider a water bucket that has a hole at the bottom. Water is constantly flowing into the bucket from one or more sources with a possible burst flow at times. But water flows out of the bucket from the hole at the bottom at a constant speed, regardless of the volume of water coming in from the source. Understandably, the size of the outflow hole is much smaller than the top opening of the bucket. At a certain point, a situation may arise when the bucket is completely full because of incoming water volume. At this point, any more water coming into the bucket will require different handling, i.e., it will be wasted or preserved elsewhere. Regardless, water inside the bucket is still streaming out from the hole at a constant speed.

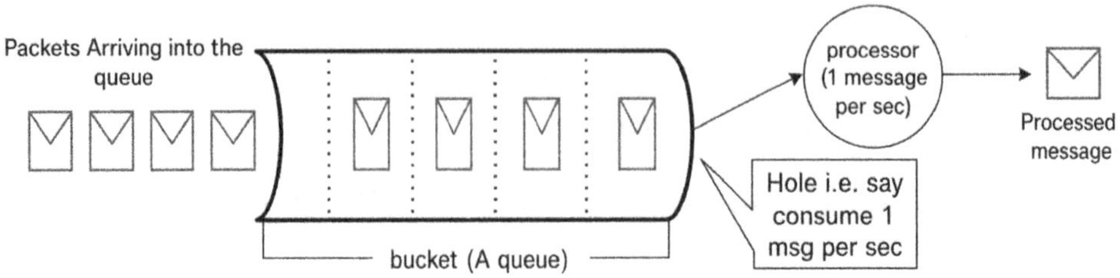

Figure 3.9: The leaky-bucket approach to rate limiting

In this approach, you maintain a bucket (i.e., a defined storage layer, say a queue) to store incoming requests/packets from a source. The requests/packets are picked and processed by workers at a constant (configured) rate. If the packet arrival rate is greater than the worker's processing rate (as shown in *Figure 3.9*), then the queue can fill to match its capacity. After this point, any incoming packet(s) will be discarded outright, if not handled. In the diagram above, there are 4 new packets arriving in the queue with one empty space. Since the queue has space to accommodate one packet, one will be accepted for processing; the other three will be discarded outright.

This algorithm is very simple to implement and quite effective for rate-limiting. Use cases where it can be used include API gateways, streaming services (such as video processing), message queues, other service-based architectures. The trade-off here is the possibility of packet loss without notifying the packet creator, leaving a permanent information miss.

Token bucket algorithm

It is another simple but powerful mechanism for controlling traffic flow and enforcing rate limits. This approach supports occasional bursts while controlling the overall average request rate.

Let us understand the idea using a simple example and illustration (*Figure 3.10*). Consider the following scenario:

- Maximum capacity of the container = 10 tokens
- It self-generates tokens at a constant refill rate (say, 5 tokens/second)
- Condition: A request is only placed in the container in exchange for a token. If no token is available, then incoming request(s) will be dropped (or queued elsewhere as per your implementation).

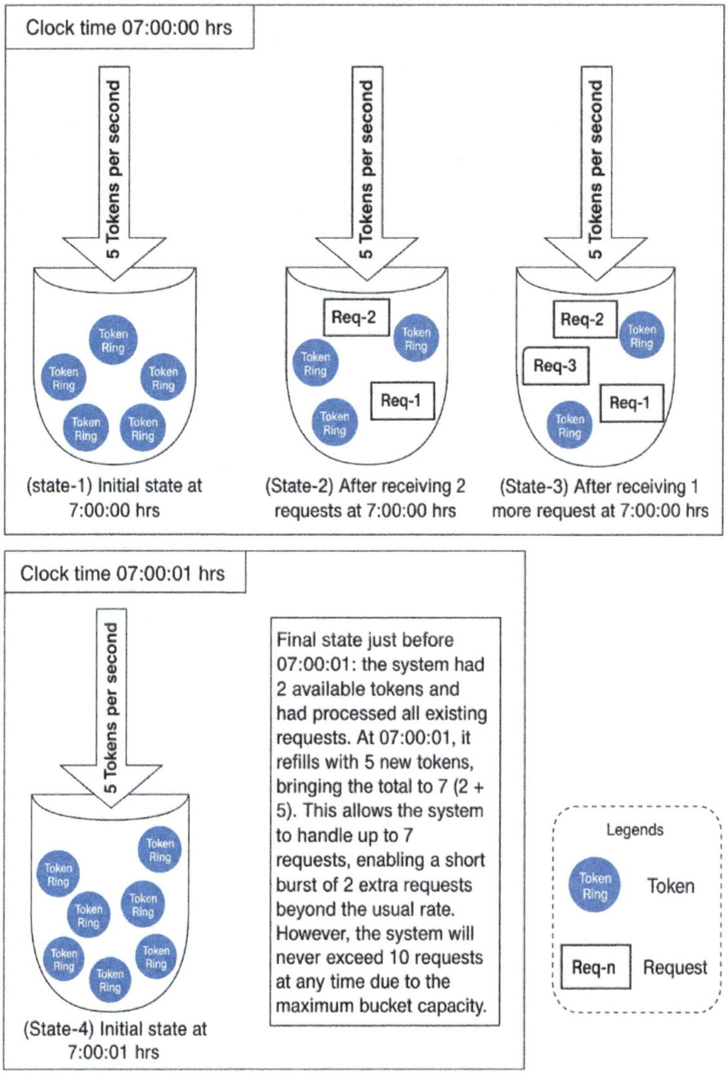

Figure 3.10: The token-bucket approach to rate limiting

As per *Figure 3.10*, on an average, the implementation allows up to 5 requests per second in the container for processing. There can be a case where all 10 tokens are available within a time window (because of the max capacity).

In such a case, a total of 10 requests can exchange a token to secure a place for processing. Since the system is built to process all the requests in the bucket, all 10 requests will be picked for processing, allowing short bursts in traffic handling.

Also, if there is no token left in the bucket within a particular time window, then any incoming request will either have to wait (e.g. queued) for the next interval or they are dropped.

In our example, there are 5 refill tokens generated every second, enabling the system to serve up to a five requests per second.

Fixed window counter

One of the simplest mechanisms to implement rate limiting is the fixed window counter. In this implementation, a time chunk(window) is determined, e.g., per second, per minute, or per hour. A defined number of requests are accepted within that time window.

Assume the limiter accepts 100 requests per minute. Requests beyond this limit are rejected. In the fixed window counter, let's say the timer starts at 07:00:00 hrs. The system can accept a total of 100 requests between 07:00:00 hrs. and less than 07:01:00 hrs. At 07:01:00 hrs., the counter resets for the next 100 requests, allowing the next 100 requests. All the requests, up to the imposed limit, can appear in one go, i.e., in our example, all 100 requests can appear at 07:00:59 hrs.

The simplicity of this approach comes with a trade-off. Even though the system constrains the total number of requests within a fixed time frame, it can still allow bursts of traffic around the boundary of two windows. As per our example scenario mentioned earlier, the system receives 100 requests at 07:00:50 hrs. When the counter resets at 07:01:00, it can accept another 100 requests immediately. In this scenario, the system serves 200 requests within a 20-second period (between 07:00:50 hrs and 07:01:10 hrs), even though the configured limit is 100 requests per minute. This makes fixed window counters simple and efficient, but less effective when strict control over traffic bursts is required. If strict control over traffic bursts is required, 'Sliding window' is a better choice.

Sliding window

The sliding window approach addresses a limitation of fixed-window counters. Rather than keeping a fixed time window, it considers a moving time window, i.e., if the system is built to accept 100 requests per minute. When a request arrives, it will check if the total number of requests in the last minute is under 100. If not, then the request is rejected; else, it is accepted.

The two main approaches under this umbrella are as follows.

Sliding window log

It maintains the request arrival timestamp for all the past incoming requests to look back and count the total number of served requests in the defined timeframe from now when a request arrives. If the total count (including the new request) is not more than the defined limit, the request will be allowed. This technique generates a precise result by keeping system processing within limits all the time. Log entries beyond the current timeframe are discarded. So if the time window is 1 minute and a request arrives at 07:01:01 hrs., then it will check all the request logs/ timestamps until 07:00:01 hrs. to count the number of requests the system has served. If the max limit has been reached, the new request will be discarded; else, the new request will be accepted and its timestamp will be recorded. In this example, logs earlier than 07:00:01 hrs. will be removed.

Sliding window counter

It shows a slight improvement in terms of performance over the sliding window log. In this case, not the entire timestamp is maintained. Rather, the aggregated counters for the current and previous time windows are maintained. With the arrival of a new request, an approximation exercise is performed to determine if the request falls within the limit count. If not, then the request is rejected.

Token bucket with sliding window (hybrid approach)

This approach combines the core features as supported by the token bucket and sliding window mechanisms. In this approach tokens are refilled at a constant rate into the bucket to serve requests. This allows a short burst of traffic. If the number of requests is more than the number of available tokens, then they are rejected. A sliding window also maintains a count of the overall number of requests that are served in the given time window. If the overall count goes beyond the limit, the requests are discarded within that window, maintaining the fair usage policy.

For example, say the total bucket capacity=60 tokens; token refill rate is 10 tokens/sec; the maximum requests allowed by the system in a minute is 500, respectively. In this case, the system allows a short burst of traffic by exchanging up to 60 tokens for requests. As per the refill rate, the system can support up to 10 (refill rate) x 60 (seconds) = 600 requests in a minute. But since the max limit imposed is 500 per minute, if at any point the request count goes over 500 within a minute's length, the request will be rejected because of the sliding window.

The algorithms above decide how a system behaves however it is the design patterns that decide how the system holds together when things go wrong.

Distributed systems fail constantly in small ways, a slow dependency, a dropped message, a replica that has drifted out of sync, and a good design assumes this rather than hoping otherwise. These patterns are the reusable moves for that reality: they contain a failure before it cascades, keep replicas honest, and combine work spread across many nodes. Where the algorithms make a system fast and scalable, the patterns make it resilient and consistent. So, let's move to some common prevailing patterns that you might come across while designing many systems.

Failing fast: The circuit breaker pattern

Circuit Breaker is a software design pattern commonly used in distributed environments to prevent cascading failures during remote calls. A cascading failure can happen when a remote dependency stops responding to the incoming requests against their expected time limits. It can occur if the remote dependency is overwhelmed, unavailable or faulty. In such cases, the calling system will wait until a timeout threshold is reached, resulting in critical resource wastage like memory, connections, threads, and other resources, at the caller's side, leading to cascading failures across the system.

A circuit breaker addresses this problem by temporarily blocking access to a failing service after detecting repeated failures, resulting in improved system reliability [20][21]. Unlike consensus algorithms that help multiple nodes agree on the same state, circuit breakers focus on preventing failures from spreading between services [22].

A circuit-breaker is a three-state machine, 'closed', 'open', and 'half-open':

- **Closed** state indicates that the system (machine) is operational as expected, and hence, requests can be sent. This is the normal operating mode.
- **Open** state indicates that the dependency is experiencing failures. Requests are immediately rejected without calling the system, allowing the caller to fail fast and avoid consuming unnecessary resources. In case of such an appropriate exception, a fallback response will be returned to the caller.
- **Half-Open** - In this state, a limited number of requests from callers are sent to the system to execute. Based on the outcome, the circuit breaker either returns to the Closed state or moves back to Open.

Circuit breaker states and workflow

The circuit breaker maintains a default state of 'Closed.' While serving requests, it maintains a counter that keeps track of the number of failed requests in a given time period. If the number reaches the threshold, the state will change from 'Closed' to 'Open' preventing requests from going through. Any request arriving to the system during the 'open' state will receive an exception response immediately. During the 'Open' state, the system starts a time-out timer and tries to recover from the failure before the timer runs out. When the timer expires, the state will be moved to 'Half-Open' when a limited number of requests will be sent to the system for execution.

If all the requests during the 'Half-Open' state are served as expected, the system will change its state to the default 'Closed' and reset the counter. Meaning, the system will return to normal operation. If from the limited number of requests allowed, any request during the 'Half-Open' state fails, the state changes back to 'Open' along with the time-out timer, and the steps are repeated until all the requests allowed to pass through within the 'Half-Open' state return a success.

A circuit breaker protects a system from a failing dependency. The last one, scatter-gather, handles a different task: sending one request to many nodes and combining their answers into a single response.

Scatter-gather pattern: Fanning out and combining results

Scatter-gather is a message-routing pattern that involves sending (or broadcasting) similar or related requests to multiple recipients for a response, and once responses are received, aggregating them into a single response. Along with other use cases, the pattern is quite useful in achieving parallel processing, reducing response latency while dealing with multiple systems in a distributed environment.[28][29]

The pattern consists of two main phases:

- Scatter phase: In this phase, a request is sent over to multiple recipients in parallel. The recipients will then independently work upon the request and then share the result with the coordinator.
- Gather phase: In this phase, the responses from all the participants will be collated using desired business processing logic to generate a single final outcome.

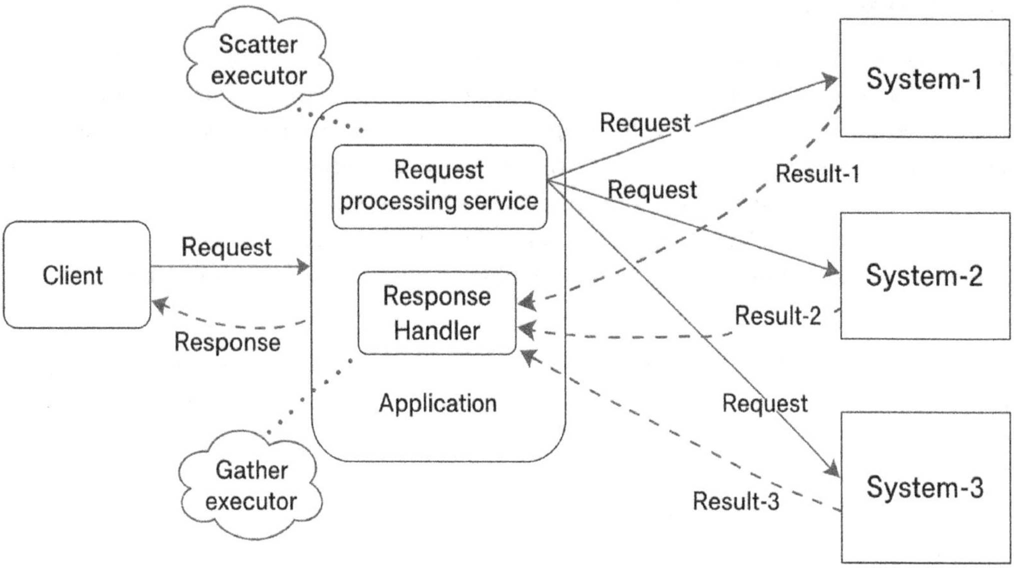

Figure 3.11: The scatter and gather phases of the scatter-gather pattern

Figure 3.11 is a representation to explain the pattern. The scatter and gather phase can be executed by two entirely different application components or using a single component. Although this pattern can be implemented to support both synchronous and asynchronous communication mechanisms, it is quite commonly used in the latter.

This pattern is of particular importance while designing a system like a key-value store during a key search. In such a case, a query processor can broadcast a key search request to all the relevant participating nodes. This will facilitate parallel key search execution by all the nodes. Results returned from these nodes can then be aggregated to respond to the caller. Other use cases include the following:

- Optimizing query executions on multiple shards of a distributed system
- Fetching, aggregating and consolidating results involving multiple discrete API-based systems
- Implementing map-reduce processing where the data request is routed to multiple data processing endpoints.

What we learnt in the later part of the chapter on design patterns: In a distributed system, something is always failing or drifting. The circuit breaker stops a struggling dependency from dragging its callers down with it. Anti-entropy, Merkle trees, and read-repair are three views of one job, detecting and closing the gaps between replicas cheaply. And scatter-gather turns many partial answers into one. These patterns all answer the same worry.

None of them make failure impossible; they make it survivable, which is the quiet difference between a design that looks good on a whiteboard and one that stays up in production.

Summary

Knowing the vocabulary of distributed systems is one thing; knowing the algorithms and patterns that make them work is another. This chapter crossed that line, moving from concepts you need to understand into techniques you can apply, reason about, and defend in a real implementation or an interview.

The first half covered the core algorithms: generating globally unique, time-ordered IDs at scale with schemes like Snowflake; spreading data evenly across a shifting set of nodes with consistent and rendezvous hashing; reaching agreement despite failures and delays with consensus algorithms like Raft; testing membership cheaply with Bloom filters; and shaping traffic with rate limiters from the leaky bucket to the sliding window.

The second half turned to design patterns for resilience and consistency: the circuit breaker that stops one failing dependency from cascading into an outage, and the family of techniques, anti-entropy, Merkle trees, and read-repair, that quietly keep replicas in agreement, together with the scatter-gather pattern for fanning a request out and combining the results. Each carries a trade-off, and the skill is recognizing which one a given problem is asking for.

The next chapter takes this further, moving from these algorithms into the architectural building blocks that hold large-scale systems together: how data is stored, replicated, and retrieved across distributed environments.

Quiz

Q1. What problem does Snowflake ID primarily solve?

A) Scaling caches

B) Generating globally unique, ordered IDs across distributed systems

C) Encrypting data

D) Maintaining user sessions

Q2. What are the main components encoded in a Snowflake ID? Select multiple if applicable.

A) Machine ID

B) Timestamp

C) Sequence number

D) Database ID

Q3. Which of the following is NOT a Raft server role?

A) Follower

B) Candidate

C) Leader

D) Coordinator

Q4. What is the primary purpose of the Raft algorithm?

A) Distribute traffic evenly across servers

B) Leader selection and achieve consensus in a replicated log

C) Encrypt messages between nodes

D) Detect and recover from node crashes

Q5. Horizontal scaling typically involves the following:

A) Upgrading storage capacity of one server

B) Running multiple database nodes to share the load

C) Optimizing SQL queries only

D) Reducing consistency requirements

Q6. In the token bucket algorithm, tokens are added to the bucket at a fixed rate. What happens if the bucket is empty when a request arrives?

A) Request is delayed until a token is available

B) Request is dropped/rejected

C) A new bucket is created

D) The system bypasses rate limits.

Q7. If the bucket size is 10 and the refill rate is 5 tokens/sec, what's the max burst size the system can handle?

A) 5

B) 10

C) 15

D) 20

Q8. The sliding window algorithm is often preferred over fixed window counters because:

A) It's easier to implement

B) It requires less memory

C) It allows unlimited bursts

D) It avoids sharp boundary effects and is smoother.

Q9. In a sliding window log implementation, what data structure is commonly used to store request timestamps? Select multiple if applicable. Tick all that apply.

A) Queue

B) Sorted list

C) List

D)Array

Q10. What is the main purpose of a Snowflake ID generator (like Twitter's)?

A) Rate limiting API requests

B) Encrypting database records

C) Generating globally unique, time-ordered IDs at scale

D) Synchronizing distributed clocks.

Q11. In its default Snowflake ID **format, how many machines can be used per** data center **for unique ID generation -**

A) 28

B) 32

C) 48

D) 64

Q12. What is the time complexity of locating the correct node for a given key in a consistent hashing ring with N nodes?

A) O(1)

B) O(log N) (with binary search)

C) O(N)

D) O(log log N)

Q13. Which failure scenario can consistent hashing handle more gracefully than modulo-based partitioning?

A) Network partition

B) Node crash/removal

C) Disk failure

D) CPU spike

Q14. While finding a host node on the hash ring, you traverse in which direction?

A) Clockwise

B) Counter clockwise

C) None

D) Random

Q15. What problem does consistent hashing primarily solve in distributed systems?

A) Preventing SQL injection

B) Reducing cache misses when nodes are added or removed

C) Ensuring encryption of data

D) Improving CPU utilization

References

Unique ID generation

[1] Leach, P., Mealling, M., & Salz, R. (2005). "A Universally Unique Identifier (UUID) URN Namespace." RFC 4122, IETF. `https://www.rfc-editor.org/rfc/rfc4122`

[2] Twitter Engineering (2010). "Announcing Snowflake." `https://blog.twitter.com/engineering/en_us/a/2010/announcing-snowflake`

[3] Segment. "KSUID - K-Sortable Unique Identifier." `https://github.com/segmentio/ksuid`

Distributed hashing

[4] Karger, D., Lehman, E., Leighton, T., Panigrahy, R., Levine, M., & Lewin, D. (1997). "Consistent Hashing and Random Trees." Proceedings of ACM STOC '97.

[5] Thaler, D. G., & Ravishankar, C. V. (1998). "Using Name-Based Mappings to Increase Hit Rates." IEEE/ACM Transactions on Networking, 6(1). [Rendezvous / Highest Random Weight hashing]

[6] Stoica, I., Morris, R., Karger, D., Kaashoek, M. F., & Balakrishnan, H. (2001). "Chord: A Scalable Peer-to-peer Lookup Service for Internet Applications." Proceedings of ACM SIGCOMM '01.

[7] DeCandia, G., et al. (2007). "Dynamo: Amazon's Highly Available Key-value Store." Proceedings of ACM SOSP '07. [consistent hashing with virtual nodes]

Consensus algorithms

[8] Howard, H., & Mortier, R. (2020). Paxos vs Raft: Have we reached consensus on distributed consensus? Proceedings of the 7th Workshop on Principles and Practice of Consistency for Distributed Data. `https://dl.acm.org/doi/10.1145/3380787.3393681`

[9] Lamport, L. (2001). "Paxos Made Simple." ACM SIGACT News, 32(4).

[10] Ongaro, D., & Ousterhout, J. (2014). "In Search of an Understandable Consensus Algorithm." Proceedings of USENIX ATC '14. [Raft] `https://raft.github.io/raft.pdf`

[11] Junqueira, F. P., Reed, B. C., & Serafini, M. (2011). "Zab: High-performance Broadcast for Primary-backup Systems." Proceedings of IEEE/IFIP DSN '11.

[12] Castro, M., & Liskov, B. (1999). "Practical Byzantine Fault Tolerance." Proceedings of USENIX OSDI '99.

[13] Raft consensus algorithm - papers, animations, and implementations. `https://raft.github.io/`

Membership testing - Bloom filters

[14] Bloom, B. H. (1970). "Space/Time Trade-offs in Hash Coding with Allowable Errors." Communications of the ACM, 13(7).

[15] Broder, A., & Mitzenmacher, M. (2004). "Network Applications of Bloom Filters: A Survey." Internet Mathematics, 1(4).

[16] Fan, B., Andersen, D. G., Kaminsky, M., & Mitzenmacher, M. (2014). "Cuckoo Filter: Practically Better Than Bloom." Proceedings of ACM CoNEXT '14.

Rate limiting

[17] Stripe Engineering. "Scaling your API with rate limiters." https://stripe.com/blog/rate-limiters

[18] Blake, S., et al. (1998). "An Architecture for Differentiated Services." RFC 2475, IETF. [token bucket / leaky bucket traffic conditioning] https://www.rfc-editor.org/rfc/rfc2475

[19] Cloudflare. "How we built rate limiting capable of scaling to millions of domains." https://blog.cloudflare.com/counting-things-a-lot-of-different-things/

Circuit breaker

[20] Nygard, M. T. (2018). Release It! (2nd ed.). Pragmatic Bookshelf. [origin of the circuit-breaker pattern]

[21] Fowler, M. (2014). "CircuitBreaker." https://martinfowler.com/bliki/CircuitBreaker.html

[22] Netflix Technology Blog (2012). "Fault Tolerance in a High Volume, Distributed System." https://netflixtechblog.com/fault-tolerance-in-a-high-volume-distributed-system-91ab4faae74a

Anti-entropy and gossip

[23] Demers, A., et al. (1987). "Epidemic Algorithms for Replicated Database Maintenance." Proceedings of ACM PODC '87.

[24] van Renesse, R., Dumitriu, D., Gough, V., & Thomas, C. (2008). "Efficient Reconciliation and Flow Control for Anti-Entropy Protocols." Proceedings of LADIS '08.

Merkle trees

[25] Merkle, R. C. (1987). "A Digital Signature Based on a Conventional Encryption Function." Advances in Cryptology - CRYPTO '87, Springer LNCS 293.

Read repair and eventual consistency

[26] Apache Cassandra. "Read repair." https://cassandra.apache.org/doc/stable/cassandra/managing/operating/read_repair.html

[27] Vogels, W. (2009). "Eventually Consistent." Communications of the ACM, 52(1).

Scatter-gather and aggregation

[28] Hohpe, G., & Woolf, B. (2003). Enterprise Integration Patterns. Addison-Wesley. [Scatter-Gather pattern]

[29] AWS. "Scatter-gather pattern." `https://docs.aws.amazon.com/prescriptive-guidance/latest/cloud-design-patterns/scatter-gather.html`

Background

[30] Cachin, C., Guerraoui, R., & Rodrigues, L. (2011). Introduction to Reliable and Secure Distributed Programming (2nd ed.). Springe

4

The Building Blocks of System Design

System design is not merely about assembling components; it's about understanding why those components exist, how they interact, and what trade-offs they introduce. Concepts such as latency, throughput, consistency, and fault tolerance are the lenses through which we evaluate design choices. Similarly, the roles of clients, servers, APIs, databases, caches, etc. form the vocabulary of every system you will build in your real-life projects as well as during an interview. In this chapter we are going to elaborate on some core building blocks in depth. For most of the system designs presented, these building blocks can be stitched together for your use case. The most important decision you will have to make during your interview will be which combination of building blocks to use, based on a clear understanding of why.

Before taking a deep dive into this chapter, it is recommended to have a good grip on the concepts presented in *Chapter 2*. References to a few algorithms and patterns from *Chapter 3* have also been used here, and hence *Chapter 3* is a recommended prerequisite as well.

By the end of this chapter, you should be confidently able to:

- Choose between stateful and stateless architecture with reasoning
- Talk about scalability, its different dimensions, and when you would choose one over another
- Understand load balancers, their types, and some common algorithms that are used
- Compare SQL/NoSQL trade-offs to make an informed selection in your architecture
- Sketch a sharding strategy

- Explain the CAP trade-off in basic terms
- Evaluate multiple tools and techniques that can be bundled together to produce a meaningful architecture

Stateful and stateless application

It is an important architectural decision to choose between stateful and stateless patterns for your presented business problem. This choice fundamentally affects how an application scales, how users are managed, and how failures are handled. You must know the goal in the context of the problem you are solving as well as the trade-offs associated with the mentioned architecture patterns.

Stateful

A stateful application (also see *Stateful vs. stateless*, from *Chapter 2*) is an application where the server keeps the state information of clients' previous interactions, sessions, and other relevant information to determine or execute the next request. A stateful service becomes more relevant where low-latency and in-memory performance is a non-negotiable requirement.

Think of a multiplayer game system where the state of each active user changes on average 50-60 times per second. Here, latency is the most critical requirement. To reduce latency, you would attempt to minimize the size of data packets being exchanged between the client and the server. At the same time, you would want to precisely know a player's current state, like exact coordinate location, rewards, remaining lives, scores, etc., for an optimal user and gaming experience. To achieve this, the server will need to maintain a lot of information about players in memory for faster reaction and response. Hence, a stateful approach is ideal in this scenario. If we choose a stateless approach instead, the size of data packets that a client will exchange with the server will be larger. Also, the server will need to perform some complex and maybe repetitive calculations for each request, slowing down the overall response time.

In an environment with more than one node, you would require a traffic manager to efficiently manage request propagation. This is achieved with the help of a load balancer. We have discussed *load balancing* at length, in a later section of this chapter. For the purpose of this section, we cover an important load balancing behavioral aspect needed for a stateful application.

Stateful applications and load balancing

In a multi-server environment, load balancers are used to distribute client requests to servers. To ensure that a client's request is always handled by the same server in a session for a stateful application, load balancers are configured with **'sticky sessions'**.

Note

Sticky sessions (or session affinity) ensure that all requests from a client are routed to and served by the same server. It is a common implementation practice when client session state is managed by servicing components, i.e., the backend server locally, and hence not shared. Some common use cases where you would implement a sticky-session approach include a system using WebSocket connections and gaming applications like multi-player games.

Some common mechanisms to implement sticky sessions -

Cookie-based: It is a simple and common type of implementation that can be found at the load balancer. In this case, when the load balancer receives the first request from a client, it inserts additional cookie information in the response to the client. In each subsequent call, the load balancer uses this additional cookie information to determine the target server. It is easy to implement, but the main trade-off is rebalancing issues when new servers are added. The new server might not be able to participate in request handling until a new client session is established.

Session ID-based: In this approach, the server adds identifying information as a suffix to the client's session ID. When the client sends any subsequent request, the load balancer parses the suffix information and forwards the request straight to that server. It reduces the need for the load balancer to maintain a mapping table as the server information is embedded in the session ID. Also, if additional load balancers are added to the ecosystem, they can start functioning without any prior context, as the server information is always available in the request. A real-world example is Apache Tomcat, which generates JSESSIONID with a 'jvmRoute' suffix added for server identification. The limitations of this approach are tight coupling of routing logic to a defined text format; if an active server is removed from the group, then all the clients previously served will need to be remapped. Similarly, adding a new server to the group cannot help share the load of active requests.

IP-based: We have covered this in detail in the section Load balancing.

Figure 4.1 illustrates a typical representation of a stateful application:

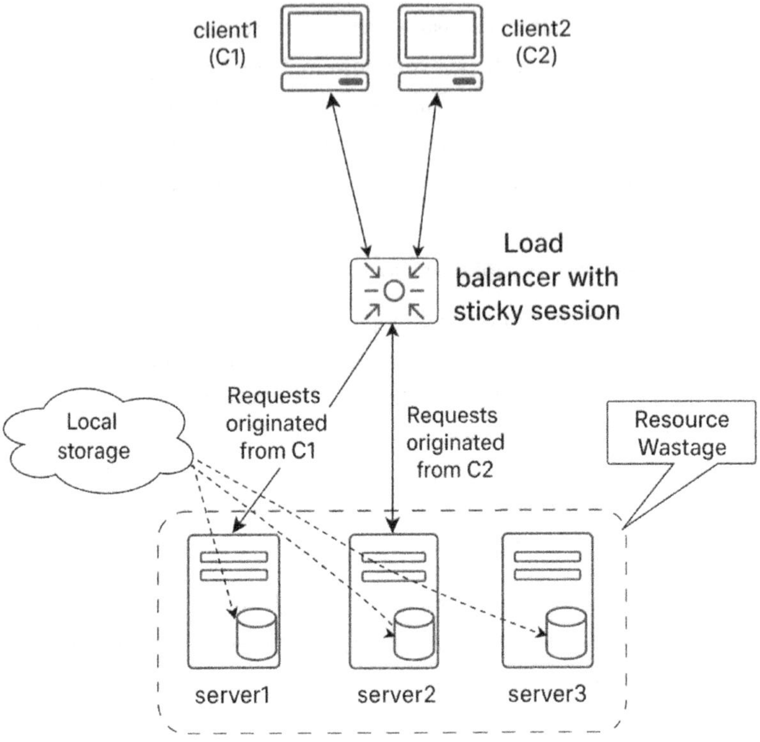

Figure 4.1: A high-level representation of a stateful application

In the preceding figure, you can observe that 'server3' is not able to contribute to request handling within the current session, resulting in resource wastage. Some practical examples and use cases for stateful applications are as follows:

- **A real-time chat system:** In this case, generally a client and server will interact using a stateful connection over the WebSocket protocol for a stable, low-latency, full-duplex conversation. This is still a strong use case for choosing a stateful implementation.
- **Video/audio streaming**: Some video/audio streaming services need to maintain session state to ensure continuity, quality of service, latency, etc. Examples include live streaming platforms, music streaming platforms, etc.

Drawbacks and challenges

The following are some trade-offs to consider while assessing this approach:

- **Resource-intensive:** High resource usage, as the setup requires the capability to store and manage users' session information. Each active session consumes server memory, and for an application with thousands or millions of concurrent users, memory requirements can become substantial. Maintaining session states requires CPU cycles for state management operations.
- **Scaling:** Since the servers within a stateful environment maintain users' session information in-memory or in local storage, it complicates scaling out. This is because until a client ends its session, all its requests will continue to land on the designated server for that session regardless of whether more servers are added to the cluster.
- **Server failure or fault tolerance:** In the event of a server issue, e.g., a crash, all associated sessions become irrecoverable, leading to a negative user experience as well as permanent data loss in some cases. For example, a subsequent request from a client might trigger an authentication challenge. A player may also be dropped from a multiplayer game.
- **Deployment Complexity**: Rolling updates and deployments become more complex with stateful applications. Draining sessions from servers before taking them offline, ensuring graceful handling of in-flight requests, and coordinating deployments without disrupting user sessions require sophisticated orchestration.
- **Data Consistency:** In scenarios where sessions need to be replicated for high availability, ensuring consistency of session data requires additional overhead around synchronization, conflict resolution, and eventual consistency considerations.

Stateless

Stateless applications are those where servers do not retain session information of their clients. That means each client request is treated independently of any previous request by the same client. This makes the overall application lightweight from a deployment perspective, as it enables it to scale out easily. Any server from the cluster can now perform request processing, regardless of whether the server processed the previous request by the same client. A common example is a RESTful service. In this case, each REST call by a client can be served by any server in the cluster. The trade-off here is that to serve a request, the server relies on the client to supply all the relevant information within the request. This means the request payload is slightly larger than in the case of a stateful application. Externalizing this information from the server also impacts overall latency.

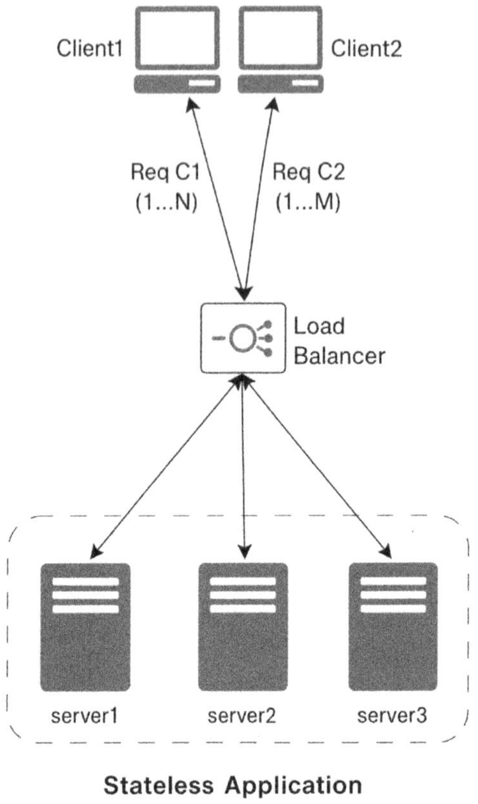

Figure 4.2: A sample multi-server stateless application

As shown in *Figure 4.2*, requests originating from clients during a session can be directed to any server for processing. This means that if more servers are added to this cluster, they will be picked seamlessly and can start contributing to load sharing immediately.

Foundational principles of stateless design

Stateless architecture represents a paradigm shift from stateful application design. In this architecture, every request contains all the information necessary for the server to process, as the server does not rely on information from previous requests, nor does it maintain any context about the client between requests.

The advantages of a stateless system extend to dependent systems in the ecosystem as well; for example, since any server can handle any request, load balancers can distribute traffic using simple round-robin or least-connections algorithms without worrying about session affinity. When traffic spikes, new server instances can be added immediately to serve requests without any warm-up periods or state synchronization.

Stateless models align with modern cloud-native architectures, containerization, and microservices patterns. Containers can be started and stopped dynamically based on demand, with no concerns about losing state, unlike stateful applications.

Authentication in stateless systems

Authentication is one of the primary challenges in stateless architecture. Since the server does not maintain session state, each client request must include authentication credentials. In most applications, users are identified by their unique usernames or email addresses and passwords, but it is inefficient and insecure to send these on every request. This challenge has been addressed through token-based authentication mechanisms. Some patterns include JSON Web Tokens, refresh tokens, OAuth 2.0, and OpenID Connect. The *Authentication* section in *Chapter 5* provides more detail on these topics.

The hybrid approach

A common mechanism to overcome the limitations of a stateful application while leveraging the flexibility offered by stateless architecture is decoupling locally managed server state by using an external data store. In this approach, servers do not hold session information locally but in a common centralized or decentralized store (as shown in *Figure 4.3*). Such a repository can be Redis or another suitable storage mechanism. A server will consult such storage to extract and store the client's state information as needed. By doing so, the servers can scale independently, demonstrating the same level of flexibility as in the case of a stateless architecture. Some benefits of this approach are:

- Freedom for the server to scale out with ease.
- A more reliable mechanism in case of a server failure in a stateful system.
- Deployment on a server is simpler and more controlled because of other servers' resilience in serving requests during deployment.
- Abstraction of layers. The storage layer and the application layer can scale independently without creating a bottleneck for each other.

The trade-offs this approach brings are -

- Increased latency: This approach introduces some time delay in request processing as servers need to consult an externalized storage for each request.
- Increased resource and management overhead: Additional infrastructure costs and management overhead are introduced for storage.
- Data management for sustained availability: Availability of stored session data across servers in a multi-region distributed environment requires more complex

implementation and comes with some implicit trade-offs, e.g., consistency model, replication strategy, etc.

- New single point of failure (SPoF): If a single external storage is used without failover configuration, it can become a new single point of failure that can bring the entire system down.

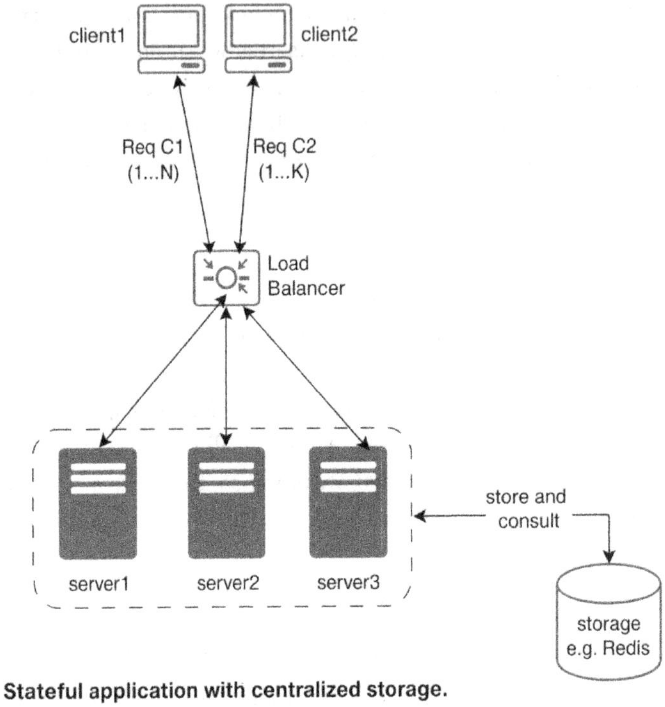

Figure 4.3: Architecture of hybrid applications

As shown in *Figure 4.3*, all session information is stored in external storage. Whenever there is any state change, the server will store it in this storage. While rendering or serving a request for a client, the same storage will be consulted by a server.

Some best-practice recommendations for maintaining such storage (*Figure 4.3*):

- For disaster recovery, regular backups of the storage with an appropriate recovery plan should also be implemented.
- Choose redundant external storage

- Implement session store connection pooling
- Set up appropriate **Time to Live** (**TTL**) as an additional eviction measure to prevent unbounded data growth

Techniques for externalized session management

Redis: A widely adopted choice for session storage, Redis has become a de facto standard for high-performance, distributed caching and in-memory data access. As an in-memory data store, it provides microsecond latency for read and write operations, making it ideal for session storage that requires fast access. Redis has several features that make it valuable for session management, such as high performance, rich data structures, automatic expiration, persistence, replication, high availability, and atomic operations.

Cloud-managed session stores: Cloud platforms such as AWS, Azure, and Google Cloud provide services that support Redis engines. They offer multiple tiers for different performance, availability requirements, and automatic failovers, and they can integrate seamlessly with other cloud services.

Database-backed session storage: Traditional databases can serve as session stores for applications that prioritize durability over raw performance. Relational databases like MySQL provide **ACID** guarantees and can serve as session stores; while they are slower than in-memory stores, they offer strong consistency and can be appropriate for applications with less stringent latency requirements. NoSQL databases like MongoDB or DynamoDB also offer flexible schemas, making them a good fit for applications with unstructured session data.

> **Tip**
>
> If it is becoming difficult for you to determine whether the service you are creating should be stateful or stateless, we recommend starting with a stateless approach. If your use case is showing signs that in-memory state is needed, then consider the **hybrid approach**. A stateful approach usually comes with a specific use case and hence should be easy to identify.
>
> Some use cases for stateless patterns include APIs serving a very high-volume user base, microservices-based scenarios, and CDN-dependent scenarios.

Scalability

Scalability refers to a system's ability to efficiently adjust and respond to changes in its internal or external environment, such as increased user traffic, growing data volumes, and other operational complexities. While there are factors that may drive the need for a system to scale, one of the primary goals is to ensure business continuity. Let us look at a few characteristics [3]:

- **Flexibility:** The ability to adapt to changes in demand and operating conditions.
- **Performance**: There exists a functional relationship between scalability and performance. That is, we cannot be absolutely sure that a scalable system will show good performance, but if carefully implemented, scalability can contribute positively to performance. [4]
- **Reliability**: By showing high uptime and better disaster recovery, the system becomes more reliable to users.

Scalability (scale-up or scale-out) can be achieved by implementing any combination from the following [5]:

- **Software-based scalability**: Implementing an approach without changing the existing hardware configuration, while allowing the system to serve more requests. Think of a time when you are tasked with optimizing your database query to reduce the response time/cost of execution. The trigger for database query optimization could be to improve performance, but it also serves as a very basic use case of software-based scaling. Other more apt examples include the use of L1, L2, or another local cache.
- **Hardware-based scalability**: In this case, the number of physical components, e.g., processing power, web server, app server, and datastore, is increased to handle more requests.

Let's take an example to expand this –

Case 1: You want to build a web-based application to show the latest news and trends for employees of your company. The overall requirement looks something like:

```
Existing total number of employees = 10,000
Expected number of regular readers every morning = 50% i.e., 5000.
Each user makes roughly 10 requests in a 5-minute window.
Occasional peaks = An additional 20%, i.e., 2000. Total users during peak period
5000+2000 = 7000 users
Newsletter Content: Text and image based. Images are stored in S3.
Availability requirement: The system should remain available most of the time
during the day.
```

To keep this section focused, we cover only the read journey here. Let's start with identifying the technical details you would need to build this system –

A datastore to store the latest news and trends content for a particular day – For this volume we can use a SQL database. (Say it can handle = 400 QPS)

An application tier service will be needed to interact with the backend store to retrieve content. Say your application service can accept 500 RPS.

We will need a web server to host our application as well as static assets, except images. Say the web server you have used can support 250 RPS.

It is an internal application, so you can rely on the company's firewall and other security setups to ensure no external user can access the network, and hence, authentication/authorization is not a day-1 requirement.

For this scenario, a basic setup is sufficient (as shown in *Figure 4.4*):

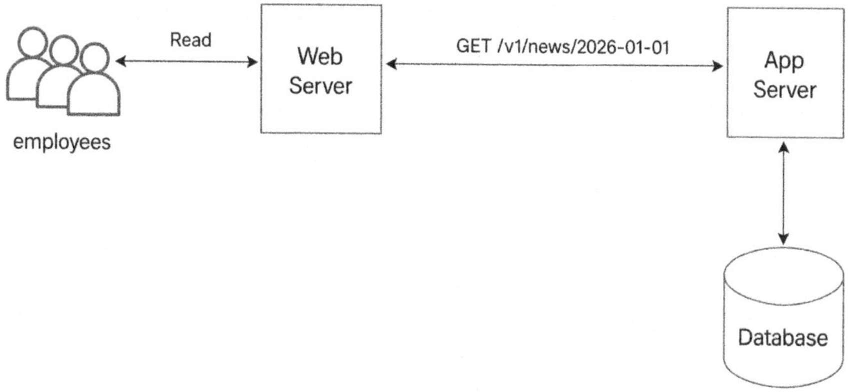

Figure 4.4: News web application (high level view)

The first step is to work through the estimates so that we can better understand the requirements for different infrastructure components that will be used to build this system:

```
User Volume = 7000 (Peak)
Number of requests per user = 10 / 5 = 2 requests per minute
Total number of requests the system will observe = 7000 x 2 = 14000 requests per
min
```

Throughput calculation:

```
Web server = 250 RPS = 250 x 60 = 15000 requests per min
Application server = 500RPS = 500 x 60 = 30000 requests per min
Database = 400QPS = 400 x 60 = 24000 queries per min
```

The maximum throughput the system can generate is 15,000 requests in a minute, i.e., the minimum of all participating components.

For our given use case, we are confident that the selected infrastructure is sufficient to meet the need. Our confidence is supported by the numbers we have derived above.

In this implementation the area of special interest is that each user request reaches the database for rendering a response.

Case 2: The company has been acquired by another company, leading to a total employee headcount of, say, 50,000. Your news and trends are a big hit, and the new management wants to continue with it. The regular article reader base has also increased to 60% with the same occasional peak. All other requirements are the same.

In this case the existing setup might work for some users. But the web server might not cooperate with the increased user volume, leading to employee frustration. Let's work through the numbers again to understand the problem in depth:

```
Number of employees = 50,000
Daily active user = 50,000 x 60% = 30,000
User volume, including peak time active users = 30,000 + (20% of 50,000) = 40,000
users
Number of requests per user = 10 / 5 = 2 requests per minute
Total number of requests the system will observe = 40,000 x 2 = 80,000 requests
per min
```

Throughput calculation:

```
Web server = 250 RPS = 250 x 60 = 15000 requests per min
Application server = 500 RPS = 500 x 60 = 30000 requests per min
Database = 400 QPS = 400 x 60 = 24000 queries per minute
```

From the preceding calculations, we can see the problem now exists at every layer of your original system. We would require an appropriate mechanism to scale the system to match the demand. This is shown in *Figure 4.5*.

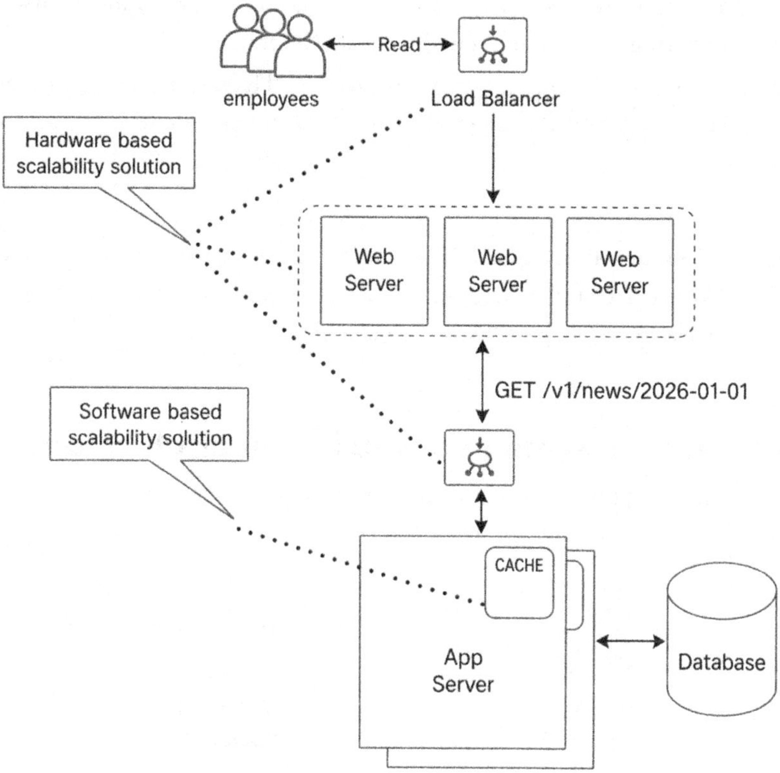

Figure 4.5: A high-level scaled view of the News web application

To keep your system up and running, you might want to make a few changes -

- If possible, replace the web server with a higher-capacity one, i.e., vertical scaling that might require more upfront investment, or add additional instances of your web servers, i.e., scale horizontally to increase the overall throughput of this layer. These web servers can be backed by a load balancer for traffic management.
- Add more application servers in the middle layer cluster to start accepting the increased number of requests or replace it with a more powerful server.
- Add more database instances to meet the overall QPS requirement. But this might not be as simple as it appears. This is because with a new database instance, you would need to define a replication strategy, data synchronization and backup plans, etc., to name a few concerns unique to this layer. A simpler and more efficient mechanism for this use case can be to add an in-memory or local caching layer within the application server. By using an appropriate caching and eviction management system, we can reduce overall

read load on the database by up to 80% in this case. It will enhance user experience without performing any changes to the backend storage layer.

In *Figure 4.5*, adding physical components at any layer, load balancers, servers, etc. are examples of hardware-based scaling. Introducing local cache at the application layer represents software-based scaling.

> **Note**
>
> The example is presented to explain the concept. If needed, you can further scale the existing infrastructure, including web, app, database servers. You can also think in terms of introducing distributed cache, CDN, and similar options.

Different layers to scale in a web-based application

A typical web-based application uses multi-tier architecture consisting of three main components: web, application, and storage (*Figure 4.6*).

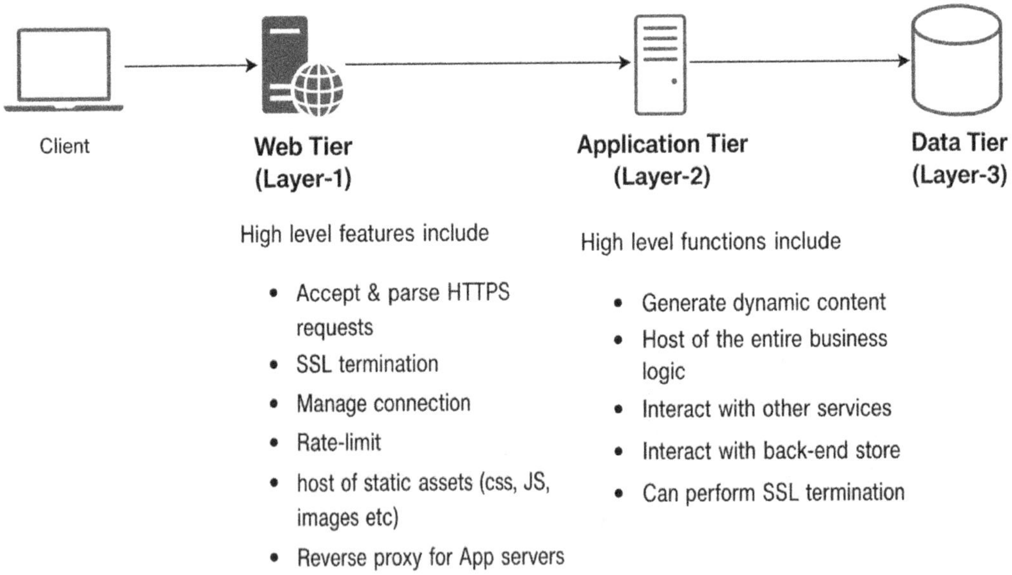

Figure 4.6: A typical three-layered web architecture

Hardware-based scaling can be implemented on each tier as shown in *Figure 4.6*. But to select the right scaling tier and strategy, let us look at some additional details associated with each tier:

Web Tier: This is the first interaction layer in a 3-tiered web application model. This layer does not hold any critical business logic. Along with other things, it mainly serves as a reverse proxy for your backend application servers. Since it does not hold a lot of dynamic, custom knowledge, it is the layer with the least risk to implement scaling. Some symptoms that indicate a need to scale this layer include when the number of valid requests reaching application servers is lower than expected, when request latency through this layer is consistently higher than expected, or when you expect a high, persistent surge in user volume accessing your application's static assets. The overall cost and complexity to plan scaling at this layer is low.

Application Tier: Scaling an application server is relatively complex. This is the layer that holds all your complex business logic, third-party integrations, caching, data store interaction management and many other business-critical activities needed to render the dynamic content. And hence, scaling this layer requires more careful planning. The overall cost and complexity involved in scaling the application tier is much higher than the web tier. To minimize the risk associated with scaling here, it is a better strategy to assess and identify sub-components (e.g., cache) that must be scaled for the given scenario.

Data Tier: This is the most sensitive tier and therefore the most complex to scale. A critical analysis must be done to ensure that the data tier is the point of contention. Also, there is no viable alternative to scaling this layer. Scaling this tier means dealing with actual data too. Data is something that is ultimately used for creating a dynamic response. Even a small accidental change at this tier can create massive trouble overall. And hence a thorough analysis is recommended. We will discuss database scaling in the *Database* section, later in this chapter, where we will also elaborate the concept of data partitioning, and sharding.

Scalability – tools and techniques

Each layer of a typical three-tier web architecture as shown in *Figure 4.6* can be scaled to meet a system's need. The main tools and techniques covered in this book are:

- **Load balancers**: We've discussed this in the upcoming section, *Load balancing*.
- **Caching:** Discussed in the section *Caching*, later in this chapter.
- **Horizontal and Vertical scaling** techniques: The term has been explained in *Chapter 2*. Applying the concept to the database for scaling is covered in a later section, *Database scaling*.

Scalability challenges

Data Consistency: Ensuring data consistency across multiple nodes in a distributed system is a major challenge. Replication lag, network partitions, and system failures can all lead to inconsistent data.

Network latency: In a distributed system, servers may be located in different geographic regions. This can lead to delays when servers need to communicate with each other, affecting system performance.

Bottlenecks: Even in horizontally scaled systems, certain components may become bottlenecks. For example, if all nodes rely on a single database, that database can become overwhelmed, causing system-wide slowdowns.

Cost: Scaling horizontally can require more servers, which increases costs. While cloud platforms offer pay-as-you-go models, organizations need to carefully balance the trade-off between performance and cost.

State management: Stateless components (e.g., web servers) are easy to scale horizontally, but stateful components (e.g., databases) are much harder to scale. Managing state across multiple servers can become complex and requires strategies like sharding, replication, and session management. [1][2]

Tip

When you are working through a system's scalability during an interview, you need to clearly understand and evaluate different dimensions associated with it. The dimensions to consider include -

- Traffic dimension, i.e., number of requests the system will handle
- System presence dimension, i.e., local/regional/global user base and hence system presence
- Data dimension, i.e., storage, sharding, partitioning etc.
- Features dimension, i.e., functional enhancement with ease

Depending on this knowledge, you can plan your approach to the problem. For example, if the problem focuses on the traffic dimension, you might consider adding load balancers, more machines, or other ways to increase throughput. If the dimension is system presence for a global user base, you might consider CDNs, edge gateways/ proxies, multi-region data management, and similar approaches.

Asynchronous communication

Traditional web interactions mainly rely on a synchronous request-response model where clients send requests to the server, which processes each request and sends the response back to the client. It all happens in a single journey. In this model, the client waits until the server processes the request and generates and sends a response. That server response completes the loop that frees the client to continue. In most cases, this works well. The issue appears when the servicing platform or server cannot process a request independently. Let's understand it with an example.

A client clicks a send email button to notify its users from your web page. You would want the system to generate and send the desired email as soon as possible but your server might not be able to execute it instantaneously. Also consider the case where the email needs to be sent to a million recipients. To add some complexity to this case, consider that the list of recipients is stored in a database from which you will first read the details and then send them an email.

We might build something to fulfill this task in a synchronous fashion, but:

a. It might not create a good user experience as sending such a bulk email is time-consuming and can leave the client hanging, and

b. Do we really want to execute this task synchronously?

A better way to handle this problem would be to record the client's intent and show a confirmation such as 'your email request has been accepted'. Then process the request in the background while the client can continue their work.

Asynchronous communication is a mechanism through which two or more systems interact with each other through data exchange to fulfill tasks without blocking each other (i.e., control flow inversion or inversion of control, IoC). The interacting systems can execute their business functions at different times. This communication model improves a system's throughput, scalability, fault tolerance, and load management. The interacting entities can be part of the same system bounded context, or they can be in their own independent context. Each participating entity does not need to know each other's underlying implementation or technology. This flexibility makes it an ideal approach to implement loose coupling while maintaining system integrity in a distributed environment. The following sections discuss techniques to implement it [6].

Message and message queue

In simple terms, a **message** is a unit of communication that conveys information from a sender to a receiver. *It can be transmitted through various forms, such as spoken or written words, signals, or electronic data, and can range from simple instructions to complex information.*

A **message queue** is an asynchronous service-to-service communication enabler. It is heavily used with microservices. It facilitates modular software development by offering application decoupling in a distributed environment, enabling participating systems to scale independently.

A message queue is essentially a temporary, lightweight store to hold messages created by one or more producers until they are retrieved by a consumer for processing. A message in a queue should be retrieved and processed by a single consumer, and hence generally, consumer applications guide how a message is formulated, i.e., the message structure within the queue.

But obviously there are implementation variations you will find in the real world, and hence you see the word 'generally'. Message queue communication is also called one-to-one, or point-to-point, communication, as a producer will create a message for a consumer to ingest. This is shown in *Figure 4.7*.

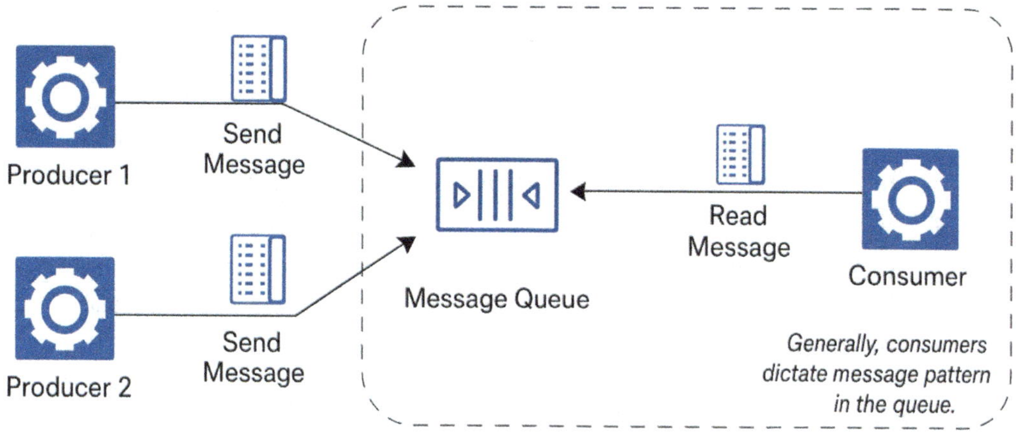

Figure 4.7: Message queue journey

In summary, benefits of a message queue include:

- **Decoupling**: The producer can continue its operation without waiting for the consumer to process it because of its asynchronous handshake.
- **Load Leveling**: A message queue acts as a temporary buffer that helps distribute messages. If more than one consuming instance is attached to the same queue, then it ensures no two consumers are processing the same message. This is because each message is delivered to exactly one consumer. It facilitates smooth horizontal scaling for consuming services.
- **Reliability**: If a consumer is not available for any reason, data is retained within the queue for some time (depending on the implementation mechanism) so that when the consumer application is back, the message can be processed.

Note

Using persistent storage, for example, a database-based implementation, does not represent a message queue, although with correct measures it can mimic the queue behavior and solve some problems. To understand some main differences,

1. A database is persistent storage with high durability; a message queue keeps data temporarily.
2. Load leveling is implemented manually with a database, which impacts horizontal scaling, whereas it is an implicit behavior in a message queue.
3. Writing and reading data from a persistent store can become a bottleneck if you think about scaling your system. This is because of the cost associated with the end-to-end database connection as well as underlying data management. Such complexity becomes a lightweight operation with a queue.

In terms of similarities, both a queue and a database can be used for decoupling and reliability.

In summary, a queue is much more lightweight and purpose-built to achieve asynchronous communication between systems.

An AWS native example of a popular queue-based system is **Amazon SQS** [9].

Events and topics (publish-subscribe pattern)

Another popular mechanism to achieve asynchronous service-to-service communication in a distributed environment is using **'events'** and **'topics'**. It is a variation of a message queue and also has a slightly different (**fan-out**) use case. [7]

An event is explained in Wikipedia as:

> *In computing, an* ***event*** *is a detectable occurrence or change in the system's state, such as user input, hardware interrupts, system notifications, or changes in data or conditions, that the system is designed to monitor. Events trigger responses or actions and are fundamental to event-driven systems.*

The phrase 'change in the system's state' means that an event is an outcome observed because of a change in a system's state, for example, application received, payment succeeded, or order dispatched.

'Topic' has been explained by Kafka creators as:

> *"The closest analogies for a topic are a database table or a folder in a filesystem. Topics are additionally broken down into a number of partitions. Messages are written to it in an append-only fashion and are read in order from beginning to end."* [8]

In this model, the event (message) creator is known as the 'publisher,' while the consumer of an event is called a 'subscriber'. *Figure 4.8* shows a generic pub/sub model.

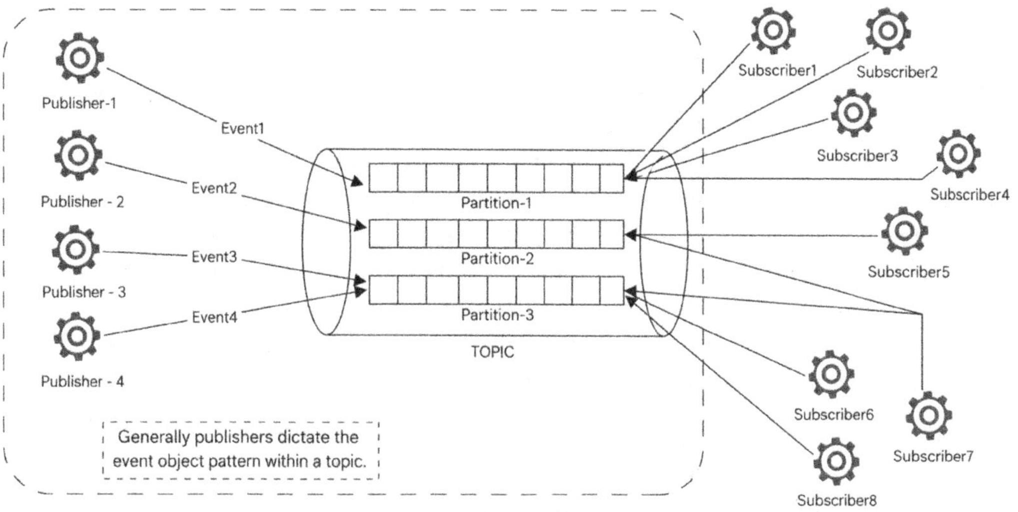

Figure 4.8: Architecture of a publisher-subscriber model

Publishers create 'Events'. These events are placed in a temporary store called 'Topic'. There are interested subscribers who listen to such events for downstream activities. There can be more than one publisher generating events for a single subscriber **(fan-in)**, one publisher generating events for multiple subscribers (fan-out) or multiple publishers generating events for multiple subscribers **(many-to-many)**.

It might feel a bit confusing as to why two different terminologies are used by Message-Queue and Pub/Sub to describe similar kinds of behavior. The answer lies in the intent and responsibilities of the systems involved.

In a pub/sub pattern, when a publisher experiences a change in its state, it will publish the change to a topic designed to capture such a change of state. Once stored, the publisher's journey ends. Any (subscriber) application that is interested in such a change of state of a publisher will subscribe to the topic (meaning monitor it for new data) and react accordingly. A publisher does not expect anything back from any downstream applications after this stage. In this alignment, publishers are the communication initiators without depending on downstream consumers. Hence, the event (message) format generally reflects or is guided by the publisher's implementation.

For example, an 'Order' service creates an *Order-Received* event. When an order is received, the service will store the necessary information in its persistent store and then add an 'order-received' event to its associated topic. At this stage, this service does not make any further attempt to know what happens to that event. Theoretically, there may be no subscriber to this event, and the publisher does not depend on any subscriber. In reality, there can be an 'Inventory' service interested in an order-received event that will react by reducing the number of items with the order quantity so that customers can see the updated available quantity before placing an order. A few more services will also be interested in 'Order-Received' events, for example, a 'PaymentService' to ensure the payment for the order has been successfully received, or a 'Notification' service to inform the customer about success or issues in order placement, etc.

In the case of a message-queue pattern, the producer can either request or command a consumer application to perform some action. It is the consumer who will decide when to pick a message and how to respond. This means that, in the case of a queue, there is always at least one associated consumer for the produced message. This is not a requirement in the case of a pub-sub pattern.

Let's say, in the preceding example, 'PaymentService' wants a confirmation of successful payment. This service cannot directly interact with the third-party payment providers like VISA, MasterCard. But there is a 'PaymentMediator' service that can interact with the actual payment providers to get this information. 'PaymentService' will send a request to the 'PaymentMediator' service to confirm the successful payment using a point-to-point message queue.

Obviously, the 'PaymentMediator' service will have its own request format and hence when requesting this information, 'PaymentService' will use the message format that 'PaymentMediator' service can consume.

Some limitations of pub/sub systems are –

- Complex implementation that is hard to test end to end
- For consistency-based applications, pub/sub can only support eventual consistency
- Little to no visibility into subscribers, making it hard to refactor
- No workflow control, i.e., in its basic form, it is not possible to define the order in which subscribers of a topic should process data (there are ways to achieve it, e.g., the mediator pattern).
- It is not a recommended pattern if strict message ordering is needed at the global level.

Message Queuing Telemetry Transport

Message Queuing Telemetry Transport (**MQTT**) is a lightweight pub/sub messaging protocol for unreliable networks mainly suited for **Internet of Things (IoT)** devices. It must run over a transport protocol that provides an ordered, bidirectional connection with reliable packet delivery and hence is typically used with TCP/IP.

Figure 4.9 shows how Message Queuing Telemetry Transport (MQTT) works:

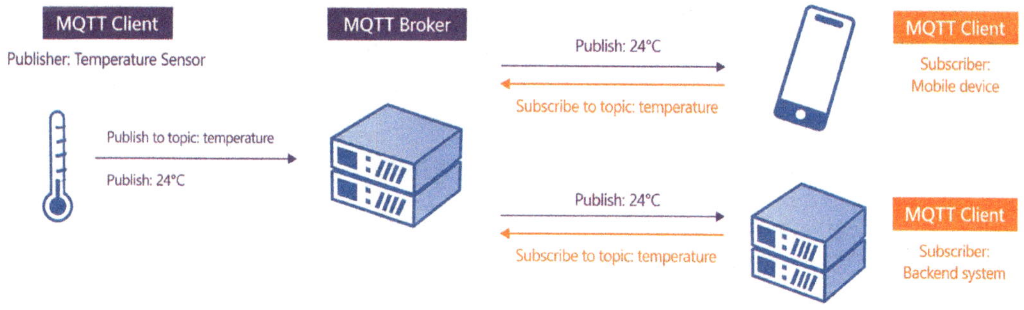

Figure 4.9: Message Queuing Telemetry Transport

Entities involved in MQTT communications are [11]:

MQTT Message Broker: It is a server that receives all the messages from originating clients and then routes all these messages to their desired destination clients. It is a single message facilitator, meaning it is also a single point of failure. If a broker goes down, then the entire communication stops. A distributed broker approach should be considered.

Client: A client is any device (e.g., mobile phones, sensors) that can connect to an MQTT message broker over the network. Since MQTT supports bidirectional communication using the publish-subscribe model, both the publisher and subscriber to the broker are called clients.

> **Tip**
>
> Generally, use cases that involve an unreliable or low-signal network are an early indication to plan for MQTT over REST (or a similar protocol). This is because MQTT maintains a lightweight TCP connection, reducing the handshake overhead during interactions. Also, this protocol is purpose-built to handle unreliable, low-signal network use cases, supporting resilience through handling signal drops and graceful reconnection.

Some system design use cases where MQTT can be a good fit are:

- Design a messaging system for IoT devices or millions of sensors in a parking lot
- Design a system to monitor and control traffic lights within a busy city

Message broker

A message broker is an enterprise-level service module that facilitates asynchronous communication between senders and receivers. It performs additional tasks beyond a simple queue or pub/sub implementation such as validating, routing, storing, and delivering messages. It guarantees message delivery to the recipient; that is, it holds the data until the end consumer(s) processes it. This is a great tool for achieving high reliability in an asynchronous environment where data loss can be a setback.

A well-known example of a message broker is RabbitMQ [10].

RabbitMQ enables applications to communicate asynchronously. It is highly configurable, supporting various messaging patterns like direct exchange, fanout exchange, and topic exchange, as well as a rich set of plug-ins to extend its services. It is also a highly reliable system; for example, it monitors whether a message from a sender reaches its intended recipient through message delivery tracking, creating better transparency and overall visibility. On the other hand, in Message-Queue or Pub/Sub patterns, the producers publish messages to the queue/topic without knowing whether consumers have retrieved them. If a message is not picked by the desired consuming application and the maximum retention time of a message in the queue/topic is met, then the message is deleted without getting processed.

Load balancing

The functioning of hardware components, such as a server or computational node, is influenced by a combination of internal and external constraints. Internal constraints arise from the device's constituent resources, including processing capacity, memory, and storage subsystems, whereas external constraints stem from environmental and infrastructural dependencies, such as power availability, network infrastructure, and connectivity conditions. Together, these constraints govern the node's response-delivery capabilities and affect system-level attributes, including performance, availability, and operational reliability.

A **load balancer** acts as a traffic manager that distributes incoming network traffic/workloads across multiple redundant servers (or nodes) in a system. The goal is to prevent a single point of failure (SPOF) as well as any single server from becoming overwhelmed, ensuring that all requests are handled smoothly and efficiently [12]. *Figure 4.10* shows the impact of introducing a load balancer in distributing traffic.

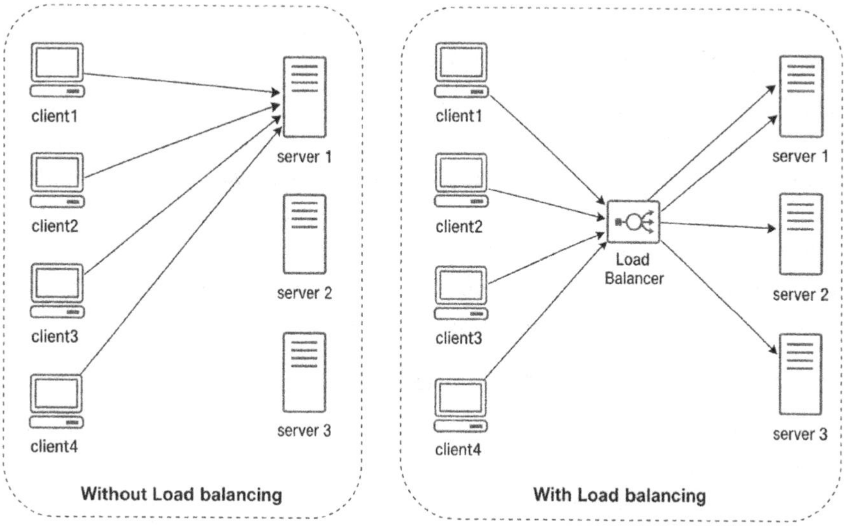

Figure 4.10: Systems with and without load balancing

Why load balancing is important

To enhance business continuity and achieve fault tolerance, redundant instances of servers are typically deployed in real-world production environments. For these instances to work in tandem, incoming requests should be distributed between available instances in a structured and controlled manner. A load balancer solves this business problem. Without it, incoming requests can only be routed to a preconfigured set of server(s). Traffic management while adding and removing instances will become a complex exercise, impractical in a global distributed environment.

For example, consider you have an e-commerce website with a single backend server. It works well during a normal business day and hence does not require any additional traffic manager. During a holiday sale period, the system might observe 10 times the usual traffic. The server might become overwhelmed and struggle to maintain the response rate or it may crash. To maintain business continuity without making a huge upfront investment, you might think about increasing the number of servers. To create a balance, the servers will be fronted by a load balancer to ensure smooth traffic distribution among the available servers. It also creates flexibility to add more servers, if needed, or remove servers from the group if they no longer serve the purpose.

A load balancer also helps improve the overall security posture for an organization by reducing the attack surface of its backend applications. It helps to minimize the impact of a **distributed denial-of-service** (**DDoS**) attack as it intelligently spreads traffic to avoid a server from becoming overwhelmed.

High availability and fault tolerance

'High availability' is about the operational uptime of your system to match an agreed expectation whereas 'Fault tolerance' is about operational uptime even in case of partial component failures. Fault tolerance has stricter operational requirements than high availability. As a traffic manager, a load balancer can perform a periodic health assessment of target nodes determining if they are healthy to serve a request and hence directing traffic only to healthy nodes. That means, in a multi-node environment, a system can continue functioning even if some nodes fail. Such an arrangement also helps while executing hardware and software maintenance.

Load balancer implementations

A load balancer can be hardware-based, software-based, or virtual (cloud technology). Here we are going to discuss the first two because the virtual load balancers also implement the same properties as achieved using the two explained below.

Hardware based

Hardware load balancers are dedicated physical devices that sit in front of the servers and distribute traffic based on pre-configured rules. They are typically used in enterprise environments where high performance is a core requirement. The benefits include high reliability, making them suitable for mission-critical applications, low latency, high throughput, and SSL offloading (depending upon the product selection). The trade-offs that you should consider include higher cost to procure and maintain, flexibility of the load balancer itself is limited to selected hardware, and vendor lock-in that is ultimately tied with the cost element we mentioned earlier.

Software based

Software load balancers run on standard servers or cloud instances and distribute traffic based on configurable algorithms. They are more flexible than hardware load balancers and are used in cloud-based and many modern distributed systems [13][15]. Benefits here include lower installation costs, configuration flexibility once it is up and running, and ease of installation as all you need is a server that can host an application. The trade-offs are dependency on the chosen host machine CPU, memory, and other resource capacity, performance overhead since constrained by the host server capacity, and operational overhead as you are on your own to manage it.

Examples of popular software load balancers include Nginx, a widely used open-source software that functions as a web server, reverse proxy, and load balancer, and HAProxy, another open-source load balancer known for its high performance and low resource consumption.

Load Balancer types

In this section we are going to cover the two most common types: Layer 4 (Transport Layer) Load Balancers, and Layer 7 (Application Layer) Load Balancers. Let's dive into each type in more detail.

Layer 4 Load Balancers (Transport Layer)

Also known as a **Network Load Balancer** (**NLB**), it operates at the transport layer of the OSI model and routes traffic based on network information such as IP addresses and TCP/UDP ports. It does not consider the content of the traffic (packet) while making the routing decision. Because there is less decision logic involved in routing, these load balancers demonstrate massive speed. NLBs are relatively simple to configure and operate. SSL offloading is not supported by NLBs, and hence, you have to consider your use case in choosing this load balancer.

> **Note**
>
> SSL Offloading: It is a term used to explain the overall process when an encrypted message is received at a location, a corresponding decryption key will be used at the receiving location to extract the message in plain text format. The message journey might terminate at this point or might go further down the chain for processing, depending upon your use case.

Figure 4.11 shows a Network Load Balancer (NLB):

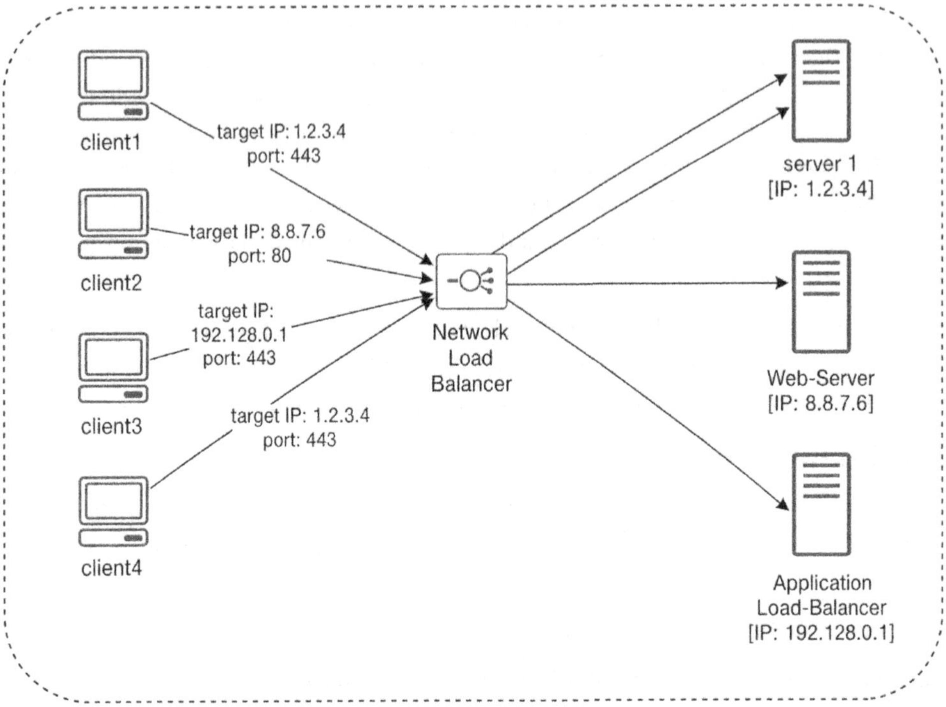

Figure 4.11: Network Load Balancer

In *Figure 4.11* the load balancer makes a routing decision depending upon target IP address and the port number as mentioned in the client request. A load balancer can further send requests to another load balancer down in the chain.

Layer 7 Load Balancers (Application Layer)

Also known as **Application Load Balancer (ALB)** [14]; it operates at the application layer of the OSI model. It is used to make more intelligent routing decisions based on the content of the request. These load balancers can inspect application data such as HTTP headers, cookies, and URLs to determine how to distribute traffic.

These load balancers are more sophisticated, and hence, they involve a relatively complex configuration. They are generally slower than the network load balancers, because they can perform fine-grained routing. ALBs are more secure as compared to NLBs because of the content inspection capabilities. ALBs support SSL offloading that can significantly reduce the workload for underlying servers as one of their main responsibilities is executed by the load balancers, giving more bandwidth for application servers to perform their core processing exercise.

Load balancing algorithms

Load-balancing algorithms are divided into two main categories:

- **Static load balancing**: Works on fixed or pre-configured rules and does not account for a server's current state within the group. Examples of static load balancing are - Round Robin, Weighted round robin, IP Hash
- **Dynamic load balancing**: Load balancing is performed by considering the current state of each server within the group that makes it adaptable. Examples are - Least connections, Least response time, Weighted least connection, and Resource-based.

The choice of algorithm depends on the use case and the type of system being deployed. Here are some of the most common load-balancing algorithms:

Static load balancing

Round Robin is one of the simplest load-balancing algorithms. In this method, the load balancer forwards each incoming request to the next available server in a cyclic order. When it reaches the last server, it loops back to the first server and continues the cycle. It is simple to implement, making it a good choice for small-scale systems. It also evenly distributes traffic across all available servers in the group. The approach is also used to manage stateful traffic with sticky session. In such a case it is called sticky round robin. The round-robin technique sometimes leads to inefficiencies, especially when servers within the group have varied capacities.

Use this technique when the servers are identical in terms of capacity and performance. Otherwise, it is better to look at other available options. It is not a recommended approach if your system is dealing with long-lived connections.

IP Hashing involves using the client's IP address to determine which server will handle the request. The load balancer applies a hash function to the IP address, and the resulting hash is used to consistently route requests from the same IP address (i.e., the client) to the hash-determined target server. This approach can lead to uneven traffic distribution as the distribution becomes dependent on the hash function to determine the target. Also, adding or removing a server might require hash redistribution that can be complex. The benefit it adds is that a client request will always be served by the same servicing backend without any actual sticky-session implementation.

It is recommended to use IP Hashing when you want to achieve session-affinity-like behavior, perhaps because of a local caching implementation on your server. But if multiple clients' IPs are masked because of network topology (for example, all requests originating from a corporate environment might show the same IP because of an external-facing proxy) the server accepting the request might become overwhelmed, failing the traffic management purpose.

Weighted Round Robin is an extension of the basic Round Robin algorithm. It assigns a weight to each server based on its capacity or performance. Servers with higher weights receive more requests, while those with lower weights receive fewer requests. It is a useful technique when there are servers of different configurations in the group. If servers in the group are identical, then using this approach adds unnecessary complexity over round-robin with no added gain.

Dynamic load balancing

The least-connections algorithm directs traffic to the server with the fewest active connections. This ensures that servers that are already handling more traffic don't get overloaded, making it ideal for systems where the traffic load varies greatly across servers. Systems that manage long-lived connections, such as video streaming or chat applications, benefit from this method because it avoids overloading specific servers. Although it routes traffic dynamically, with identical servers, this approach does not add much value for the implementation complexity over simple Round Robin.

The least-response-time algorithm routes traffic to the server with the lowest response time for health monitoring requests. It considers both the number of active connections and the current response time of each server to decide which server should handle the next request. This can improve the overall user experience by minimizing latency and response times. But the algorithm is quite resource-intensive, as it needs to continuously monitor the response times of all servers. Also, if response time is not the prime requirement, then this algorithm does not add much value.

A geolocation-based algorithm performs traffic routing based on the geographic location of the user (client machine IP address) and the closest server that is hosting the content requested. This approach is of great significance in multi-location cloud-based environments where servers can be hosted in different countries. It does not necessarily work as a traditional load balancer but achieves similar results. Examples include Akamai, Cloudflare, AWS Global Accelerator.

Figure 4.12 captures some commonly used load-balancing mechanisms for reference.

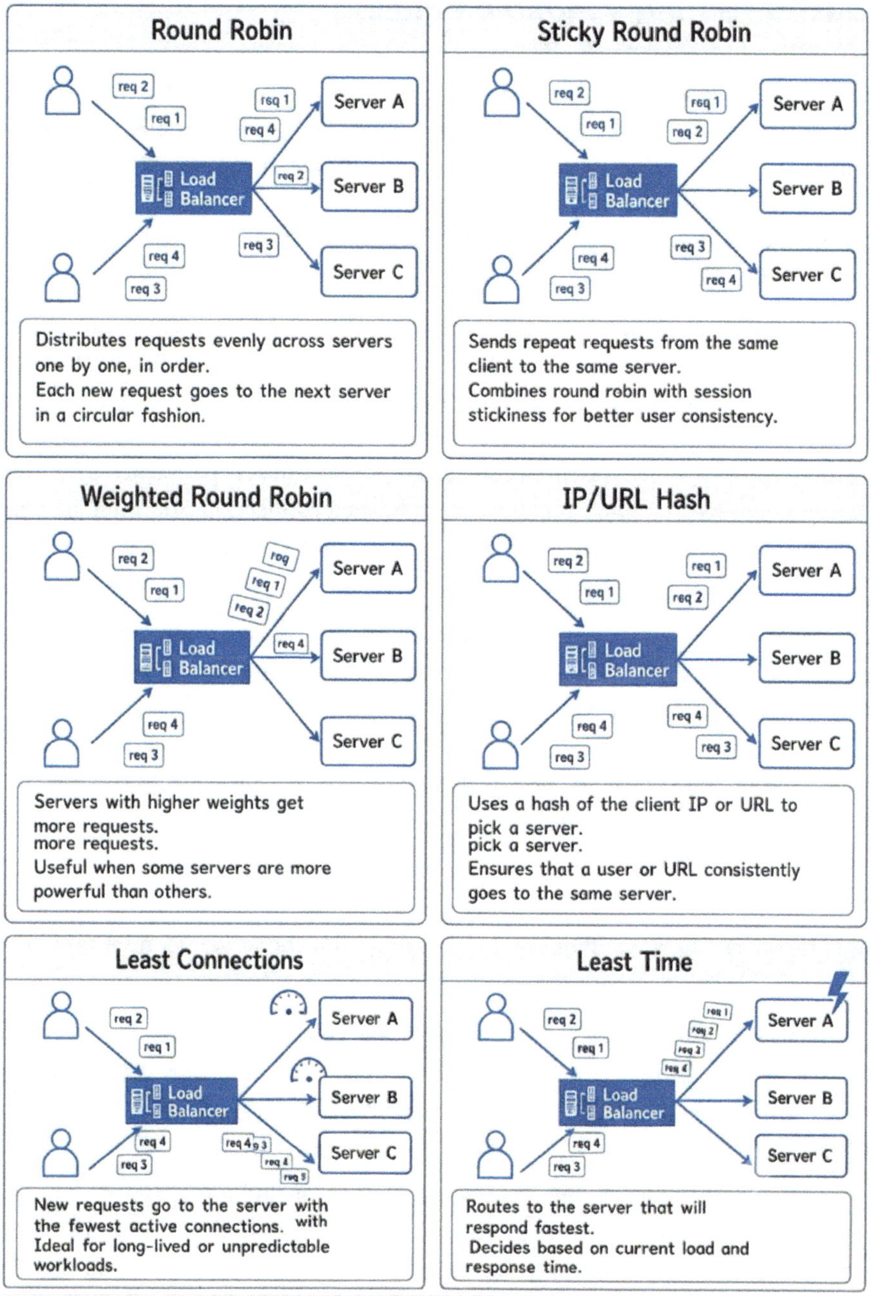

Figure 4.12: Load Balancing algorithms at a glance

DNS-based routing vs load-balancing

In distributed computing environments, DNS-based routing is a commonly adopted mechanism for directing client requests. It is primarily employed to achieve global traffic distribution in multi-location architectures. This approach relies on pre-configured mappings between domain names and target IP addresses, and in some cases, designated failover IPs, to satisfy specific business or availability requirements. Consequently, request routing strictly follows these predefined DNS configurations, with the client independently initiating the connection to the resolved endpoint.

In contrast, load balancing determines the target server through dynamic and sophisticated evaluation of available resources, based on built-in algorithms and real-time health assessments. While DNS-based routing and load balancing exhibit certain functional similarities, they differ fundamentally in their operational semantics. DNS routing merely resolves where a request should be directed, after which the connection attempt to the host is performed by the requester. Load balancing, however, operates on already-established connections, deciding how incoming requests should be distributed across backend servers and forwarding them to healthy service instances accordingly.

In general, DNS-based routing is well-suited for global traffic distribution across geographically dispersed regions, whereas load balancers are more effective for localized traffic distribution within a region or data center, where fine-grained control, health checks, and real-time load awareness are required. An example of DNS-based routing would be a use case dealing with multi-cloud environments or global applications with regional presence, using a CDN. Within the AWS cloud, Route 53 is used to configure this routing.

Caching

In a large-scale system, where millions of requests might hit the server per minute, accessing the data from its origin, e.g., a database, for every request can be costly. [16]

Caching is a mechanism to temporarily store and serve copies of data subsets, whose source of truth resides in another store, so that future requests can be served faster. Cached data reduces the load on databases and other services, improves response times, and enhances user experience.

Caching can be applied at various technology layers, including operating systems, web applications, databases, and networking, which covers Content Delivery Networks (CDNs) and Domain Name System (DNS) layers. Following are some common caches highlighting their behavior and native placement in general. It should help you choose the right one or in combination for your design problem:

Content Delivery Networks (CDNs): CDNs cache static content like images, videos, and scripts at various geographical locations. CDNs serve cached content to users from the nearest edge server, reducing latency and speeding up content delivery. Use case: CDNs are widely used for high-traffic websites, video streaming platforms, and applications that serve large amounts of static data, ensuring faster load times for users regardless of their geographic location. [18]

Edge cache and Origin cache: Both of these terms are quite commonly used in the industry. They both represent gateway-level caching. The placement of the gateway component in the overall ecosystem determines if it is an edge or an origin gateway. Depending on the placement, the purpose of the cached data changes. An edge gateway is something closer to the user base and hence the cache at this layer is created to hold data to support the user demand e.g. public data that does not change per user. The origin gateway (e.g., API Gateway), on the other hand, resides close to the backend server and hence the cache created here is with the intent to reduce load on the backend server, for example, the user-specific response.

In-Memory Caches: They reside in the host's RAM; for example, Memcached. Depending upon the need, the cache can reside on the same node as your application server or be installed on a dedicated host close to the application server. When installed on a dedicated host, network latency and cache duplication are factors to take into account. If it is installed on the same host where your application runs, a clear separation of RAM space is configured between cache and application usage. The in-memory placement reduces network and disk I/O latency during data access, making it the fastest in the application journey performed on your host. The trade-off is that since the data does not persist in a disk, there is the potential of losing cache data in cases such as a power outage or node crash. Primary use cases include - session management, storing most frequently accessed data that is not too large in size.

Local caches: They reside on the local disk of the server where the application is running. Being native, they offer lower latency than making any remote or persistent storage call, but higher latency than the in-memory cache explained earlier because of the involved disk I/O. They are most suitable for use cases that do not require blazing-fast speed and involve relatively large data volumes. Since the data resides on the local disk, they can be recovered after a power outage or server crash. But this data is not shared with other nodes in the group. The use case may include a periodic snapshot of in-memory cache for resilience during a node crash, frequently accessed file data if your files are stored in the persistent storage.

Note

The terms 'Local cache' and 'In-Memory cache' are often used interchangeably during normal chats within the industry. Although fundamentally they point to different storage locations, in abstraction they are both local to a server or node.

Distributed caches: In simple terms, a distributed cache provides the behavior of an in-memory cache at a distributed scale. It involves storing data across multiple nodes in a cluster. This type of cache can span geographic regions and hence it is a suitable choice in designing a multi-node application. Data is replicated among cache nodes within the cluster to ensure it is available close to a running application server for speed. It also means that regardless of the location where a data element has originated, once in the cache, the data can be accessed globally. It is a highly specialized and complex grouping of multiple cache nodes. Because of the availability of more than one cache node maintaining the same data replica, the system can recover itself in case of a node crash or similar failure, enhancing the overall reliability. One notable downside to highlight is a delay in data replication or sync between nodes because of factors including network delay. Some market-leading solutions that offer distributed cache include Redis [17], Hazelcast, and Apache Ignite.

Example use cases for such a cache include a read-heavy application, e.g., a news feed system; a global microservices-based application that stores static lookup data; and a key-value cache store.

CPU-level cache: It includes L1, L2 & L3 caching where L1 demonstrates the highest speed but the lowest data storage, and L3 demonstrates the lowest speed, compared to other L caches, but more storage in the group.

> **Tip**
>
> Default order in which an application server consults different caches to perform data lookup -
>
> ```
> L1 -> L2 -> L3 -> In-Memory
> ```

Caching strategies

Selecting the right caching strategy makes the overall solution look elegant and also reduces the response latency. Some of the caching strategies are (reference *Figure 4.13*):

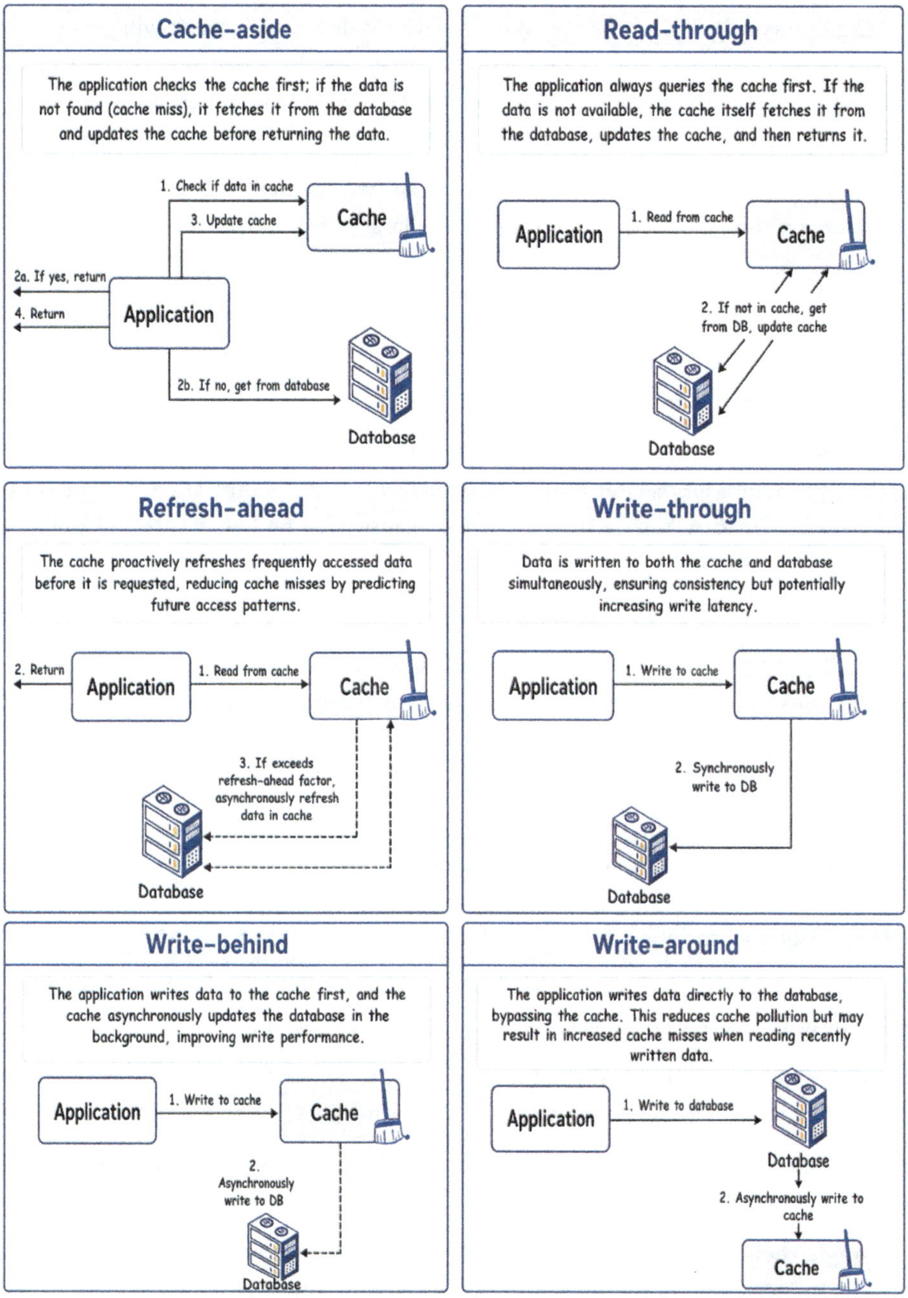

Figure 4.13: Common caching strategies

Write-Through Caching: It ensures data consistency as both the cache and database are updated simultaneously. Trade-offs are: A) it is relatively slow to write as it will generate a write response after updating both the cache & the database, and B) If there is a route that directly updates the database without updating the cache, then the cache becomes outdated pretty soon. A careful implementation is needed to ensure both the cache and database are in sync.

The strategy is useful when data consistency is your key requirement, e.g., a read-heavy workload where each reader should have the same copy of the data.

It is not a viable strategy when write latency is critical or your system deals with a write-heavy workload.

Examples of systems where such a caching mechanism is commonly useful include financial transactions and inventory management.

Write-back or write-behind caching: In this case, data is written into the cache first and updated into the database at a later stage. It offers a faster write confirmation response but poses a risk of data loss in case the cache fails, e.g., because of a node crash before updating the backend.

The strategy is useful where write performance is critical and the system can tolerate eventual consistency

It is not a viable approach if immediate consistency is the prime focus, i.e., the system cannot tolerate any data loss. Example use cases where this strategy is used are analytics data and user activity logs.

Cache-aside: In this approach, the application first checks the cache for the requested data. If the data is found (cache hit), it is returned immediately. If not (a cache miss), the application retrieves the data from the database and stores a copy in the cache before returning the response data. It is a widely used caching mechanism.

The strategy is useful when you need some flexibility in cache invalidation logic implementation as your application layer controls the caching logic implementation.

It is not an optimal approach when you have a dedicated, external caching infrastructure where the cache is shared by multiple consuming applications for the same set of data.

Example use cases where this strategy is used are maintaining user profiles and product catalogs for listing.

Read through cache: Here, in case of a cache miss, the cache will itself interact with the backend storage to populate the request data rather than the application doing it. Use cases include a content management system's dynamic content caching.

The strategy is useful when you want a level of transparency in caching and your caching libraries handle database interactions for cache population.

It is not a great strategy if you are looking to implement any complex or bespoke cache invalidation logic.

Example use cases for this strategy are a content management system's dynamic content caching and configuration data.

Cache eviction policies

Eviction policies dictate when cached data should be removed from the cache to make room for new data. Below are some common cache eviction strategies [19]:

- **Least Recently Used (LRU)**: removes the data elements with the oldest access timestamp when the cache storage needs to make some space. This approach assumes that recently accessed data is more likely to be accessed again, while older data can be discarded. Use case - user session management.
- **First-In-First-Out (FIFO)**: In FIFO, the data elements are removed from the cache in the order they were created. This policy does not consider the last access time, i.e., access frequency of the data element in the cache. The FIFO approach is used in systems where data access patterns are predictable and time-bound, such as event logs
- **Time-to-Live (TTL)** or Expiry-Based Eviction: In this, each object that enters the cache is assigned a time duration (called time to live or TTL) after which the object is auto-removed. This is an efficient technique to automatically remove any stale data in a timely fashion. The approach is not space dependent, meaning even if the underlying cache storage is almost empty, resident objects will be removed when the TTL expires. Many cache providers implement TTL as a default property associated with objects entering into the cache. They will additionally configure another use-case-specific eviction policy. A TTL-based implementation is commonly found during DNS caching, caching dynamic content, such as news articles, where old content can become irrelevant after a certain period. It is the most common type of policy.

Key metrics to monitor

Cache Hit Rate: The percentage of requests that are served from the cache. A higher hit rate indicates that the cache is effective.

Latency: The time taken to serve a request from the cache. Lower latency is crucial for improving user experience.

Eviction Rate: The frequency at which items are evicted from the cache due to capacity limits.

Common operational and architectural challenges

While caching can significantly improve performance by reducing load on your backend systems, it introduces several challenges to consider during cache implementation. Below we have captured some of the challenges along with the strategies to handle them -

Over-caching and stale data: Over-caching is about storing more data than needed, which can overwhelm the underlying storage. Stale data (cache drift) is about data residing in the cache for longer than needed, giving clients access to the outdated data.

Some strategies to overcome these problems:

- TTL-based cache expiration: Associate a time-to-live duration marker with objects before adding them into the cache. The cache auto-expires the objects after the expiration time.
- Event-based cache invalidation: Implement a strategy to invalidate data objects in near real time from the cache as soon as the data state in the underlying persistent storage changes.

Cache stampede and Cache avalanche: Stampede happens when a popular cache key expires, resulting in an overwhelming number of requests reaching the backend system to get the data/ regenerate the cache. An avalanche, on the other hand, happens when multiple cached keys expire simultaneously or a complete cache node fails, creating a sudden surge in traffic to the backend system. It can have quite an adverse effect on a system, potentially causing a system crash as well in some scenarios.

Some strategies to overcome these problems:

- Implementing a preventive approach to limit the number of requests that reach the backend system for cache regeneration. This can be controlled by rate-limiting, mutex, or a similar implementation.
- Randomized TTL, for example, by adding random jitter for such key(s), works well. In this case, the keys expire in a staggered manner.
- Probabilistic pre-refresh, where such hot keys are refreshed earlier based on their data refresh probability before expiration.

Hot key bottleneck: In this scenario, a cache node becomes overwhelmed because it holds a data object that is very popular with the user base. It is also known as a 'Popular key' bottleneck or a 'Celebrity problem' where everyone wants to see the updated news about a celebrity in the city.

Some strategies to overcome this problem:

- Distribute and serve the hot keys from multiple nodes. If needed, randomize the key expiration or use a probabilistic approach

- Consistent hashing approach (discussed in *Chapter 3*)
- Create additional application-level local memory arrangements for such hot keys to distribute the load. When the load balancer distributes the traffic to the application server, then the request will be served locally from the server cache instead of reaching out to the cache node.

Cache Penetration: Penetration happens when the requested key does not exist in the cache and has no corresponding database record. In such cases the database query will return an empty/null response for an invalid key. By default, an empty/null result is not stored in cache. A large volume of such requests can lead to degraded backend server performance or might crash it. Malicious applications generate such requests to overwhelm backend servers.

Some strategies to overcome this problem:

- Cache the returned null value with a relatively short TTL for the queried key or ID. This can be used to serve any subsequent request for the same key or ID, reducing load on the backend server
- Bespoke key or ID validation in combination with the Bloom filter (explained in *Chapter 3*), as needed, to ensure the presence of the requested key/ID before querying the backend server.
- IP blacklisting of request-originating clients at the edge location, if it appears to be from a malicious origin.
- Rate-limiting to protect the backend server from becoming overwhelmed

Database

A well-designed system can overcome any bottleneck imposed by slow-performing services, handle traffic spikes, or even deal with certain component failures. But a weak selection of data storage and its handling can cause even the best design to underperform. This is the component where data is maintained. The selection of the database dictates how data will be written, read, replicated, and secured. It is also an important component for attaining a level of consistency, availability and scalability. In this section we are going to take a deep dive to explore the principles that can guide us in making the right decision while selecting a database. We will also explore data partitioning, the associated consistency guarantees, trade-offs and handling techniques to build our confidence.

SQL vs NoSQL

An extremely popular discussion and decision in system design interviews is whether to use a relational (SQL) or a non-relational (NoSQL) database. First of all, it is important to understand that these databases can be supplementary to each other and should be used as per the use case you have. If need be, they can be used together to meet their relevant purposes rather than choosing one over another.

SQL databases, or relational database management systems (RDBMSs), are best for systems that deal with structured data, i.e., a well-defined schema for data stored in tabular format (represented in tuples), and require consistency guarantees, high transaction reliability, high security, and data integrity. They use Structured Query Language (SQL) for data handling and facilitate complex joins in doing so with efficiency. Some associated trade-offs are that an RDBMS is not as scalable as a distributed NoSQL database; horizontal scalability can be achieved by sharding, but it is complex to implement; read and write operations are more expensive (also driven by the presence of redo and undo logs and dynamic locking for concurrent access) because it ensures consistency and security; and hardware and management costs are higher. RDBMSs are ideal for business domains such as banking and insurance. [20]

NoSQL databases, on the other hand, are CAP compliant and work on eventual consistency models. Their primary focus is availability and scalability while keeping a balance between overall hardware cost and management overhead. They can tolerate a data node failure gracefully with the help of replication, making them ideal for cloud-native distributed architecture implementation. They provide significantly better data throughput than SQL databases. They handle very high-volume data and come in multiple flavors to match data demand. Such systems can handle structured, semi-structured, and unstructured data. These datastores are most suitable for use cases where strict consistency is not a primary requirement, for example, maintaining a user's session data.

By design, SQL databases are best suited for Online Transaction Processing (OLTP) requirements as they are Atomicity, Consistency, Isolation, and Durability (ACID) compliant. NoSQL databases, on the other hand, are best for throughput, speed, scalability and eventual consistency requirements. So while answering the question of which database to select, start by looking at the main properties and trade-offs of these data stores and map them with your core requirements. For instance, if your system is dealing with users, can your system afford the delay of new user registration information reaching other stakeholders, or if you are maintaining a client's session information, does it need to be strictly consistent or even persistent? What is the trade-off if you lose such session data? You should also consider its implications, recovery plan, and overall impact on the system you are building. If you start by asking such questions, then the selection process of the desired datastore will become more informed. *Figure 4.14* shows some properties associated with SQL and NoSQL databases.

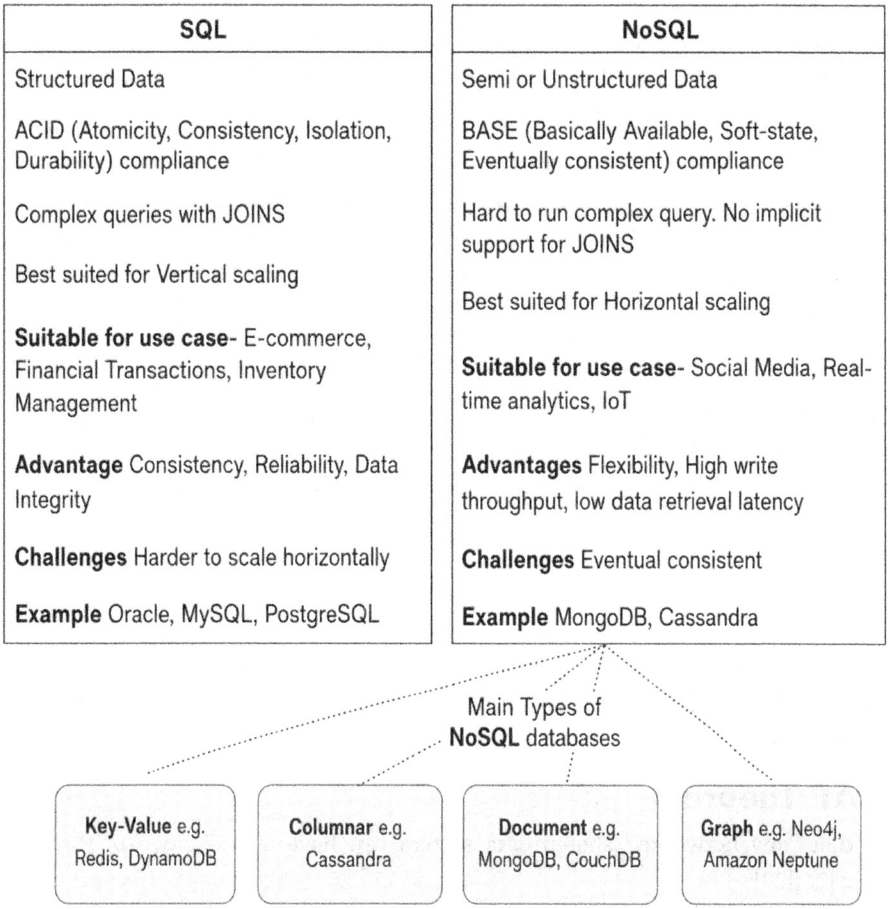

Figure 4.14: About SQL vs NoSQL database

Popular NoSQL databases

Key-Value: A key-value database uses a simple key-value method to store data. It uses a string-based key and stores actual data as a value. The key serves as a unique identifier. Both keys and values can be anything, ranging from simple objects to complex compound objects.

Columnar or column-oriented: A columnar database stores data by columns rather than by rows, which makes it suitable for analytical query processing and thus for data warehouses also. This is quite an important shift from the usual tuple-based architecture for updates because most of the time an update only includes a change of a subset of attributes from a row. [21]

Document: NoSQL document databases store data in the form of a 'document' supporting a flexible schema scheme. At its core, such databases also fall under the key-value category, where a key is the document identifier and the value is the actual document. Examples of document formats include JSON, XML, PDF, and others. Such stores enable data handling by the use of APIs or other inbuilt mechanisms that are different from the traditional SQL-based approach. Example: MongoDB, CouchDB. [25]

Graph: In the Graph database, the entity is stored as a node with the relationship as edges. An edge gives a relationship between nodes. Every node and edge has a unique identifier. Compared to a relational database where tables are loosely connected, a Graph database is multi-relational in nature. The behavior makes it a suitable choice for social media-type use cases. Example: Neo4j, Amazon Neptune.

Note

Graph databases are available in ACID as well as BASE consistency compliance models. It is the use case that decides which Graph database is suitable while designing a system. Graph databases, including Neo4j and Amazon Neptune, are ACID-compliant

With so many variations of a NoSQL datastore available, another important choice is how to choose one datastore over another. The CAP theorem helps in answering this question during decision making. Before taking a deep dive into the CAP theorem, you will appreciate that nodes or network partitioning (availability of multiple nodes distributed over a network) is a constant in a distributed environment.

The CAP Theorem

It states that "any networked shared-data system can have at most two of three desirable properties: [26][27]

- consistency (C) equivalent to having a single up-to-date copy of the data;
- high availability (A) of that data (for updates); and
- tolerance to network partitions (P)."

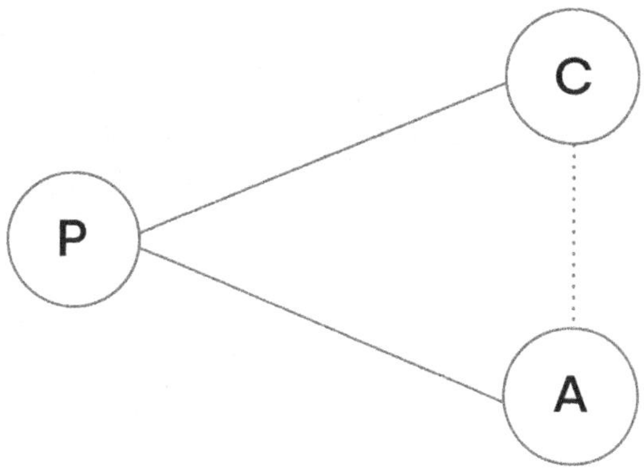

Figure 4.15: CAP Theorem

As shown in *Figure 4.15*, the theorem highlights trade-offs in designing a distributed, that is, network-partitioned system.

In a network-partitioned 'P' environment, if a system claims guaranteed 'C' then it can only optimize itself to support best effort 'A'. In this situation, in case of some inconsistencies within any node (say a node failure), write operations may be affected. A read request in this model will always return the consistent outcome.

If a system in this environment claims a guaranteed 'A' then it can only demonstrate the best-effort 'C,' e.g., in a CDN or web-content caching use case. In this case the system continues to accept write requests from users regardless of some node failure. But when performing a read operation all clients might not get the same, i.e., most up-to-date value because of the lag in achieving the eventual consistency.

If network partitioning 'P' is not a factor for a system then both 'C' and 'A' can be guaranteed, e.g., a traditional database, such as PostgreSQL or MySQL in a non-clustered setup. *Table 4.1* summarizes the key takeaways:

Distributed (Network partitioned) system - Must have	**Guaranteed outcome**	**Best effort outcome**	**Example database**	**Ideal for example use-cases**
Availability	P with A	C	Cassandra, DynamoDB, Couchbase	Social media feeds, Recommendation engine

Distributed (Network partitioned) system - Must have	Guaranteed outcome	Best effort outcome	Example database	Ideal for example use-cases
Consistency	P with C	A	MongoDB, HBase, CockroachDB	Banking systems, Inventory management system

Table 4.1: CAP Theorem availability vs consistency trade-off with example

The CAP theorem applies more broadly when considered in the context of different layers involved in a distributed system and is not limited to databases.

Note

'Consistency' as per the CAP theorem is slightly different from consistency in ACID transactions. 'C' in ACID means that a database preserves all the database rules, e.g., primary key constraints whereas 'C' in CAP refers to a single up-to-date copy of the data (a subset of behavior from ACID)

Choosing the right database

Selecting a database is the most important decision that depends on the nature of the data and its intended usage. A traditional comparison to help in making such a decision is captured in *Table 4.2*.

Use-Case contains ↓	SQL	NoSQL
Data need	Structured (Rows and Columns i.e., tuple-based) and relational	Semi or Unstructured (Hierarchical, highly interconnected or sparse data)
Throughput	Good	Generally much higher than SQL stores
Query Patterns	Complex joins and ad-hoc queries support	Complex joins and ad hoc queries are difficult to support

Use-Case contains ↓	SQL	NoSQL
Scaling	Vertical scaling is fit for the use case	Horizontal scaling is better for the use case
Data volume	Data growth can be handled by database resizing (vertical scaling). It can be limited by the physical server's capacity, or another complex data fragmentation technique will be required to meet volume needs	Intended use is to deal with a very large volume of data. Theoretically, it can scale to accommodate infinite data volume.
Performance	Good performance that can be enhanced using indexing and relevant caching techniques.	Very low data retrieval latency with built-in caching support
Consistency & Reliability	Strong requirement of overall ACID behavior	Eventual consistency is sufficient
Security	Built-in security for both reads and writes.	May require additional security controls to secure the data journey.
Default choice during interview	Suitable for most of the use cases.	Consider as a first choice for distributed data where partition tolerance is important

Table 4.2: Traditional comparison: SQL and NoSQL store

A more pragmatic way to make this decision is to think in terms of the data model that you will use for storing the data as well as to better understand the trade-offs presented by these data stores in the context of your system needs. Data is always an important aspect of a system. To summarize the thought:

In a NoSQL context, eventual consistency does not mean you will lose data; it only means a delay can be observed in reaching consistency. There are mature mechanisms that can be used to minimize the impact. Its power includes the presence of different types of storage systems that can match your specific needs. Also, it brings overall flexibility to the backend implementation in terms of data models, latency, throughput, scalability, etc. Data security is relatively high in the case of SQL databases, but that does not make NoSQL insecure. Some indicators for choosing this datastore include: your problem is not about structured data, you have to support a very high-volume non-warehouse data use case, your problem statement is availability over consistency, you have a very specific use case e.g. social media connections, a key-value store.

In a SQL context, scalability is a concern, but it is achievable using alternatives, including sharding. Performance and throughput of RDBMSs are relatively lower by comparison, but they are not always the bottleneck in context to your use case. Also consider introducing different caching layers to gain performance benefits. Moreover, it is much more mature than the NoSQL space of data stores. It is also easier to explain to someone. Some indicators for choosing this datastore include data consistency, business domain for example, banking or insurance, structured data, highly available system but main focus on consistency. [28][29]

In many cases, a combination of SQL and NoSQL stores are used to solve parts of a business problem. For example, for a distributed social media system you might like to use a SQL database for user management but a NoSQL database for user relationships, that is, connection management as well as post management. [24]

Database scaling

As your system grows, you'll need to scale your database to handle more data and traffic. Scaling a database follows the same fundamental concept as we have discussed in *Chapter 2* with regard to hardware-based scaling. With databases it becomes more focused and sensitive, as we need to put extra effort to ensure your data remains unaffected while scaling the underlying hardware.

Vertical scaling

In this strategy, an existing database server is replaced by an upgraded one with more computational power and/or storage capacity as needed. In such a scenario, a lift-and-shift of the entire underlying data architecture can be performed from the existing to the new server. It is considered as a safe approach to scale your database as the underlying architecture (e.g., storage principle, data handling techniques, entities) remains as is. It is an effective and desirable way of scaling up your database. It suffers from the hard limits imposed by the underlying hardware on which the database instance runs.

Horizontal scaling and sharding

Scaling a database horizontally means introducing more database instances of desired capacity into the ecosystem and then grouping them together to work as a single unit. Adding more units of servers comes with its own underlying complexity, e.g., replication, consistency, and failover. To enable efficient use of data and to improve data management goals, we often distribute (i.e., partition) data across multiple database servers (or nodes), a process also known as **sharding**. Each participating data node or server in this arrangement is called a shard. Each shard contains a portion of the data, allowing the system to scale out by adding more nodes as needed (also see

Consistent hashing, in *Chapter 3*). Data partitioning can reduce query response time significantly, as the query will run on a significantly smaller data set hosted per node.

Example: If you have a table with a million users, you can distribute the user data to multiple shards by `userID`, if we consider a key-based partitioning strategy. In an environment involving two shards, users with IDs 1-500,000 may go to one shard, and users with IDs 500,001-1,000,000 may go to another. Each shard contains the same schema but different rows. In this case, any query running on a shard will only have to scan through half of the overall dataset and, hence, show faster execution.

Sharding techniques: There are multiple techniques available to implement sharding. Here, we have touched upon some of them:

- **Range-based:** It involves dividing the entire dataset based on a key and then distributing each divided set on one server as explained in the example above. It can lead to hotspot problems. [*Chapter 3* discussed some ways to generate unique keys (IDs).]
- **Location-based:** Mainly used in the case of applications that have a global presence and require low-latency region-based data. Data of a specific region will be placed in a relevant partition located near the region for quick access.
- **Hash-based:** In this case, a hash is created for the data, and then the hash is used to determine the node where it will be stored. An elaborated technique is described as part of *Consistent hashing* in *Chapter 3*. An example of a datastore that uses a hash-based sharding technique is DynamoDB
- **Directory-based:** It is a more dynamic form of partitioning. Instead of relying on predefined rules (like ranges or hash-based partitioning), the system uses a directory or lookup service to determine where data should be stored. It maintains a mapping of data records to their respective partitions. When a new record is added, the directory is consulted to determine which partition will store the record. For example, Dropbox

Sharding comes with a cost of node rebalancing and sometimes resharding, e.g., when new nodes are added, a node fault occurs, or a more efficient data distribution strategy is needed. Rebalancing has been discussed in *Chapter 3*, highlighting multiple techniques that we can use for a problem.

Sharding Trade-offs: It is important to understand the trade-offs associated with data sharding. A better knowledge of the trade-offs will enable you to make an informed selection of the technique for the given problem. Below are a few such points highlighted -

Query performance while dealing with complex joins: Queries on a single shard are usually faster in the case of sharding, but some queries might span multiple database nodes, e.g., determining the top 'K' famous songs globally. A complex query spanning through multiple shards might encounter a performance bottleneck because of network latency or other contributing factors. To mitigate this trade-off, some recommendations are to identify such scenarios and create a denormalized data structure to handle such scenarios, scatter-gather pattern where the system queries all the shards and then merges their results

Skewed data (hotspot problem): It is possible that a single node or some nodes end up holding data elements that are the most frequently accessed, attracting high-volume traffic. It can overload those nodes, which might result in a degraded response. To mitigate, you can consider approaches like shard replication, load balancing to include additional replicas, use of consistent hashing, etc. in some combination.

Consistency across shards: One of the most important aspects to consider. A wider explanation is presented under the 'Data Replication' & 'Handling Data Inconsistency' sections of this chapter. This is a trade-off where the key question is whether the goal is to achieve strong consistency or whether eventual consistency is sufficient. Most of the modern systems follow the principle of strong consistency within a shard and eventual (asynchronous) consistency across the shards. To achieve the desired level of consistency, the use of two-phase commit, Raft, Consistent hashing and other such protocols helps.

Shard Router: A shard router is a component sitting before your database/shards layer that determines which shard or shards a query should be routed to for its execution. This means that this component is data-aware and can make such decisions. It might appear to be similar to a load balancer, but the main difference is, load balancers are not generally data-aware. A shard router maintains information such as your shard key, metadata information, partitioning information, etc. to match the sharding strategy you have incorporated. Such information helps this component to choose the target shard(s) where a query should be directed for its execution. For a given use case, it is possible for your application server to be a shard router. A specialized router is generally needed for a complex environment. A shard router is shown in *Figure 4.16*.

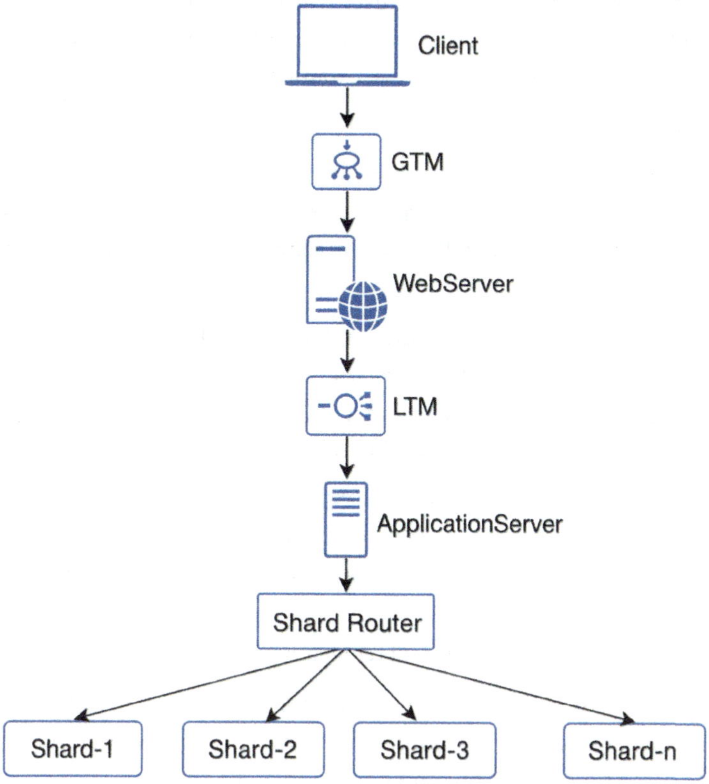

Figure 4.16: Function of a Shard router

Resharding

To explain the concept, let's take a scenario where you are running an e-commerce business. You have customers and their orders. Their information is stored in a distributed environment. You chose to use a range-based sharding technique to organize customers and their order data so that you have information of all the orders placed by a user in one place. This works well initially. Over time, say there is a shift in some requirement, and now you want to see (near real-time) all the users who have ordered any item during the day. Your existing data distribution mechanism might give you a tough time to gather this information in near real time because of the presence of multiple data hosts in making such a decision, and hence you might consider resharding based on order date if you are maintaining a range-based technique.

This is just an example; there could be many other real-world scenarios where you will have to consider resharding to maintain business continuity, for example, in a financial system where one entity/institution is making ten million transactions compared with an average of a thousand, indicating the possibility of hotspot problems. Dynamic or automated resharding is one technique where the database itself adjusts and redistributes data among nodes when a change in workload is encountered, for example, MongoDB. But it needs database readiness to support such implementation; also, during redistribution, query performance can go down.

Data replication

Replication refers to the process of duplicating data across multiple servers or data centers. It is implemented to ensure that the system remains operational in the event of failures, increases its read performance, and can scale to handle a growing number of users. Benefits of data replication include –

- Mitigates SPoF (Single point of failure) and increases data availability. If one server goes down, a replica takes over to serve user requests. For example, Netflix uses data replication extensively to ensure that if a data center in one region fails, viewers in that region can still stream shows from a different data center.
- Disaster recovery ensures the system can recover from catastrophic events like data corruption, hardware failures, or hacking attempts. By maintaining replicas in different regions or availability zones, organizations can recover data quickly and restore services after an outage.

In terms of control flow and consistency, data replication can be achieved by one of the two ways.

Synchronous: In this method, the system waits for all replicas to acknowledge the write operation before considering the transaction complete. This ensures that all replicas have the latest data at the same time, **guaranteeing consistency**. Because the system must wait for all replicas to acknowledge the write, it introduces additional latency

Asynchronous: Here, once the data is written on a primary node, the transaction is deemed to be complete. The data then gets propagated to the replicas later. This approach is faster in terms of response time for users performing write operations but leads to **eventual consistency**, where replicas might temporarily have outdated information.

Some well-known data replication patterns are:

- ***Primary-secondary***: In this pattern, the primary server handles all write operations, and the secondary servers replicate the data from the primary server to all secondaries to handle read operations. This pattern is widely used for systems that have a much higher ratio of reads to writes. It facilitates clear separation of write and read but suffers from replication lag. E.g., MySQL
- ***Primary-primary***: It allows multiple servers to act as primary. This means that both read and write operations can be performed on any of the servers, and the changes are propagated to the other primary nodes. This replication model is often used in systems where high availability is critical, and the system cannot afford to have a single point of

failure. It is a great fit for a highly available, fault-tolerant, and high-write-throughput system but suffers from conflict resolution overhead if two primary servers try to update the same record at the same time. Conflict resolution can be achieved using 'last-write-wins (LWW)' or another implementation. E.g., CouchDB uses a combination of revision tracking and conflict resolution to handle conflicts in its multi-primary replication model

- ***Quorum-based replication:*** In this case a certain number of participants (write-quorum) from a group of nodes must agree to a write operation to be successful. Also, during data read operation, a group of nodes are queried (read-quorum). The number of participating nodes that formulate a read-quorum & write-quorum are determined intelligently. Examples of systems using such replication are Cassandra, Amazon DynamoDB, and Riak [22][23].

Handling data inconsistency

Managing data inconsistency is crucial to ensure data sanity as well as the system's reliability to respond to user actions. Dealing with inconsistency involves two main steps – conflict detection and conflict resolution/reconciliation.

Conflict detection

There are multiple mechanisms available to detect inconsistency within data being stored within a distributed environment. Some well-known approaches include:

- ***Vector Clock and Dotted Version Vector:*** Vector clock (or dotted version vector, an extension of vector clock) implementation is a well-known technique in maintaining different versions of data as and when they appear. A Vector clock (covered in *Chapter 8*) is a data structure that achieves the goal of determining the causality of events occurring on different nodes in a distributed system. That is, it helps us to determine the order of events whenever their node communication creates a causal link.
- ***Hash comparison***: e.g. checksum

Conflict resolution/reconciliation

Conflict resolution deals with the system's behavior in case of a conflict. Multiple mechanisms exist to achieve this task. These include:

- **Use of data structure**: This technique is only suitable if the data type of the data being stored is supported by the chosen data structure, e.g., Set, Map. Not suitable for all the use cases. [30]

- **Last Write Wins (LWW)**: It uses versioning and timestamps associated with data. It is an effective mechanism overall but misses some data/action in certain cases. The weakness of LWW is - It is server-clock-dependent i.e. it assumes all server clocks in the distributed system use exactly the same time. There can be multiple triggers that can fail this assumption, leading to some catastrophic outcome. **NTP (Network Time Protocol)** is widely used to keep system clocks in sync in a distributed environment, but it is still not guaranteed.
- **Read repair**: In this technique, data is merged during a read data call. It works pretty well for most of the use cases. The main problem it leaves is that of stale data, i.e., if data is not read by a consumer for a long time, it will stay in an inconsistent state within the persistent store. Refer to the section *Proactively reconcile inconsistent data: Read-repair*, from *Chapter 3*.
- **Merkle Tree based**: It is used to periodically identify data mismatch between nodes. If a mismatch is found then appropriate corrective measures will be built to attain consistency. Discussed in detail in the section *Detecting differences between replicas: Merkle trees*, in *Chapter 3*. It is primarily a passive, resource intensive journey and hence runs in the background. The benefit it offers is that all data objects will receive the latest copy of the data regardless of when they were last accessed, keeping the entire database consistent.

Gateways and API gateway

A gateway can be described as a device or a software component that connects two or more discrete networks, regardless of their protocols, to enable data exchange. Some gateway components that are commonly used in designing systems are –

Reverse Proxy: It acts as an intermediary to abstract server details from clients, e.g., HAProxy and Envoy

Edge Gateway: A commonly found component within cloud-hosted environments, it handles traffic at the edge location. This component is slightly more feature-rich than a reverse proxy in the sense it can perform device authentication, protocol translation, etc. to mention a few.

Security Gateway: It is used to protect your systems from threats over the network. Main features to use this component include – Allow or block traffic based on rules, including DDoS prevention, Packet inspection, and prevention of malware injection for example, AWS Network Firewall, CISCO AnyConnect, ZScalar Internet Access.

Message Gateway: A message gateway is primarily used for asynchronous communication and facilitates the movement of messages between different systems. Beyond basic message transfer, a message gateway provides a range of supporting capabilities such as protocol translation (for example, HTTP to JMS or JSON to XML), security features including message filtering and encryption, intelligent message routing, and delivery guarantees through mechanisms like status tracking, retries, and failure handling.

Specialized message gateways also exist to address specific communication needs, such as SMS gateways, email gateways, and event gateways.

At its core, a message gateway is conceptually different from a message queue. The gateway is responsible for aspects related to message handling - such as validation, transformation, routing, and delivery. In contrast, the primary responsibility of a message queue is to provide temporary but durable message storage and buffering.

In practice, many messaging platforms that provide message queue functionality also include an associated gateway component to manage ingress, egress, and integration concerns. Common examples include RabbitMQ and ActiveMQ.

API gateway

An **API (Application Programming Interface) Gateway** is a specialized implementation of a gateway for enabling API interactions between a client and an underlying servicing environment. It acts as a reverse proxy while serving any request that involves one or more backend services. It creates an abstraction by enabling a single point of entry for clients making API requests. [31]

How it works

A client makes an API request using the exposed URI. The request reaches the API gateway that fronts the underlying services. The gateway processes the request based on the defined policies (including authentication, authorization, encryption, protocol translation, etc.), and directs the call to one or more underlying services. If more than one service is involved in request fulfillment, the gateway collects and aggregates the response, and sends the response back to the caller/client. *Figure 4.17* shows an API gateway and some core functions it handles.

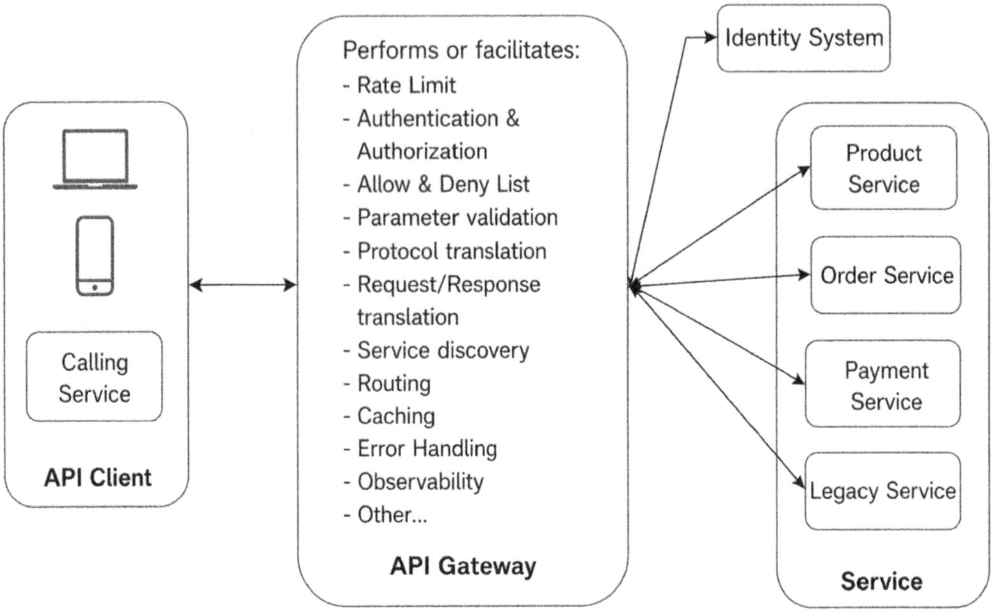

Figure 4.17: Architectural representation of API Gateway with some core responsibilities

An API gateway is a go-to component if you are working on a microservices-based system design. In *Figure 4.17*, components on the right-hand side represent microservices. An API gateway can also perform traffic management to some extent but it should not be looked at as a replacement for a load balancer in your architecture. Some commonly used API gateways are NGINX, ZUUL, APIGEE. [32]

Trade-offs

Like any other component, an API gateway comes with some trade-offs to know. Some key trade-offs are –

1. **Cost**: Most of the enterprise-grade API gateways come with vendor lock-in. This can lead to high licensing and operational costs.
2. **Increased latency**: At a minimum, an API gateway introduces an additional network hop before the backend service can be called. Also, being a sophisticated system, there are a number of activities being executed here that might increase overall latency.
3. **Complexity**: When self-managed, it requires expert knowledge to configure an API gateway. A small misconfiguration can lead to a bigger problem, especially around security configuration, logging, and monitoring.

API design

API (Application Programming Interface) design allows different parts of a system to communicate. It also enables external systems or clients to interact with your system. In interviews, designing robust, scalable, and secure APIs demonstrates your ability to think holistically about how users and systems will interface with your application.

APIs can be designed using REST, SOAP, GraphQL, gRPC, WebSocket, or MQTT (detailed in the *Message broker* section, in this chapter) styles, depending on your use case. It is recommended to understand all of them so that you can confidently apply one style during your interview. Here we are going to expand the RESTful API and *WebSocket* in more detail.

RESTful API design

REST is a stateless architectural style that leverages standard HTTP methods to interact with resources in a client-server model. Let's see a sample request with annotation [35].

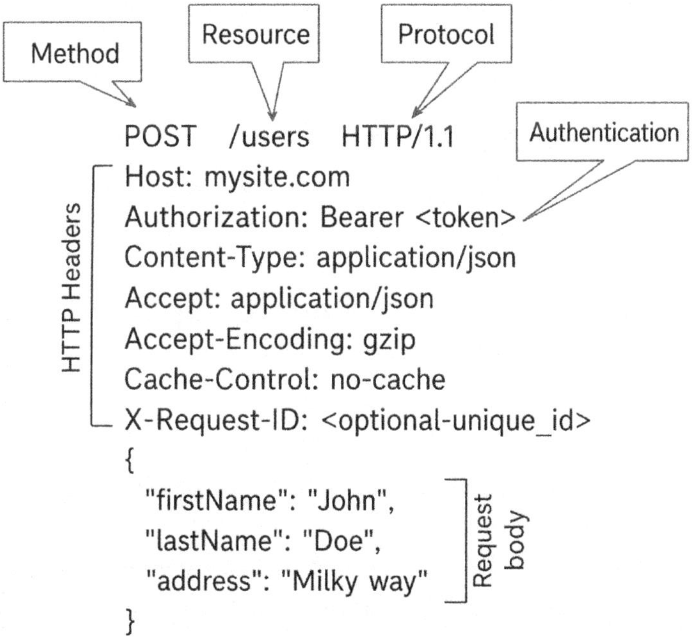

Figure 4.18 HTTP Request sample

From *Figure 4.18*, let's understand the components –

Details of the URI:

- *Endpoint* is `'POST /users'`,
- *Protocol* used is HTTP/1.1,
- *HTTP Method* used is POST,
- *Resource* is user (represented as plural as per standard naming convention)

HTTP header consists of:

- Server location is represented by the 'Host' key-value pair,
- `'Authorization'` key-value pair is where you specify your authentication mechanism, for example, JWT token, OAuth2 token, etc.
- `'Content-Type'` key-value pair in this example points to the JSON media type. There are other types, e.g., Text, XML, supported as well. JSON is the most widely adopted data exchange type in RESTful implementations because of its easy-to-understand structure and lightweight format.

Request body:

- Also called the payload, contains the actual data, in this case the user to create.

REST APIs best practices

Resource: A resource is an entity, object, or service that will be acted upon. As a standard, plural terms must be used, e.g., /user**s** rather than /user. The method determines the action that the endpoint should execute.

Methods: REST APIs must conform to the HTTP methods specification [33][34]. Some common HTTP methods and their purpose while writing an API are:

- GET for reading data without modifying the state of any underlying resource. E.g. GET /users or GET /users/{id}
- POST for creating new resources. POST is not idempotent (sending the same request multiple times could result in multiple resources being created).
- PUT for updating existing resources. PUT is idempotent, meaning sending the same request multiple times will produce the same result. Caution: if you use PUT to update a resource that does not exist, the resource will be created.
- DELETE for removing resources.

Response: It should return the requested data or appropriate feedback on the operation's success or failure. Successful responses often include the created resource, a status message, and any other relevant information.

Example Response for creating a user:

```
HTTP/1.1 201 Created
Content-Type: application/vnd.api+json
{
"data": [ {
"userId": "123456",
"firstName": "John",
"lastName": "Doe",
"address": "Milky way",
"createdAt": "2025-06-30T12:32:56Z"
   } ]
}
```

Notice the response code `201` is the standard HTTP response status when an object, entity, or record is created. Also notice additional attributes returned in the payload.

Query parameters and patterns

There are patterns associated with APIs that are implemented using query parameters in the URL. This concept is very useful to understand because if you create some APIs during your interview and you need to demonstrate how you can accommodate certain features, they will be handy. It is also important to understand that the implementation of these patterns is bespoke, i.e., the system owner will control; hence, you can use your appropriate thought to expand them if needed. Here are some examples:

Sorting: You can implement result sorting in an order, say lexicographical order by first name, as `GET /users?sort=firstNameℴ=asc`

Filtering: `GET /products?category=electronics`

Pagination: `GET /users?limit=20&page=1`

There are variations available as well, e.g., cursor-based and offset-based.

API security

There are some standard mechanisms to build your API securely. Remember that security should be demonstrated intentionally within APIs rather than as a side activity.

- ***Authentication*** mechanism must be clearly mentioned.

- ***Data encryption:*** Ensure to encrypt all your sensitive information using appropriate mechanisms. TLS/SSL is the best to mention/implement.
- ***Apply rate limiting*** to your APIs to prevent their misuse, including minimizing the threat surface from DDoS attacks.

Example:

```
X-RateLimit-Limit: 100
X-RateLimit-Remaining: 50
X-RateLimit-Reset: 60
```

Here, the client is limited to 100 requests per minute, and the header informs them how many requests are remaining and when the limit will reset

API versioning

You might need to demonstrate how to maintain multiple versions of APIs as well as the best way to phase out the previous version. There is no direct answer to it. When it comes to versioning your APIs, as per the best practice, the first change you will make is to include a version number before your resource name, i.e., in our previous example, `/users` will become `/<version-no>/users` such as `/v1/users`, `/v2/users` etc. It ensures business continuity by allowing backward compatibility, and then you can choose a mechanism to shift your customers to the new version of APIs using a phased transition or a big-bang approach, depending on your use case.

Note

A REST-based API approach is not an ideal approach if your use case is dealing with complex nested data or it requires multiple round trips to the backend for your data requirements.

Managing API versioning requires some good documentation practices. They are an addendum to the versioning strategy. Within documentation, you would need to clearly define what each version does and which version will be deprecated.

Also, when learning about API versioning, an understanding of "Canary" and "Blue-Green" deployment can be useful, as it might help you during some later conversation with interviewers.

WebSocket, Server-Sent Events (SSE) and Webhooks

These technologies enable different forms of real-time communication between clients and servers. This section explores WebSockets, Server-Sent Events (SSE), and webhooks, and how each supports different communication needs.

WebSockets

It is a communication protocol that provides full-duplex (data can be transmitted and received simultaneously) and bidirectional (meaning from a server to a client and vice versa) interaction between a web client and a server over a long-lived TCP connection. It is ideal for real-time, very low-latency communication between the two systems, especially when the server needs to push data to client(s) without any client having to request it. Main use cases where WebSocket is a suitable mechanism include chat applications (e.g., WhatsApp Web, Discord, Slack), real-time collaborative editing (e.g., Google Docs). There are a few more use cases where

WebSockets can work but there are less resource-intensive alternatives available as well. Some such use cases include real-time sports updates (e.g., live cricket scores) and news feeds [36].

How it works for a web client:

1. **Handshake**: This is the first stage where a web client and a web server perform a handshake, upgrading the connection from HTTP to WebSockets. The web client always initiates the handshake.
2. **Data exchange**: After the handshake, each side (client or server) can independently send data as needed. The WebSocket connection acts as a persistent full-duplex channel.
3. **Close the connection**: It can be initiated by the client or the server. Once done, the connection breaks and the communication stops.

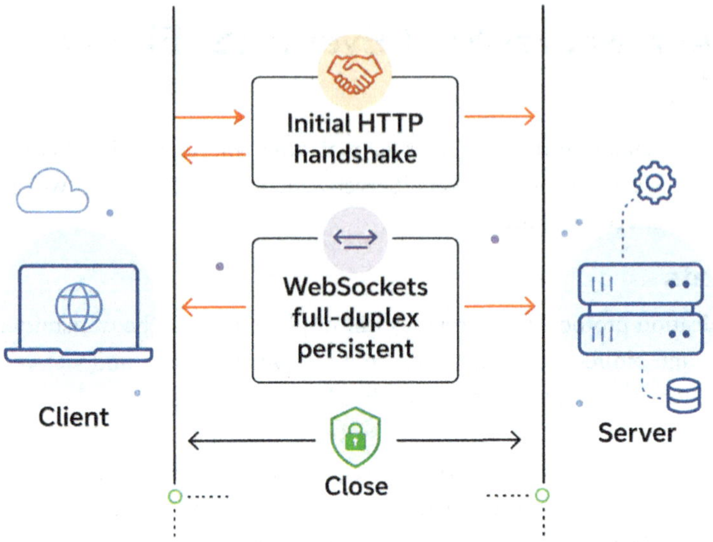

Figure 4.19: An example of WebSocket connection

Figure 4.19 depicts how a WebSocket connection is established. In its originating form (native to HTTP/1.1), a WebSocket handshake request is a specially formatted GET request that contains some mandatory pre-defined **header** information.

A client-initiated handshake request might look like this:

```
GET /chat HTTP/1.1
Host: nobleapproach.co.uk
Upgrade: websocket
Connection: Upgrade
Sec-WebSocket-Key: <some_key_in_base64>
Sec-WebSocket-Version: <some_supported_version>
```

The last four header entries in the above handshake request are the mandatory ones for WebSocket upgrade requests from the client. On receipt of this request, the server performs its validation to ensure that the upgrade request is valid in all respects and then returns a response similar to-

```
HTTP/1.1 101 Switching Protocols
Upgrade: websocket
Connection: Upgrade
Sec-WebSocket-Accept: <some_hash_for_the_client>
```

The preceding response completes the journey and a WebSocket connection is established between the client and the server. Equivalent mechanisms are available to support WebSockets over HTTP/2 and HTTP/3 for WebSocket upgrade.

We will explore further the usage of WebSocket with the help of a case study in *Chapter 7.*

> **Note**
>
> In the context of client-server communication, two other available mechanisms to mention here are – short polling and long polling.
>
> Short polling is a simple client-server interaction where a client requests new data from a server over HTTP. To stay up to date with the latest information, clients initiate such requests iteratively and/or periodically. It is not a suitable technique for a real-time response scenario but still a good choice for its class of problems. Common examples where short polling can be used are - job execution status check, email checks, weather updates.
>
> Long polling is similar to short polling with the difference that the server keeps the connection open for a relatively longer period of time. During this extended time frame any new information known to the server will be sent back to the client. Ignoring WebSockets, it was a famous implementation during a period before SSE & Webhooks to generate near-real-time updates. Use cases include - email checks and notifications

Server-Sent Events (SSE)

Server-Sent Events (SSE), introduced as part of the HTML5 specification, is another standard HTTP-based protocol to enable real-time data push from server to client. It is achieved using a single long-lived HTTP connection. The connection request is invoked by the client to a server (supporting SSE) over HTTP. Even though the main interaction use case for this approach is from a client (browser) to a server, the approach can be implemented for any client that can consume the streaming data over a long-lived open connection [37].

Because of this nature of communication, it is an ideal choice for systems that do not require bidirectional communication and need the latest information from the server e.g., a live scoreboard.

Since this is an HTTP-based RESTful call, it is lightweight and works well with corporate firewalls. On its first connection request the server opens a long-lived connection and sends a 'Content-type: text/event-stream' response to the client, indicating that the client should expect a stream of data from the server going forward, rather than a single response. From this point onward, the journey becomes uni-directional from server to client. The connection so established between the client and server comes with an automatic reconnect feature where the client will send the ID of the last received data packet and the server will continue sending the next one as soon as the connection is re-established.

The trade-off for this approach is - It strictly supports UTF-8 encoded messages. Also, the communication is uni-directional.

Some use cases for SSE are - live game updates, news feeds, push notifications, stock price updates, etc.

Webhook

A webhook is another push-based (but not polling-based) mechanism available for data exchange between systems over HTTP. It enables event-driven communication where a serving system (henceforth called server) automatically sends information about a change in state for the subscribed event, to a listening system (henceforth called client) using an API. It is a server-to-server communication but message flow is uni-directional.

In this approach, a client shares a callback URL to the server API to subscribe to a specific event. Once this communication is established, the client no longer polls the server. When the server observes a state change for the subscribed event, it will send the new state to the client using the shared callback URL (usually via HTTP POST method with payload).

Summary

Algorithms tell you how distributed systems think. Building blocks are what you actually assemble when you sit down to design one. This chapter introduced the core components that appear in virtually every system design interview - not as isolated concepts, but as interconnected pieces that work together to make systems scalable, secure, and observable.

At the beginning we discussed stateless versus stateful services to help you decide which one is the best fit for your problem domain. Stateless services scale horizontally without much effort, whereas stateful services require more care and thought. Scaling vertically is quick and relatively easy, but horizontal scaling wins at internet scale. Horizontal scaling comes with its own complexities around partitioning, distribution, and tolerance of partial failure. Load balancers play an important role in achieving horizontal scaling.

We explained asynchronous communication as the way to decouple interacting systems so that they can be scaled independently, and how it can improve latency. To improve a system's latency, we also discussed maintaining data freshness within the cache with the help of different eviction and data population techniques. We established that the choice of a database is based on the system requirements, access patterns, and most importantly the data itself. The CAP theorem helps us make such decisions in a more structured way.

We looked at how to create APIs using industry best practices, and how an API gateway abstracts multiple mission-critical concerns including authentication, rate limiting, and logging by providing a common place for implementation. We also took a detailed look at specific near-real-time interactions that can be achieved using WebSocket for full-duplex communication, SSE for one-way streams, and Webhooks for service-to-service interactions.

The next chapter talks about security and observability, the two cross-cutting concerns that span everything that we have learned so far. We will take a deep dive to understand why security and observability should be planned from the beginning rather than at a later stage.

Quiz

Q1. In consistent hashing, what is the purpose of virtual nodes (vNodes)?

A) To speed up token generation in OAuth2.

B) To reduce hotspots and balance load across physical nodes.

C) To reduce the cryptographic weakness of hashing functions.

D) To avoid duplicate keys in JWT payload.

Q2. Which load balancing algorithm sends requests to the server with the least active connections?

A) Random

B) Least connections

C) Round robin

D) Hash-based

Q3. Which replication strategy ensures strong consistency but may reduce availability?

A) Asynchronous replication

B) Synchronous replication

C) Multi-master replication

D) Lazy replication

Q4. What is a common benefit of replication?

A) Slower writes

B) Reduced read throughput

C) Lower storage costs

D) Higher availability and fault tolerance

Q5. Which load balancing method is best when servers have different capacities?

A) Weighted round robin

B) Least connections

C) Random

D) FIFO

Q6. Which of the following is NOT a characteristic of databases?

A) Data persistence

B) Query support

C) Session management

D) Data indexing

Q7. Which of the following is a relational (SQL) database?

A) MongoDB

B) Cassandra

C) Redis

D) Oracle

Q8. Which NoSQL database is commonly used as a document store?

A) MySQL

B) PostgreSQL

C) MongoDB

D) SQLite

Q9. Which NoSQL type is most suitable for social network graphs?

A) Document store

B) Graph database

C) Wide-column store

D) Key-value store

Q10. A document-oriented database stores data in which format?

A) Tables and rows

B) Plain text files

C) Graph edges and vertices

D) XML or JSON-like structures

Q11. The CAP theorem states that in the presence of a network partition, a system must trade off between:

A) Consistency and scalability

B) Availability and partition tolerance

C) Consistency and availability

D) Durability and latency

Q12. What does PACELC add to CAP?

A) A focus on cost and performance

B) A distinction between failure and normal operation trade-offs

C) A new category for graph databases

D) Security considerations

Q13. According to PACELC, if there is no partition, what trade-off is considered?

A) Consistency vs Availability

B) Latency vs Consistency

C) Performance vs Security

D) Partition tolerance vs Replication

Q14. Which database type is best suited for a financial transaction system requiring ACID compliance?

A) Document store

B) Relational database

C) Key-value store

D) Graph database

Q15. For a recommendation engine that relies heavily on relationships between entities, which database type is best?

A) Relational database

B) Graph database

C) Wide-column store

D) Key-value store

Q16. Your e-commerce application requires catalog storage where product details vary widely (different fields for electronics vs. clothes). Which database is the best fit?

A) MySQL

B) Redis

C) Oracle DB

D) MongoDB

Q17. A social networking app requires efficient traversal of user relationships (e.g., "friends of friends"). Best choice?

A) MongoDB

B) Neo4j

C) Cassandra

D) MySQL

Q18. A machine learning pipeline requires quick access to JSON documents describing users. Best DB?

A) MongoDB

B) Oracle DB

C) Redis

D) Neo4j

Q19. A supply chain system must ensure product inventory counts are always correct, even under concurrent updates. Which DB type?

A) Relational DB (ACID-compliant)

B) Wide-column store

C) Key-value store

D) Document DB

Q20. What HTTP response code is sent to rejected requests

A) HTTP 500

B) HTTP 429

C) HTTP 403

D) HTTP 401

Q21. What mechanism is used by the service platform to inform clients regarding their quota information?

A) HTTPS handshake

B) with heartbeat response

C) HTTP response header

D) separate service to find out quota information

Q22. The first bit of Snowflake ID is reserved. It is also known as -

A) signed bit

B) unsigned bit

C) zero bit

D) one bit

Q23. What is the 10-bit machine identification made out of:

A) data center id and auto-generated number

B) machine mac-id and auto-generated number

C) data center id and mac-id

D) 10-bit timestamp

Q24. In a queue, every message is consumed by exactly one consumer.

A) True

B) False

Q25. What is the main difference between a message queue and pub-sub?

A) Queues are synchronous, pub-sub is asynchronous

B) Queue delivers to one consumer, pub-sub can deliver to many

C) Queues guarantee ordering, pub-sub does not

D) Queue is only for small data, pub-sub is for large data

References

Stateful and stateless applications

[1] Fielding, R. T. (2000). "Architectural Styles and the Design of Network-based Software Architectures." Ph.D. dissertation, University of California, Irvine. `https://ics.uci.edu/~fielding/pubs/dissertation/top.htm`

[2] Redis. "Session management." `https://redis.io/solutions/session-management/`

Scalability

[3] Abbott, M. L., & Fisher, M. T. (2015). The Art of Scalability (2nd ed.). Addison-Wesley.

[4] Amdahl, G. M. (1967). "Validity of the Single Processor Approach to Achieving Large-Scale Computing Capabilities." Proceedings of AFIPS '67. https://dl.acm.org/doi/10.1145/1465482.1465560 and https://en.wikipedia.org/wiki/Amdahl's_law

[5] Gunther, N. J. (2007). Guerrilla Capacity Planning. Springer. [the Universal Scalability Law] https://doi.org/10.1007/978-3-540-31010-5

Asynchronous communication and messaging

[6] Hohpe, G., & Woolf, B. (2003). Enterprise Integration Patterns. Addison-Wesley.

[7] Eugster, P. T., Felber, P. A., Guerraoui, R., & Kermarrec, A.-M. (2003). "The Many Faces of Publish/Subscribe." ACM Computing Surveys, 35(2). https://doi.org/10.1145/857076.857078

[8] Kreps, J., Narkhede, N., & Rao, J. (2011). "Kafka: a Distributed Messaging System for Log Processing." Proceedings of the NetDB Workshop. https://notes.stephenholiday.com/Kafka.pdf and Narkhede, N., Shapira, G., Palino, T. Kafka: The Definitive Guide — Real-Time Data and Stream Processing at Scale. O'Reilly Media, 2017. Confluent-sponsored edition, 20170707-EB-Confluent_Kafka_Definitive-Guide_Complete.pdf https://assets.confluent.io/m/1b509accf21490f0/original/20170707-EB-Confluent_Kafka_Definitive-Guide_Complete.pdf

[9] AWS. "Amazon Simple Queue Service Developer Guide." https://docs.aws.amazon.com/AWSSimpleQueueService/latest/SQSDeveloperGuide/

[10] RabbitMQ. "RabbitMQ Documentation." https://www.rabbitmq.com/documentation.html

[11] OASIS (2019). "MQTT Version 5.0." OASIS Standard. https://docs.oasis-open.org/mqtt/mqtt/v5.0/mqtt-v5.0.html

Load balancing

[12] NGINX. "What Is Load Balancing?" https://www.nginx.com/resources/glossary/load-balancing/

[13] Eisenbud, D. E., et al. (2016). "Maglev: A Fast and Reliable Software Network Load Balancer." Proceedings of USENIX NSDI '16. https://www.usenix.org/sites/default/files/nsdi16-paper-eisenbud-update.pdf

[14] AWS. "Elastic Load Balancing - Application Load Balancers and Network Load Balancers." https://docs.aws.amazon.com/elasticloadbalancing/

[15] HAProxy. "HAProxy Configuration Manual." https://docs.haproxy.org/

Caching

[16] Nishtala, R., Fugal, H., Grimm, S., Kwiatkowski, M., Lee, H., Li, H. C., McElroy, R., Paleczny, M., Peek, D., Saab, P., Stafford, D., Tung, T., & Venkataramani, V. (2013). "Scaling Memcache at Facebook." Proceedings of USENIX NSDI '13. `https://pdos.csail.mit.edu/6.5840/papers/memcache-fb.pdf`

[17] Redis. "Redis Documentation." `https://redis.io/docs/`

[18] AWS. "Amazon CloudFront Developer Guide - Caching content." `https://docs.aws.amazon.com/AmazonCloudFront/latest/DeveloperGuide/`

[19] Podlipnig, S., & Boszormenyi, L. (2003). "A Survey of Web Cache Replacement Strategies." ACM Computing Surveys, 35(4). `https://dl.acm.org/doi/10.1145/954339.954341`

Databases - relational and NoSQL

[20] Codd, E. F. (1970). "A Relational Model of Data for Large Shared Data Banks." Communications of the ACM, 13(6). `https://dl.acm.org/doi/10.1145/362384.362685`

[21] Chang, F., et al. (2006). "Bigtable: A Distributed Storage System for Structured Data." Proceedings of USENIX OSDI '06. `https://doi.org/10.1145/1365815.1365816`

[22] DeCandia, G., et al. (2007). "Dynamo: Amazon's Highly Available Key-value Store." Proceedings of ACM SOSP '07. `https://web.stanford.edu/class/cs244/papers/amazon-dynamo-sosp2007.pdf`

[23] Lakshman, A., & Malik, P. (2010). "Cassandra: A Decentralized Structured Storage System." ACM SIGOPS Operating Systems Review, 44(2). `https://www.cs.cornell.edu/projects/ladis2009/papers/lakshman-ladis2009.pdf`

[24] Corbett, J. C., et al. (2012). "Spanner: Google's Globally-Distributed Database." Proceedings of USENIX OSDI '12. `https://research.google/pubs/spanner-googles-globally-distributed-database-2/`

[25] MongoDB. "Sharding." `https://www.mongodb.com/docs/manual/sharding/`

CAP, consistency and replication

[26] Brewer, E. (2012). "CAP Twelve Years Later: How the 'Rules' Have Changed." IEEE Computer, 45(2). `https://ieeexplore.ieee.org/document/6133253`

[27] Gilbert, S., & Lynch, N. (2002). "Brewer's Conjecture and the Feasibility of Consistent, Available, Partition-Tolerant Web Services." ACM SIGACT News, 33(2). https://doi.org/10.1145/564585.564601

[28] Pritchett, D. (2008). "BASE: An Acid Alternative." ACM Queue, 6(3). https://doi.org/10.1145/1394127.1394128

[29] Vogels, W. (2009). "Eventually Consistent." Communications of the ACM, 52(1). https://cacm.acm.org/practice/eventually-consistent/

[30] Shapiro, M., Preguica, N., Baquero, C., & Zawirski, M. (2011). "Conflict-free Replicated Data Types." Proceedings of SSS '11. [conflict resolution via data structures] https://link.springer.com/chapter/10.1007/978-3-642-24550-3_29

Gateways and API gateway

[31] Richardson, C. "Pattern: API Gateway / Backends for Frontends." https://microservices.io/patterns/apigateway.html

[32] NGINX. "Deploying NGINX as an API Gateway." https://www.nginx.com/learn/api-gateway/

API design

[33] Fielding, R., Nottingham, M., & Reschke, J. (2022). "HTTP Semantics." RFC 9110, IETF. https://www.rfc-editor.org/rfc/rfc9110

[34] Masse, M. (2011). REST API Design Rulebook. O'Reilly Media. https://www.oreilly.com/library/view/rest-api-design/9781449317904/

[35] Richardson, L., & Ruby, S. (2007). RESTful Web Services. O'Reilly Media.

Real-time transports - WebSocket, SSE, Webhooks

[36] Fette, I., & Melnikov, A. (2011). "The WebSocket Protocol." RFC 6455, IETF. https://www.rfc-editor.org/rfc/rfc6455

[37] WHATWG. "Server-sent events." HTML Living Standard, Section 9.2. https://html.spec.whatwg.org/multipage/server-sent-events.html

5

Cross-Cutting Concerns: Security and Observability

A system is not truly production-ready simply because it works and scales. It also needs to protect its data and users and give engineers enough visibility to understand its behavior in production. This chapter explores these two essential aspects of system design: security and observability. Security protects data and access at every layer, from network transport through authentication, authorization, application logic, and data. Observability provides insight into a running system through logs, metrics, and traces, and turns that insight into reliability practices such as SLOs, alerting, and incident response that help keep the system healthy.

Both security and observability are cross-cutting concerns. Neither belongs to a single service or component, and both are easier to implement when they are designed in from the beginning rather than retrofitted later. They are also areas that are often overlooked until something goes wrong, making them essential considerations in any production system.

In this chapter, we are going to cover the following topics:

- **Security**: This section will provide an overview of why security should be deliberate rather than an afterthought. We will discuss best practices, including:
  - Zero trust
  - Data encryption in transit and at rest
  - Authentication and authorization
  - Rate limiting and more
- **Observability**: In this section, our main focus will be on logging and monitoring. We will see types of logs and learn about metrics and practices that play an important part in monitoring.

Security

As modern systems become more interconnected, they also become increasingly vulnerable to attacks, data breaches, and unauthorized access. Security isn't just about protecting data; it is also about ensuring the overall integrity, availability, and confidentiality of a system.

Proper security implementation must be an integral part of system design, not an afterthought. It ensures that systems are resilient against a variety of threats, including:

- **Data Breaches**: Unintended exposure of sensitive data (personal information, financial records, etc.).
- **Unauthorized Access**: Attackers gaining access to systems they shouldn't have access to.
- **Denial of Service (DoS)** Attacks: Overloading systems to the point where legitimate users cannot access services.
- **Malware and Exploits**: Malicious software and vulnerabilities that can compromise a system's integrity.

Security must be considered at multiple layers, such as the network, application, and data layers, to safeguard against a wide array of threats.

Why security is critical

Data Privacy Regulations: With laws such as **GDPR (General Data Protection Regulation)** and **CCPA (California Consumer Privacy Act)**, organizations can face legal consequences if they fail to remain compliant.

User trust: Users expect their data to be handled securely. A security breach can destroy trust and cause irreversible damage to a company's reputation.

Financial impact: Security breaches often result in fines, legal fees, and the cost of mitigating the attack.

If security has to be deliberate, the place to start is a mindset for it, and that mindset is zero trust.

Zero Trust (security strategy)

It is a security strategy, a comprehensive approach that consists of several principles. It outlines the need to explicitly establish trust between interacting systems (users, devices, data, and applications), regardless of whether they are internal or external to the network [1]. A few commonly adopted principles are:

- **Principle of least privilege**: A subject (say, a user) should be granted only the minimum permissions needed to execute the desired task.
- **Multi-Factor Authentication** (**MFA**): It identifies a user by requiring more than one challenge to prove their identity. For example, a 2FA mechanism can require 1) a password and 2) a code received via text message or an in-app code.

Data encryption (in-transit, at-rest)

Zero trust assumes the network is hostile, which makes protecting the data itself non-negotiable, starting with encryption.

Encryption at Rest: This ensures that data stored in persistent or intermediary storage, e.g., databases, files, queues, and other backup systems is encrypted, protecting it from unauthorized access, even if the storage medium is compromised. For example, many cloud providers, such as AWS, Google Cloud, and Azure, offer services that encrypt data stored in their persistent storage by default.

Encryption in Transit: Data packets traveling over the network must always remain encrypted to prevent interception by attackers, e.g., a **man-in-the-middle** (**MITM**) attack. For example, HTTPS (using TLS/SSL) is the most common way to encrypt data in transit. A banking website encrypts all communications between the user's browser and the server, preventing eavesdropping or data tampering. [6]

Authentication

Encryption keeps data from those who should never see it. The next question is proving who someone is in the first place, which is what authentication does. Authentication verifies that a user or system is who they claim to be, i.e., it verifies identity. Implementing strong authentication practices ensures that only legitimate users can access your application.

This topic is often discussed alongside authorization (described next). It is quite a specialized area of study. For the purpose of this book, we are going to touch upon a few authentication methods that are widely used in the industry. This should give you a strong understanding of the working fundamentals of these techniques, allowing you to make the right selection when needed:

Password or credential-based

Users authenticate by providing a unique username and a password. Password-based systems must enforce strong password policies, such as requiring complexity (length, special characters) and secure storage. This approach is vulnerable to brute force attacks and phishing without additional security measures.

JWT (JSON Web Token)

From RFC-7519 – "**JSON Web Token** (**JWT**) is a compact, URL-safe means of representing claims to be transferred between two parties. The claims in a JWT are encoded as a JSON object that is used as the payload of a **JSON Web Signature** (**JWS**) structure or as the plaintext of a **JSON Web Encryption** (**JWE**) structure, enabling the claims to be digitally signed or integrity protected with a **Message Authentication Code** (**MAC**) and/or encrypted." [4]

In summary, it is a token format for encoding JSON data. It is cryptographically signed, which makes it secure for its purpose. It is commonly used with microservices and API-based architectures.

From the RFC definition, the JWS part is commonly found in the system since it acts as a public pass during data access, i.e., anyone with a valid token can access data. On the other hand, JWE is private, stricter, and requires both the token & the secret key to gain access. In general conversation, JWT is usually used to refer to the JWS structure.

Figure 5.1 shows how it works:

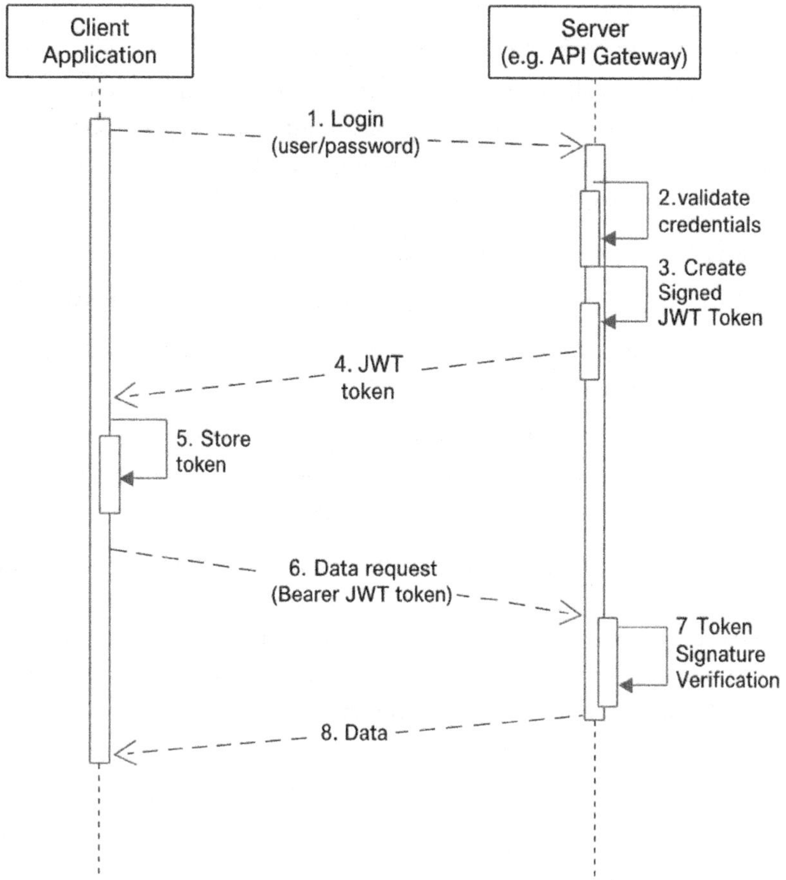

Figure 5.1: JWT Token journey

A typical JWT authentication flow involves the following:

1. The user logs in with credentials (username/email and password)
2. The server validates credentials and generates a JWT, using its secret key, containing user information and claims
3. The server returns the JWT to the client
4. The client stores the JWT (either in any secure local storage, or a secure cookie)
5. The client includes the JWT in the authorization header of the subsequent requests.
6. The server validates the JWT token using the same secret key used to create the token and extracts claims without querying a database. It rejects the requests if the JWT is not valid

7. The server processes the requests based on the claims in the token
8. The server returns a response to the client

Since JWT handles token validation on the server itself without consulting an underlying persistent store, it can provide lower latency. As a best practice, JWTs are transmitted over encrypted connections to prevent interception, appropriate expiration times are set, and sensitive data is not stored in the payload.

The structure of a JWT consists of three parts separated by dots (.):

- Header - contains the token type and the signing algorithm (e.g., HS256)
- Payload - contains the claims, i.e., user details and additional metadata such as expiration time, issuer, and subject.
- Signature - used to verify that the token has not been altered.

JWT authentication is completely stateless, as the server does not store any information related to the token issued or client session, making it quite a scalable approach.

Since a JWT token contains all the claims inside the token, it brings an associated vulnerability. If it is stolen, the holder can use this token as a valid ticket to access data from the resource server. This is the reason the use of a JWT token is not considered a general-purpose secure authentication approach. Secondly, it is not easy to invalidate or revoke an issued JWT token to avoid its misuse. These limitations make this approach less favorable for sensitive domains, e.g., banking and healthcare web applications.

Tip

JWT is a token format and not an authentication or authorization framework in itself. Comparing JWT with security frameworks like OAuth 2.0 or OIDC is not a like-for-like comparison. Security frameworks like OAuth2.0 and OIDC can internally use JWT tokens as access tokens.

OAuth 2.0 (Open Authorization) and OIDC (OpenID Connect)

OAuth2.0 is an industry-standard protocol for delegated authorization. In the process of gaining access to the requested resource, the user also needs to complete an authentication step.

As per RFC 6749, "The OAuth 2.0 authorization framework enables a third-party application to obtain limited access to an HTTP service, either on behalf of a resource owner by orchestrating an approval interaction between the resource owner and the HTTP service or by allowing the third-party application to obtain access on its own behalf." [3]

Different roles and terms associated with OAuth:

- ***Resource Owner***: If you are the user initiating a web interaction, then it is 'you'; think of it as the user whose credentials will be used during the authentication step.
- ***Client***: The interfacing application where you are accessing a resource, e.g., `anysecuresite.com`. Simply put, your browser or mobile app.
- ***Resource server***: The server that holds the protected resource that you want to access via 'anysecuresite.com'; e.g., you want all your documents from Google Docs to be listed on 'anysecuresite.com'.
- ***Authorization server***: The server where the Resource Owner will need to authenticate, e.g., `google.com`, `facebook.com`, `amazon.com`. On successful authentication, this server will issue an 'authorization code' (to be exchanged for an access token later) or an 'access token' directly, depending on what has been requested by the client. The token is usually stored on the application server (in our example, the application server of `anysecuresite.com`) making it more secure.

Figure 5.2 shows how the authorization code journey works:

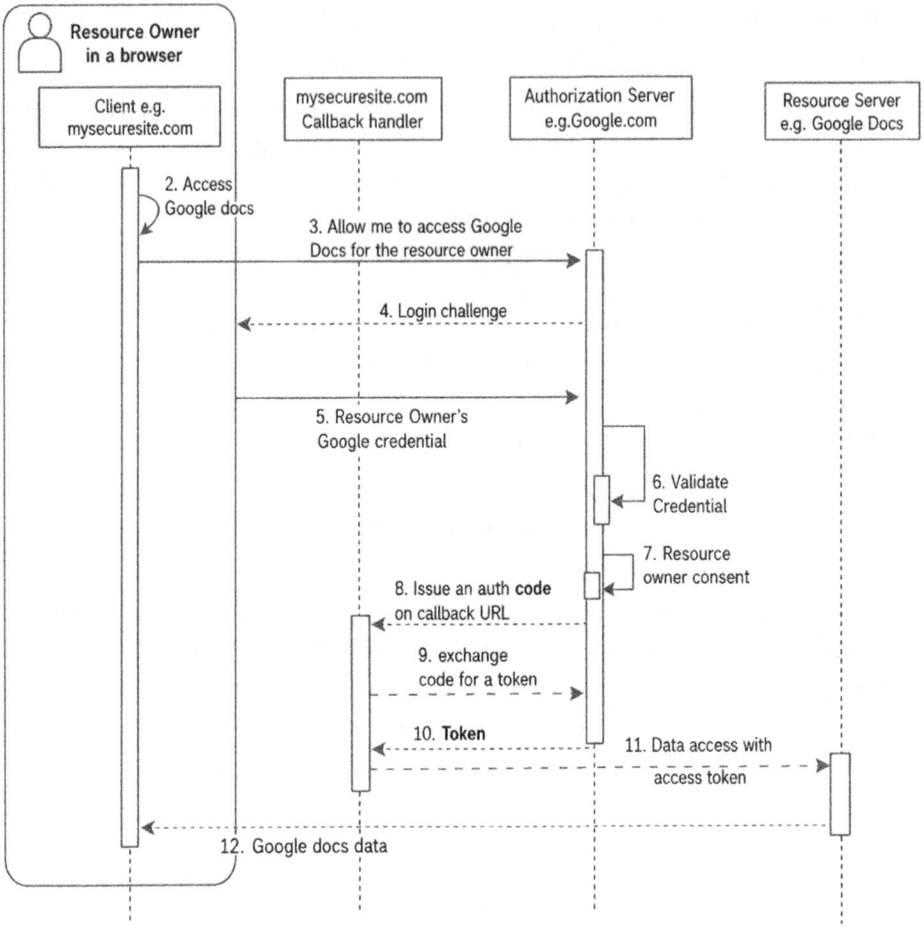

Figure 5.2: OAuth2.0 journey

Figure 5.2 captures a generic flow of a web client getting an access token in an OAuth journey. There are different variations available to match different client requirements, e.g., mobile apps and single-page applications. Underneath, they all follow this pattern in one form or another. The token so granted does not hold user profile information, i.e., user identity.

1. The resource owner (henceforth called the 'user' of the system) opens up her browser to access the site `mysecuresite.com` (henceforth called the 'client') - This step is not shown in the diagram.

2. The web page of the site is presented on the browser. The page has a feature to access your Google Docs while being on the site. The user clicks on that action.
3. The user request is forwarded to the authorization server, i.e., `google.com`. The request to the authorization server consists of some instructions, including a callback URL, type of response ('code' type in our example), and scope (to define the extent of the access request, i.e., read item, write, delete, etc.).
4. On receiving this request, the authorization server presents the user with its native hosted challenge screen. This is to enter her username and password for authentication.
5. The user enters her credentials and submits the page.
6. The authorization server validates the entered credential.
7. On successful credential verification, the authorization server presents the user with consent information so that she can explicitly give consent for the resource server to share the desired information.
8. Once consent is granted, the authorization server sends a 'code' to the configured callback URI.
9. The URI is hosted on the client backend (call it 'AppServer'). The AppServer sends a follow-on request to the authorization server for an access token for resource access. This request contains the code received in the previous step.
10. The authorization server grants an access token.
11. The client then interacts with the resource server with the access token to retrieve requested data.
12. The resource server grants access to the data requested if the requested access is within the remit of the 'scope'.

It is a secure way to delegate authorization to get access to protected resources in a controlled manner by the use of a token, and hence, you will find it implemented for various use cases. This is a recommended approach primarily for authorization, while authentication can be added through related protocols such as OIDC.

OpenID Connect (OIDC) is an identity layer built on top of OAuth 2.0 that adds authentication capabilities [5]. OIDC provides standardized ways to obtain user information and maintain authentication state while preserving application design. The token used by OIDC is known as an ID token. Although OIDC is built on OAuth 2.0, it uses different terminology to identify the entities associated with the journey:

- **User**: This is the resource owner in OAuth2.0 flow. Once authentication is successful, the ID token contains information about this user.
- **Relying party (RP)**: This is the 'client' as per OAuth2.0.

- **OpenID provider (OP)**: Takes the responsibility of the authorization server in case of OAuth journey. It is an entity that has implemented OpenID Connect on top of the OAuth 2.0 protocol.
- **ID Token**: Identity Token with user and authentication claims issued by the provider after authentication success.
- **Claims**: Information, or say attributes, in the token.

Note

Refresh tokens

To implement access security within the modern distributed environment, token-based authentication is widely used. Tokens can have various formats, but two are mainly used in the industry: opaque tokens and JWTs. An opaque token is a random token that bears no tangible information inside; e.g., think of a complex random string. Only the issuer of the token can decode the worthiness and purpose of such a token. This means the holder of the token must always contact the issuer for validation. They are also very easy to revoke. Since only the issuer can decode, it is included as one of the favorite security mechanisms within the distributed environment. One of the main use cases for an Opaque token is as a Refresh Token.

Refresh tokens are long-lived and are implemented to balance security and user experience, especially for mobile applications. The pattern is simple - upon successful authentication, the server issues two tokens:

Access token: Short-lived tokens used for accessing protected resources

Refresh token: Long-lived token stored securely and used only to obtain new access tokens

When the access token expires, the client uses the refresh token to request a new access token without requiring the user to re-enter their credentials. The server validates the refresh token (usually stored in a secure, durable storage, e.g., a database, keychain or keystore for mobile) and issues a new access token. If the refresh token is compromised, it can be revoked by system admins.

OAuth use cases include social media integration, healthcare, e-commerce, mobile application authentication, and banking.

SAML (Security Assertion Markup Language)

It is an XML-based markup language for security assertions. It is an open standard for authentication and authorization data exchange between parties. These parties are called an 'Identity Provider (IdP)' and a 'Service Provider (SP)'.

Identity Provider (IdP) – Is the service that performs user authentication and, after successful authentication passes the user's identity and associated authorization details to a service provider, e.g., Okta, Azure cloud identity.

Service provider (SP) – Is the application owner that you are trying to access, e.g., your company portal. A service provider will trust the identity provider for authentication purposes and use associated authorization to determine the user's action while being on the site. Remember, authentication is performed by the IdP, but authorization implementation still sits within the scope of the SP.

This approach is considered one of the most secure ways of authentication, as in this journey a user's client, e.g., browser, is authenticated. When you change the client, you will need to reauthenticate, and hence there is no fear of token theft, as we discussed in other mechanisms.

A simple SAML journey is shown in *Figure 5.3:*

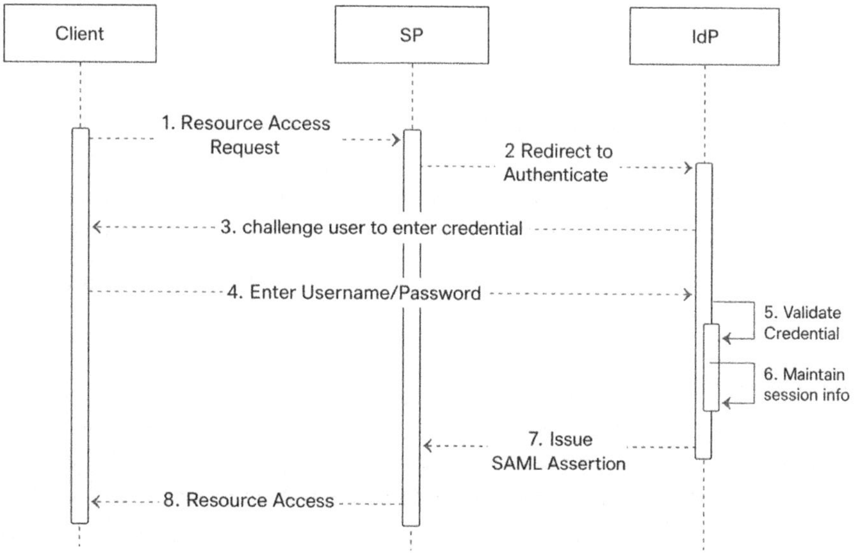

Figure 5.3: SAML authentication journey

In *Figure 5.3*, the client, i.e., user, requests some resource access from the service provider (SP). The SP could not recognize the user and in turn forwards the request to the agreed Identity Provider (IdP). The IdP could not see a valid session of the user and, hence, presents the user with a login challenge. The user enters her credentials. The IdP then validates the credential, and once successful, it stores the client's session information for future reference. The IdP then returns SAML assertions to the SP. The SP trusts the assertion received and verifies the authorization information received within the assertion. The client can use resources and perform actions on the SP resources as guided by the authorization granted.

If the client tries to access a different resource hosted by the same SP, then she will not be challenged to reauthenticate (i.e., SSO) as long as the session of the client is still active with the IdP. There are a few factors that play a deciding role with regard to SSO, but in most cases, the journey works as outlined.

Since the assertion never leaves the IdP or SP application area, this approach removes the risk of token theft. It is slightly complex to implement end-to-end as compared to OAuth. The complexity increases significantly when you try to integrate it with any mobile-based application where there is no browser/session.

> **Note**
>
> There are a few other ways to achieve authentication between two parties. We encourage readers to explore the available mechanisms. One option worth exploring is SSL certificate-based authentication that is commonly used within a corporate environment.

Single Sign-On (SSO) is a technical solution to the business problem that allows a user to access multiple related but independent applications using a single credential, i.e., the user authenticates herself once and gets access to multiple discrete applications. There are a few mechanisms available to achieve it, most importantly SAML and OIDC, discussed earlier.

Authentication confirms who you are. Authorization decides what you are allowed to do once you are in.

Authorization

Authorization works in conjunction with the authentication we discussed earlier. While authentication is a solution to determine 'who are you?', authorization establishes controls that explicitly enforce 'what can you do?' To expand it further, with authentication you get the ticket to access a system, but during the access, what actions you can perform on the available digital resources within that system, is controlled by authorization. To formalize, authorization determines what actions a user can perform on the protected resources with the help of a permission model enforced to each subject accessing the system. The permission model is one of the complex research areas for further elaboration here. Permission models can be divided into two broad access models:

1. Coarse-grained access control, where access privilege is grouped or configured at a wider level for accessing entities e.g. RBAC, and
2. Fine-grained access control, where access privileges are configured at a per-user, per-resource level, e.g., ABAC. It enforces least-privilege principles, ensuring users only access what they need to execute their desired task.

Role-Based Access Control (RBAC): Users are assigned roles, and roles are given permissions to access certain resources. This is commonly used in corporate environments where different teams need different levels of access to company systems.

Attribute Based Access Control (ABAC): Attribute-based access control, also known as policy-based access control for IAM, defines an access control paradigm whereby a subject's authorization to perform a set of operations is determined by evaluating attributes associated with the subject, object, requested operations, and, in some cases, environment attributes.

Knowing what a caller may do still leaves the question of how much they may do, and that is where rate limiting and throttling come in.

Rate limiting and throttling

Rate limiting and throttling help prevent misuse of system resources by limiting the number of requests a client can make or a system can serve in a specified time window. This practice prevents **Denial of Service (DoS)** attacks, protects against excessive usage, and ensures fair use of resources, resulting in improved reliability of the system.

Rate Limiting: It is usually implemented by an application that provides services to a user or other systems. It sets a cap on the number of requests allowed during a period. For instance, a user might only be able to make 100 API requests per minute. Exceeding the limit **results in rejected requests**.

As per Wikipedia, 'In computer networks, rate limiting is used to control the rate of requests sent or received by a network interface controller. It can be used to prevent DoS attacks and limit web scraping.'

> **Note**
>
> Web scraping in general refers to data extraction techniques over the web using automated processes implemented using bots or crawlers.

Example: APIs from services like Twitter (now X) and GitHub implement rate limiting to prevent abuse. If a user tries to access the API more than the allowed quota over time, they will receive an HTTP 429 "Too Many Requests" response.

Algorithms to implement rate limiting include the leaky bucket, token bucket, sliding window, fixed window counter, etc. [*Explained in section 3.5 of the book*]

Throttling: Can be explained as another implementation to attain diligent system use. It is similar to what we have discussed in the case of rate-limiting with a simple but crucial difference. In throttling, excess requests are not dropped but deferred, i.e., queued and then picked up subsequently. It is a helpful technique to avoid request dropping in case the servicing system is not able to process requests for reasons beyond request count, e.g., network latency or something similar that can impact processing power.

Throttling is an efficient implementation choice at the request originator (sender) side as a technique that manages outgoing requests at the source by gradually reducing the rate or quality of service to maintain servicing application-defined thresholds. Unlike rate limiting, which strictly blocks requests beyond a set threshold, throttling allows for controlled, gradual adjustments. This helps to prevent sudden drops in performance and ensures a smoother experience, especially under heavy load, by slowing down requests or prioritizing essential requests rather than fully denying access. Ways to implement throttling include ring buffers and delay queues. These implementations can be used in conjunction with the techniques discussed in the *Controlling request flow with rate limiting* section in *Chapter 3* of the book.

Example: Cloudflare uses throttling to manage sudden traffic spikes. If a website experiences a surge in traffic, Cloudflare might throttle access for non-critical users to ensure the core functionality remains available.

Even with every control in place, some incident eventually gets through, and what matters then is how you respond.

Handling data breaches

Even with robust security measures, data breaches remain a possibility. A prepared response plan can help minimize damage and expedite recovery. This section covers essential practices for managing data breaches effectively. [2]

Regular Backups: Maintaining regular backups is essential to ensure data can be quickly restored if needed. Backups should be encrypted and stored securely, ideally off-site or in a different geographic location, to prevent data loss in a breach.

Example: AWS provides automated snapshot services for their cloud databases. These snapshots can be configured for regular intervals and are stored in multiple availability zones, ensuring secure and reliable recovery options if data is compromised.

Disaster Recovery Plans: A **disaster recovery plan (DRP)** outlines the steps for restoring systems and data in the event of a breach. Two critical parameters in a DRP are the **Recovery Time Objective (RTO)** and **Recovery Point Objective (RPO)**

RTO: The maximum time allowed for restoring systems to operational status after failure.

RPO: The maximum acceptable data loss measured in time, a guiding element to determine how often backups should be taken. E.g., if RPO is 10 mins, then the system must ensure a mechanism to retain data older than 10 mins from the current time (say, delta backup every 10 mins).

Example: After Target's 2013 data breach, which compromised over 40 million credit card records, the company overhauled its DRP to prioritize data integrity, encryption standards, and timely recovery. As part of these improvements, they set RTO and RPO goals to minimize downtime and data loss.

Centralized logging, **real-time monitoring and alerts**, and **anomaly detection** are a few additional practices to manage data breaches. The observability section provides more detail on these practices.

Example: AWS GuardDuty uses machine learning and threat intelligence to detect abnormal behavior and flag it. For instance, if it detects that sensitive data is being accessed from an unusual location or under unusual conditions, it can alert administrators for further investigation.

By defining RTOs and RPOs and using tools like AWS GuardDuty, organizations can create a layered, resilient approach to detecting and managing potential data breaches. This ensures both a rapid response and an ongoing enhancement of security measures.

Responding to a breach depends on noticing it in the first place, and noticing anything at all is the job of observability. If security is about keeping a system safe, observability is about being able to see inside it, and the next section of the chapter is all about that.

Observability

Observability refers to the collection and analysis of data such as logs, metrics, and traces from a wide variety of sources to provide detailed insight into application behavior [13]. In system design evaluations, these are among the most common operational topics discussed. The purpose of observability in system design is to answer a simple but important question, i.e., when something goes wrong in production, how quickly and effectively can an engineer diagnose the problem and resolve it? *Table 5.1* introduces the three pillars of observability and explains what each provides.

Pillar	What it records	The question it answers
Logs	Discrete, timestamped events	What happened, and when?
Metrics	Aggregated numeric measurements over time	How much, how often, how healthy?
Traces	One request's path across services	Where did the time go, and which service failed?

Table 5.1: The three pillars of observability

Let us understand the mentioned concepts one by one in a bit of detail.

Logging

It is the practice of recording discrete events that occur inside the system during process execution. It attempts to record one event at a time, with enough information to reconstruct the event occurrence. A log tells what happened in the system and why it happened.

A log is a timestamped record. In a modern distributed system, logs are emitted by every layer e.g., load balancer, gateway, web, application, cache, and database. The logs are then shipped to a centralized pipeline for search, correlation, and observability as needed [9][10]. A sample JSON-style log is presented below:

```
{
"time": "2026-05-14T10:11:42.318Z",
"level": "INFO",
"service": "order-service",
"event": "order_placed",
"user_id": UID2217,
"order_id": 11002345,
"order_value_gbp": 35.10,
"latency_ms": 156,
"trace_id": "4bf92f3577b34da6a3ce929d0e0e4736"
}
```

JSON-style logs are popular as they allow querying capability with ease, e.g., 'find all orders where order_value_gbp is more than 30 in the last 30 mins'. Frameworks such as Logback, structlog, and Zap emit JSON by default while logging.

Note

Correlation ID

In certain architectural decisions e.g. microservices based architecture, a request might pass through multiple services for its task(s) execution. To understand the full journey of a request you would like to know the complete trace. If these services are deployed independently, as in the case of microservices, service logs from these independent domains will not serve the entire purpose of an event recreation. A 'CorrelationID' solves this purpose. In this case, the first service that receives the request will generate a unique identifier, universally accepted to all other downstream services. The new ID is added into the request header or likewise. All the services involved in serving the request will include this new ID while creating a log record.

Log storage types and retention

Log files are high volume as they originate from multiple layers within an application. They can quickly overwhelm the storage space creating cost and management overhead. Within corporate environments, logs are stored using a typical tiered policy:

- **Hot logs:** The purpose of this tier is to hold the latest logs to perform searching in case some incident is reported on any latest activities. The retention period depends upon the company's policy. Generally, it holds records from the last 30 days that are quick to search, in seconds. It is stored in a hot SSD for the purpose and is therefore the most expensive. Elasticsearch, Loki, and ClickHouse are some common tools used to enable indexing and searching.
- **Warm logs:** Retention period is 30 to 90 days. Records can be searched in minutes. Stored in relatively slower disk such as S3. Data can be stored in compressed form for optimal cost.
- **Cold logs:** Such logs are kept for audit and compliance. Not actively used for searching, monitoring and hence their retrieval time is higher (can be in hours). Suitable storage for such logs is S3 Glacier Deep Archive.

Some logging stages, their purpose, and tools associated with centralized logging architecture are captured in *Table 5.2*:

Stage	Used for	Example tools
Emit	Application writes structured logs to files	Logback, Bunyan, Structlog, Zap
Collect/ Forward pipeline	Read logs and ship them to a destination	Fluentd, FileBeat, Vector
Buffer	Intermediary store to maintain log capture	Redis stream, AWS Kinesis, Kafka
Index store	Keeps logs indexed for searching	OpenSearch, ElasticSearch, Loki
Visualization	Executing search queries for visualization usually by operation team members or dedicated staff	Kibana, Grafana [11]

Table 5.2: Logging stages, their purpose and tools to implement

Caution: When speaking about logging, explicitly mention that PII and sensitive information (such as payment card data) should not be logged, as doing so can be a deal breaker during an interview. The application must mask or tokenize the data field before it reaches the logging library. Also, if the data field appears in a request payload, the logger should ignore capturing it. It is a mandatory regulatory requirement as per GDPR and PCI-DSS and hence should not be taken as a preference.

Logs tell you what happened after the fact. Monitoring watches the system in real time, so you can act before users feel the problem. Let's move on to monitoring.

Monitoring

It is the practice of measuring the aggregate behavior of numeric quantities, called metrics, at regular intervals. An expected value or range is configured in such a system. In case of deviation between expected and actual, the system uses alerting to send a notification for potential action. It is the first line of operational activity that indicates something has gone wrong.

Depending on the system being monitored, different methods are used to get the desired outcome. Some popular methods are captured in *Table 5.3*:

What is being monitored	Metrics to use	Example use-cases
User/Client facing systems	Latency, Traffic, Errors, Saturation (Also called the four golden signals as popularized by the Google SRE Book) [7] [12] *[SRE - Site Reliability Engineering]*	Services tied to service level objectives (SLO)
Request driven services	Rate, Error, Duration (also called the RED method) [8]	APIs, Microservices, Web interfaces
Hardware tools	Utilization, Saturation, Error (also called the USE method)	CPU, Memory, Disk, Network interfaces

Table 5.3: Monitoring metrics and their use case

Based on the metrics, there are a few important reliability concepts and operational practices in use. Together they work as an established framework that can be used to get a holistic view of a system and can be leveraged for contractual commitments. *Table 5.4* captures the concepts and practices along with their purpose.

Concepts / Operational Practice	Purpose
SLI (Service Level Indicator)	It is a measurement concept that talks about the direct measurement of one aspect of user-visible service behavior. An example aspect can be the proportion of HTTP requests that complete successfully. E.g. total request received in a day = 100M, total requests served within 50ms time during the day = 99.999M Some aspects here can be - Availability, Latency, Throughput
SLO (Service Level Objective)	It talks about an internal target (goal) for an SLI over a defined window. E.g. for SLI aspect - 200ms Latency, 99.5% of the requests in a month period complete in 200ms.

Concepts / Operational Practice	Purpose
SLA (Service Level Agreement)	It is a contractual commitment to a customer. It is often tied with financial consequences if missed. To maintain some room for operational activities beyond the normal execution or unforeseen, SLAs are kept slightly lighter than SLOs. So, if the SLO is 99.5% then SLA is usually kept at 99% or less.

Table 5.4: System reliability operational practices and their purpose

An important derivative of an SLO is the **error budget**. If the availability SLO commitment is 99% for a year then the remaining 1% is the error budget that determines how long a service can remain unavailable in that year. Let us take a hypothetical example to understand why it is important:

```
A service availability SLO = 99% per year
It gives error budget = 1% per year
Number of hours in one year = 365 × 24 = 8760 hrs.
Error budget in hours = 8760 × 1% = 87.6 hrs.
```

Suppose deploying new features or enhancements requires some application downtime, and your system experienced 20 hours of downtime last month due to these deployments. You know your error budget could be exhausted in 4-5 months if more such deployments happen. Hence, you might freeze new deployments to meet the target or introduce process improvements and automation to reduce downtime.

Metrics and logs are only useful if someone can see them, and that is what dashboards are for. A dashboard turns raw metrics into charts a team can read at a glance, and logs into searchable views. Grafana (commonly over Prometheus metrics) and Kibana (over Elasticsearch logs) are the usual choices. A good dashboard answers a specific question, for example 'is checkout healthy right now?', rather than crowding the screen with every metric a system emits.

Alerting

Alerting is what turns monitoring from something you watch into something that reaches you. An alert fires when a metric crosses a threshold or an SLO is at risk, and pages the on-call engineer. The art is in what you choose to alert on. Alert on symptoms your users feel, such as rising error rates or latency, rather than on every internal cause, and tie the threshold to the error budget so you are paged when the budget is burning too fast rather than on every transient blip. The failure mode to avoid is alert fatigue. When alerts are noisy or not actionable, people learn to ignore them, and the one alert that matters gets missed. A good alert is rare, urgent, and comes with a clear next step.

Distributed tracing

Logs tell you what happened and metrics tell you how much, but in a system spread across many services, neither tells you where a single request spent its time. That is where tracing helps. A distributed trace follows a request from end to end as it travels through different services and records how long each step takes.

A trace is made up of spans. A span represents a single unit of work, such as the order-service handling a request or making a call to a payment provider. Each span records a start time, duration, and status, along with three identifiers that connect the spans:

- `trace_id`: A single ID shared by every span belonging to the same request. This is the same `trace_id` you saw in the earlier log example, allowing a log entry to be linked to its trace.
- `span_id`: A unique ID for each individual span.
- `parent_span_id`: The span that called the current span, allowing the spans to be arranged in a parent-child hierarchy.

These identifiers travel between services in request headers, allowing downstream services to associate their work with the same trace. The W3C Trace Context standard, which uses the traceparent header, provides a common way to propagate this information across services written in different languages.

Figure 5.4 shows a single request as a trace. Each bar represents a span, its length shows the time spent, and the indentation shows the parent-child relationship. This becomes particularly useful when a request is slow. Instead of searching through multiple log files and trying to work out where the delay occurred, the trace can show which service or call is responsible.

Example: A checkout request looks fast in the web tier but takes 950 ms overall. The trace shows that the API gateway and order service returned quickly, while a single call to the payment provider took 780 ms. Without the trace, that delay may be difficult to identify. With the trace, the source of the slowdown is clear.

Popular tools include Jaeger and Zipkin for storing and viewing traces, while OpenTelemetry provides vendor-neutral libraries and APIs for generating and exporting traces, metrics, and logs.

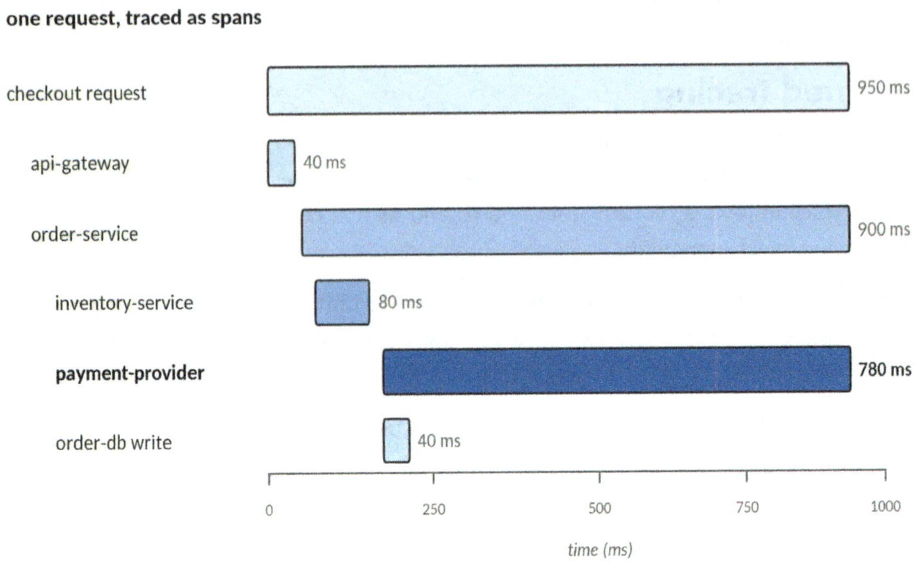

Figure 5.4: A distributed trace

Together, these elements provide end-to-end visibility into requests, making it easier to pinpoint latency and performance issues across services.

Summary

This chapter covered two important cross-cutting concerns. On security, it explained why security must be explicit and not an afterthought. We looked at multiple authentication mechanisms and how each serves the same goal while not being interchangeable, and at authorization through the principle of least privilege, which shrinks the blast radius when something goes wrong. We saw why data must be protected both in transit and at rest, and how zero trust, rate limiting, and a plan for handling data breaches round out a defensible design.

On observability, we saw that it rests on three kinds of data. Logs record what happened, metrics measure how much and how often, and traces follow a single request across services to show where its time went. We looked at how logs are structured, stored, and retained, how metrics feed dashboards and alerts, and how SLIs, SLOs, and SLAs, together with an error budget, turn all of that into a concrete standard for reliability. Together, security and observability are the difference between a system that merely works and one you can trust and see into.

The next chapter takes everything covered so far and puts it to work by walking through the elements of a real system design interview, from gathering requirements all the way through to managing your time under pressure.

Quiz

Q1. What is the biggest security risk if a JWT is not signed or verified properly?

A) Token replay

B) Token tampering (claims modified by attacker)

C) Token compression attacks

D) Token caching

Q2. In OAuth2, what is the difference between an access token and an ID token (OpenID Connect)?

A) Access token is for authentication, ID token is for authorization.

B) Access token is for authorization, ID token is for authentication.

C) Both are used for authentication only.

D) Both are opaque tokens.

Q3. What's the key difference between a JWT access token and a refresh token?

A) JWT access tokens are encrypted, refresh tokens are plain text.

B) JWT access tokens are short-lived and self-contained, refresh tokens are long-lived and used only to request new access tokens.

C) JWT access tokens contain the refresh token inside them.

D) Refresh tokens are always JWTs as well.

Q4. In OAuth2, what is the role of the Resource Server?

A) Authenticate the end user.

B) Store refresh tokens securely.

C) Serve protected resources and validate access tokens.

D) Issue both access and ID tokens.

Q5. In OAuth2, which entity issues the access token?

A) Resource Server

B) Authorization Server

C) Client Application

D) End User

Q6. Which statement is true? Select multiple if applicable.

A) Rate limiting rejects requests once a threshold is crossed.

B) Throttling queues or delays requests instead of outright rejecting them.

C) Both rate limiting and throttling are identical.

D) Throttling only works in distributed systems.

Q7. Which messaging pattern is most suitable for logging and monitoring pipelines?

A) Message Queue

B) Publish-Subscribe

C) Request-Response

D) Point-to-Point

Q8. Your API can handle 100 requests/second. A client tries 200/sec. If extra requests are dropped, what mechanism is used? If they are delayed, what mechanism is used?

A) Rate Limiting

B) Throttling

C) None

D) Both

Q9. The Four Golden Signals from the Google SRE book are:

A) CPU, memory, disk, network

B) Latency, traffic, errors, saturation

C) Rate, errors, duration, throughput

D) Logs, metrics, traces, events

Q10. An SLO of 99.99% availability over a 30-day month gives an error budget of approximately:

A) 43 minutes

B) 4.3 hours

C) 4.3 minutes

D) 26 seconds

References

Security

[1] Rose, S., Borchert, O., Mitchell, S., & Connelly, S. (2020). "Zero Trust Architecture." NIST Special Publication 800-207. `https://doi.org/10.6028/NIST.SP.800-207`

[2] OWASP. "OWASP Top Ten" and "OWASP API Security Top 10." `https://owasp.org/`

[3] Hardt, D. (Ed.) (2012). "The OAuth 2.0 Authorization Framework." RFC 6749, IETF. `https://www.rfc-editor.org/rfc/rfc6749`

[4] Jones, M., Bradley, J., & Sakimura, N. (2015). "JSON Web Token (JWT)." RFC 7519, IETF. `https://www.rfc-editor.org/rfc/rfc7519`

[5] Sakimura, N., Bradley, J., Jones, M., de Medeiros, B., & Mortimore, C. (2014). "OpenID Connect Core 1.0." OpenID Foundation. `https://openid.net/specs/openid-connect-core-1_0.html`

[6] Rescorla, E. (2018). "The Transport Layer Security (TLS) Protocol Version 1.3." RFC 8446, IETF. `https://www.rfc-editor.org/rfc/rfc8446`

Logging & Monitoring, Observability

[7] Google SRE Book - "Monitoring Distributed Systems" (Chapter 6): `https://sre.google/sre-book/monitoring-distributed-systems/`

[8] Tom Wilkie - "The RED Method": `https://www.weave.works/blog/the-red-method-key-metrics-for-microservices-architecture/`

[9] "What is the ELK Stack?": `https://www.elastic.co/what-is/elk-stack`

[10] "Centralized Logging on AWS" reference architecture: `https://aws.amazon.com/solutions/implementations/centralized-logging-on-aws/`

[11] "Best practices for dashboarding": `https://grafana.com/docs/grafana/latest/best-practices/`

[12] Beyer, B., Jones, C., Petoff, J., & Murphy, N. R. (Eds.) (2016). Site Reliability Engineering. O'Reilly Media / Google. [especially "Monitoring Distributed Systems"]

[13] OpenTelemetry. "OpenTelemetry Documentation - logs, metrics, and traces." `https://opentelemetry.io/docs/`

6

Elements and the Method to Design a System

Designing a real system can feel open-ended, but experienced engineers treat it as a sequence of well-understood moves rather than a blank canvas. Whatever the problem, the same elements recur: you clarify what is being asked, size the system with rough numbers, shape the interfaces and the data, assemble a working design, and then stress-test and refine it. This is what you actually do when you set out to design a system in the real world, and it is exactly what a system design interview asks you to walk through, only compressed into an hour.

This chapter covers those elements one by one, so that whether you are at a whiteboard on the job or across the table in an interview, you have a repeatable structure to lean on instead of improvising. Master these building blocks, and the specific problem, whether a chat app or a payment system, becomes a matter of applying them in the right order.

For the purpose of this chapter, we will take the simplest example, a share-link service, focusing primarily on its structure. Later chapters will use the same structure but the design problems will become more complex.

In this chapter, we will cover the following topics:

- Requirement clarification: Functional and non-functional requirements, and the constraints that shape your solution
- Estimation: Traffic, throughput, storage, bandwidth, and latency primitives, and the pitfalls to avoid
- API and database design
- System design: bringing the components together into a coherent architecture

- Resolving bottlenecks and handling follow-up questions
- Effective time management

Requirement clarification

Before we start discussing requirements clarification, let's take a high-level look at the key elements of system design. *Figure 6.1* brings them all together in one place:

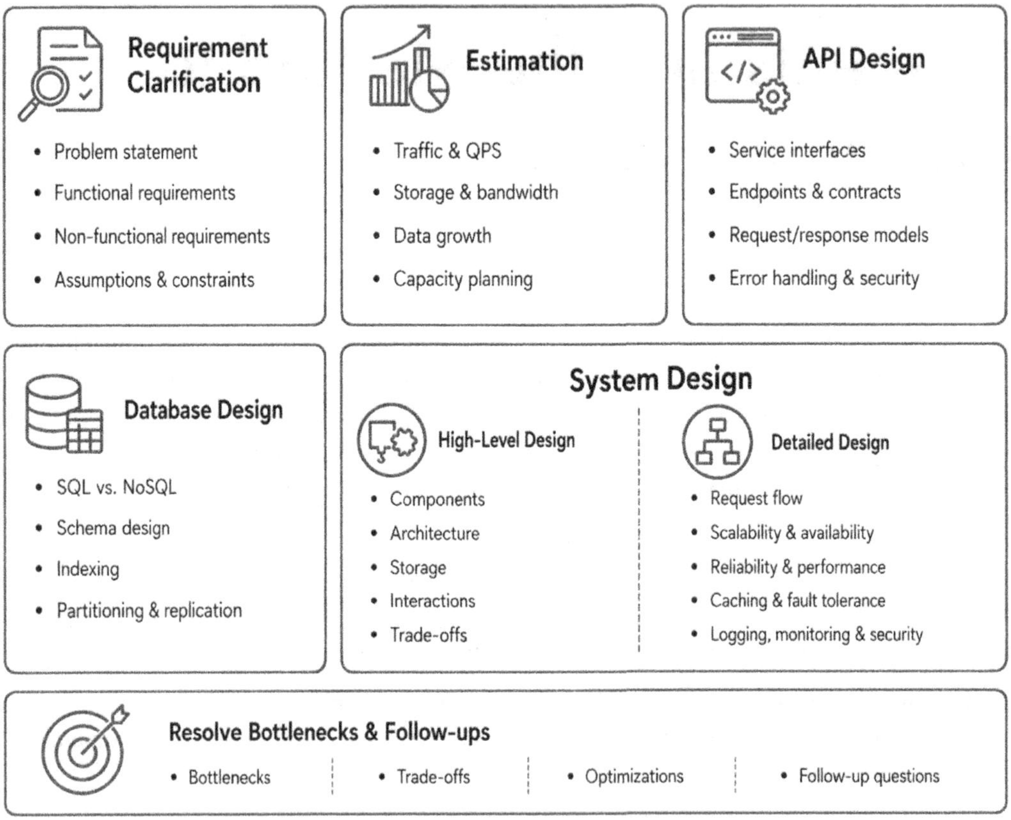

Figure 6.1: The elements of a system design

Keep this figure handy as you work through the chapter. It will serve as a guide each time you approach a new system design.

The sequence begins where every sound design does, with requirement clarification. Before drawing a single component, good engineers spend their first minutes aligning with the people who own the outcome, the stakeholders in real work or the interviewer in a design round, on what the system must do and how well it must do it. It is the foundational step in system design, the one that keeps everything built afterward tied to the real need instead of a guess at it [2].

This is where you agree on scope: the functional requirements (what the system must do, the happy path), the non-functional requirements (how well it must perform), and the key constraints that shape the solution space. In real projects the same step widens into identifying stakeholders and then eliciting, documenting, and validating requirements across the lifecycle, but the goal is constant, e.g., a shared understanding and a clear roadmap before design begins. Skip it, and later steps like estimation or database selection rest on assumptions instead of a clearly defined request; jumping in without clear requirements is how even capable teams ship misaligned or inefficient solutions [1].

Two habits sharpen this stage. First, agree on what success looks like before you design anything by defining the concrete targets the system must hit, such as a latency ceiling, an availability percentage, or a scale number, so that good enough is measurable rather than a matter of opinion. Second, name the single hardest part of the problem early, the constraint or scale factor that will shape every later decision, so your limited time goes where the real difficulty lies.

Requirements answer two big questions:

- **Functions**: *What* should the product let people do, i.e., what business or real-life problem is it being built to solve?
- **Qualities**: How good must the experience be while they do it?

Without these answers, any solution you build matches the actual need only by luck.

Here are the two buckets of requirements:

Bucket	Covers	Examples for a photo-sharing app
Functional	What does this system allow its user/ consumer to execute/perform?	Upload and tag photo, view a feed, create an account, search by tag
Non-functional or Qualities	How smooth, safe, or cost-efficient those actions must be	Feed loads in under 300 ms; 99.9 % of requests succeed. Data should remain available for at least 10 years; Private albums stay private

Table 6.1: The two buckets of requirements, functional and non-functional

Next, we look at techniques for gathering clear functional requirements, useful when you scope real work and when you clarify scope in an interview.

Functional requirements

Simple, testable requirement statement(s).

The interviewer says: "*Users should be able to upload large photos.*" –This statement is too ambiguous to serve as a requirement

Problem you can work with: "*A user can upload JPEG or PNG files up to 25 MB in size.*" – This is what you need, i.e., your target state.

Your clarification question to remove the ambiguity can be: Should a JPEG or PNG file be the minimum requirement? What would be an ideal file size? Is there a limit to consider?

> **Tip**
>
> If you have a file size in mind, then you can formulate your question accordingly.

Describe the trigger, the action, and the result

The interviewer says: "*When a user clicks on the 'post' icon, the image should be saved.*" This is an incomplete statement because it leaves out information needed to form a complete requirement.

Problem you can work with: "*On clicking the 'post' icon, the image should be saved. Once saved, a public URL for the image will be generated that can be shared through other channels*". – This is your target state.

Your clarification question to remove the ambiguity can be: "*Is the saved image accessible via a public link? Can it be shared on some other channels?*"

Add edge cases early

Ask questions like: "*What will be the system's behavior if the image file used for upload is of the incorrect type or the file size is greater than the max limit?*" Such questions will help you identify how to handle known edge-case scenarios. It also shows how thoroughly you consider all aspects of a problem before getting into the solution mode. It might impact your design, or it might add to it during the conversation when you elaborate on your design.

Non-functional requirements

Non-functional requirements require careful consideration to ensure a complete and robust system design. *Figure 6.2* shows some of the most commonly used non-functional requirements during system designs:

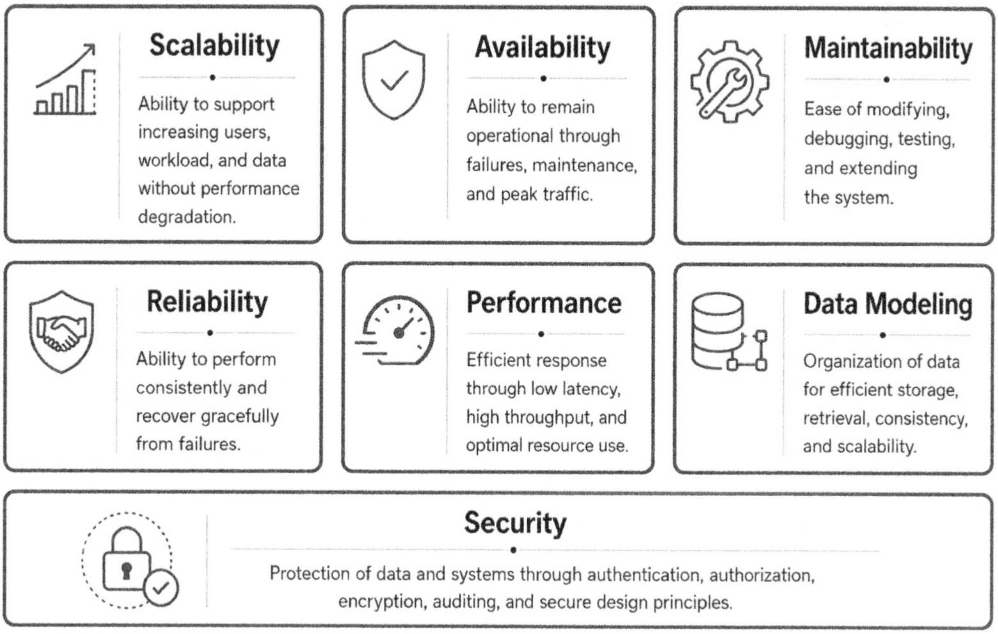

Figure 6.2: Common non-functional requirements

Let's see each one of these in more detail.

Scalability

Scalability means the ability and readiness of a system to deal with changes in request volume, usually considered in terms of spikes/increases in system load. It means a system can handle increased demands by either adding more machines (horizontal scaling) or enhancing existing ones (vertical scaling). One of the primary goals of a system design exercise is to design a system that can scale efficiently [16]. *Chapter 4* covers scalability in detail.

Example: A social media platform must be able to handle a growing number of users without significant degradation in performance. The system can scale horizontally to handle this increased load by employing techniques like database sharding.

Reliability

A reliable system is one that can perform its intended function consistently and accurately for a specified time under a given set of operating conditions. There are multiple components that contribute to a system's reliability. These include redundancy, replication, failover and disaster recovery plans, testing and quality control, system monitoring and alerting, and an improved security posture. *Asynchronous Communication* from *Chapter 4* covered reliability in detail.

Example: In a banking application, reliability is critical because even a small data inconsistency could result in financial losses or user mistrust. Techniques like distributed database replication, reconciliation, audit, disaster recovery plans, and failover mechanisms help to ensure the reliability of the system.

Performance

System performance is often measured by how fast it can respond to user requests. Low-latency systems are crucial for applications like real-time gaming or stock trading platforms where every millisecond counts. A well-performing system should deliver good results across percentile-based measures while also reducing tail latency. *Chapter 4* covered the topic across multiple sections.

> **Note**
>
> For a system (especially in a distributed environment), some requests take longer than expected to return a response to the caller/user. **Tail latency** is a performance metric that captures the latency experienced by such requests/request groups. Some of the requests from the group might experience an exceptionally slow response and may time out before the page renders. This is a bad user experience for a critical system.

Example: For an e-commerce website, users expect product pages to load within milliseconds. Implementing caching strategies (like storing frequently accessed data in a cache rather than fetching it from the database each time) improves performance.

Availability

Availability measures how often a system is accessible and functional. A highly available system ensures continuous access, even during peak usage or some hardware failures, by leveraging redundancy and automatic failover mechanisms. A stricter measure is **fault tolerance,** where the system remains operational even in case of one or more data center failures. *Chapter 4* covered the topic across multiple sections.

Example: For a platform like Netflix, availability is essential. If one server or data center fails, a backup system kicks in without the user noticing any disruption, ensuring smooth streaming at all times.

Data modeling

Data modeling defines how information is structured and managed within a system. It includes choosing the right database type, creating schema designs, and planning data partitioning for scalability and performance.

Example: An online store might use a relational database like MySQL to store structured data, such as customer orders, and a NoSQL database like MongoDB to manage product reviews. This combination offers both consistency and flexibility.

Security

Security ensures that data and systems are protected from unauthorized access and cyber threats. This includes authentication, authorization, encryption, and secure communication protocols to safeguard user information. Section 4.10 covered it in detail.

Example: A payment platform must protect sensitive data like card information through encryption. Multi-factor authentication and secure communication channels like TLS ensure that data remains safe while in transit.

Maintainability

A maintainable system is easy to update and debug. This involves creating clean, modular architectures where individual components can be updated without affecting the entire system.

Example: A microservices architecture breaks down the system into independent components, allowing each service to be updated or scaled independently. This increases the maintainability of the system.

We will cover some of these concepts in the following chapters in detail along with appropriate examples to help you understand and implement them when needed. With the requirements and their quality targets pinned down, the next question is one of size: how much traffic, data, and load the system must handle. That is what estimation answers.

Estimation

The importance of estimations cannot be overstated in system design. These numbers drive nearly all major design decisions, from selecting databases and servers to configuring load balancers and caching mechanisms. Miscalculations can lead to system failures, performance bottlenecks, or unnecessary costs. In a system design interview, making estimations demonstrates that you can think critically about scalability, performance, and resource allocation.

Key reasons why estimates matter

Architectural impact: The right estimates guide decisions about the hardware and software choices to meet the overall expectation from it. It helps to balance the solution building blocks within your design by providing confidence that the design component you are using is the one that is needed. For example, a traffic estimate will give you an early indication if a basic web-server, a single high configuration server, or a group of servers working in tandem is needed for your use case. The knowledge can span all the layers in your application. Also, it helps in many other areas including hardware sizing, choosing correct caching location & strategy etc.

System stability: By predicting traffic spikes and data growth, you can design a system that doesn't buckle under unexpected load. For example, by the use of appropriate estimation you can make an upfront informed decision on how much compute you need to deal with your immediate requirement and how to plan for its scaling.

Cost efficiency: Overestimating resources leads to expensive infrastructure bills, while underestimating causes service outages and downtime. A balanced resource usage creates a predictable cost model including just enough management overhead on those resources.

Performance tuning: Estimations help you optimize for response times and throughput. They guide the use of caching, CDNs, database indexes, etc.

Below are some primitives you can use to derive estimates for any real system, and to size one quickly in an interview.

Estimation primitives

You'll often be asked to estimate metrics such as Queries Per Second (QPS), storage, bandwidth, and other performance factors in your design. These *back-of-the-envelope* calculations showcase your ability to understand the scale of a problem and offer practical solutions.

Decimals to Power of twos

1 Thousand = 1 KB = 2^{10}

1 Million = 1 MB = 2^{20}

1 Billion = 1 GB = 2^{30}

1 Trillion = 1 TB = 2^{40}

1 Quadrillion = 1 PB = 2^{50}

Availability Numbers

Availability Percentage	Downtime Per Year	Downtime Per Month	Downtime Per Day
90% (one nine)	36.53 days	73.05 hours	2.40 hours
99% (two nines)	3.65 days	7.31 hours	14.40 minutes
99.9% (three nines)	8.77 hours	43.83 minutes	1.44 minutes
99.99% (four nines)	52.60 minutes	4.38 minutes	8.64 seconds
99.999% (five nines)	5.26 minutes	26.30 seconds	864 milliseconds
99.9999% (six nines)	31.56 seconds	2.63 seconds	86.4 milliseconds

Object Storage

char: 1 byte
char (Unicode): 2 bytes
UUID: 16 bytes
Thumbnails: 20-30 KB
Website image: 200-300 KB
Mobile image: 2-3 MB
Documents (books etc.): 1-3 MB
Audio files (songs): 4-5 MB
1-minute 720p video: 60 MB
1-minute 1080p video: 130 MB
1-minute 4K video: 350 MB

Latency Numbers

L1 cache reference: 0.5 ns
Branch mis-predict: 5 ns
L2 cache reference: 7 ns
Mutex lock/unlock: 100 ns
Main memory reference: 100 ns
Compress 1K bytes with Zippy: 10,000 ns (10 μs)
Send 2K bytes over 1 Gbps network: 20,000 ns (20 μs)
Read 1 MB sequentially from memory: 250,000 ns (250 μs)
Round trip within the same data-center: 500,000 ns (500 μs)
Disk seek: 10,000,000 ns (10 ms)
Read 1 MB sequentially from network: 10,000,000 ns (10 ms)
Read 1 MB sequentially from disk: 30,000,000 ns (30 ms)

Figure 6.3: Estimation reference numbers: powers of two, availability-to-downtime, common object sizes, and canonical latencies.

Below are key estimates that every engineer should be familiar with.

Number scales

There are different scales used in human conversation and in terms of machine understanding. It is absolutely important to understand how these terms are related so that when you are using these as a basis for estimation, you can work with complete confidence.

Scale used in human conversation:

- 1 thousand (1K): 3 zeroes
- 1 million (1M): 6 zeroes
- 1 billion (1B): 9 zeroes
- 1 trillion (1T) : 12 zeroes
- 1 quadrillion (1Q) : 15 zeroes

Scale used by machine:

- 1 KB (Kilobyte): 2^{10} = 1,024 bytes ~ 1K
- 1 MB (Megabyte): 2^{20} = 1,048,576 bytes ~ 1M
- 1 GB (Gigabyte): 2^{30} = 1,073,741,824 bytes ~ 1B
- 1 TB (Terabyte): 2^{40} = 1,099,511,627,776 bytes ~ 1T
- 1 PB (Petabyte): 2^{50} = 1,125,899,906,842,624 bytes ~ 1 Q

Comprehending the conversational and machine **Scales** together:

Volume requirement		**Binary equivalent for system design**	
Conversational Term	**Power of 10 (number of zeros in decimal representation)**	**Binary term**	**Power of 2 (bytes representation)**
1 thousand (1K)	3	1 KB (Kilobyte)	2^{10}
1 million (1M)	6	1 MB (Megabyte)	2^{20}
1 billion (1B)	9	1 GB (Gigabyte)	2^{30}
1 trillion (1T)	12	1 TB (Terabyte)	2^{40}
1 quadrillion (1Q)	15	1 PB (Petabyte)	2^{50}

Table 6.2: Conversational (power of ten) and machine (power of two) number scales

These number scales are used during almost all the estimation tasks you will perform e.g. Traffic, Throughput, Storage. For example, if your use case is dealing with 1 million users each consuming 10KB of storage space per day. There is a mismatch between the scales (million vs KB). To perform the estimation, we have to bring them to the same scale i.e. bytes (1 million = 2^{20}) and (10KB = 10 x 2^{10}). This will give us a precise daily storage need as (10 x 2^{30} bytes = 10GB).

Latency numbers

In this section, we have captured some latency (introduced and defined under *section 2.11*) numbers as a ready guide for you to keep in mind while designing a system. It covers two aspects

1. It gives you the number that you can use while estimating, and
2. It also provides a comparative study on which component is faster over another.

These numbers (absolute value) may have slightly changed because of hardware improvements in recent years but using them as presented below during an interview will be completely acceptable [3][4].

Note

Common system latencies [15]

L1 cache reference: 0.5 ns

Branch mis-predict: 5 ns

L2 cache reference: 7 ns

Mutex lock/unlock: 100 ns

Main memory reference: 100 ns

Compress 1K bytes with Zippy: 10,000 ns (10 µs)

Send 2K bytes over 1 Gbps network: 20,000 ns (20 µs)

Read 1 MB sequentially from memory: 250,000 ns (250 µs)

Round trip within the same data-center: 500,000 ns (500 µs)

Disk seek: 10,000,000 ns (10 ms)

Read 1 MB sequentially from network: 10,000,000 ns (10 ms)

Read 1 MB sequentially from disk: 30,000,000 ns (30 ms)

Send packet CA (California) → Netherlands → CA: 150,000,000 ns (150 ms)

[Credit: Jeff Dean "Numbers everyone should know"]

Knowing these latency figures helps when designing systems that need quick response times, such as real-time messaging apps. For instance, to achieve sub-200 ms p95 latency for an API, you might use in-memory caching to avoid slower disk seeks.

Availability numbers

Achieving high availability is critical for services that must be online 24/7. When a problem requires high availability at a specific percentage, it becomes quite important to understand what that percentage means in terms of downtime.

Following table captures a breakdown of availability percentages and the corresponding downtime (you can use 'error budget' technique explained in the previous chapter to derive it yourself) [6]:

Availability percentage	Downtime per year	Downtime per month	Downtime per day
90% (one nine)	36.53 days	73.05 hours	2.40 hours
99% (two nines)	3.65 days	7.31 hours	14.40 minutes
99.9% (three nines)	8.77 hours	43.83 minutes	1.44 minutes
99.99% (four nines)	52.60 minutes	4.38 minutes	8.64 seconds
99.999% (five nines)	5.26 minutes	26.30 seconds	864 milliseconds
99.9999% (six nines)	31.56 seconds	2.63 seconds	86.4 milliseconds

Table 6.3: Availability percentages and the downtime per year, month, and day

For systems that require 99.99% availability, the design should include features like replication, load balancing, and failover strategies to ensure minimal downtime, as covered in previous chapter. This also ties into your storage and traffic estimations, as you need to ensure that replication across multiple regions doesn't affect performance [7].

Blob/object storage sizes

Storage estimate is a key one that can be created for almost any type of system design problem you have. But if the system is dealing with high volume data or any data intensive use case such as images, videos, and documents, storage estimates become indispensable. You must prepare such an estimation and present it in front of the interviewers.

Below we have captured some commonly used data types that might help you prepare the estimates, if needed. A note of caution, some of these numbers are variable depending upon the underlying technology you choose and hence you should be aware of those numbers with technology selection. In general, you can use the following numbers to approximate your estimation:

> **Note**
>
> char: 1 byte
>
> char (Unicode): 2 bytes
>
> UUID: 16 bytes
>
> Thumbnails: 20-30 KB
>
> Website image: 200-300 KB
>
> Mobile image: 2-3 MB
>
> Documents (books, reports, etc.): 1-3 MB
>
> Audio files (songs, recordings): 4-5 MB
>
> 1-minute 720p video: 60 MB
>
> 1-minute 1080p video: 130 MB
>
> 1-minute 4K video: 350 MB

There are a few different types of estimations that we perform to get various insights on the given problem. We are now going to capture some of them in a bit more detail highlighting their purpose, when to use them, and how to work out the numbers.

> **Note**
>
> In every calculation in this chapter and later in the book we round 1 day = 24 × 60 × 60 = 86,400 seconds to 100,000 and 1 year = 365 days to 400. This trades a small loss of precision for a large gain in mental arithmetic speed during an interview.

Traffic estimates

This is the foundational estimate that drives many other estimations down the line. You must get this right. This is used to understand how much traffic the system will handle over a given period, usually per second. The interviewer might present this information in the form of **DAU (Daily Active Users)**, **MAU (Monthly Active Users)**, or likewise. Your **goal** here is to **calculate the number of RPS**(Requests per Second). If your use case requires separate estimation for read vs. write traffic, you should do so. While calculating this number, you must consider peak time traffic estimates. One way to do this is to know the 'peak-to-average' ratio. You can either ask your interviewer for it during requirement clarification, or you can assume and validate. It is perfectly acceptable to ask such questions even after you have moved on from the requirement clarification phase.

Following is an example of performing Back-of-the-Envelope traffic estimates for an e-commerce website with 100 million registered users. We are considering for the following:

```
DAU=30%, Peak Traffic factor=10x during the festive season.
100 million users × 30% = 30 million daily active users (DAU)
Peak traffic = 10 × 30 million = 300 million requests
Requests per Second (RPS) = 300m / 100000 = 3000 RPS
```

Therefore, your system needs to handle a minimum of **3000 RPS** to support peak traffic.

As we dive deeper into other estimates, we will see the significance of the traffic estimate and why it is so important to get it right.

The same method sizes the running example we return to through the rest of this chapter: a share-link service, the kind of service behind an app's Share button that turns a content URL into a short link. If it creates 100 million new links a month and each link is followed on average 100 times, that is 10 billion redirects a month, roughly 3,000 to 4,000 reads per second on average and several times that at peak, against only a few dozen writes per second. That lopsided read-to-write ratio is exactly what later pushes the design toward caching and read replicas.

Throughput estimates

Throughput estimates should be driven entirely by the use case you are solving. It helps you determine how to plan different areas within your system to meet traffic demand. This estimate spans all the layers of the system you are creating. A careful selection is needed to perform just enough estimation during your interview [8].

Some areas where this estimate helps include:

- **Database query throughput**: Read QPS (or queries per second) & Writes per second. Reading QPS helps to understand how we can scale the database to increase read efficiency, e.g. Adding cache layer, Read Replica. Write throughput helps to define scaling strategies, e.g., data partitioning, sharding, and active-active write.
- **Cache throughput QPS**: This helps us determine how a cache should be set up to reduce load on the backend system. It is used to determine an ideal hit ratio as well as cache eviction policies.
- **Message queue throughput**: Used to determine ingress vs egress messages. It helps in determining how many instances will be used to serve the desired traffic.
- **Application/service layer throughput**: Used to determine how many instances of the service we might require to serve the desired traffic volume. It considers how long it takes for the service to process a single request, and then we can scale that information.

Let's take the example used during the traffic estimates derived above and then work out back-of-the-envelope throughput estimates.

3000 RPS = The traffic estimate = 3000 RPS = 3000 RPS.

Consider that each request makes 5 queries to the database server for reading.

Read throughput = 3000 × 5 = 15000 QPS.

This number will provide you with an indication if your database can handle this many queries or you should think about some alternate mechanism like implementing caching to reduce the number of database hits or redundant storage, e.g., read-replicas. Also, if you choose to establish redundant storage you will have to plan the replication mechanism etc.

Similarly, Back-of-the-Envelope calculation example of a Social Media Platform

Requirement summary: A social media platform with 10 million active users per day, where each user makes 5 posts and views their timelines 10 times, fetching 50 posts per view. Consider peak time traffic as 5x.

Let's estimate the QPS for:

```
Posts Traffic estimates = 10M users × 5 posts = 50M posts/day
RPS = 50M posts /100,000 seconds = 500 posts/second
Assuming each post makes one write query
Write QPS: 500 posts per second
Peak Write QPS = 5 × 500 posts/second = 2500 posts/sec
```

Timeline View Requests (viewing a timeline):

```
Timeline views per day = 10M users × 10 views = 100M views/day
Read QPS = 100M / 100,000 seconds = 1,000 queries/second
Peak is 5x and hence Peak time Read QPS = 5 × 1000 = 5000
```

Post fetch QPS for fetching 50 posts per view:

```
Read QPS = 1,000
Post read QPS = 50 × 1000 = 50,000
Peak post fetch QPS = 50 × Peak time Read QPS = 50 × 5000 = 250,000
```

For estimation purposes the final numbers you will consider are:

```
Write QPS: Average = 500, Peak = 2500
Timeline Read QPS: Average=1000, Peak=5000
Posts Read QPS: Average = 50,000, Peak = 250,000
```

Storage estimates

This estimation helps you understand how much storage you should plan in advance for the system to continue functioning for a defined period, say 5-10 years. During data storage estimation, also consider data growth per year, metadata storage, backup, space needed for indexing and other business-as-usual activities as per applicable data retention policies. This requires an understanding of the nature of the data, how it is structured, and how it grows over time.

Example: Estimating Data Storage for a Social Media Platform

Let's estimate storage needs for a social media platform with 10M users making 10 posts daily, consisting of text and images, every day. User growth 10% YoY. Data must be available for 5 years.

Assuming unit data

User profile data size = 5 KB, Post content data size = 2 KB, and image metadata size = 1 KB.

Abstract: Consider that the image is uploaded directly to a CDN location that you are not accounting for in this calculation.

Storage need for user profile information:

Base storage for user profiles = 10M × 5 KB = 50 GB. Profiles are stored once per user, so unlike posts this figure does not accumulate each day.

Allowing for 10 percent user growth a year, that base grows to roughly 80 GB after five years.

Total storage need for user profiles is about 80 GB.

Storage need for posts:

```
Daily = 10M × 10 posts × 2KB = (10 × 2²⁰) × 10 × (2 × 2¹⁰) = 200 × 2³⁰
Yearly = 200 × 2³⁰ × 365 = 73000 GB = 73TB
5 years = 5 × 73TB = 365TB
10% YoY growth = 36.5TB (approx.)
Total storage need for posts = 365 + 36.5 = 401.5TB
```

Storage need for image metadata:

```
Daily = 10M × 10 posts × 1KB = (10 × 2²⁰) × 10 × (2 × 2¹⁰) = 100 × 2³⁰
Yearly = 100 × 2³⁰ × 365 = 36500 GB = 36.5TB
5 years = 5 × 36.5TB  = 182.5TB
10% YoY growth = 18.25TB (approx.)
Total storage for image metadata = 182.5 + 18.25 = 200.75TB
```

Total storage for 5 years for the given use case = 80GB + 401.5TB + 200.75TB ≈ 603TB

If you create one redundant copy of this storage, then the estimates will become double.

Tip

A year has been taken as 365 days on purpose here for two reasons:

1. To take the precise value in one calculation
2. To show how it complicates the calculation under time pressure.

This is the reason working with the ceiling value of 400 is a better trade-off.

Bandwidth estimates

Bandwidth estimates are required when dealing with large amounts of data transfer, suchas streaming services or file-sharing applications. It is used to plan your system ahead to answer - how your system will support required data transit over a network. This ensures system efficiency by assisting in calculating the necessary network bandwidth to manage user requests, data streaming, and API interactions without experiencing performance bottlenecks. It is measured in units like Mbps or Gbps. For a high data volume system, it helps you decide if there is a need to consider any data compression strategy, use of a CDN, etc.

For bandwidth estimates you should always consider the peak traffic RPS.

Estimating bandwidth for a video streaming platform

Let's estimate bandwidth for a video streaming platform like Netflix for 100M users with 40% DAU and 5x peak.

> **Note**
>
> An average 1080 stream video in its compressed form requires a 5 Mbps-8 Mbps bandwidth range. We can use this as a benchmark during the interview to determine the bandwidth requirement.

```
Traffic estimate DAU = 40% of 100M = 40M users
Average video watch time = 2 hours
Total watch hours = 40M × 2 = 80M hours per day = 80M × 4000 = 320,000M seconds
per day [rounding to the ceiling value for an hour (60 × 60) = 3600 seconds ≈ 4000
seconds]
The system must support an average concurrent views per second = 320000M/100000 =
3.2M views/sec
Peak concurrent traffic (5x) = 3.2M × 5 = 16M = 16 × 2^20
Total Bandwidth = 16 × 2^20 × 5 Mbps = 16 × 2^20 × 5 × 2^20 bps = 80 × 2^40 bps = 80
Tbps
```

Thus, the network must handle **80 terabits per second** of data transfer during peak times for this system to work.

Performance/latency estimates

It is another important type of estimation that spans through all the components you will be using to build a system. It uses latency as a performance lens to assess how responsive the system is. It is an indicator for worst-case and target latency expectations from the system. It helps early identification of 'tail latency' & its amplification issue so that appropriate remediation actions can be taken [5].

For the given problem you will use different building blocks and glue them together to yield the desired outcome. Performance estimates will help you predict the overall system response time so that you can assess if the building blocks used are fit-for-purpose.

Say the system (an API) you are building uses a load balancer, an API Gateway, an external cache, an application server, and a database. For each component, we can determine an ideal response time, and the sum of it will show the performance estimate for the API you are building. Let's look at the following table that shows estimation for the API:

Component	**Use**	**Estimated performance (p50)**
Load Balancer	Traffic manager	< 5 ms
API Gateway	Single entry point	< 50 ms
Cache	Distributed cache (Memcached)	< 5 ms
Application server	Business logic	< 50 ms
Database	Data persistence	< 90 ms
Total predicted time		< 200 ms

In the preceding example, the system will take approximately 200ms to generate a response. If your use case requires a p50 response time of <150 ms then this setup might fail. In this case you might introduce some strategy to reduce the number of interactions with the database to enjoy the performance gain.

When it comes to performance benchmarking, the industry standard is to use percentile-based measures such as p50, p95, and p99. A percentile tells you the latency a given share of requests stays under: p99 means 99 percent of requests are faster than that number, and the higher percentiles capture the slow tail that a few requests hit. That tail is easy to overlook. If the user base is 100M and the system meets its target only at p99, then 1 percent, which is 1M users, are getting a bad experience, and the business feels it if their latency runs high. This kind of tail latency, accumulating across the many building blocks in your solution, is what produces tail amplification [11][12].

Resource capacity estimates

This estimation is more closely tied to infrastructure planning, e.g., how many CPU cores are needed, how many database shards, read replicas, etc. The traffic estimates done earlier in this section play a vital role in performing this estimation [9][10].

During our traffic estimation, we calculated RPS = 3000.

Consider that you are doing resource capacity planning to find out how many CPUs will be needed to process the incoming requests.

On average, consider 1 request takes 5 ms of CPU time for processing. Then 3000 requests will require 3000 × 5 = 15,000 ms = 15000 ms = 15 seconds for their processing using a single CPU. If we have to achieve sub-second processing, then we would need at least 16 CPU cores to run at near 100% capacity. For CPU planning, it is a good idea to consider some extra capacity to remain ready for unexpected spikes. An additional 40-50% capacity should provide sufficient headroom. The final result = 16 + (50% of 16) = 16 + 8 = 24 CPUs.

Estimation pitfalls

Overestimating traffic: While it's important to account for growth, overestimating traffic can lead to over-complicating your design.

Ignoring data growth: Always consider how data grows over time, especially in systems that need to store historical data like analytics or logs. These numbers tell you how big the system has to be. The next step is to define how the outside world talks to it, beginning with its APIs.

API design

This is an optional step as it is not required for all the system design problems presented in front of you. But if you use microservices or API-based approach in your solution then it becomes mandatory to highlight. Designing an API is covered at length, including best practice recommendations in *Chapter 4*.

When APIs are in scope, treat them as the contract between the client and your system. Defining them early is a forcing function: you cannot specify an endpoint without deciding what the system actually does, so a clean API often exposes gaps in the requirements before they become gaps in the design. Keep the set small and purposeful, one endpoint per meaningful action, and let the request and response shapes mirror the entities you identified during data modeling.

The important points for this phase are:

- Identify all the endpoints needed for your system.
- Define the request and response format as required. This makes it clear to anyone reading the design, a teammate in review or an interviewer, how an endpoint will work. You can skip this bit for trivial endpoints, e.g., GET /products (Reference: For HTTP methods and status-code semantics.
- Ensure you highlight any important error handling you have considered, e.g., response code 429 in case you have implemented rate-limiting.
- Ensure you have considered and highlighted endpoint security.

As a worked example, the share-link service needs only two endpoints that matter. A write path, `POST /links`, takes the target URL (and optionally a custom alias and an expiry) and returns the short code with a `201Created`. A read path, `GET /{short_code}`, performs the redirect, returning a `301` or `302` to the original URL, or a `404` if the code is unknown or expired. Naming just these two, with their status codes, shows where the traffic actually goes—reads far outnumber writes, which is why the redirect path is the one you optimize.

A few concerns cut across every endpoint and are worth naming even briefly: versioning, so you can evolve the API without breaking existing clients; idempotency on writes, so a retried request does not create a duplicate; pagination on anything that can return a list; and consistent authentication and rate-limiting at the edge. You will not design all of these in an interview, but calling out the ones your problem needs signals that you have shipped real APIs, not just drawn them.

One more choice is worth a sentence in an interview, and that is the API style. REST over HTTP is the sensible default for public, resource-shaped APIs like the shortener. gRPC suits low-latency, high-volume calls between internal services, where a binary protocol and generated clients pay off. GraphQL fits when many different clients need to fetch different, aggregated slices of data and you want to avoid a sprawl of endpoints. You will rarely design the protocol in depth, but naming the style and one reason for it shows that you treat APIs as a design decision, not a default.

Keep the payloads honest to the data model: the create request carries the target URL and any options, and the response returns the short code and its expiry, the same fields that live in your URL entity. Small touches, such as returning a Location header on the redirect or a clear 409 when a custom alias is already taken, are the difference between an API that looks drawn and one that looks built.

Once the interface is clear, attention turns to what sits behind it: how the system stores and retrieves the data those endpoints move.

Database design

The database is where you will persist your data and hence it becomes quite important to keep this part of the design as precise as possible, matching your requirement. Any unnecessary use of jargon or lack of clarity in your reasoning can turn out to be a deal breaker. You have to meticulously plan and deliver the details in front of interviewers. Belowwe have attempted to outline a structured way of thinking so that each layer of your thought can contribute to the next stage. Together they can help you achieve the result. It is only a recommendation. Different people have different ways of handling a problem. Feel free to choose what suits you the best.

Identify key entities

Based on the requirements (functional and contributing non-functional) you have captured about the system; you should start building your thoughts on what entities will persist in this storage. But go a step further and also think about the minimum attributes an entity should possess, in terms of schema, to keep it meaningful. Also, start identifying any relationship that can exist between the entities and, most importantly, their storage and access patterns that will create business value. We will leave it to you to decide how the entities should be structured i.e. in case of a SQL database you want to keep the entire data completely denormalized, that might introduce some redundant copy of data per tuple or you want to keep it in a normal form (NF) in which case you might use joins to fetch the data. There is no single right or wrong approach here. There are only trade-offs, and the approach that creates the most value for your use case wins. An example entity schema for share-link service design problem can be [14]:

ShareLink table

```
`id` (Primary Key)
`target_url` (VARCHAR)
`short_url` (VARCHAR, unique)
`user_id` (Foreign Key, references Users table)
`created_at` (TIMESTAMP)
`expiration_date` (TIMESTAMP, optional)
```

User table

```
`id` (Primary Key)
`url_id` (Foreign Key, references ShareLinks table)
`username` (VARCHAR, unique)
`email` (VARCHAR, unique)
`password_hash` (VARCHAR)
`created_at` (TIMESTAMP)
```

Analytics table

```
`id` (Primary Key)
`url_id` (FK, references URL table)
`access_count` (INTEGER)
`last_accessed` (TIMESTAMP)
OR
```

User_URL_Access table

```
`id` (Primary Key)
`url_id` (FK, references URL table)
`user_id` (FK, references User table)
`last_accessed` (TIMESTAMP)
```

At the end of this exercise, you should have a better understanding of actual data in use and how you will interact with data [14].

Choose your storage

We have presented detailed information on storage, in *Chapter 4* that should help you in making this decision. But the most important at this stage will be the knowledge that you have developed during the entity identification stage above. If you know your entities, their schema, and access patterns, then it is a relatively easier task to bring contributing non-functional requirements into the overall thought map to decide the database that will fit your use case.

When you decide which database you are going with, you must be able to explain the reasoning behind the choice, to your team in the real world or to the interviewer in a design round. The details you present should be mapped to the non-functional requirement e.g. desired consistency level, scaling vertical or horizontal, read/write latency impact, data management, interoperability etc. It is also better to highlight any related technology choices in your design, e.g., the use of Snowflake ID to achieve uniqueness in your distributed dataset, database indexes to improve performance, and in-memory, local, or distributed caches to reduce database load.

The choice between SQL and NoSQL is not a matter of fashion; it follows from the access patterns you identified. A relational store earns its place when data is highly structured and you need multi-entity queries, joins, and strong transactional consistency. A NoSQL store, whether key-value, document, wide-column, or graph, earns its place when one dominant access pattern, very large scale, or a flexible schema matters more than ad hoc querying. State the pattern first and let it choose the store, rather than naming a database and reasoning backward.

Take the share-link service as a worked example. Its dominant operation is a redirect: given a short code, return the target URL. That is a simple key lookup that happens far more often than any write and has to be fast, which points to a key-value store, or a relational table keyed on the short code, fronted by a cache so popular links are served from memory. Writes are comparatively rare and small, so they are seldom the bottleneck. If the product later needs rich analytics, such as click counts by region and time, that is a different access pattern, better served by a separate analytics store than by bending the redirect path to answer reporting queries.

Two more decisions usually follow. First, indexing: an index on the short code turns a lookup from a scan into a direct hit, at the cost of slightly slower writes and extra storage—a trade-off worth making in a read-heavy system. Second, scale: when a single database can no longer carry the load, you shard by the short code so related reads stay on one node, and you add read replicas to spread redirect traffic. Naming these choices and the trade-off behind each is what separates a schema on a whiteboard from a data layer that would survive production.

With the data layer decided, you have all the pieces in hand. The next step is to assemble them into a working system, first at a high level and then in detail.

System design

The design phase is where you architect the system and lay out all its components to meet both functional and non-functional requirements including scalability, fault tolerance, and audit capabilities. You can choose either a top-down or bottom-up approach to lay out your design components. For many system design problems, it is a better choice to fix your backend system first and then create the ecosystem around it i.e., a bottom-up approach. Also, as we know by now, databases are the most complex to scale. But before choosing the approach, ensure you have adequate requirement understanding and your back-of-the-envelope estimates (if needed) are done.

The design phase consists of two components – high-level design and detailed design.

High-level design (HLD)

High-level design is important for laying out your initial thoughts on the board, making sure you are moving in the right direction. Usually, a high-level design represents a happy path of the system depicting the core functional coverage. You should continually interact with the interviewer in the process. You will end this stage with all your major building blocks identified and an affirmation by your interviewer.

A high-level design should reflect:

- **Clarity of vision**: A high-level design shows you have understood the problem correctly and can picture the whole solution: the major components, how they connect, and the journey a request takes through them. It proves you can hold the system in your head and describe where it is going before zooming into any one part.
- **Effective communication**: A well-articulated high-level design shows that you can communicate complex systems in a way that is easy for others to understand. This is an important skill in real-world scenarios where you need to align with other engineers, managers, and stakeholders. In the interview, it also helps ensure that both you and the interviewer fully understand each other's thoughts before you proceed to more detailed discussions.
- **Problem-solving approach**: This is about how you reason, not what you picture. A high-level design shows you can take an open-ended problem, break it into tractable pieces, and weigh the trade-offs between competing approaches, committing to one and being explicit about what you gave up. It is the difference between knowing the destination and showing your method for reaching it.
- **Buy-In from stakeholders**: In real-world projects, securing buy-in from stakeholders, including engineering teams, product managers, and business leaders, is central to success. A high-level design that fits the system's needs shows that you know how to build and maintain consensus in team settings. Getting stakeholder buy-in should be the goal of the HLD stage.

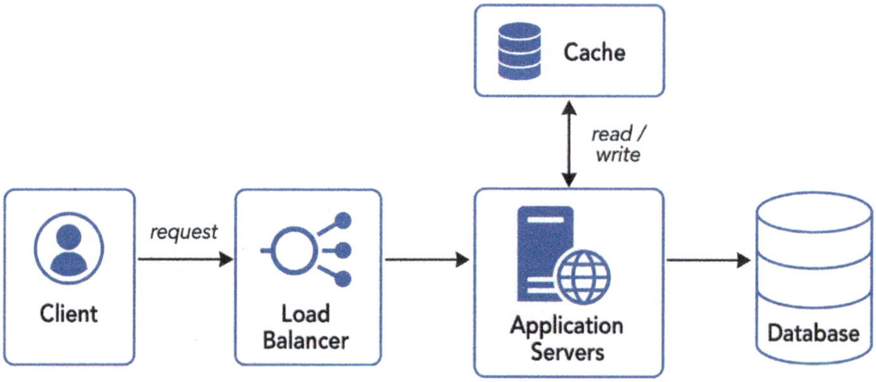

Figure 6.4: A high-level design for a share-link service.

Detailed design

Detailed design is the phase where you expand on your initial design. Demonstrate the system's end-to-end journey, outlining detailed responsibilities of chosen components, API endpoints (if not covered separately), the database, and the use of schema (if not covered separately) design. Align your work with the core functional and non-functional requirements.

This is the stage where you go deeper into the work so far and detail the key components. Expand each key component to a level that lets anyone reading the design, including an interviewer, see the depth of your solution. For a share-link service, a few key areas that will leave a lasting impression include expanding on the mechanism you will use to generate the short code, a specific caching strategy, and a redirection mechanism.

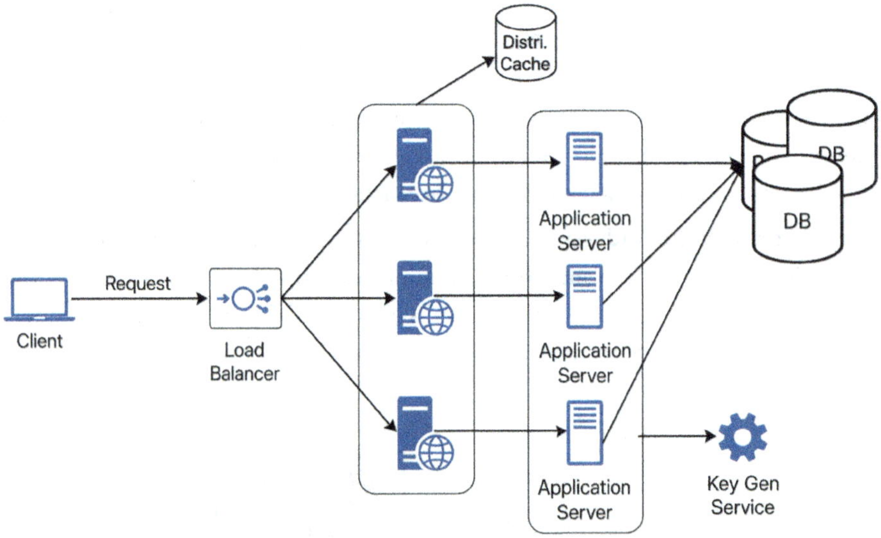

Figure 6.5: A detailed design for a share-link service

For the share-link service, that move from high level to detailed is concrete. The high-level design in *Figure 6.4* is deliberately sparse: a client, a load balancer, a tier of application servers, a cache, and a database. The detailed design in *Figure 6.5* then fills in the parts that carry the load and the risk: how short codes are generated (a dedicated key-generation service, or a counter encoded in base 62), how the read path is served (cache first, then database, with the redirect returning a `301` or `302`), and how the data scales (the database sharded by short code, with read replicas behind the cache). Each added detail earns its place by answering a specific requirement or removing a specific bottleneck, which is what turns a diagram into a design.

A complete detailed design also answers three non-functional questions:

- **Designing for scale**: name the levers that keep the system fast as load grows, load balancing across a tier of stateless servers, caching hot data (with a CDN for static content), sharding and read replicas on the database, and moving any work that does not need an immediate answer onto a message queue for asynchronous processing. *Chapter 4* covers these building blocks in depth; here you pick the few your numbers actually call for.
- **Designing for failure**: assume every component eventually fails and show what happens when it does. Retries with backoff and circuit breakers stop a struggling dependency from dragging the caller down with it, replication and failover keep a datastore available when an instance dies, and autoscaling absorbs traffic spikes before they turn into outages. The aim is a system that degrades gracefully rather than all at once [17].
- **Designing for observability**: a design you cannot see into is a design you cannot operate. Say how you would know the system is healthy, the metrics you would watch (latency, error rate, saturation), the logs and traces you would keep to debug a bad request, and the alerts that would page someone before users notice. Naming this is a strong senior signal, because it shows you think past launch to the day the system misbehaves.

A design is rarely finished the moment it is drawn. The next step is to turn a critical eye on it, finding the points most likely to break and showing how you would resolve them.

Resolving bottlenecks and follow-up questions

This is where a strong candidate pressure-tests their own work. With a first design on the board, you walk back through it looking for the places most likely to strain or fail, a database absorbing every read, a single service everything depends on, or a hot key that could swamp one node, and for each you propose a concrete way to relieve it.

That instinct, hunting for the weak point before it finds you, is exactly what a senior engineer brings to a real system long before it reaches production. In an interview this is also the final phase, when the follow-up questions arrive and your design is tested from angles you did not choose, so it rewards a deliberate approach rather than a scramble at the end.

You will hear this step called different things, resolving bottlenecks, optimizing the design, or scaling for the next order of magnitude, but the activity is the same: find what limits the system and remove the limit.

Steps to follow

- **Identifying bottlenecks**: Look for areas in your system where your non-functional requirement e.g. performance or scalability could be affected. Bottlenecks can occur at various points, such as:
- **Single points of failure**: Say your system relies on a single database instance, a failure of that instance could bring down the entire service. In case of a single database, you can propose a database replica or an active-active setup as per the use case.
- **Database load**: If the system queries the database too frequently, this could lead to performance degradation. To minimize the impact, caching might be an effective proposal as per your use case.
- **Hot partitions or hot keys**: When one key or shard receives a disproportionate share of traffic, for example a single viral item, that node becomes a hotspot even though the system as a whole is lightly loaded. Spreading the load through consistent hashing, replicating the hot entry, or fronting it with a cache usually relieves it.
- **Thundering herd on cache miss**: When a popular cached entry expires, many requests can miss at once and stampede the database together. A short-randomized jitter on expiry, request coalescing, or serving slightly stale data while one worker refreshes the entry keeps the database from being overwhelmed.
- **Synchronous coupling**: When one service blocks waiting on another, a slowdown in the dependency becomes a slowdown everywhere, and a single failure can cascade. Introducing a queue, an asynchronous call, or a timeout with a fallback contains the blast radius.
- **Resolving bottlenecks**: For each bottleneck, propose a solution. This could involve adding redundancy, caching, or load balancing to distribute the load as described above [17].

On the share-link service, the bottleneck that bites first is a viral link: one short code suddenly draws a huge share of reads, and a single row or shard turns into a hotspot. The fix layers defenses, serving the redirect from a CDN or an in-memory cache so most requests never reach the database, adding read replicas for the rest, and replicating that one entry if it still dominates.

A second candidate is the key-generation service: if every write waits on it, it becomes both a single point of failure and a throughput ceiling, which you resolve by pre-generating a pool of keys or partitioning the key space so no single instance sits on the critical path.

The follow-up questions are not an attack; they are how the interviewer probes the edges of your design. They tend to push on a few things: how the system behaves at ten times the load, what happens when a component fails, where the data could drift out of sync, and what you would do differently with more time. Handle each the same way: restate what is being asked, reason out loud from the requirements rather than reaching for a memorized answer, and name the trade-off in your reply. When you do not know, say so and describe how you would find out. A calm account of how you would investigate lands better than a confident guess, and it mirrors how the work actually goes on the job.

All of this has to happen inside a fixed window. The final element governs the rest: managing your time so each step gets the attention it deserves.

Effective time management

Time is the one resource the interview will not give you more of. Candidates rarely fail for running out of ideas; they fail for running out of minutes, having spent too long polishing the requirements or the estimates and then rushing the architecture, which is where most of the signal actually lives. A rough plan for the hour keeps the clock from making that call for you.

Here is a general guideline for dividing your time during a sixty-minute system design interview. The same habit of budgeting attention across each step serves you in any time-boxed design session at work:

- **Requirement clarification** (5-7 minutes): Begin to engage with the interviewer by driving the conversation. Your prior domain knowledge on the given problem can play a vital role. At the end of this stage, you should try to have a workable functional understanding of the system, a possible must-have/should-have categorization of the solution you will produce, all your assumptions stated and validated, and a non-functional understanding associated with the use case. Many candidates rush through this part, but in reality, not asking the questions would mean skipping a part where you can get a score from interviewers.

- **Estimations** (3-5 minutes): Depending upon the non-functionals associated with your use case, work on back-of-the-envelope estimates as relevant. Keep working aloud so your interviewer knows what estimates you have picked up and how each estimate will inform a decision. At the end of this stage, along with presenting the number(s), also explain how you are using these numbers in your solution.
- **Database Design** (5-7 minutes): Translate the requirements into data. Identify the key entities, their essential attributes, and the relationships between them, then choose a store that fits the access patterns you expect. Say the reasoning aloud, tying the choice to a non-functional need such as consistency, the read/write ratio, or scale. At the end of this stage, you should have a workable schema and a defensible database choice, not just a named technology.
- **API design** (5-7 minutes): If the problem is API-driven, define the handful of endpoints that carry the real traffic, with their request and response shapes and status codes. Skip the trivial ones and highlight anything that signals maturity, such as error handling, idempotency, or rate-limiting. At the end of this stage the interviewer should see the contract between the client and your system, and where the load actually flows.
- **End-to-end design** (15-20 minutes): This is where most of your time, and most of your score, lives. Start with a high-level design to agree on the major building blocks, then deep-dive the components that matter, walking a request through the system from entry to storage and back. Cover the non-functional concerns as you go, such as caching, replication, and fault tolerance, and keep checking in with the interviewer so you stay on the path they care about. At the end of this stage, you should have a coherent architecture that visibly satisfies both the functional and the non-functional requirements.
- **Resolving bottlenecks and follow-up questions** (3-5 minutes): Reserve time to pressure-test your own design before the interviewer does. Call out the weak points, single points of failure, hot spots, or database load, and propose concrete fixes such as redundancy, caching, or sharding. Use the remaining minutes for follow-up questions, reasoning aloud and naming trade-offs rather than reaching for memorized answers. Ending on a clear-eyed view of the design's limits usually lands better than pretending it has none.

All interviews are different, and hence it is possible that you might not require to allocate time on every head mentioned here.

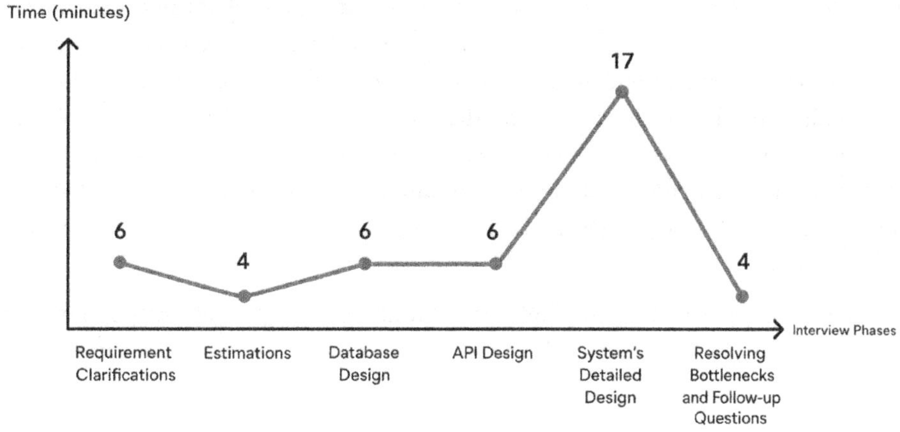

Figure 6.6: A suggested time allocation across the phases of a system design interview.

Each section should be approached methodically, ensuring that you address the most critical elements of the design while staying within the time limits.

Put together, these elements are less a checklist than a way of thinking. Requirements set the target, estimation grounds it in numbers, and the API, data, and end-to-end design turn it into something concrete before you pressure-test the result and manage the clock. Worked in order, a blank whiteboard stops being intimidating: each step narrows the problem and feeds the next, so that by the end you hold not just an answer but a defensible line of reasoning behind it. That reasoning, more than any single diagram, is what a strong system design leaves behind, on the job and in an interview alike.

Summary

Designing a system is less about knowing every technology than about moving through a dependable sequence, and this chapter laid that sequence out. It begins with requirement clarification, separating what the system must do from how well it must do it, and then turns those requirements into rough numbers through estimation, so that the decisions ahead rest on evidence rather than instinct. Together these two steps fix the constraints that everything else is built to satisfy.

From there the design takes shape: you define the APIs that expose what the system does, choose and structure a data layer around real access patterns and consistency needs, and connect the pieces into a coherent end-to-end architecture rather than a scatter of boxes. The closing moves are where judgment shows, finding the bottlenecks in your own design and resolving them, meeting follow-up questions with composure, and pacing yourself so every part gets its due. None of this is interview theater; it is how careful engineers approach a real system, which is exactly why a design interview tests it. Learn the sequence once, and it serves you on both sides of the whiteboard.

The next chapter puts this framework into action, walking through a full end-to-end design of a distributed messaging system like Slack, so you can see exactly how each element plays out in a real problem.

Quiz

Q1. In a distributed banking system, which two NFRs are most likely to be in conflict?

A) Maintainability & Observability

B) Availability & Consistency

C) Scalability & Elasticity

D) Durability & Security

Q2. A healthcare records system must never lose patient data. Which NFR is most critical?

A) Availability

B) Durability

C) Performance

D) Scalability

Q3. Which NFR is most directly measured by "requests per second" a system can handle?

A) Availability

B) Scalability

C) Performance (Throughput)

D) Reliability

Q4. A social media platform must handle billions of daily posts. Which NFR is most critical to ensure the system continues functioning under sudden traffic spikes?

A) Availability

B) Scalability

C) Durability

D) Observability

Q5. The feed system must show new posts with minimal delay. Which NFR is most directly relevant?

A) Latency

B) Security

C) Maintainability

D) Reliability

Q6. A social media platform must prevent permanent loss of user-generated content (photos, posts, videos). Which NFR is most critical?

A) Availability

B) Consistency

C) Durability

D) Elasticity

Q7. Users complain that sometimes they see outdated likes and comments in real-time feeds. Which NFR is being compromised?

A) Performance

B) Consistency

C) Reliability

D) Maintainability

References

[1] Wiegers, K., & Beatty, J. (2013). Software Requirements (3rd ed.). Microsoft Press. https://www.microsoftpressstore.com/store/software-requirements-9780735679665

[2] Donne Martin. "The System Design Primer." https://github.com/donnemartin/system-design-primer Estimation - latency and the canonical numbers

[3] Dean, J. (2009). "Designs, Lessons and Advice from Building Large Distributed Systems." LADIS keynote. [the source of the "numbers everyone should know"] https://brenocon.com/dean_perf.html

[4] Bonér, J. "Latency Numbers Every Programmer Should Know." https://gist.github.com/jboner/2841832

[5] Gregg, B. (2020). Systems Performance: Enterprise and the Cloud (2nd ed.). Addison-Wesley. https://www.pearson.com/en-us/subject-catalog/p/systems-performance/P200000000297/9780136821656

Availability and service-level objectives

[6] Beyer, B., Jones, C., Petoff, J., & Murphy, N. R. (Eds.) (2016). Site Reliability Engineering, Chapter 4, "Service Level Objectives." O'Reilly / Google. https://sre.google/sre-book/service-level-objectives/

[7] Beyer, B., et al. (Eds.) (2018). The Site Reliability Workbook, Chapter 2, "Implementing SLOs." O'Reilly / Google. https://sre.google/workbook/implementing-slos/

Throughput, queuing and capacity

[8] Little, J. D. C. (1961). "A Proof for the Queuing Formula: L = lambda W." Operations Research, 9(3). https://doi.org/10.1287/opre.9.3.383

[9] Gunther, N. J. (2007). Guerrilla Capacity Planning. Springer. https://doi.org/10.1007/978-3-540-31010-5

[10] AWS. "AWS Well-Architected Framework - Performance Efficiency Pillar." https://docs.aws.amazon.com/wellarchitected/latest/performance-efficiency-pillar/

Tail latency and percentiles

[11] Dean, J., & Barroso, L. A. (2013). "The Tail at Scale." Communications of the ACM, 56(2). `https://cacm.acm.org/practice/the-tail-at-scale/`

[12] Tene, G. "How NOT to Measure Latency." Conference talk on latency percentiles and coordinated omission. `https://www.infoq.com/presentations/latency-response-`

7

Designing a Slack-like Messaging System

A distributed messaging platform enables high-volume users to exchange messages in real time. This may include file exchange, audio and video calls, etc. Many such platforms exist in both free-to-use and subscription-based models. Examples include Slack, WhatsApp, Microsoft Teams, Zoom, and Discord.

Someone in London types a message and it appears on a screen in San Francisco a heartbeat later, in the right order, even though the two devices never communicate directly. Making that happen reliably, across regions and at scale, is the real challenge behind the design. This chapter walks you through the systematic approach to designing a distributed messaging platform during a technical interview. The same approach can also be applied when designing real-world systems. Rather than jumping directly into architectural diagrams, we'll follow the methodology that experienced engineers use.

We will start with problem clarification, gathering requirements, estimating scale, and then progressively building toward a comprehensive solution. This structured approach not only demonstrates technical competence but also shows your ability to think critically about product requirements and make informed trade-offs - skills that are invaluable in real-world engineering roles, as discussed in the previous chapter.

The goal is not to recreate the platform in its entirety, but to design a system that captures its core capabilities while demonstrating structured thinking, sound architectural choices, and strong fundamentals.

In this chapter, we will go over the following steps to solve the problem:

- Requirement clarification
- Approach
- Estimates
- Database design
- System design
- Resolving bottlenecks and follow-up questions

Here's a sample problem statement: Design a Slack-like messaging system that supports millions of distributed users to enable real-time communication through channels and direct messages.

Understand the problem domain

The current system design problem specifically mentions building a Slack-like messaging platform. Let us first look at the main capabilities of a platform like Slack and the types of interactions the system needs to support for context building [5]. This context will help you ask the right clarifying questions, define the scope, and make informed design decisions during the interview.

- Support for multiple clients, for example, web, mobile. A user can be on more than one device simultaneously. Messages sent from one device are auto-synced to the other device.
- User authentication and authorization to allow system access
- Channel-based messaging: One-to-many (fan-out) messaging for a channel.
- Group messaging
- One-to-one or direct messaging
- Audio/video calls
- File upload/download
- Maintain message order with instant delivery
- Message persistence in a durable way to enable message history

- Perform search on messages
- Display users' presence, for example, online/offline
- Manage state and events – persistent, for example, reactions/emojis and members joining/leaving a channel; and transient, for example, a user typing status message.
- Notification to users via app (i.e., push notification) [16]
- Low latency

Once you have a clear understanding of the system design problem for building a Slack-like messaging system, the next step is clarifying the requirements. The capability list above is deliberately long. No design could deliver all of it in one go, so the first real decision is not how to build, but what to leave out. That is the work of requirement clarification.

Requirement clarification

If you closely inspect the problem domain, you will realize there is broad functional coverage involved in this system. Within an interview setting, it is quite important to clearly understand the core functional aspects you are expected to cover in your solution, as it can become a challenge to build everything in the given time limit. For this design activity, we will consider the following requirements:

Functional	Ability to send real-time text-only messages in a channel and through direct messaging. An average of 100 messages (1 KB each) per day per user Multiple devices support User online/offline presence display Message persistence Maintain message ordering per channel Only registered, authenticated users can access the system. [Note: User management, authentication journey although important but can be abstracted for this work]

System qualities/Non-functional	Secure access Ultra-low latency, real-time message delivery Highly scalable Message durability and availability (5 years of instant access, then archived but available when needed) High user volume (10 million DAU), a read-write ratio of 10:1, and daily short-period spikes of 30% Highly available infrastructure for a geographically distributed user base Year-on-year growth in the user base is 10%

Table 7.1: Functional and non-functional requirements

Approach

With the scope fixed, each requirement now has to become a design choice. Rather than committing to any one straight away, it helps to lay each requirement beside the options that could satisfy it and weigh the trade-offs. These requirements indicate the following key questions for which an approach is required to formalize the solution. *Table 7.2* summarizes these:

Problem	Possible approach(es)
Online messaging system for channel-based and direct chat	Channel-based chat indicates the need for a fan-out implementation. Also, to achieve direct chat, a WebSocket-based implementation can be leveraged.
Geographically distributed user base for an ultra-low-latency chat system	It indicates the need for a real-time interaction component at a location close to the users. Also, this component should be scalable to match a growing client base.

Problem	Possible approach(es)
When the two requirements mentioned are considered jointly: 1) Authenticated user access 2) Direct chat Together, they implicitly indicate an additional requirement for 'user discovery' functionality to enable such chat. Moreover, when a new user is added to a channel, the user should start receiving the messages from that channel.	It requires the presence of a user management module in the system. Users should be discoverable by some lightweight attributes, e.g., first name, last name, and email. There are two high-level ways to maintain user information: • A centralized user base module, or • A distributed module. The first approach keeps all users in a common place, making it a single source of truth. The trade-off here is the potential for a bottleneck as volume increases. The second approach scatters user information at multiple connected primary stores. The trade-off here involves syncing user information, including new joiners, leavers, or any profile update to enable their discovery efficiently. **Assume and clarify with stakeholders:** A user will either be part of a company, i.e., an organization or they will be implicitly assigned to an organization named 'Anonymous'. Communication among users is only possible within the same organization boundary.

Problem	Possible approach(es)
Maintaining message ordering while reading	Some possible ways to achieve this are: • Client machine timestamp: This is dependent on the location and time of the clients' machines, which are geographically distributed. It does not appear to be a reliable option. • Web or Application Server: It can be a potential option. To implement ordering at this layer, all the distributed nodes must agree on a leader. For this, an approach like ZAB or Raft can be implemented. A vector clock-based implementation might also be needed. So, overall, it is possible, but with implementation complexities [14]. • A dedicated system that can provide an ordering guarantee in some form e.g., Kafka per partition **Database-level implementation**: This can be thought in two different ways: • A single relational database where built-in ID generation methods can be used to ensure ordering. But with the number of users, message data volume, and distributed client locations, the use of such databases might become impractical or constrained over time. • A partitioned SQL database where each message is assigned to a dedicated shard for high-throughput writes and reads. We can build a cluster of each shard with asynchronous replication to achieve redundancy, reliability, and improve read latency. This can be a possible approach if all user messages from an organization are strictly maintained in a single shard. This approach further requires in-depth thinking to make the system functional.

Problem	Possible approach(es)
Messaging persistence	It can be either SQL or NoSQL. Such a system requires very high data-access throughput and is latency-sensitive. A range-based read pattern is a common way to achieve this. A SQL database can be used for the purpose but it will come with the additional complexity of sharding the data per organization, writing shard-aware queries, using shard routers and so on. Range-based read queries are simple to implement and are highly efficient for the purpose. A wide-column NoSQL store, e.g., Cassandra, natively supports data persistence and querying in the desired way. Also, to strengthen our storage selection we should perform estimates to get a clear understanding of traffic, query volume, etc.

Table 7.2: Design problems and possible approaches

Based on our understanding of the problem and the approach identified to address it, the design can follow the path below:

1. Perform relevant estimates to better understand the volume this system will have to handle.
2. Define REST-based interactions for synchronous communication
3. Use of WebSocket-based architecture to facilitate real-time messaging. It should be created in multiple geographic locations, close to the high-volume user base for latency benefits.
4. Leverage Kafka-supported fan-out technique to get near-real-time message consumption. Also, it offers ordered, immutable data per partition that will be helpful for achieving message ordering [10][11].
5. Messages can be stored in a wide-column NoSQL database to get high write and read throughput (more details covered with database design). Consistent hashing-based technique can be incorporated for node management.
6. Centralized (abstract), replicated user management module backed by a traditional SQL database for storing users' data and their discoverability. It also provides consistency

guarantees. Relevant indexes as well as caching should be implemented for latency gains and scalability.

7. Along with the centralized user module, a multi-node centralized web module can be considered to enable users' first interaction, i.e., login to the system. A redundant copy of this module should also be deployed in at least another location for failover.

Two of those choices - the database and how many serving nodes to run—cannot be settled by reasoning alone. They depend on volume. So before going further, we put rough numbers to the load.

Estimates

Before making architectural decisions, it is useful to estimate the expected scale of the system. These estimates help us understand the request volume, storage needs, and throughput the design must support.

Traffic estimates

Each number below decides something concrete; for example: how many web nodes, which class of database, and how much storage to provision. We work through traffic first, then throughput, then storage.

```
Daily active users = 10 M
Number of messages per day by a user = 100
Requests per second for writes = 10 M x 100 / 100,000 rounded seconds in a day =
10000 RPS
The stated daily peak is 30% of 10000 RPS = 3000
Total daily peak traffic = 10000 + 3000 = 13000 RPS
```

Throughput estimates

Database write query throughput = total daily peak traffic = 13000 QPS

Read query throughput:

- Read-write ratio given = 10:1
- Read QPS = Write QPS x 10 = 13000 x 10 = **130,000 QPS**

An inference from this calculation is that a single instance of a web, proxy, or gateway component is not enough to serve this request volume. Also, the persistent storage should be built carefully to allow very high-volume data writes and reads.

Storage estimates

Storage needed per day = 10 million daily active users x 100 messages x 1 KB = (10 x 2^{20}) x 100 x (1 x 2^{10}) = 1000 x 2^{30} = 1 TB.

```
Annual storage need = 400 x 1 TB = approximately 400 TB
Total storage need for 5 years = 5 x 400 TB = 2000 TB = 2 PB
Total storage (without replication) for 5 years, including 10% year-on-year growth
with a simplified calculation = 2 PB + (2 x 10/100) = approximately 2.2 PB
Storage with replication factor (assume 3) = 2.2 x 3 = 6.6 PB
```

These estimates tell us three things: the system will have heavy writes, reads will need to be ordered, and users will be spread across multiple regions. Together, these requirements make the data store the next key decision to address.

> **Note**
>
> Although we are not expanding much on the user authentication side of the journey, we cannot ignore the presence of registered users. During your storage estimation you are also expected to calculate the storage space that will be needed to maintain the user information. This is left here as a do-it-yourself exercise.
>
> **Hint**: You should first think about what minimum information (attributes) about an organization and user you would want to store and then estimate from that point on.

Database design

Let us begin by examining the choice of data store for persisting messages. In practice, both SQL and NoSQL data stores are used to implement distributed messaging systems. For example, Slack relies on MySQL, whereas Microsoft Teams uses a native NoSQL backend. Each of these approaches involves distinct trade-offs, which merit closer examination [7][8].

The choice of database depends on a few key requirements:

- Data volume
- Scalability
- Latency, i.e., write throughput and data access needs
- Message ordering

The system should support high write throughput as well as ordered reads. There are multiple ways in which a message-ordering guarantee can be achieved. We will cover one way in our solution. To achieve high availability as well as to support a growing user base, horizontal scaling should be our primary consideration. In terms of data access patterns, for a chat system, a range-based query implementation is usually a better choice as it returns ordered data sets with very low latency. A wide-column NoSQL database, for example, Apache Cassandra, supports all of these by default. Selecting a SQL database will require data sharding that is relatively complex to scale. It can also add overhead in meeting the latency expectation. A relational database, however, does offer strong consistency. For the purposes of this exercise, we have used a NoSQL data store for message persistence. The following captures some details on the storage layer [12].

For message persistence, a shard can be created per organization. This will keep data of a single umbrella entity together. Each shard's data will be replicated to multiple redundant instances in a cluster. Adding or removing nodes can be achieved using a consistent hashing-based technique [13].

A basic data model for chat tables can be presented as follows:

Table to handle channel messages: `Channel_Message`

Partition Key: `organization_id, Channel_id`

Cluster Ordering: `message_timestampDESC, message_idDESC`

Table structure:

```
(
    organization_id,
    Channel_id,
    Message_id,
    posted_by_user_id,
    message,
    message_timestamp
)
```

Table to handle direct messages: `User_Conversation`

Partition Key: `organization_id`, `conversation_id`

Cluster Ordering: `message_timestampDESC`, `message_id DESC`

Columns:

```
(
    organization_id,
    conversation_id,
    message_id,
    posted_by_user_id,
    message,
```

```
    message_timestamp
)
```

In the next section you will see the actual system design using the information gathered so far. All the stages carried out up to this point become important contributors to the decisions that shape the final architecture.

System design

In system design, we will first create a high-level view of the main building blocks that will be used to solve the problem. We will then take a deep dive into individual journeys the system supports to match the requirement. Let's dive into it.

High-level design

With the selected NoSQL database, challenges related to strict message ordering and consistency require some additional handling. Such aspects are implemented through complementary techniques in the system.

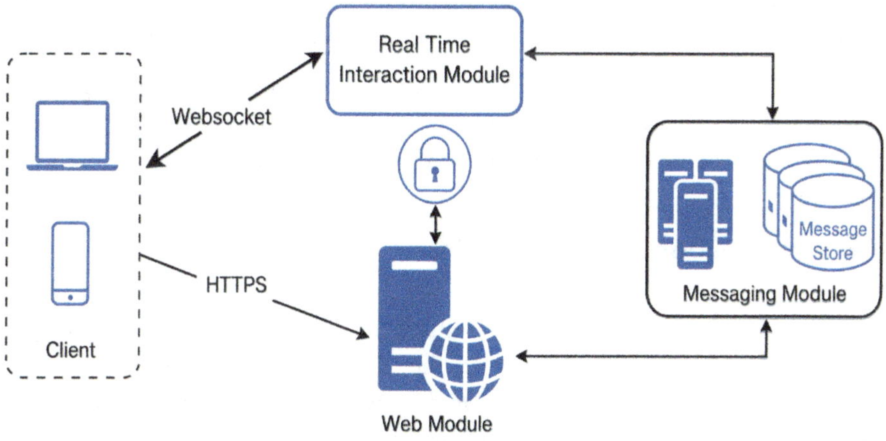

Figure 7.1: High-level design for a Slack-like system

As you analyze *Figure 7.1*, you can see that it captures three main high-level modules to solve the given problem. Below we have added some functional details of these components for you to better relate to them during the detailed design.

Component details

In the following sections, we describe each module's detailed responsibilities and rationale for their presence in the overall solution. The information builds a foundation that will become key contributing factors when performing a detailed design.

Web-module

It is the main facilitator, the first touchpoint for any user to interact with the system. It is a stateless REST-based module to be deployed as a multi-node application within a core (single) region.

A redundant setup of this module will be deployed in a different region for failover. The two environments will be configured in active-passive mode for automatic failover. Main responsibilities of the module include:

- Users and organization management
- Authentication and authorization
- Channel message facilitation including send initiation, etc.

Trade-offs to consider here include latency and handling bottlenecks. The latency can be noticeably high during a system outage in the event of a regional failure. This is because the new environment might take some time to start responding to its full capacity. On successful authentication, this module returns all the information needed for the user to start using the system, including a WebSocket URL to connect to the 'Real-Time Interaction Module'. Other details in the response might include the user's channels, chat history, and access privileges.

The web module also plays a pivotal role in facilitating the message-sending action to a channel when initiated by a client. The 'send message to a channel' action makes a call to this module where the message is stored in memory before being passed to the 'messaging module' for further handling.

Real-Time Interaction Module (RTIM)

This is a stateful, WebSocket-based module for real-time message interaction with clients in the nearby region of its service. The module is stateful for ultra-low latency benefits [1]. Its main responsibilities include message delivery to the clients, observing client presence, typing indicator, rendering messages in order, and multi-device sync. It will be deployed in multiple regions (including the core region) to match client locations.

It maintains the list of all active connections for each client to relay fan-out messages to the available clients. For offline clients, it can send a push notification, indicating that a new message is pending delivery. It subscribes to the messaging module to receive all new messages for a channel in near-real time. Once it receives a message, it will relay the message to all connected recipients immediately.

This module is also responsible for enabling one-to-one direct messaging, group-based messaging, as well as user presence indicator for clients.

Messaging-module

This module is responsible for overall message management. It dictates message ordering for all the channel messages as well as facilitates message fan-out to subscribers. A topic for each organization will be created for the purpose. Each topic will consist of multiple partitions, one for each channel. `Channel_id` will be used as the partition key to achieve strict message ordering per channel. All subscribers will pick up messages in the order they are placed within their 'partition' to relay them to their clients.

Messages are also persisted into their respective shards at this layer. Sharding is performed based on the user's organization to ensure message isolation by organization which also enhances the security posture. A consistent hashing-based algorithm can be used for adding or removing shards in the persistent group.

If you are designing for this in an interview, at this stage, ensure that the interviewer is fully aligned with your overall approach and there are no other expected functional aspects missing. If it is relevant, you can highlight that the data archival will be explained as part of the detailed design or later during the journey.

Detailed design

The high-level design shows what the pieces are. The detailed design shows how they behave when a real request moves through them, one journey at a time. In *Figure 7.2*, the RTIM module is only depicted in the core application region. This is to keep the diagram simplified. As explained earlier, this module will have multi-region presence. For example, if your high-density user base is distributed across, say, San Francisco, Delhi, and London, then you can expect one RTIM instance in each of the mentioned regions. However, in this example, if San Francisco is your core location, then your web-module and messaging-module will only be hosted here.

There are multiple core journeys associated with the problem. As part of the detailed design, it is more meaningful to highlight those journeys while expanding the components. Within the design, all user interactions will be logged (excluding or redacting sensitive information) and shipped to a common ELK stack for monitoring [18].

Session establishment

Establishing a session is the first step before a user can start using the system. *Figure 7.2* captures the detailed journey:

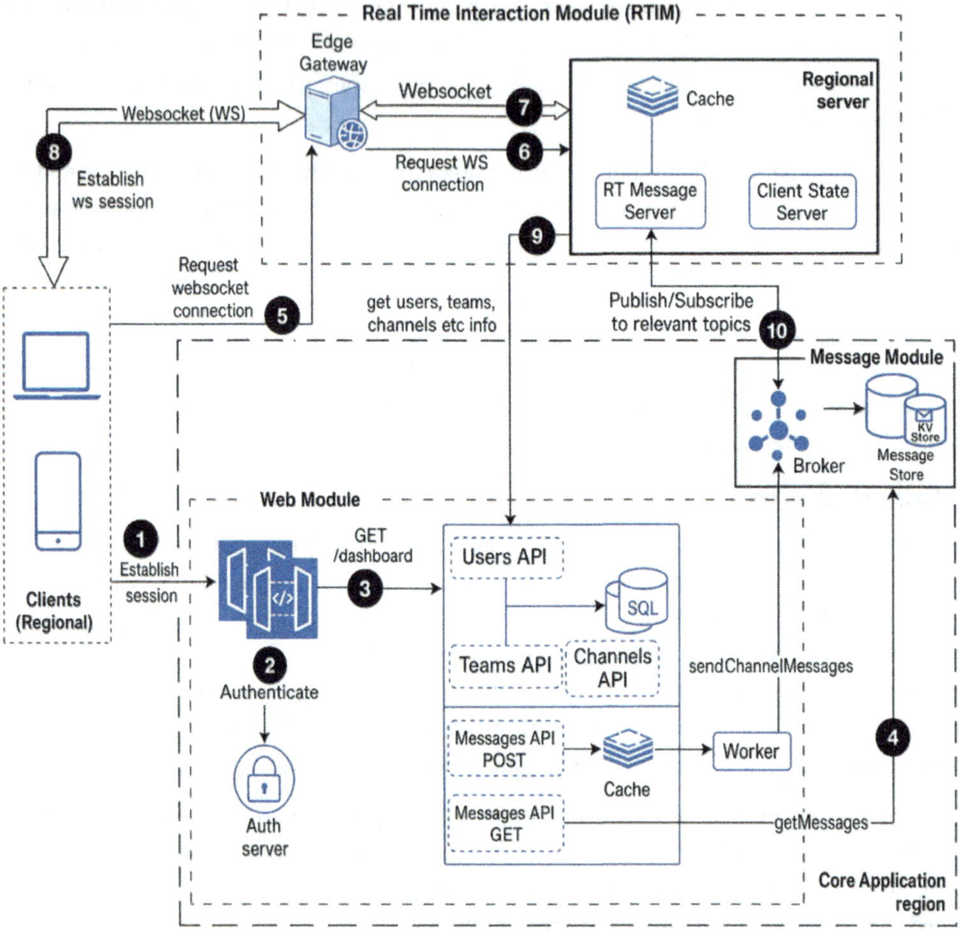

Figure 7.2: The user session establishment journey

Let's try to understand the journey here. A client tries to connect to the system by accessing a public web URL. It goes through DNS resolution and passes through the network firewalls, load balancers, and other components as per industry best practices. These components are purposefully abstracted in the preceding diagram to keep the focus on mainstream components.

After completing all the initial hops to reach the host server, the user's request lands on the API gateway where the authentication token gets verified. If there is an invalid token or no token available, the user will be challenged to authenticate. On successful authentication, the API gateway will make a call to the REST API 'GET /dashboard' (shown in the figure). The API will gather comprehensive information as needed to render the login success page. The information, at a minimum, will include the user's basic details, their organization details, and linked channels. Internally, an additional call will be made to retrieve identified channel messages (including from persistent storage) matching their profile. Our use of NoSQL stores will become a better choice in terms of executing high-performance range-based read queries. The response object will include an additional WebSocket URL for the client to establish a connection with RTIM.

To complete the session establishment journey, the client uses the WebSocket URL from the web-module's response to make a connection request to the edge gateway component of RTIM. The edge server interacts with the 'Regional Server' components hosted within the region. A WebSocket connection will be established between the client and the RTIM. While establishing the WebSocket connection, the 'RT Messaging server' component performs two additional tasks:

- It interacts with the web module to retrieve the user's channel association information to store it in its local cache [2].
- If a new channel is found, it subscribes to the 'broker' component of the 'Messaging Module'.

The subscription is created for all the topics depending on the user's channel association [15].

Note

Good to know

There are some challenges that the stateful WebSocket connection poses [6]. These challenges are listed here with relevant techniques to overcome them:

- **Connections break and reconnect**: There are too many factors that can influence the connection stability within a WebSocket connection. Some examples are: client machine accidental shutdown, mobile phone out of network/data coverage area, server health check not received within a bounded time limit and hence temporarily discarded from the group, and more. Once a server recovers from an outage, all the clients previously associated with that server try to reconnect to it instantly (almost at the same time). This might overload or crash the server again. To overcome this challenge, 'Exponential backoff with jitter' should be implemented. Exponential backoff is an established algorithm to manage retries after failure by increasing wait time exponentially after each unsuccessful attempt. The maximum time is usually bounded by a maximum. A jitter component is added to further reduce the number of clients attempting to connect simultaneously on server recovery. You can learn more about this problem at https://websocket.org/guides/reconnection/
- **Scaling WebSocket horizontally**: Scaling WebSocket horizontally requires more careful planning because of the stateful nature of the connection. For a connection to work in a stateful manner, each client request must be served by the same server that served its first request. This is because the server maintains some additional information, for example, TCP connection, client session state, and message queue management of the client. A strategically chosen sticky-session implementation during load balancing helps in achieving traffic management during scaling. Introduction of a 'WebSocket Gateway' component can also help improve scalability. The gateway component itself can scale horizontally, and it also abstracts many underlying responsibilities of a WebSocket server, like connection management, state management, etc., giving the server more room to perform its core task. [3]
- **Latency**: Use of WebSocket does improve the overall latency between the communicating systems, but the placement, that is, the location of the server component and its distance from the client machine might take away this benefit. To mitigate this, the server components should reside as close to the client system as possible.

Channel message delivery

Sending a message to a channel is different from sending one-to-one messages or group messages. The difference lies in the nature of communication. The latter two communications are temporary or ad-hoc in nature. *Figure 7.3* captures the channel message journey. Here, we assume that the user session has already been established using the previous journey.

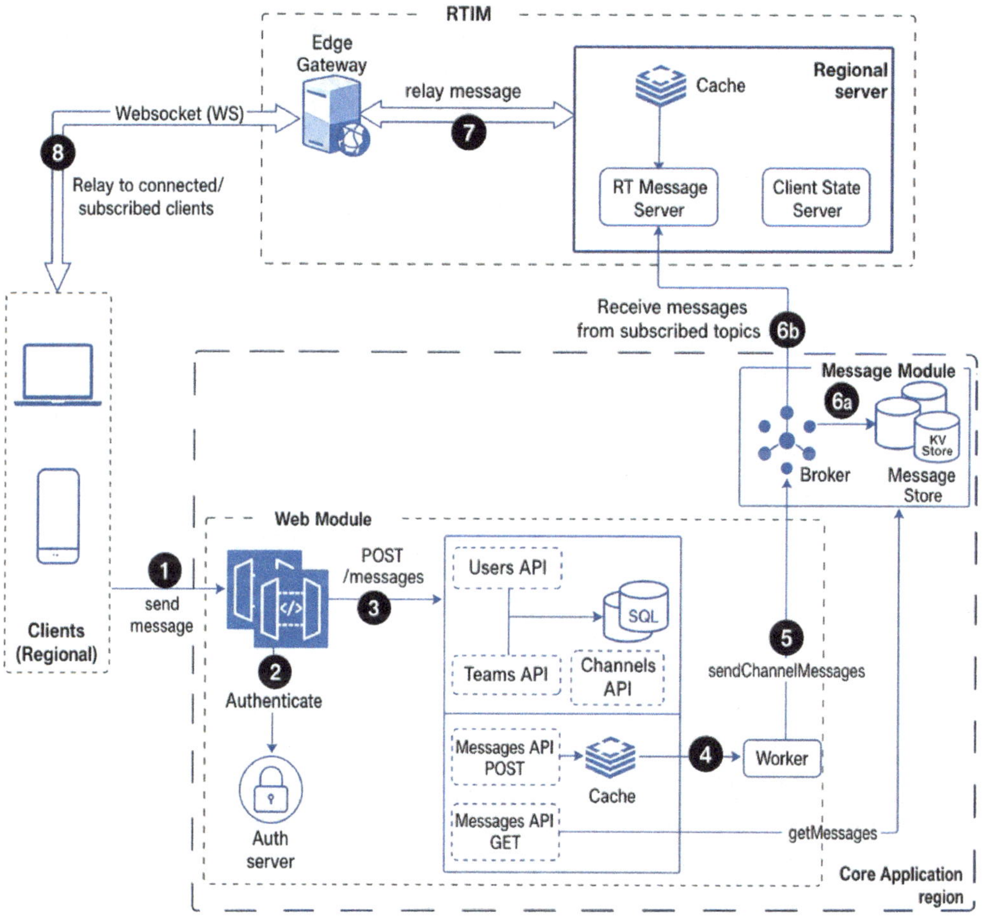

Figure 7.3: Message send journey

A user opens a channel on their client and initiates a send-message action in that channel. The request first reaches the web-module's API Gateway component. The user request is validated using an active authentication token. On a happy path, the action makes a call to the 'POST / message' API (as shown in figure).

It is important to understand that the request contains message metadata, including organization and channel information, along with the original message the user has posted. The message object is stored in memory or in a distributed cache backed by a persistent store for temporary message storage. We have considered a distributed cache in this design. At this point, we can send a success response to the client stating the message has been accepted. We should understand the trade-off of this response. If the cache fails before the message is fully processed by the worker, then the response sent earlier to the client becomes misleading. The likelihood of such a scenario with a distributed cache like Redis is minimal. [17]

A 'worker' from the cluster is constantly monitoring the cache entries. As soon as a message is received, the worker sends that message to the 'Broker' component of the 'Messaging Module' where it is placed into its desired topic determined by organization, channel_id, and other parameters, along with the metadata information associated with the message. As mentioned earlier, the broker maintains a single partition per channel identified by the channel_id. The order in which the message enters the topic is the final order assigned to the message for display. A copy of the message is saved to persistent storage here.

The regional server's 'RT Message server' within RTIM will receive a copy of the message via its channel subscription. The message will then be immediately relayed to online clients over the web and/or app.

User presence and state journey

User presence is part of the wider set of state changes that a system observes. A state change can be online, away, offline, user typing a message in a window, and so on. *Figure 7.4* captures the overall journey explaining how a change of state information is propagated to the connected user base. The details below are in the context of the user's presence journey but the same semantics apply to other mentioned states.

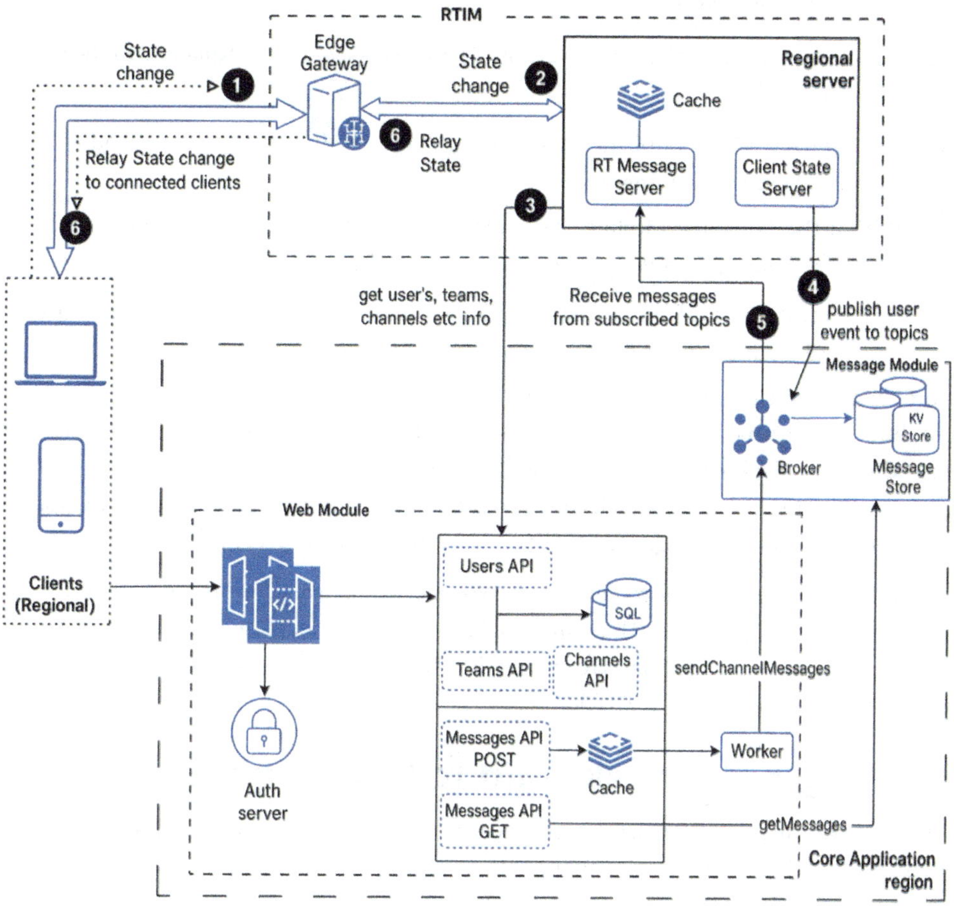

Figure 7.4: User state change, e.g., presence indicator

A client's state change is first observed by RTIM over the WebSocket connection. A corresponding state change event is sent to the 'Regional Server' of RTIM. The user's latest channel information is retrieved, and then the 'Client state server' publishes the state change event to the 'Broker' component of the 'Messaging Module' where the new event is captured in an appropriate topic. The new published information will immediately become available to the subscribing RTIM module components. Such *transient* state change events will not persist in the database.

The 'RT Message server' components in all regions that are subscribed to the topic will receive that information, and the state change is relayed to all the connected clients.

Direct and group messaging

This type of messaging takes the same route as 'User Presence journey' explained in the preceding sections. The steps are:

- The sender's RTIM publishes the message directly to the 'Message Module' via the 'Regional Server' component.
- Within the 'Message Module', separate topics/partitions will be created for handling messages from such routes. The partition key can be '`conversation_id`'.
- These messages will be persisted and delivered to clients via the same subscription journey explained above (steps 6a, 6b onwards in *Figure 7.3*).

The problem specifically asks to design a Slack-like application. The components presented here might differ from actual Slack. The most important difference to highlight is the message store. As stated earlier, Slack uses a MySQL database cluster to persist messages. Data sharding is implemented, but the shards are selected at random for resilience. Data-to-shard mappings are maintained in a separate MySQL cluster that is used for shard discovery [4].

To provide enough functional requirement coverage in this solution, the problem asks about archiving data over 5 years old. This can be achieved with the help of an ETL routine or similar process that can run on a daily basis to extract data from the persistent store and move it to other low-cost storage, for example, S3 Glacier.

Resolving bottlenecks and follow-up questions

No design stays unchanged once it meets real traffic. Some parts of this design will feel the pressure before others, and identifying those areas shows that you have thought beyond the ideal scenario. This design is no exception and can be enhanced in several ways to handle real-world demands. For example:

- Implementing rate limiting at your gateway layer to improve the security posture
- The system can be scaled to support file handling. For this purpose, a CDN backed by an S3-based approach can be implemented to host all uploaded files
- Logging and monitoring touchpoints can be made more explicit. They are needed to keep track of the system's health as well as identify tail-latency-related insights
- An acknowledgement-based message-seen marker can be built (e.g., two blue ticks)

Not every improvement needs to be part of the core design. In an interview, you will rarely have enough time to build everything, so what matters is knowing what you would add first and why. Rate limiting is a good example. It protects the services behind the gateway, so it is likely to come before less critical features. File handling, on the other hand, only becomes important if the product actually needs it, so you can reasonably leave it for later.

It is also worth thinking about where the system might struggle under real traffic. That is often where the follow-up questions begin. Imagine a channel with millions of members. One message now needs to reach a huge number of users, creating a difficult fan-out problem. Or consider thousands of long-lived WebSocket connections reconnecting at the same time after an outage. This is where the backoff and jitter approach discussed earlier becomes important. And because the design uses eventual consistency, an interviewer may also challenge you on message ordering and delivery guarantees. Thinking through these pressure points in advance helps you move from a design that works on paper to one that can handle the harder questions.

Summary

Reading about system design and actually designing a system are two very different things. This chapter bridged that gap, taking everything covered so far and applying it to one of the most commonly asked and genuinely complex design problems you will encounter - a distributed messaging system like Slack.

In this chapter we showed how to open this problem by identifying functional and non-functional requirements, scoping the design, and aligning on what the system actually needs to do before diving in. We then moved to the approach where you learned how to think through the high-level architecture, the key components, communication patterns, and design decisions that shape the entire solution. Later, you saw how the pieces come together end to end, covering message delivery, storage, real-time communication, scalability, and fault tolerance at the component level.

If you take only a few ideas from this chapter, remember the following. Real-time delivery depends as much on where the system is placed as on the protocol it uses, which is why the WebSocket layer stays close to users rather than in a single central region. Strict ordering does not always require a complex algorithm. An append-only log with one partition per channel can provide it naturally. Most importantly, good system design is about making trade-offs explicit. Whether choosing a NoSQL store for higher write throughput or accepting a short window before an acknowledged message becomes durable, explain why you made the choice and what you are giving up. That is what makes a design credible both on paper and in an interview.

The next chapter tackles a different class of problem - designing a distributed key-value datastore, one of the most fundamental and frequently tested system design challenges you will face.

References

Slack's real architecture

[1] Slack Engineering. "Real-time Messaging." https://slack.engineering/real-time-messaging/

[2] Slack Engineering. "Flannel: An Application-Level Edge Cache to Make Slack Scale." https://slack.engineering/flannel-an-application-level-edge-cache-to-make-slack-scale/

[3] Slack Engineering. "Migrating Millions of Concurrent WebSockets to Envoy." https://slack.engineering/migrating-millions-of-concurrent-websockets-to-envoy/

[4] Slack Engineering. "Scaling Datastores at Slack with Vitess." https://slack.engineering/scaling-datastores-at-slack-with-vitess/

[5] "Scaling Slack." GOTO Amsterdam 2018 conference talk. https://gotoams.nl/2018/sessions/440/scaling-slack

WebSocket transport

[6] Fette, I., & Melnikov, A. (2011). "The WebSocket Protocol." RFC 6455, IETF. https://www.rfc-editor.org/rfc/rfc6455

Messaging at scale - other platforms (further reading)

[7] Discord Engineering. "How Discord Stores Billions of Messages." https://discord.com/blog/how-discord-stores-billions-of-messages

[8] Discord Engineering. "How Discord Stores Trillions of Messages." https://discord.com/blog/how-discord-stores-trillions-of-messages

[9] Reed, R. (2012). "Scaling to Millions of Simultaneous Connections." Erlang Factory SF. [WhatsApp's connection-scaling architecture] https://www.infoq.com/presentations/whatsapp-scalability/

Message broker and the ordered log

[10] Kreps, J., Narkhede, N., & Rao, J. (2011). "Kafka: a Distributed Messaging System for Log Processing." Proceedings of the NetDB Workshop. https://notes.stephenholiday.com/Kafka.pdf

[11] Apache Kafka. "Documentation - Design (topics, partitions, and ordering guarantees)." https://kafka.apache.org/documentation/#design

Message store

[12] Lakshman, A., & Malik, P. (2010). "Cassandra: A Decentralized Structured Storage System." ACM SIGOPS Operating Systems Review, 44(2). https://www.cs.cornell.edu/projects/ladis2009/papers/lakshman-ladis2009.pdf

[13] Apache Cassandra. "Documentation - Data modeling and the storage engine." https://cassandra.apache.org/doc/latest/cassandra/architecture/storage-engine.html

Ordering, consistency and pub/sub

[14] Lamport, L. (1978). "Time, Clocks, and the Ordering of Events in a Distributed System." Communications of the ACM, 21(7). https://lamport.azurewebsites.net/pubs/time-clocks.pdf

[15] Eugster, P. T., Felber, P. A., Guerraoui, R., & Kermarrec, A.-M. (2003). "The Many Faces of Publish/Subscribe." ACM Computing Surveys, 35(2). https://doi.org/10.1145/857076.857078

Supporting infrastructure

[16] Apple. "Apple Push Notification Service." https://developer.apple.com/documentation/usernotifications

[17] Redis. "Redis Documentation." https://redis.io/docs/

[18] Elastic. "The Elastic (ELK) Stack." https://www.elastic.co/elastic-stack

8

Designing a Distributed Key-Value Datastore

A distributed key-value store is a classic design problem that may be presented in various forms, such as designing a key-value store like Redis, a key-value database like DynamoDB, or a NoSQL database. It brings together several core concepts in one example, making it a natural choice to include in the book. It is also important to understand that there are several approaches to addressing this problem and there may not be a single *correct* solution. Someone may ask you to solve this problem and they may be interested in finding out how well you identify and bring together the core components while ensuring adequate functional and non-functional coverage in your proposed solution.

In this chapter, we will cover the following topics for the distributed key-value store:

- Requirement Clarification
- Approach
- Estimates
- System design
- Resolving bottlenecks and follow-up questions

Problem statement: Design a distributed key-value store like Amazon DynamoDB. The system can see a rapid growth in the user base over time.

Understand the problem domain

A key-value store is a fundamental building block in a distributed system. It is needed to demonstrate (ultra) low-latency while dealing with data, scalability, and high availability. The system must also demonstrate a fair balance between consistency and availability as per the CAP theorem. In such a datastore, data is stored using an identifier (obviously, which has a unique value) called **a key** and then the data itself as **a value** in a <key, value> (like in the case of a hash table) pair.

The mechanism to determine the key is one of the most important steps, as it needs to uniquely identify a record as well as demonstrate low latency in overall operation. Such systems are best used for high throughput, low latency use cases, including caching, user preferences, and session storage, with Redis being a common example.

Requirement clarification

Questions you should have answers to include:

- How does the desired system work? With this question, A) you gain an understanding of the problem domain if you do not know it already, and B) if you know the problem domain, this question ensures there is no gap between your understanding and the stakeholders' expectations.
- What is the expected user volume? – This is to establish whether the system needs to support high-volume usage.
- Is consistency the prime consideration or high availability? – In reference to the CAP theorem, this question is to establish whether the system needs to demonstrate strict consistency level (ACID compliance) or eventual consistency level (BASE compliance) is just fine [2].
- What should be the latency considerations? - This is to establish whether you should use p99, as is common for such use cases, or consider something else.
- What should the read-write ratio be? - This question will help you understand if it is going to be a read-heavy system or write-heavy.

Here's a summary of the requirements:

- We need to build a distributed key-value datastore for a high-volume user base, say millions of users.
- Daily active users can be 10 million with 3x peak.
- The read/write ratio is 10:1.
- Availability and Partition Tolerance: The system needs to remain available all the time.

- The system must be reliable.
- Data should be durable.
- Data should be retained for a minimum of 5 years.
- Year-on-year data growth is 10%.
- The read operation p99 latency should be < 10ms.

Assumptions

In the interest of remaining relevant to the core functionality, we will assume appropriate authentication and authorization mechanisms are in place.

We will also assume that we are not considering large data objects (such as blobs) for the purpose of this exercise. An ideal data object size is 100 KB, which is a reasonable size for storing session data or JSON-type documents.

Approach

This system design problem is about building a data store in a distributed environment. Relevant data-storage best practices need to be maintained, including data integrity, durability, and reliability. The best way to deal with such problems is to capture individual requirement line items and then align each one with an approach that is best suited to the need.

Connecting the dots

Table 8.1 has been created for this purpose and can be used as a working reference during the design:

Requirement	Can be achieved using...
Data Partitioning to support high-volume data & user growth	'Consistent hashing'/'Virtual Node' can be a good fit. This is because of the flexibility it supports while adding/removing nodes i.e., flexibility while scaling. Also, overall time complexity for the approach is quite low, making it an ideal solution for the use case.
Key generation mechanism for the Key-value store	A key generation mechanism is needed. Any approach, from *Generating unique identifiers at scale*, from *Chapter 3* of the book, will work. A hash-based key of manageable size will be a better option because of its simplicity, lightweight nature, and speed.

Requirement	**Can be achieved using...**
Ability to store and read data	The API-based approach is a good option. It supports an easy-to-implement authentication and authorization module, if needed. It is lightweight to implement. A `get(key)` method for reading and put<key, value> method for writing will do the trick. A `put` will be sufficient because we can use it for both `create` and `update` operations.
Reliability, including during nodes' temporary & permanent failure	Write reliability: Write reliability can be improved by replicating data to more than one node during a write operation. A quorum-based technique is a great fit to improve data consistency. To deal with the scenario of temporary node(s) failure while writing, a 'sloppy quorum' and 'hinted-handoff' can be implemented. For permanent node failures or new nodes joining the cluster, a Merkle tree-based approach is a good fit. Read reliability: Read-repair while rendering a read data request and Merkle tree-based approach in the background to perform data reconciliation can be helpful.
Scalability	Consistent hashing is a suitable choice here too.
High Availability for both read and writes	The presence of multiple request-serving nodes (i.e., a consistent hash-based approach) will ensure high availability of the backend system. To achieve the level of consistency balance during such operations, a vector clock-based approach will be useful, where the client application will deal with any conflict resolution during reads, or a **last-write-wins** (**LWW**) approach can be implemented during writes.

Requirement	Can be achieved using...
Ultra low latency and durability	For latency purposes, an in-memory approach, such as Memcached, is a good fit but lacks durability. In such a case, using an **LSM (log-structured merge)** tree-based approach ensures durability and makes the solution robust. It supports both in-memory data for speed and disk-based storage technique for durability.

Table 8.1: Mapping different requirements to a target solution approach

The next important stage in understanding the problem is to work through the different estimates. The estimates will help you in many ways, including determining your cluster size, bandwidth requirements, and throughput during real-world implementation. From an interview standpoint, the storage estimates matter most. The next section provides a detailed estimation and walks through the calculation approach.

Estimates

The estimates below are anchored to the given set of inputs. The derivation steps mentioned are standard. If you are working through a different set of inputs, you can change the input. The derivation steps remain identical.

For simplicity of calculation, 1 day is approximated as 100,000 seconds, and 1 year as 400 days.

Traffic estimates:

```
Daily active users (DAU) = 10 million
Average number of writes per user per day = 10 (assumed)
Read/Write ratio = 10:1
Average number of reads per user (derived) = 10 x 10 = 100
Total number of (read + write) operations per user = 100 + 10 = 110
Total number of queries in a day = DAU x total read-write operations = 10 million
x 110 = 1,100 million
Average queries per second = 1,100 million / 100,000 = 11,000 QPS.
Peak QPS (3x average QPS) = 11,000 x 3 = 33,000 QPS
```

Throughput estimates:

```
Read/Write ratio = 10:1
Peak QPS = 33,000
Peak Read throughput = 33,000 x 10 / (10 + 1) = 30,000 QPS
Peak Write throughput = 33,000 x 1 / (10 + 1) = 3,000 QPS
Average QPS = 11,000
Average Read throughput = 10,000 QPS
Average Write throughput = 1,000 QPS
```

Storage estimates:

```
The following estimation is purely for data storage:
Average Write throughput = 1,000 QPS
A write operation will require storage space for the 'key', 'metadata', and
'value'. Assume the total unit data size of the three = 1 KB = 2^10 bytes.
Storage
per day = average write QPS x 100,000 x unit data size = 1,000 x 100,000 x 1 KB =
100 x 2^30 = 100 GB/day
Storage per year = 100 GB x 400 = 40 TB/year
Storage requirement for 5 years = 5 x 40 TB = 200 TB
With 10% year-on-year growth, the approximate storage requirement becomes 200 TB +
(200 TB x 10%) = 220 TB.
The requirement mentions that "the system should remain available all the time".
To remain aligned with this requirement, the data replication factor should be at
least 3.
Total average storage requirement for 5 years (with replication factor) = 3 x 220
TB = 660 TB.
Total peak storage requirement (3x peak) = 3 x 660 TB = 1,980 TB = approximately 2
PB.
```

The derived range for provisioning the storage layer is between 660 TB and 2 PB. To create enough headroom for peak demand and year-on-year growth, baseline storage of between 1 PB and 1.5 PB for 5 years should serve the purpose.

Looking at the throughput estimates, we can establish that the system is read-heavy. Also, we now have a better understanding about the overall storage size of the data store. Based on the information gathered, we can now start working through the design.

System design

In this section, we will first create a high-level design that provides an abstract view of the system. We will then move on to the detailed design, where our focus shifts toward more precise read and write journeys. The level of information we present in the high-level design should clearly demonstrate the wider functional coverage. Stakeholder buy-in must be received before taking it further to the detailed level.

High-level design

The high-level design for this system can be represented with a relatively simple diagram. The important aspect is the level of coverage you provide and explain during this phase. Let's look at *Figure 8.1*:

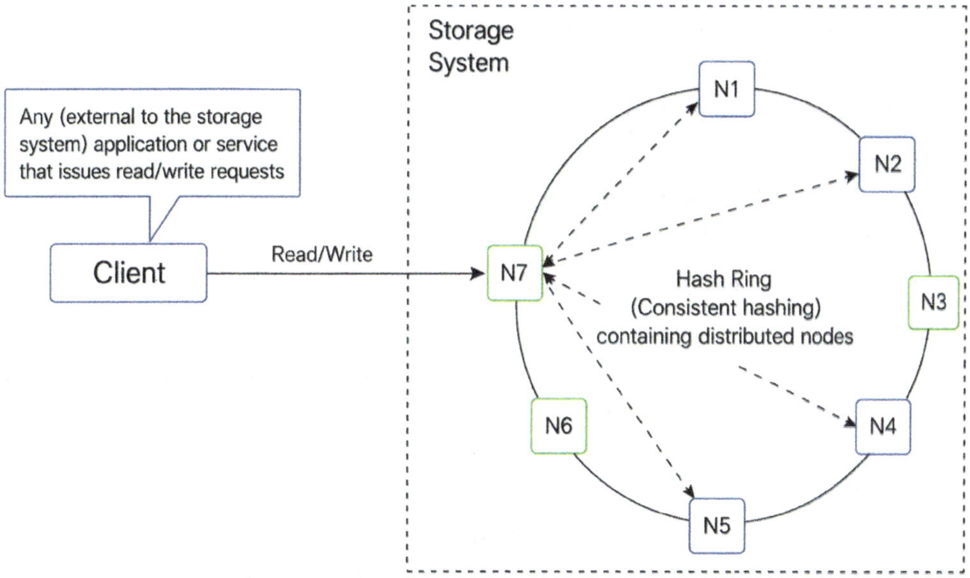

Figure 8.1: A high-level view of distributed key-value store

We'll first walk through the components shown in the diagram:

Client: It can be any application or service that is external to the storage system and that sends read or write requests to the storage system. To make this more concrete, let's consider a few examples of what a client can be. A client could be a backend service or a client library provided (or supported) by a storage system provider.

Between the client and the storage system, traffic can be routed using a load balancer that decides which coordinating node should accept the request, or by a more specialized partition-aware client library that sends requests directly to a coordinating node. When a client request is sent to a coordinator node but does not receive a response within a defined time window, it can resend the request to the storage system. In this way, if a coordinator node fails midway during processing, a new node can take over as a new coordinator to serve the replayed request.

Coordinator node (N7 in the diagram): The storage system follows a leaderless architecture, meaning all the nodes shown in the diagram share equal responsibility. Hence, any node can be a coordinator node for serving a request. Maintaining symmetry in responsibility creates greater transparency and management efficiency.

Nodes N1, N2, N4, and N5: They are the quorum nodes. Considering the data key is replicated to all the nodes; for a simplified understanding, we have used the same quorum nodes for both read and write operations. We have purposefully kept a total of 4 quorum nodes in the 7-nodes ring. This is to ensure that the combined number of nodes in the read and write quorums is greater than the total number of nodes in the system. For instance, in a seven-node system, (4+4) > 7. This helps achieve consistency in a BASE-compliant distributed environment [5].

Now, we'll dive deeper into the *Figure 8.1*.

The circle in the diagram represents a virtual ring (refer *Distributing data across nodes with hashing*, from *Chapter 3*). It will support high availability as well as easy scaling of the environment by enabling seamless node addition or removal.

As mentioned earlier, any node in the ring can accept user requests. For example, in the preceding diagram node-7 (N7) is accepting the request.

The blue-colored nodes are quorum nodes. This is to achieve consistency and to allow data replication during create and update operations. This will enhance system reliability by implementing resilience. Sloppy quorum approach with a hinted handoff is used for speed and high availability.

To maintain data consistency during reads, we have used the Read-Repair technique. The read-repair can handle temporary node failure in the system. To handle permanent node failures or new nodes joining the ring, we are also going to implement a Merkle-tree-based data synchronization mechanism as a background process to keep data in sync.

All the nodes in the cluster will communicate with one another, say, once per second, using the gossip protocol to remain failure-aware.

The preceding discussion provides a foundation that can be used to further expand our solution. Before taking a deep dive, it is worth referring back to table 8.1 to refresh requirement line items and their suggested approach. Below, we are going to elaborate on these identified approaches. This should help you understand the 'why' behind the selection of solution building blocks.

Data storage management

In a distributed environment where system scalability is of prime importance, you would like to implement data sharding to distribute data elements across multiple servers in smaller chunks. This enhances system performance and overall system maintainability. Consistent hashing (refer to *Distributing data across nodes with hashing*, from *Chapter 3*) is an appropriate approach that is suitable for the given problem. A benefit of using consistent hashing includes the seamless addition/removal of additional nodes to the system, improving overall elasticity.

Handling data inconsistencies (vector clock)

In a multi-node read-write environment, it is important that all nodes operate on data elements atomically to avoid accidental corruption. It is also important to build a mechanism that ensures the data read from disk is the most up-to-date version available. For a system that supports eventual consistency and where each node shares the same responsibility to facilitate read and write operations, it is possible that a `'put()'` request might not have propagated to all replicas before another `put()` or `get()` request is received by one of them. This might lead to result inconsistency.

For this, a robust technique is needed to:

a. Avoid such situations of data inconsistency, and
b. If it does happen, have enough information to reconcile and resolve the inconsistency to bring the system into a consistent state.

There are different ways to handle such inconsistency. Let's take a closer look at the vector clock-based approach [7]. A vector clock is a list of ('node', 'counter') pairs. It is associated with each data object. The idea here is to capture inconsistency while allowing writes from multiple nodes without performing any lock, i.e., mutex, for performance benefits. When a conflict is detected, a system-specific correction or mitigation approach can be built to achieve the desired consistency. Let's understand it with the help of a possible scenario-based example. We will use multiple diagrams (*Figures 8.2* to *8.5*) for this purpose.

In *Figures 8.2* through 8.5, C1, C2, and C3 represent distributed client applications, while N1, N2, and N4 are distributed data-serving nodes. The rightmost box in each diagram shows the vector clock state of the data element as a result of an operation.

All updates to a data element are propagated to the available nodes asynchronously. When a client reads a data element for update, it also receives the vector clock of that data element as maintained by the serving node. With every update request, the client sends the vector clock it holds for the data element.

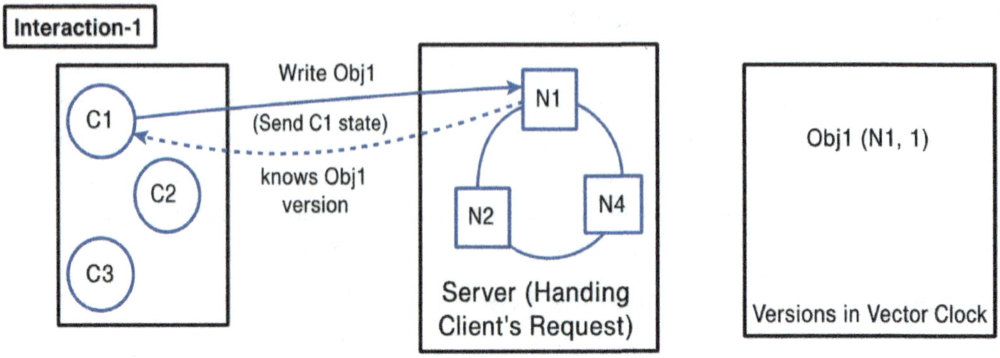

Figure 8.2: Vector clock (first write action)

In *Figure 8.2*, a user executes a write action that is picked by client C1. The client interacts with a node say, N1 to store the data object. Node N1 processes the operation, creates a vector clock for the data element and sends the success acknowledgement and object's vector clock back to C1. At this stage, all the nodes and C1 are fully aware of Obj1's vector clock. Now, client C1 reads the same data object with the intent to update the value. Let's assume that the request is picked by the same node N1 again, as shown in *Figure 8.3*:

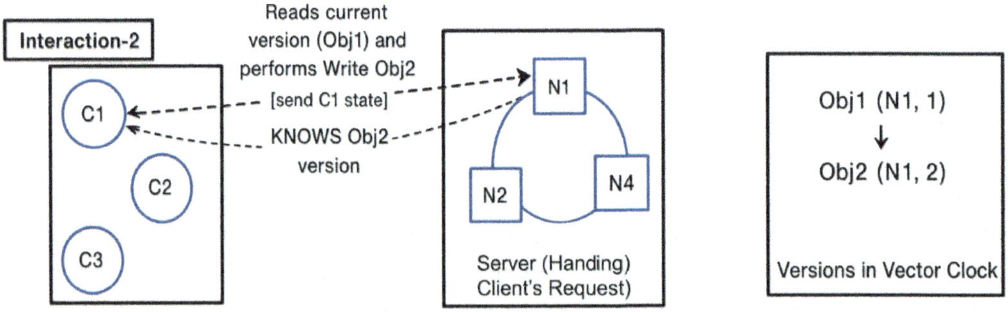

Figure 8.3: Vector clock (second write action)

In *Figure 8.3*, C1 gets the latest of 'Obj1' along with its vector clock during the read operation. C1 makes some changes in Obj1's value (referred as Obj2). An update command is issued from C1 that is picked by N1 again. Node N1 matches the received vector clock from C1. It finds everything in sync and executes the update. The data element's (now Obj2) vector clock is updated and returned as a confirmation to C1. The new vector clock for that data element is Obj1(N1, 1), Obj2 (N1, 2)

At this stage, consider two different clients, C2 and C3, performing a read operation on the data item '`Obj2`' with the intent to update its value, as shown in *Figure 8.4*.

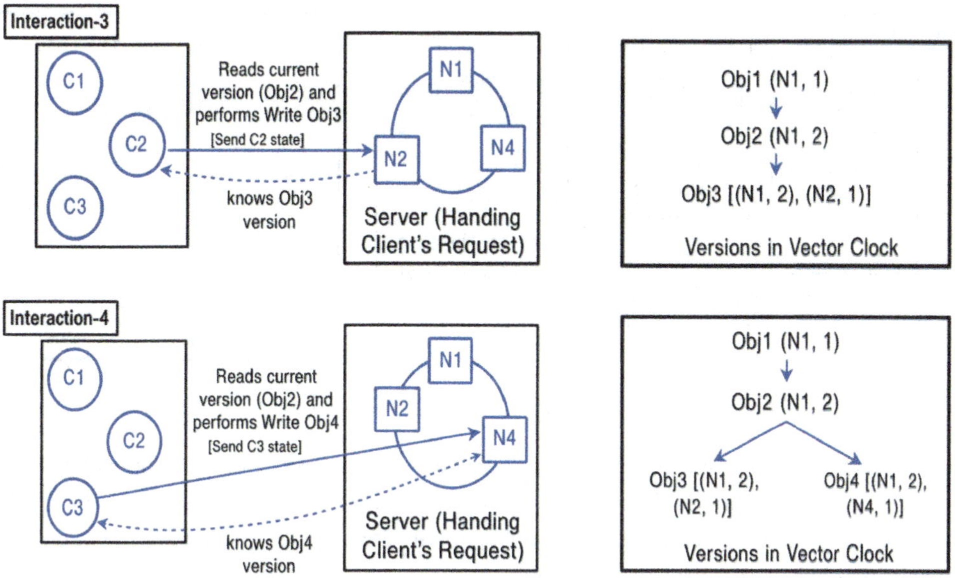

Figure 8.4: Vector clock (consecutive third and fourth write action)

As per *Figure 8.4*, both the clients C2 and C3 read the same object 'Obj2' and its associated vector clock. Assume C2 is served by node N2 and C3 is served by node N4. Both C2 and C3 make changes to the object and issue an update. When C2 sends its update and associated vector clock for the data element, node N2 executes the update. The vector clock for this data element is changed to Obj3[(N1, 2), (N2, 1)]. At this point, client C3 also issues an update on the same data element. C3 shares the currently held vector clock of the data element. The request is picked by node N4.

When N4 matches the vector clock entries received from C3 to the vector clock entry present in the data nodes, it finds a mismatch. Vector clock as per C3 still shows Obj2(N1, 2) whereas as per data nodes it is Obj3[(N1, 2), (N2, 1)]. Node N4 identifies the mismatch and creates a branch at Obj2(N1, 2). The presence of a branch highlights some discrepancy during update after the second update.

At this point, say C1 again issues a read on the same data element with the intent to update it (*Figure 8.5*).

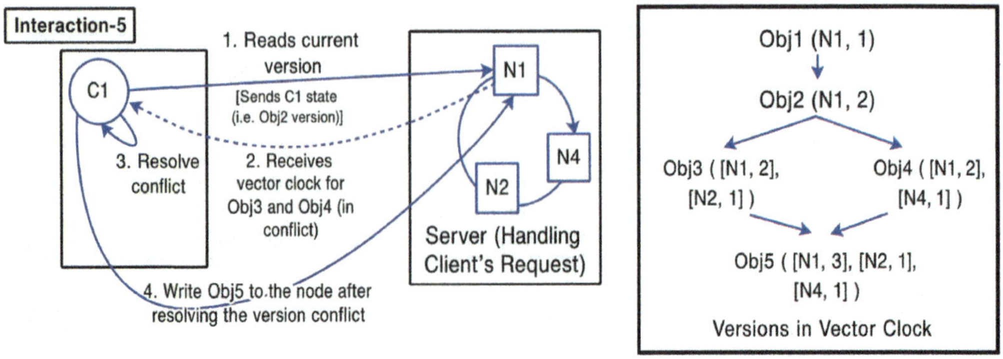

Figure 8.5: Vector clock (conflict resolution)

When C1 issues a read request as shown in *Figure 8.5*, it receives the conflicting vector clock. At this stage, client C1 can implement a conflict resolution technique to match the business requirement e.g. merge or discard the value. The updated value will be sent back to the data node with an updated vector clock, shown as Obj5. As an alternative to the client performing conflict resolution, a mechanism such as **Last Write Wins** (**LWW**) can be incorporated at the data nodes.

The size of vector clocks may grow if many servers coordinate the writes to an object. It is not likely in practice but possible in case of say, multiple server failures. Dynamo limits this growth by removing the oldest entries once the vector clock reaches a defined threshold. [1]

The benefits of this approach are that it does not require clock synchronization between participating nodes; also, there is no need to maintain multiple revisions of a data element on different nodes.

Also refer to the section *Handling data inconsistency*, in *Chapter 4*, which discusses such cases in detail.

Key-generation

As discussed in *Generating unique identifiers at scale*, *Chapter 3*, any of the techniques can be used to generate a unique ID for a distributed data store. Specific to the key-value store requirement, the key can also be generated using some hash function (refer to *Hashing and Hash Functions*, in *Chapter 2*). The benefits of a hash-based key are:

1. The same object will generate the same hash key, eliminating the need to implement deduplication within the system;
2. A smaller-sized key is better for performance, and
3. It will be difficult for someone to guess the key to retrieve any value, creating a better security posture.

Another simpler approach can be auto-increment ID generation, but it will lead us to a weaker security posture, and data might be duplicated if an appropriate mechanism is not created to handle it. In this book, we assume a hash-based key, as it provides a simple and deterministic approach to key generation that works well in a distributed environment.

> **Note**
>
> Amazon DynamoDB "treats both the key and the object supplied by the caller as an opaque array of bytes. It applies a MD5 hash on the key to generate a 128-bit identifier, which is used to determine the storage nodes that are responsible for serving the key."

Interactions

The primary function of a key-value store is to store and retrieve values. An API-based approach is most suitable because of its simplicity, distributed nature, and ability to scale. To store a value, **'put'** can be used. Similarly, to retrieve stored data, **'get'** is suitable.

Here, we are using 'put' because it can perform both create and update operations for a given key. A simple function to save data can look like **put(key, value)**. A read function will appear as **get(key)**.

If you plan to implement delete functionality, you should include the delete API as well. For the purpose of this chapter, we are limiting our focus to read and write functionality only.

Ensuring system's availability

Ensuring availability (the CAP Theorem in *Chapter 4*) means the system must remain operational and continue supporting read and write operations, even if a data center or one or more nodes in the cluster fail. In other words, there should be no interruption in interaction with the data store despite failures.

It leads us toward two important aspects of the system:

- Node state management
- Ensuring data consistency in the event of node failures

Node state management

There are a couple of ways in which node state management can be achieved:

1. A centralized approach where a dedicated system maintains nodes' state, e.g., Apache ZooKeeper. In this case, if the centralized system fails, all transactions halt. It is mainly suitable where consistency is desired over system availability and
2. A peer-to-peer approach to managing node state. It is suitable for systems where availability is more important than consistency; this also means it supports best-effort consistency. This approach is highly scalable. The gossip protocol is a widely used mechanism for implementing peer-to-peer heartbeat communication.

Gossip protocol (rumor-mongering)

Gossip-based protocols require each node of the system to periodically exchange information with a number of its peers. The choice of which peer nodes communicate with is crucial to how information gets disseminated through the network. Theoretically, a node could randomly select a sub-set of all the available nodes in the network. In practice, however, this is not feasible since it would require each node to keep a complete network membership table, which is expensive to store and maintain. Here's a simplistic journey to understand its working:

- Each node maintains a list of basic information and a heartbeat counter about other nodes in the group.
- A node will randomly select a list of neighboring nodes (from its subset list) to send a heartbeat event.
- If neighboring nodes return a reply, the heartbeat counter is increased; all good. If a neighboring node does not reply, then it is 'marked' by the initiator node.

The initiator node then sends (gossip) this 'no-response' information to a few other randomly selected nodes from the subset list. These new nodes will then send a heartbeat message to the 'marked' node for an answer. If an answer is received, all good. If no answer is received, the 'marked' node is considered dead and removed from the cluster. Since network partitioning is a default in case of a distributed system, the randomly selected nodes should be from more than one data center for an optimal result.

Communication with this removed node will be reinstated once it recovers and starts sending its state information again.

Ensuring data consistency in distributed systems

A node failure, as explained in the previous section, can be temporary or permanent. Both of these situations should be handled appropriately for maintaining data consistency, system availability, and resilience. To minimize the impact in case of failure, data must be replicated efficiently across other nodes. 'Sloppy Quorum' is a technique that is used in conjunction with 'Hinted-handoff' to deal with temporary failures. Let us expand these concepts.

Quorum and sloppy-quorum for data replication

In a **Quorum based approach**, all the designated nodes from the distributed cluster participate in accepting both read and write requests. Each node is grouped (or paired if desired) with some other communicating nodes within the distributed system to participate in voting to allow or deny any transaction request. There can exist more than one quorum in a distributed system to decide upon write/read requests. In quorum consensus with a total of 'N' nodes, usually, there are 'K' number of 'write consensus nodes' or quorum nodes for write operations and "M" number of "read consensus nodes" i.e., quorum nodes for read operations, such that (K + M) > N.

This means that if you add the read and write quorum node counts, the result will be greater than the total number of distributed nodes. This is to allow some overlap between read and write consensus nodes. This overlap means that when a read operation is performed, at least one node from the write quorum participates in the read consensus. This ensures at least one read quorum node is aware of the latest changes that have occurred for a data item.

In quorum consensus, for a write operation to be successful, all quorum nodes, participating in the write quorum, must vote affirmative. The same applies to a read request. The problem with classic quorum consensus is—if a voter node from a quorum becomes unavailable temporarily or permanently, it will disturb the corresponding operation. There can exist more than one quorum in the system. However, to execute a specific task, one of the available quorums is used. Let's understand the concept with the help of *Figure 8.6*.

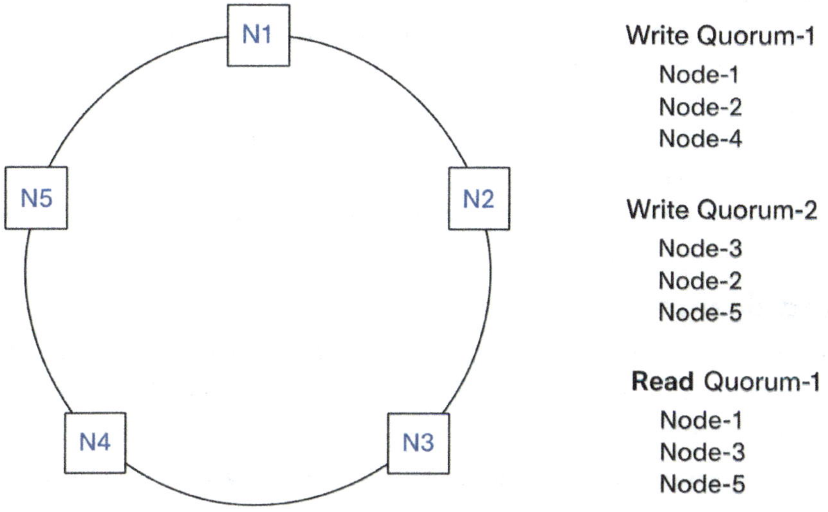

Figure – 8.6: An example quorum ring

As shown in *Figure 8.6*, the quorum size is kept as 3. All of them are participating. Meaning, at least 3 consenting nodes must vote for a transaction to take effect. You can choose to keep the participation size to any number suitable for your system. For example, if you choose participation size to be 2, then at least 2 out of the 3 quorum nodes must vote true for a transaction. Fewer consenting nodes mean a faster response time, leading to better availability and improved latency for clients. The trade-off with fewer consenting nodes is weaker consistency. It might end up consuming more time in performing inconsistency resolution internally in case there are a smaller number of consenting nodes.

As we increase the number of consenting nodes, the response time degrades, but you get better consistency. If all nodes participate in voting, then the system will become consistent. Our use-case here is about availability over strong consistency. Figure 8.6 shows there are two separate write quorums and one read quorum that exists. In this case, if a read request is made at node N4, the node will consult all the read quorum nodes (Nodes 1, 3, and 5) before returning data to the user. If you add a random node (N6) somewhere in the ring and assume a write request is received by the newly added node, it will either take a consent from 'write quorum – 1' or 'write quorum – 2' before allowing the write.

In the case of classic quorum consensus, if Node 2 is down, then all write operations will halt, as this node participates in both the write quorums. But if Node 1 goes down instead, then all reads and some writes will be impacted as the read quorum, as per our example, dies. If your system does not require this rigid behavior of classic quorum and requires some flexibility to absorb partial failures of consenting nodes, then you can implement sloppy quorum instead.

Sloppy Quorum is based on the quorum consensus technique with added flexibility for quorum participating nodes. In this approach, there is still a minimum number of designated nodes that should agree/vote upon a distributed transaction for it to take effect. But if a designated voting node is not active, its voting right is delegated to another active node in the interim. The interim node maintains a track (also called *hints*) of all the transactions it has facilitated on behalf of the unavailable node. When the designated voting node is back online, 'Hinted Handoff,' an anti-entropy mechanism, is used to replicate all tracking data (hints) from the interim node back to the main (originally targeted) node.

Detailed design

The detailed design explains read and write interactions and their impact on a node. At this stage, we can abstract the underlying multi-node environment setup including quorum consensus, sloppy quorum, consistent hashing and other related points discussed earlier.

Two concepts, SSTable and write-ahead log, are used extensively in the detailed design. We will first explain these concepts and then delve into the design.

SSTable (Sorted String Table): An SSTable is a file that contains a set of arbitrary key-value pairs [12]. Once written to the disk, it is immutable. To search for a data item within the files, the search starts with the most recently created file and can proceed sequentially to older files. To improve search performance a separate '*Index*' table can be created. The index table might contain key-offset information as metadata for lookup that can be used to facilitate random reads.

Write-ahead log (WAL): Also known as a 'commit log,' it is a durability and recovery primitive. It is a log file that sequentially holds (append-only) description of an action that results in modification of a data state onto the disk or in-memory storage. Such action descriptions are first appended to the WAL and then applied to their native storage. It improves data durability in case of data store loss. The log file can be used to rebuild the datastore. WAL also improves write speed because the system does not need to perform a real-time database or disk write for every transaction to commit.

Let's take a look at the two journeys. We are going to start with the write action first, followed by read action. This is because it is easier to visualize the read action when you know how the data has been stored.

Write journey

In the write journey, a user's request to store an object is picked by a client application that interfaces the interaction with the data store. The end-to-end write journey is depicted and explained with the help of *Figure 8.7*.

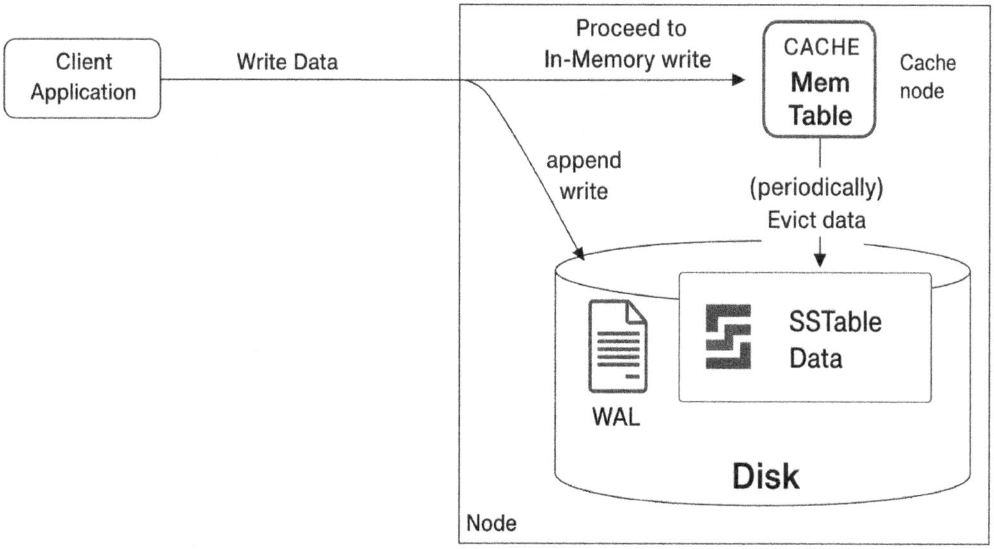

Figure 8.7: Write journey for a key-value store (single node action)

Let's walk through the key steps:

- The client invokes a write request to a node in the cluster (hash ring).
- The request receiving node sends the request to quorum nodes.
- Each request-receiving node then performs the following actions:
  - First, it captures the action in a write-ahead log (commit log) persistent store or file.
  - Then, the data is written to a memory-bound cache (e.g., Memcached) for fast access.
  - To keep the load of the memory-bound cache manageable, the node performs data eviction periodically to the associated SSTable. At the time of data eviction into the table, it can maintain a Bloom filter. This will help with quick retrieval during a read-bound operation when a data object is not found in memory. (explained later in this chapter)
- 'Write' response is sent to the client.

What happens if the eviction action results in an error? In that case, the partially created SSTable is removed from the system during the next run. WAL entries will be used to re-create the data structure and then flush it off to create a new SSTable.

Read journey

When a read request arrives at a node, the request is sent to the cache and then to the SSTables (*Figure 8.8*). Bloom's filter is used to help identify a subset of files on the disk that should serve the read request [14]. If the data is found in memory, no further action is needed. Otherwise, data from the SSTable will be used to fulfill the read journey.

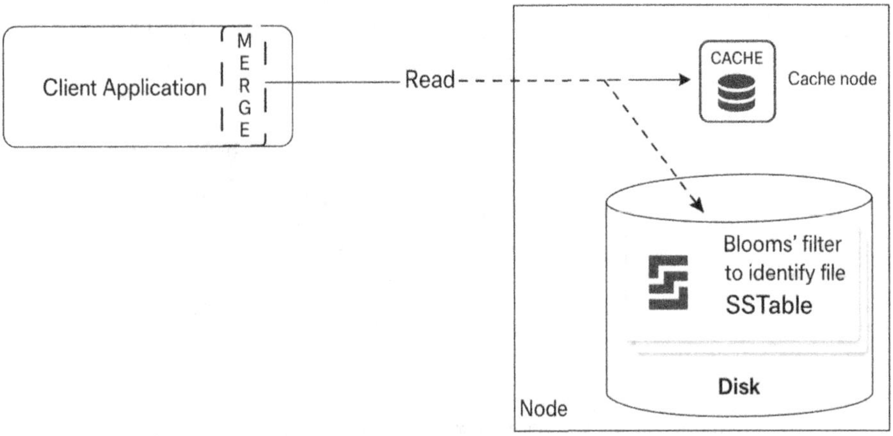

Figure 8.8: Read journey for a key-value store (single node action)

The 'Merge' action on the client is to enable either cache or disk behavior. The application first checks whether the requested object is available in the cache or not. If the object is found in the cache, then it is returned; else, SSTable disk files are queried in sequential order for the same object. To avoid costly sequential traversal of files during data file identification, Bloom's filter and/or other relevant approaches, e.g., B-trees, can be implemented for data file lookup.

Storage layout in a physical disk

In the context of the key-value store, let us elaborate on the options that can be used to optimize the storage of data objects on a physical disk with the help of a few available techniques [12]:

- **Row-Based data storage:** This is the classic relational database approach. Here data is structured as tables. The tables represent a single entity as well as their relational tables. The data will be prepared, somewhere within your application, to match the desired tabular (tuple) structure, and then for persistence, it will be flushed onto a disk. Data that is stored in this fashion takes contiguous disk space allowing faster read/write access per row. But to access data by column, you will require additional effort and will not get the same level of performance advantage by default.
- **Column based data storage:** It follows the same principle as in the case of row-based storage except for the fact that data here is not organized into the disk as tuples; rather, it is stored by grouping column information together. This kind of data storage takes contiguous disk space, allowing faster read/write access per column. But to access an entire row of data, you will require additional effort and will not get the same level of performance advantage by default.
- **Log Structured Merge Trees:** This is also referred to as LSM Trees. These use a combination of in-memory and disk storage to achieve data read/write. In this approach, any write will be first appended into a commit log file hosted on the disk, for durability. The data state change will be first captured in-memory. Any read during this period will be served from the in-memory copy of the data, providing a significant performance boost.
  Periodically, this data, held in memory, will be flushed to disk as immutable, append-only data files called SSTables, or sorted string tables. It allows sequential data file object creation that is fast to access.

  Since the data is stored in immutable, append-only files, compaction will be performed periodically to remove duplicate or deleted data. Once the compaction process is done, a new data file will be created, and the files compacted will be removed from the system. The approach does show very high write latency and a good read latency but also suffers from a high tail latency problem because of the cost involved during the compaction process.

Resolving bottlenecks and follow-up questions

A single popular key can overwhelm a node (hotspot/celebrity problem). To overcome this, application-side in-memory caching for known keys can be used. Also, using vNodes with the proposed consistent hashing approach can create a better balance for hash keys.

For background data reconciliation, a Merkle tree-based approach is proposed, but a full-tree repair can saturate the cluster. A scheduled incremental repair during off-peak periods should be planned and implemented.

Also, LSM-tree stores can stall on background compactions during heavy writes. Tiered compaction for a write-heavy system and leveled compaction for a read-heavy system are suggested. Dedicated compute resources for the LSM-tree compaction process can improve resource utilization.

Summary

A distributed key-value datastore sits at the heart of some of the most critical infrastructure in the world, from session management to configuration storage to caching at scale. This chapter worked through how to design one from scratch, using the same structured approach you would be expected to apply in real-world problem-solving or an interview setting.

In this chapter, you learned how to scope the problem by identifying what the datastore needs to support in terms of read/write patterns, consistency guarantees, availability requirements, and scale targets. You also explored how to think through the high-level architecture, including partitioning strategies, replication, and the core trade-offs between consistency and availability. Finally, you gained a deeper understanding of the design by exploring how the components come together, covering data distribution, conflict resolution, fault tolerance, and the mechanics of reads and writes across a distributed environment.

The next chapter shifts into a completely different domain: designing a real-time bidding system for advertising, where millisecond latency and massive throughput are not nice-to-haves but hard requirements.

References

The foundational design:

[1] DeCandia, G., Hastorun, D., Jampani, M., Kakulapati, G., Lakshman, A., Pilchin, A., Sivasubramanian, S., Vosshall, P., & Vogels, W. (2007). "Dynamo: Amazon's Highly Available Key-value Store." Proceedings of the 21st ACM Symposium on Operating Systems Principles (SOSP '07). [Foundational - the single most important paper for this chapter; the source of leaderless replication, sloppy quorum, hinted handoff, and the consistent-hashing-with-vnodes design.] `https://www.allthingsdistributed.com/files/amazon-dynamo-sosp2007.pdf`

[2] Vogels, W. (2009). "Eventually Consistent." Communications of the ACM, 52(1), 40-44. [Foundational - explains the eventual-consistency (BASE) model that this datastore relies on.] `https://dl.acm.org/doi/10.1145/1435417.1435432`

Partition and consistent hashing:

[3] Karger, D., Lehman, E., Leighton, T., Panigrahy, R., Levine, M., & Lewin, D. (1997). "Consistent Hashing and Random Trees: Distributed Caching Protocols for Relieving Hot Spots on the World Wide Web." Proceedings of the 29th ACM Symposium on Theory of Computing (STOC '97). [Foundational - the original consistent-hashing paper.] `https://www.cs.princeton.edu/courses/archive/fall09/cos518/papers/chash.pdf`

[4] Stoica, I., Morris, R., Karger, D., Kaashoek, M. F., & Balakrishnan, H. (2001). "Chord: A Scalable Peer-to-peer Lookup Service for Internet Applications." SIGCOMM '01. [Recommended - ring-based key lookup, the structure the chapter's hash ring is built on.] `https://pdos.csail.mit.edu/papers/ton:chord/paper-ton.pdf`

Replication and quorum consensus:

[5] Gifford, D. K. (1979). "Weighted Voting for Replicated Data." Proceedings of the 7th ACM Symposium on Operating Systems Principles (SOSP '79). [Foundational – the original quorum-consensus paper; the basis for the R + W > N rule used in the chapter.] `https://dl.acm.org/doi/10.1145/800215.806583`

[6] Herlihy, M. (1986). "A Quorum-Consensus Replication Method for Abstract Data Types." ACM Transactions on Computer Systems, 4(1). [Recommended - generalises quorum consensus beyond simple read/write registers.] `https://dl.acm.org/doi/10.1145/6306.6308`

Conflict detection:

[7] Lamport, L. (1978). "Time, Clocks, and the Ordering of Events in a Distributed System." Communications of the ACM, 21(7), 558-565. [Foundational – establishes happens-before ordering; the conceptual root of vector clocks.] https://lamport.azurewebsites.net/pubs/time-clocks.pdf

[8] Mattern, F. (1989). "Virtual Time and Global States of Distributed Systems." Proceedings of the International Workshop on Parallel and Distributed Algorithms. [Foundational - the canonical vector-clock paper; introduces the (node, counter) vector used in the chapter.]

[9] Preguica, N., Baquero, C., et al. (2010). "Dotted Version Vectors: Logical Clocks for Optimistic Replication." arXiv:1011.5808. [Recommended - the dotted-version-vector refinement the chapter mentions as an extension of vector clocks.] https://arxiv.org/abs/1011.5808

Anti-entropy and gossip protocols:

[10] Demers, A., Greene, D., Hauser, C., Irish, W., Larson, J., Shenker, S., Sturgis, H., Swinehart, D., & Terry, D. (1987). "Epidemic Algorithms for Replicated Database Maintenance." Proceedings of the 6th ACM Symposium on Principles of Distributed Computing (PODC '87). [Foundational - the canonical paper on gossip and anti-entropy; defines anti-entropy vs rumor-mongering.] https://dl.acm.org/doi/10.1145/41840.41841

[11] Merkle, R. C. (1987). "A Digital Signature Based on a Conventional Encryption Function." Advances in Cryptology - CRYPTO '87. [Foundational - the hash-tree (Merkle tree) construction used for replica comparison.] https://link.springer.com/chapter/10.1007/3-540-48184-2_32

LSM-trees, SSTables, and Bloom filters:

[12] O'Neil, P., Cheng, E., Gawlick, D., & O'Neil, E. (1996). "The Log-Structured Merge-Tree (LSM-Tree)." Acta Informatica, 33(4). [Foundational - the write-optimised storage structure behind the commit log and SSTable design in the chapter.] https://www.cs.umb.edu/~poneil/lsmtree.pdf and Todd Lipcon, Cloudera, [Just Enough Distributed Systems To Be Dangerous (slides 21 - 31)] https://static.last.fm/johan/nosql-20090611/intro_nosql.pdf

[13] Chang, F., Dean, J., Ghemawat, S., Hsieh, W. C., Wallach, D. A., Burrows, M., Chandra, T., Fikes, A., & Gruber, R. E. (2006). "Bigtable: A Distributed Storage System for Structured Data." OSDI '06. [Foundational - the origin of the SSTable (Sorted String Table) format.] https://research.google/pubs/pub27898/

[14] Bloom, B. H. (1970). "Space/Time Trade-offs in Hash Coding with Allowable Errors." Communications of the ACM, 13(7), 422-426. [Foundational - the Bloom filter used to avoid unnecessary SSTable disk reads.] `https://dl.acm.org/doi/10.1145/362686.362692`

Real world implementations:

[15] Lakshman, A., & Malik, P. (2010). "Cassandra: A Decentralized Structured Storage System." ACM SIGOPS Operating Systems Review, 44(2). [Recommended - a production Dynamo-lineage store; combines the Dynamo distribution model with a Bigtable storage engine.] `https://www.cs.cornell.edu/projects/ladis2009/papers/lakshman-ladis2009.pdf`

[16] Elhemali, M., Gallagher, N., Gordon, N., et al. (2022). "Amazon DynamoDB: A Scalable, Predictably Performant, and Fully Managed NoSQL Database Service." USENIX Annual Technical Conference (ATC '22). [Recommended - how the original Dynamo design evolved into the managed DynamoDB service fifteen years later.] `https://www.usenix.org/conference/atc22/presentation/elhemali`

[17] Apache Cassandra Documentation - Architecture: storage engine, dynamo-style replication, and read repair. `https://cassandra.apache.org/doc/latest/cassandra/architecture/`

Background and further readings:

[18] Kleppmann, M. (2017). Designing Data-Intensive Applications. O'Reilly Media. [Recommended - Chapter 5 (Replication) and Chapter 6 (Partitioning) cover the entire chapter's territory in accessible depth.]

[19] Gilbert, S., & Lynch, N. (2002). "Brewer's Conjecture and the Feasibility of Consistent, Available, Partition-Tolerant Web Services." ACM SIGACT News, 33(2). [Recommended - the formal statement of the CAP theorem that frames the consistency-vs-availability trade-off in the chapter.] `https://dl.acm.org/doi/10.1145/564585.564601`

[20] Vogels, W. - "All Things Distributed" (blog by the Amazon CTO). Ongoing commentary on the Dynamo lineage and large-scale storage. `https://www.allthingsdistributed.com/`

9

Designing a Real-Time Bidding (RTB) System for Advertising

Every technology that touches millions of people at scale has a system working quietly behind it. Real-time bidding (RTB) is no different. Understanding how that system works is not just a technical exercise. It is the foundation for understanding how modern digital advertising operates, where its vulnerabilities lie, and how better systems can be designed around it. [1][2]

Targeting consumers through online creative content to promote products and services is a standard practice in today's digital economy. This practice, commonly known as advertising (or simply ads), has evolved into a multi-billion-dollar industry.

At its core, digital advertising relies on identifying and targeting users based on specific characteristics. These characteristics can include demographic information, interests, and (commonly) browsing behavior. For instance, if you frequently visit shopping websites, you are more likely to see ads with shopping offers or some new trends.

This chapter takes you through a detailed understanding of the business and then presents an approach to designing such a system.

In this chapter, we will design this solution by following these steps:

- Requirement clarification
- Estimation
- System design
- Resolving bottlenecks and follow-up questions

Problem statement: Design a real-time bidding system for digital advertising that processes billions of advertising requests per day and runs an auction to select the highest-value eligible advertisement within milliseconds.

Along with the real-world applications, this problem may appear in system design interviews as well. Before diving into the design, let us first build a foundation by understanding the system basics and familiarizing ourselves with a few key terms.

Understand the problem domain

In the early days, consumer targeting was relatively static, where advertisers and platform (website) owners would make offline arrangements in advance to display ads. For this, user data was analyzed beforehand, and ads were placed based on the insight.

RTB takes this a step further, enabling advertisers to compete for ad placement in real time. It happens at the moment when a user opens an app or visits a site. It offers advertisers greater flexibility to perform precise targeted marketing based on a user's current behavior rather than the previous day's behavior. *Figure 9.1* captures the high-level process overview of RTB:

Figure 9.1: Process overview of an RTB System

Let's understand the workflow, step-by-step:

- A user visits a publisher's website or opens an app, creating an available ad space.
- The user's information, such as browsing history, device, and location, is shared with potential advertisers within regional regulatory compliance boundaries.
- Advertisers then evaluate this information to determine whether the user matches their target audience profile.
- In case of a match, advertisers will submit bids in real time for the opportunity to display their ad.
- A winning bid is declared instantly and the winning advertiser's ad will be displayed on the publisher's site or app to the user.

For an opportunity, not all advertisers participate in every auction. Potential advertisers for an ad space are determined by multiple factors, including bid price, content relevance, bidding history, and geographical location, among others.

Below, we have described the different entities involved in the overall journey, highlighting their roles and responsibilities:

- **Advertiser or bidder:** They are the companies or agencies that promote their products or services through ads. They are responsible for creating and owning the ad content. Such content is also referred to as creative content, creative assets, or campaigns.
- **Demand-Side Platform (DSP):** It is a third-party system that advertisers use to publish their ad campaigns. It allows them to upload creative content and define the condition under which their ads should be shown (also known as campaign targeting or trigger criteria). DSPs act on behalf of advertisers during the bidding process by automatically responding to bidding opportunities per impression level. The advantages that a DSP brings for advertisers include:
    - Advertisers do not need to register with or integrate separately with multiple ad networks, i.e., exchanges.
    - Campaigns and their criteria can be optimized at a much finer level and with greater frequency because of access to detailed impression-level logs.
    - Advertisers can focus on their core business rather than managing a complex ad delivery system
    - DSPs are flexible and customizable, allowing advertisers to tailor strategies that suit their specific goals. For example, advertisers traditionally apply a frequency cap that limits the number of times the same ad is shown to a user. With DSPs, the frequency cap can be adjusted for a user segment, an individual user, or even globally, increasing the overall flexibility and ad efficiency.
- **Ad Exchange:** It is the central coordinator that connects advertisers' needs with publishers' needs (later in this chapter, we'll look into this in more detail). Its primary role is to match the demand for ad space (from advertisers) with the available supply (from publishers). When a user visits a site, the publisher sends an ad space availability request through a supply-side platform (SSP) to the ad exchange for fulfillment. The ad exchange then broadcasts this request to multiple advertisers via their demand-side platforms (DSPs). The ad exchange receives bids from DSPs for eligible campaigns and runs an auction among them. It selects a winning bid in real time, identifies the winning advertiser, and notifies them. The winning ad is then sent to the publisher for display to the user. In addition, the ad exchange tracks ad performance, including data related to ad impressions, ad clicks, and other important parameters.

- **Supply-Side Platform (SSP):** It is used by publishers to manage and monetize their ad space. In simple terms, it is the system that announces the ad slot availability to the ad exchange for auction. SSPs work as a central management platform for publishers providing them with greater control over how their inventory is sold, to maximize their revenue. It may include:
    - Set the minimum acceptable bid price (also called reserve price)
    - Apply pricing rules for particular advertisers
    - Introduce preferences towards certain bidders (bid bias)
- **Publisher (or Seller):** A publisher is an online platform, a website (e.g., Facebook, Yahoo, Hotmail), or a mobile app that displays content to users. Publishers monetize their content by selling ad space alongside it. This is the space for which bidding is performed. The winning bid's content is displayed in this space.

Now that we have discussed the core entities, it is important to understand some key terms used in an ad bidding system. Each time an ad appears on a publisher's site (e.g., Facebook) it is called an **impression**. Similarly, click-through rate (CTR) measures the ratio of users who clicked the ad to the total number of users who viewed it. This rate is mainly used by a bidder to make a prediction (based on history) that helps them associate a price with an ad.

CTR = (Clicks/Impression) x 100%

> **Tip**
>
> Nowadays there are multiple machine learning models that exist to help with the CTR predictions.

There's also the conversion rate (CVR), which is used to measure how often users complete a desired action after clicking an ad. The desired action can be to buy a product, participate in a survey, etc.

CVR = (Conversion/Clicks) x 100%

Requirement clarification

A real-time bidding system consists of multiple entities, as explained earlier while discussing the domain. Designing each entity can be a system design problem in its own right. Therefore, the first step is to draw a boundary around what you will actually build. In this chapter, our focus is on the ad exchange and its integration with the DSPs, so the questions below are aimed at pinning down exactly what that piece must do before a single box is drawn.

Q: How does the desired system work? – By asking this question:

A) You gain an understanding of the problem domain, if you don't know it already, and

B) If you know the problem domain, this question helps identify any gaps in your understanding and design expectations.

Sample answer: In a real-time bidding system, advertisers (also called bidders) bid against other advertisers to secure a space on publishers' sites to publish their campaigns. We want to build an ad exchange that can facilitate bidding in real time.

Q: Does the bidding happen per user impression/site visitor?

Sample answer: Yes

Q: What is the expected volume the system will experience?

Sample answer: There are over 10 billion site visitors with 10% DAU. The click-through rate is 0.1%, and the conversion rate (CVR) is 1%.

Q: Should we consider only static campaigns or videos as well?

Sample answer: It can be either static or video.

Q: How long should it take for an auction to execute?

Sample answer: We are talking about a highly competitive system here, and hence, the auction response should be in milliseconds.

Q: For how long should we maintain the data in our system?

Sample answer: 5 years.

The answers above may look like small talk, but each one quietly sets a design constraint: billions of requests, a sub-second auction, and five years of data to keep. Gathering them into a clean list is what turns a vague brief into something you can design against.

Requirements summary

Based on the information gathered during the clarification phase, we can summarize our functional and non-functional requirements as follows.

Functional requirement:

- The system should allow real-time bidding by multiple bidders (DSPs) for an ad space per user impression on a site or app.
- The most suitable bid winner should be declared, and the winning campaign should be rendered in the ad space.
- The winner should receive a notification.

Non-Functional requirement:

- The system should cater to a very high-volume user base.
- The overall auction process should be completed in sub-second time.
- The system should be highly available, as any downtime will have cost implications for all the parties.
- The system should support a distributed environment.
- Analytics and reporting are the key capabilities that the system must support.
- A minimum of 5 years of data should be stored.

Assumptions

No design happens in a vacuum, and stating your assumptions out loud keeps others on the same page as you. Naming them also protects you later, when a follow-up question probes something you deliberately left out of scope. For the stakeholders to relate to your proposed approach, a number of assumptions regarding other entities should be made clearly and agreed with. We have captured some assumptions that can create a good working foundation as follows:

- Bidder registration processes are available and aligned with the requirements.
- A bid request is sent to all the DSPs registered to the ad exchange.
- DSP-side asset (campaign) storage and their management can be assumed available for this task.
- DSPs use a CDN offering that is available to the publisher's site for accessing campaigns/creative content.
- For an impression, DSPs have all the information needed to decide whether a campaign can participate in the latest bid.
- Campaign expiry is implicitly time-bound. Once expired, the bidding journey is triggered again for the ad space.
- A few functionalities non-core for an exchange including payments, admin tasks to manage users, bids and so on, elaborated separately.
- A bidder can use multiple DSPs to publish the same campaign.
- The end-to-end observability journey will be detailed through appropriate analytics use cases.

Estimation

For a system of this magnitude, some core estimates must be made. These estimates will help you plan resources appropriately. They also allow stakeholders to assess the thoroughness of your answer. To perform the estimates, we will use *Table 6.2* from *Chapter 6*, when needed.

For a real-time bidding system, two numbers matter most – one, how much data we have to store, and two, how many requests per second we have to serve. We will work through storage first, one data type at a time, and then arrive at the request rate.

> **Note**
>
> For the purpose of this exercise and to keep the calculations simple, we have considered the following:
>
> 1 day = 100,000 seconds, and 1 year = 400 days.

Storage estimates for Ad exchange

Storage is the natural place to start, because a bidding system writes constantly. Every impression, every click, and every conversion will make its way to the persistent storage, and each stream grows at a very different rate, so sizing them separately shows where the real weight sits.

Ad impression logs storage

Impressions are by far the highest-volume event, since one is created every time an ad slot appears. If ten percent of ten billion daily visitors generate an impression, that is a billion logs a day.

```
No. of requests per day = 10 billion x 10% = 1 billion = 2^30
Assume an average impression log size = 1KB = 2^10
Daily storage need for impression log = 2^30 x 2^10 = 2^40 = 1TB per day
Yearly storage = 400 x 1TB = 400TB
Storage requirement for 5 years = 5 x 400 TB = 2000 TB = 2 PB
```

At one kilobyte per impression log, the storage need is a terabyte a day, and roughly two petabytes over five years. Hold onto that number, because impression logs are what dominate storage, and every later decision about databases and retention has to answer to it.

CTR storage

An ad exchange also maintains click information for displayed ads. Clicks are a much rarer event than impressions, and the numbers show it. With a click-through rate of 0.1%, a billion impressions produce only a million clicks a day. Including CTR storage in your estimates demonstrates subject matter depth.

```
CTR is 0.1%
No. of clicks per day = 1 billion x 0.1% = 1 million
Assume the log entry size per click = 100 bytes
Daily storage for clicks = 100 x 2²⁰ = 100MB
Yearly storage = 400 x (100 x 2²⁰) = 40 x 2³⁰ = 40GB
Storage requirement for 5 years = 5 x 40 GB = 200 GB
```

Even over five years, that is about two hundred gigabytes, orders of magnitude smaller than the impression logs. The point of estimating it is less about the size and more about demonstrating that the exchange also has to capture what happens after an ad is shown.

CVR storage

An ad exchange additionally maintains the click conversion information. CTR and CVR are used by the exchange to create a better prediction. The following calculations might not add much to the total storage capacity but it provides a comprehensive storage coverage that might create a lasting impression for your design setting.

```
CVR is 1% of CTR
No. of conversions per day = 1% of 1 million = 0.01million = 0.01 x 2²⁰
Assume the log entry size per conversion = 200 bytes
Daily storage for conversion = 200 x 0.01 x 2²⁰ = 2 x 2²⁰ = 2MB
Yearly storage = 400 x 2 MB = 800 MB
Storage requirement for 5 years = 5 x 800 MB = 4 GB
```

The additional four gigabytes is small compared with the impression logs, but it completes the picture. CTR and CVR provide the data the exchange later uses to predict clicks and conversions.

QPS for Ad exchange

Storage tells us how large the system becomes over time, while throughput tells us how much traffic it needs to handle at any given moment. For an auction that must complete within milliseconds, the request rate is what shapes the system's most time-sensitive path.

Average ad requests per day = 1 billion

QPS = 1 billion / (24 x 60 x 60) = 1 billion / 100000 = **10K per second**

That puts the real-time auction path at roughly 10,000 requests per second, every one of which has to clear within the sub-second target.

These numbers are not just an exercise. Two petabytes of impression logs, a much smaller stream of clicks and conversions, and 10,000 auctions per second define the constraints the architecture must handle. Now that we understand the scale of the problem, we can start designing the system to meet these requirements.

System design

So far, we have collected the functional and non-functional requirements and worked through the estimates to plan for backend resources. In the following section, we will walk through the high-level design and then take a deeper dive into the detailed design. Although our focus is on the ad exchange, we have included some building blocks highlighting DSP-side functions as well. This allows us to present the main interacting modules and explain their relevance in the design.

High-level design

The high-level design (*Figure 9.2*) abstracts the publisher (SSP) side as the problem does not have any focus on that area. We have depicted some components related to the ad exchange as well as some important components on the DSP side that we are going to use during the detailed phase.

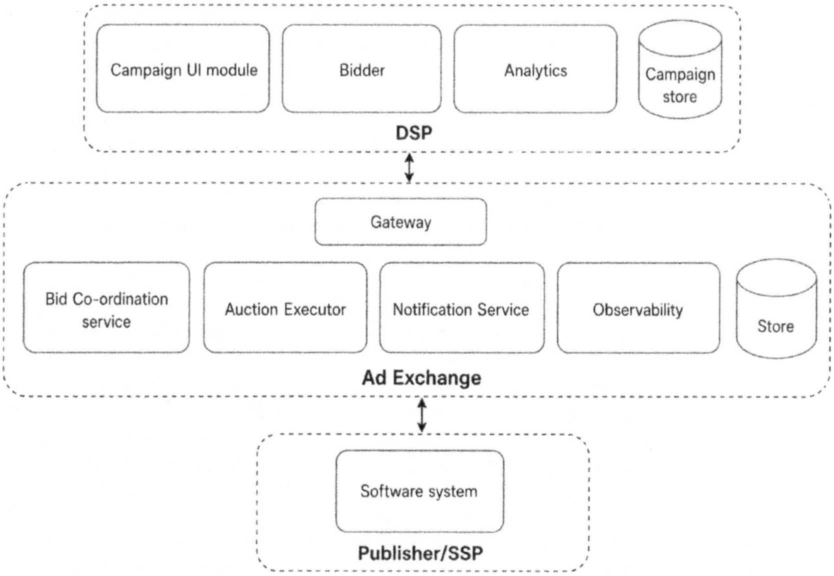

Figure 9.2: HLD for a Real time ad bidding system

As shown in *Figure 9.2*, the SSP sends a request to an 'Ad Exchange' indicating that an ad slot is available. The exchange's 'Bid Coordination Service' handles the request and orchestrates the bidding process. The orchestrator then uses its 'Gateway' component to distribute, i.e., fan out, the request, along with relevant qualifying information about the user, to all DSPs for the available ad space. The 'Bidder' component of each DSP receives and evaluates the request to decide whether to participate in the bidding. If participating, the 'Bidder' submits a bid along with campaign details back to the 'Ad Exchange' for auction. When all bids are received, the 'Auction Executor' executes the auction routine to declare a winner. Once a winning campaign is selected:

- The winner information is stored in the exchange's persistent store.
- The advertiser, DSP, and/or their proxy will be notified about the win.
- The ad content will be sent to the publisher's site for display.

Now, let's discuss the DSP side in slightly more detail. The 'Campaign UI module' is used by advertisers/bidders to create a bid. Depending on a DSP implementation, a campaign image/video can be uploaded on the DSP's own content host or a content delivery network (CDN). We will assume a CDN as a static/video content host. The 'Bidder' module is responsible for receiving ad-space availability requests from an ad exchange and executing matching criteria to determine all the qualifying bids. It considers information received from the publisher-side system and then evaluates it against the criteria created by an advertiser. Once all the bids are identified, it will send those qualifying bids to the ad exchange for an outcome.

Detailed design

This section further elaborates on what we have presented in the high-level design. The SSP side components are still abstracted but for a better understanding of the end-to-end journey, all five entities associated with an ad bidding system (as discussed earlier in this chapter) are used for clarity. Refer to *Figure 9.3*:

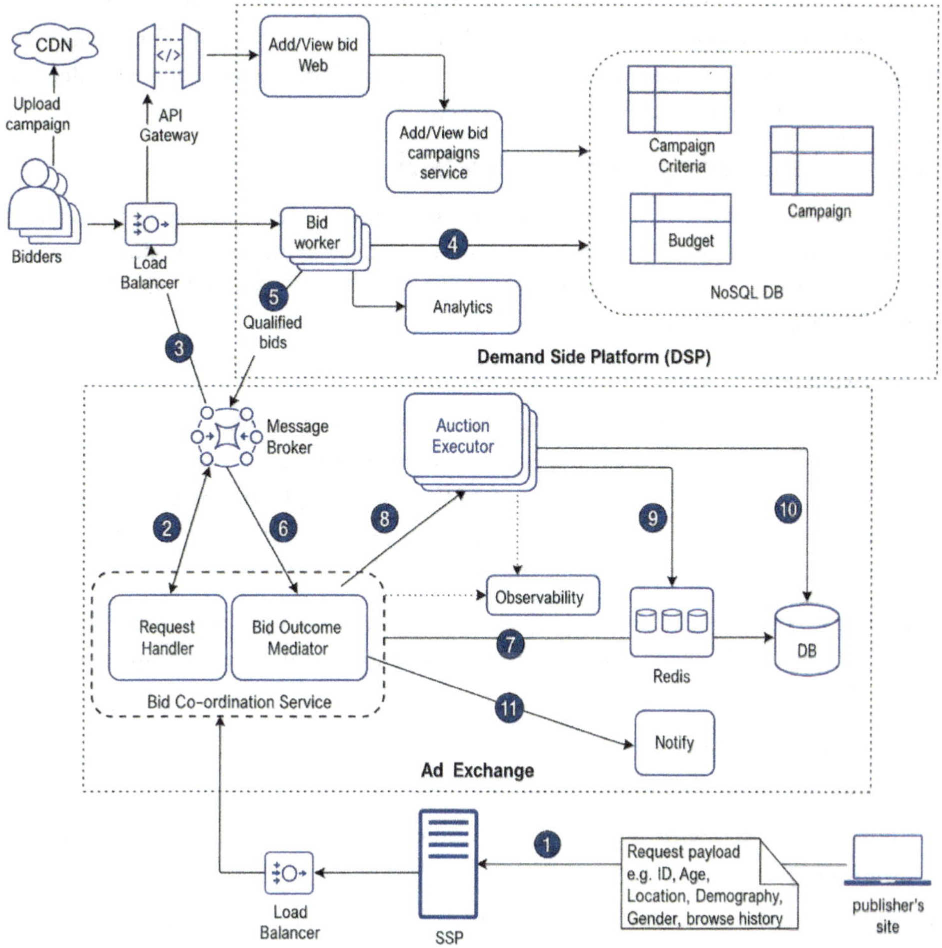

Figure 9.3: Real time bidding system - detailed design

The circular annotations in *Figure 9.3* depict the journey when an ad space becomes available for auction. Both 'Ad Exchange' and 'DSP' are set up in redundant environments. Multiple instances of a few components are shown to reflect the auto-scaling setup of these instances within a data center. In the following sections, we dive deeper into the workflow.

As shown in *Figure 9.3*, the Ad Exchange component's 'Bid Coordination Service' and 'Auction Executor' are explicitly shown as multiple nodes. This depicts a level of resiliency within a single data center. The infrastructure will be deployed across multiple regions and availability zones (AZs). Redis is used by the Ad Exchange component to allow the auction executor to gather data quickly for real-time bidding. The database component is used to persist data.

The 'Message Broker' is a single, multi-node gateway component that enables interactions with DSPs. It is configured to wait for a defined period for a response from a DSP after bid information is shared. Any response received after the defined window is discarded. Below, we detail a few mainstream journeys supported by the detailed architecture.

Bidder-side journey to create a bid

A registered bidder will access the Add/View Ad webpage to create/manage an ad. Using the screen, they will be able to set up different bidding criteria along with pricing. All campaign content, whether static or video, will be uploaded to the CDN, and a URL will be stored along with other campaign information in the associated NoSQL database.

Auction journey

When a user visits a publisher's platform (website/app), an available ad slot triggers the generation of an ad request. This request is sent via the SSP to the 'Ad Exchange'. The request to the exchange typically contains ad slot metadata (size, format, placement, etc.), user contextual data (unique ID, age, location, device, client, etc.), publisher preferences (minimum price, blocked or preferred advertisers, etc.), and other relevant information.

The exchange's 'Request Handler' component picks the request. It performs multiple operations on the request payload before it can be sent further for processing. Its responsibilities may include:

- Store impression metadata into a persistent storage
- Parse and validate incoming request
- Enrich requests with additional information, e.g., a unique request ID, internal timestamp
- Enforce regulatory compliance, e.g., data masking and privacy constraints
- Create request schema aligned with DSP agreements

The final transformed request is then forwarded to the 'Message Broker', which also serves as the gateway layer for the ad exchange. The broker fans out requests to all linked DSPs over exposed endpoints (e.g., POST `https://sample.dsp1.com/bid`) or an RPC method [11]. An RPC/gRPC-based approach is usually preferred because the underlying persistent HTTP/2 connection provides significant latency benefits. The request payload can use the OpenRTB specification in JSON or Protobuf format for uniformity and speed. The message is then picked up by the 'Bid Worker' component within the DSP. [3][9][10]

Figure 9.3 depicts only one DSP but in the real world there are multiple DSPs participating in the bidding process. Within each DSP, the bid worker must respond within a short period (usually under 50ms) to the exchange. Any delayed bid response is ignored by the exchange during the auction. For a bid evaluation, the bid worker matches incoming request attributes against the campaign targeting rules. The evaluation is performed using constraints such as:

- Budget availability
- Frequency caps
- Campaign audience target criteria

The worker generates a response to send back to the exchange. The response contains information such as bid price, campaign reference URL, campaign metadata, etc. [7]

The 'Bid Outcome Mediator' component receives all aggregated valid bid results from DSPs via the broker. Any late responses are dropped by the broker. The mediator stores the bid information in a distributed cache for resilience, and corresponding log entries are created for analytical purposes. The mediator triggers the 'Auction Executor' component (we'll explain this in detail later in the chapter) to run the auction and determine a winning bid. The winning campaign (creative content information along with a content-rendering script) is sent to the publisher's site for display.

The mediator sends a notification to the bidder stating that their bid has won, along with other information, such as the winning bid price details.

At each stage, interactions are comprehensively logged for analytics and observability purposes. This includes request/response timestamps, bid values and auction results, impressions, clicks, and conversion events. This captured information is then used for performance monitoring, campaign optimization, billing and auditing, and other tasks. [12]

Auction executor

The auction executor (also called the auction engine) is the heart of the system. Different systems assign different responsibilities to match their use cases. Its core responsibility is to execute rules and choose a winning bid from all the bids received. As a rough estimate of speed, it is expected to complete its action in, say, less than 5 milliseconds. This component is deployed in close proximity to (usually co-located with) the DSP region to improve speed by reducing network latency. Redundant instances are deployed to handle failures.

The auction executor component performs further pre-auction refinement on the bids. It applies rules to ensure that mandatory response information is included, publisher restrictions, such as blocked advertisers, are enforced, and the bid price is not lower than the floor price. The final candidate bids are then sorted based on price. Since pricing plays a key role in determining the winner, let's look at two common pricing techniques used to determine a winning bid.

First-price auction

In this approach, the bid with the highest quoted price wins [6]. If, for example:

- Bidder (B1) quotes the price as $1.50,
- Bidder (B2) quotes the price as $1.59, and
- Bidder (B3) quotes the price as $1.55

Then bidder B2 wins the bid and pays $1.59, as quoted. It is fairly easy to implement because it is straightforward.

Second-price auction

In this pricing model, the highest-priced bid wins, but the winner pays based on the second-highest bid. Some exchanges also charge a small premium amount on top of the second-highest bid price. Taking the same example as in the first-price auction above [4][5]:

- Bidder (B1) quotes the price as $1.50,
- Bidder (B2) quotes the price as $1.59, and
- Bidder (B3) quotes the price as $1.55

Here, bidder B2 wins the bid and bidder B3 has the second-highest bid price. We will consider the case of a small premium of $0.01 being added. Since the second-highest bid quote was $1.55, B2 will pay $1.55 + $0.01 = $1.56 for the bid.

Resolving ties between bids

In the event of a bid price tie, the ad exchange can implement logic to determine a winner. It can be as simple as random selection or more complex, incorporating attributes such as DSP rating, the CTR and CVR of previous DSP campaigns, or publisher preferences.

Bid worker (DSP side)

It is the most resource-intensive and complex process, performing a number of activities in a very short span of time. It sits within the DSP. In a cloud-native environment, you might consider an auto-scaling group with a defined minimum number of instances. A containerized implementation is suitable for this component. As discussed earlier, this component is responsible for sending a list of eligible bids to the ad exchange for auction. It performs an initial assessment to identify the best candidate, or a couple of candidate bids, to return to the ad exchange. A few general activities performed by this process include:

- Receive an ad-space availability request from the ad exchange.
- Fetch all the campaigns that match the ad-space size requirement.
- Match information supplied in the request with campaign criteria.

- Evaluate cost and frequency constraints (for example, a frequency constraint is enforced when a campaign has been displayed to a user for 'n' number of times already).
- Predict Click-Through Rate (CTR), Conversion Rate (CVR), and other values.

Based on these activities, the best bid (or more than one) is determined and sent back to the ad exchange as a response for the auction.

Machine learning algorithms are heavily used by bid workers to perform CTR/CVR predictions. The most commonly used algorithms are Gradient Boosted Decision Tree (GBDT) and Logistic Regression. As the industry matures, more advanced deep neural network-based algorithms are being implemented for this purpose [8][17].

Gradient Boosted Decision Tree (GBDT): GBDT uses ensemble learning's boosting technique to make a prediction. In this technique, multiple weak decision tree models are combined sequentially to develop a strong prediction model. In the sequential stage, each subsequent stage tries to reduce the error (weakness) of the previous stage [13][14][15]. Hence, for every feature, conventional implementations of GBDT need to scan all data instances to estimate the information gain of all possible split points. Therefore, their computational complexity is proportional to both the number of features and the number of instances. This approach makes the technique relatively slower but produces a highly accurate outcome.

> **Note**
>
> Ensemble learning is an approach in which a prediction is made by combining the results of a number of different models. This approach reduces bias and can generate a more accurate outcome. There are two flavors of this technique:
>
> - **Bagging**: In this approach, independent models are trained in parallel with random feature sets, e.g., the Random Forest technique.
> - **Boosting**: Here, the model is trained sequentially. Each stage tries to improve the result of its predecessor. For example, GBDT works particularly well for use cases such as click prediction, ranking-based prediction, and multi-class classification problems. XGBoost is an open-source software library that can be used to implement GBDT.

Logistic regression: Logistic regression is a type of supervised learning algorithm that uses a statistical, probabilistic approach to solve classification problems to generate a discrete outcome. It can work well with small or sparse datasets. In this model, a set of input variables such as, ad-category, geo-location, user-age, user-gender, are used to determine the probability of the user clicking the ad.

These input variables also carry some weight to represent which features are more important when determining a result. Since it is based on probability, the prediction/outcome ranges between 0 and 1, with the midpoint as 0.5. It uses the 'sigmoid function' to balance the result within this range. In this method, '0' represents the lowest chance, and '1' refers to the highest. The algorithm continues to improve by reading the user's click logs against the original prediction made, and hence, over time, it becomes more mature.

The simplest trade-offs to understand while choosing between GBDT and Logistic Regression (LR) are:

- **Speed**: LR is quite fast to generate an output compared with GBDT
- **Accuracy**: GBDT produces more accurate results than LR
- **Deployment**: LR is relatively easy to deploy compared with GBDT. [16]

In practice, both GBDT and LR are used together to combine accuracy with speed. GBDT is trained offline on historical logs, where it can learn the complex, non-linear patterns hidden in the data. When a new impression arrives, GBDT converts its raw features into a compact pattern that summarizes what the impression looks like. LR then reads that pattern and returns a predicted CTR in milliseconds, fast enough for the bid worker's time budget. GBDT is retrained nightly or weekly as new data arrives; LR is refreshed far more frequently.

For example, for a new impression, GBDT may identify a combination of user, ad, and contextual characteristics, which LR uses to predict a 15% CTR. This predicted CTR can then be used for downstream decisions such as ranking or bidding.

Resolving bottlenecks and follow-up questions

This is the section where you will identify gaps and weak points in your system and propose one or more improvements to optimize the solution. For the current design, we have assumed that the broker will fan out requests to all registered DSPs. This can be resource-intensive and may not generate the desired outcome. For instance, many ads are targeted to geographically confined user groups. Requesting bids from a DSP that operates outside that geography does not create value. To improve resource utilization, some checks can be incorporated before fanning out requests to DSPs.

Also, during requirement clarification and summarization, we assumed that the CDN used by a DSP will be natively available to SSPs. This assumption requires a better implementation to make creatives available to the SSP within the time limit. Another area for improvement could be co-locating the 'Ad Exchange' with DSPs for overall latency benefits.

Summary

Few systems in the world are as latency-sensitive as real-time bidding. Every ad auction plays out in milliseconds, at enormous scale, with revenue on the line for every request. This chapter walked through how to design an RTB system by providing an in-depth understanding of the business problem and discussing all the major entities involved in enabling bidding. We also explained some core terminology associated with the system, including impression, CTR, and CVR.

We then presented a high-level and detailed design and explained how the design works with the help of a few journeys. While discussing the ad exchange, a couple of pricing techniques were detailed as well. While discussing the DSP side, we touched upon predictions and the use of machine learning techniques for them. We finished the chapter by identifying some shortcomings in the design and proposing next steps for them.

The next chapter continues with another real-world design problem, giving you further practice applying this structured approach across a different class of system.

References

The RTB Domain and advertising ecosystem

[1] Yuan, S., Wang, J., & Zhao, X. (2013). "Real-time Bidding for Online Advertising: Measurement and Analysis." Proceedings of the 7th International Workshop on Data Mining for Online Advertising (ADKDD '13). [Foundational - an empirical study of how RTB auctions actually behave at scale.] `https://arxiv.org/abs/1306.6542`

[2] Wang, J., Zhang, W., & Yuan, S. (2017). "Display Advertising with Real-Time Bidding (RTB) and Behavioural Targeting." Foundations and Trends in Information Retrieval, 11(4-5). [Recommended - a comprehensive survey of the entire RTB field; the single best deep-dive reference for this chapter.] `https://arxiv.org/abs/1610.03013`

The bidding protocol

[3] IAB Tech Lab. OpenRTB API Specification (v2.6 and v3.0). [Foundational - the industry-standard protocol for the bid-request and bid-response payloads the chapter describes; the schema every DSP and exchange implements.] `https://iabtechlab.com/standards/openrtb/`

Auction mechanisms

[4] Vickrey, W. (1961). "Counterspeculation, Auctions, and Competitive Sealed Tenders." The Journal of Finance, 16(1), 8-37. [Foundational - the auction-theory paper behind the second-price (Vickrey) auction that historically governed RTB.] https://doi.org/10.2307/2977633

[5] Edelman, B., Ostrovsky, M., & Schwarz, M. (2007). "Internet Advertising and the Generalized Second-Price Auction: Selling Billions of Dollars Worth of Keywords." American Economic Review, 97(1), 242-259. [Foundational - the Generalized Second-Price (GSP) auction, the mechanism most ad auctions were built on.] https://www.aeaweb.org/articles?id=10.1257/aer.97.1.242

[6] Google Ad Manager (2019). "Simplifying programmatic: first-price auctions for Google Ad Manager." [Recommended - documents the industry-wide shift from second-price to first-price auctions; important context if the chapter's auction logic is to stay current.] https://blog.google/products/admanager/simplifying-programmatic-first-price-auctions-google-ad-manager/

Bidding strategy and click predictions

[7] Zhang, W., Yuan, S., & Wang, J. (2014). "Optimal Real-Time Bidding for Display Advertising." Proceedings of the 20th ACM SIGKDD Conference (KDD '14). [Recommended - how a DSP's bid worker decides how much to bid for a given impression.] https://dl.acm.org/doi/10.1145/2623330.2623633

[8] McMahan, H. B., et al. (2013). "Ad Click Prediction: a View from the Trenches." Proceedings of the 19th ACM SIGKDD Conference (KDD '13). [Recommended - Google's account of click-through-rate prediction, the model that drives campaign-targeting decisions.] https://research.google/pubs/pub41159/

Systems and infrastructure

[9] gRPC. "Introduction to gRPC." [Foundational for the chapter - the RPC framework, built on HTTP/2, that the design uses for low-latency exchange-to-DSP communication.] https://grpc.io/docs/what-is-grpc/introduction/

[10] Thomson, M., & Benfield, C. (2022). "HTTP/2." RFC 9113, IETF. [Recommended - the transport beneath gRPC; persistent connections and multiplexing without head-of-line blocking are why the chapter prefers it for the sub-50 ms bid path.] https://www.rfc-editor.org/rfc/rfc9113

[11] Kreps, J., Narkhede, N., & Rao, J. (2011). "Kafka: a Distributed Messaging System for Log Processing." Proceedings of the NetDB Workshop. [Foundational - the message broker that fans

out bid requests to DSPs and carries the impression, click, and conversion event streams.] `https://www.microsoft.com/en-us/research/wp-content/uploads/2017/09/Kafka.pdf`

[12] Ananthanarayanan, R., et al. (2013). "Photon: Fault-tolerant and Scalable Joining of Continuous Data Streams." Proceedings of the ACM SIGMOD Conference (SIGMOD '13). [Recommended - Google's system for joining ad-impression and click streams; directly relevant to the chapter's CTR/CVR analytics pipeline.] `https://research.google/pubs/pub41318/`

Machine learning

[13] Wikipedia, [Gradient Boosting] `https://en.wikipedia.org/wiki/Gradient_boosting`

[14] Wikipedia, [XGBoost] `https://en.wikipedia.org/wiki/XGBoost`

[15] Gradient Boosted Decision Trees | Machine Learning | Google for developers `https://developers.google.com/machine-learning/decision-forests/intro-to-gbdt`

[16] Logistic Regression | Machine Learning | Google for developers `https://developers.google.com/machine-learning/crash-course/logistic-regression`

[17] Wen-Yuan Zhu, Chien-Huan Wang, Wei-Yu Shih, Wen-Chih Peng, and Jiun-Long Huang Zhu, W.-Y., Wang, C.-H., Shih, W.-Y., Peng, W.-C., & Huang, J.-L. (2017). "SEM: A Softmax-based Ensemble Model for CTR Estimation in Real-Time Bidding Advertising." 2017 IEEE International Conference on Big Data and Smart Computing (BigComp). `https://ieeexplore.ieee.org/document/7881698`

10

Designing an Instagram-like Social Media System

Social media platforms have transformed how billions of people connect, share, and communicate in the digital age. At first glance, designing an Instagram-like application appears straightforward: users upload photos, browse a feed, and interact with content. However, beneath this simplicity sits a heavily read-skewed distributed system that must serve hundreds of thousands of requests per second, manage petabytes of media, and personalize content for every user in real time. The defining technical challenge of 'fan-out at scale' has shaped much of the distributed systems literature for over a decade [1]. This is why social media system design problems are among the most frequently asked and most complex questions in any technical interview.

This chapter walks you through the systematic approach to designing a social media platform like Instagram. By the end of this chapter, you should be able to scope the social media problem correctly. Furthermore, you'll be able to identify and prioritize functional and non-functional requirements for it, and design a scalable, feed-based social media system.

In this chapter, we will cover the following for an Instagram-like design:

- Requirement clarification, assumptions, and estimations
- API design
- Storage and database selection
- System design in detail
- Resolving bottlenecks
- Scaling considerations

Problem statement: Design a social media platform similar to Instagram that allows users to share photos and videos, follow other users, and consume a personalized feed at global scale.

Understanding the problem domain

Instagram and similar platforms expose a number of core concepts that any design must support. Recognizing them up front lets you scope the problem deliberately and address the key requirements systematically rather than discovering them as the design evolves.

- **Users and Profiles:** Every user has a profile, an account, a private or public visibility, followers, following lists, posts, stories, highlights, and engagement history. Authentication and authorization are assumed prerequisites.
- **Content Creation:** Users can upload images, videos, reels, and stories. These uploads often go through processing pipelines such as compression, resizing, transcoding, filtering, and moderation before becoming visible to others.
- **Social Graph:** Instagram is heavily dependent on 'directed relationships' between users. These relationships can be in the form of following, blocking, muting, close friends, and interactions, etc. Collectively they form a massive social graph that influences recommendations and visibility.
- **Feeds and Content Consumption:** One of Instagram's core strengths is the personalized feed. Users do not simply see posts chronologically. Instead, they see a ranked list of posts from accounts they follow, with the most relevant content surfaced first. The relevance is determined using factors including the user's engagement patterns, relationships, watch history, interests, and trends.
- **Engagement:** Likes, comments, saves, shares, and reactions are not just features; they are high-volume real-time events that drive notifications, analytics, ranking algorithms, and recommendation engines.
- **Search and Discovery:** Hashtags, trending topics, recommendations, creator discovery, and explore pages require indexing, ranking, and personalization systems operating at a massive scale.
- **Chat & Calls:** The platform also supports direct messaging (chats), voice and video calls between users.

It is important to recognize that building such a system is not a single problem but a composition of multiple subsystems, including account creation and authentication, photo and video uploads, viewing content posted by others, interacting with content through likes and comments, discovering and connecting with other users, consuming a personalized feed, and supporting direct messaging, audio calls, and video calls.

In an interview setting, a common mistake is to attempt to design all of them, as this will quickly lead to confusion and an overwhelming problem to solve. A strong candidate scopes the design to one or two core flows (typically content upload and feed consumption) and notes the others as out of scope or as follow-on work. As needed, make assumptions, be sure to validate them, and then proceed accordingly.

Requirement clarification

Before drawing boxes or choosing databases, pause to align on what is in scope for the design, especially when working under time constraints. Not all features carry equal weight in an initial design, and demonstrating the ability to distinguish between core functionality and nice-to-have features shows product thinking alongside technical skills.

For an Instagram-like system, the following clarifying questions are a helpful starting point:

- Is the system intended for web, mobile, or both?
- Is the target system going to be photo- or video-heavy, or should we consider them equally?
- What is the expected user volume for this application? What is the read-to-write ratio?
- What is the retention policy for posts?
- Should we consider a personalized ranked feed of posts from accounts that users follow?
- Does the system need to demonstrate 'likes' and 'comments' on posts?

You can propose some obvious requirements out of scope for the design activity, such as hashtags and search, direct messaging, voice and video calls, reels (short videos), ads, and creator analytics. Scoping the problem also demonstrates your comprehensive understanding of the problem domain and sets clear expectations by defining what the system will and will not cover upfront.

Here are the overall volumetrics used in this chapter:

- 1 billion registered users, 500 million daily active users.
- 100 million users upload at least once per day. On average, a user creates 2 posts containing a mix of photos and videos.
- 80% of uploads are photos, and 20% are videos.

If we look at it more broadly and segregate the requirement at the functional and non-functional levels, we can summarize the requirements as follows:

Functional	Non-Functional
• The system can be used via various channels, e.g., web and mobile. • Users should be able to register and log in to the platform. • Users should be able to upload and retrieve pictures and videos. • Users should be able to like and comment on other users' posts. • Users should be able to view a personalized feed on their timeline.	• The system should be highly available. • Eventual consistency for feeds, likes, etc., is acceptable, but the system must incorporate strong consistency for user creation and the social graph, i.e., followers and following relationships. • Feed read p99 latency < 300 ms and media first byte latency < 100 ms via CDN. • Posts must be durable and must never be lost unless explicitly removed by the content owner.

Table 10.1: Functional vs. Non-functional requirements

Tip

'Media first byte latency' is the time taken for the very first byte of media content to arrive at the client machine after the request for that content is initiated by that client.

Assumptions

We will use the following working assumptions to guide the design of the system in this chapter. They help define the expected scale, usage patterns, and key constraints of the system. These assumptions also provide a consistent basis for the design decisions that follow.

- Average photo size: 3 MB (after compression), video size: 50 MB (after compression and transcoding)
- Media metadata holds basic information for media identification, e.g., post ID, creator ID, timestamp, title, and media URL. Such information can be stored within 500 bytes per item.
- The average user views 50 posts per day on their feed
- During peak hours, traffic can be twice the normal level
- Posts are retained indefinitely (no deletion assumed for estimation purposes)
- Replication factor of 3 for data durability

Estimations

Back-of-the-envelope numbers drive the architectural choices that follow. All calculations round 86,400 seconds in a day to 100,000 and 365 days in a year to 400 for ease of mental arithmetic.

Traffic estimates

```
Write RPS = 100 M uploads/day x 2 posts = 200 M posts/day = 200 M / 100,000 = 2000
RPS
Peak write RPS = twice the normal level = 2 x 2000 = 4000 RPS
Read traffic RPS = 500 M DAU x 50 views/day = 25 billion views/day = 25 B /
100,000 = 250,000 RPS
Peak read RPS = 250,000 x 2 = 500,000 RPS
Read:Write ratio = 250,000 / 2,000 = 125:1
```

This information implies that the system is read-heavy, and hence caching must be used to facilitate read operations and minimize load on the origin servers.

Storage estimates

Estimating your storage resources is a non-negotiable calculation you must demonstrate while solving such a problem. This is also important because while doing this exercise you will be able to highlight different types of data presence for which a suitable store needs provisioning. Below, we have done calculations only for two main components for demonstration and to keep them relevant to this chapter. It is advisable for you to consider all the different aspects, including storage estimates for logs, in your calculations.

Media content storage

```
The average media content size per post = 80% photo + 20% video = (0.8 x 3 MB) +
(0.2 x 50 MB) = 12.4 MB
Daily storage need = 100 M x 2 posts x 12.4 MB = 2.48 PB/day
With replication factor=3, daily storage need = 3 x 2.48 = 7.5 PB/day (approx.)
Annual data storage need = 7.5 PB/day x 400 = 3000 PB/year
```

It clearly indicates that for storing media content, object storage will be an ideal choice. Cloud providers like AWS also support multiple tiering plans for cost optimization based on usage. Such plans can be used.

Media metadata storage

```
Daily metadata storage need = 100 M x 2 posts x 500 bytes = 100 GB/day
Annual storage need = 100 GB/day x 400 = 40 TB/year
With replication factor=3, annual storage = 3 x 40 = 120 TB/year
```

Cassandra can be a good choice to store metadata information.

Bandwidth estimates

For such a high-read-volume system that is exposed to external users, performing a bandwidth estimate is not an optional exercise. This is needed to ensure that the underlying infrastructure can support the number of requests it is expected to serve.

```
Read RPS = 500,000. Per post, average content size = 12.4 MB
Bandwidth to support peak read = 500,000 x 12.4 MB = 6.2 TB/s
```

The calculated bandwidth is the maximum bandwidth requirement. This is because usually, media content is served in compressed form which reduces bandwidth requirements. Keeping the maximum limit for guidance, allowing this many reads directly from an origin server (object store) can crash the server. Alternative content-caching and rendering mechanisms, e.g., CDNs, must be used efficiently to reduce the read requests reaching the backend.

API design

Our API design follows standard REST conventions with versioned endpoints (v1), uses appropriate HTTP methods (GET, POST, PUT, DELETE), and implements cursor-based pagination for list operations. All endpoints require authentication via JWT tokens and are subject to rate limiting to prevent abuse. Here are the core API endpoints for our Instagram-like system that a client can invoke:

- `POST /v1/users/register` - New user registration
- `POST /v1/auth/login` - Authentication
- `POST /v1/media/upload-url` - For uploading media binaries
- `POST /v1/posts` - Create a post
- `GET /v1/feed` - Read your feed
- `POST /v1/follows` - Follow a user. The user information will be in the body payload
- `DELETE /v1/follows/{target_user_id}` - Unfollow a user
- `PUT /v1/posts/{id}/likes` - Like a post.

- `DELETE /v1/posts/{id}/likes` - Unlike a post.
- `POST /v1/posts/{id}/comments` - Add a comment on the post

Storage and database selection

Looking at the requirement, different data classes have different access patterns and consistency expectations. In this case, a single database is not able to serve everything. These data classes also have different consistency needs and volumes. *Table 10.2* maps each class to the store best suited to it, with the reason for the choice.

Data	Data store	Justification of the choice
User profile (account, settings, password hash, etc.)	Relational, i.e., SQL database (PostgreSQL / MySQL)	Low-volume transactions per user at a given time. ACID guarantee is required for auth and account changes, along with strict unique constraints (email and/or username)
Social graph (follower/ following)	Graph store (Neo4j)	Supports ACID consistency and high write throughput for follow and unfollow operations. It is a specialized store for this purpose. A fit-for-purpose sharding technique will be used to get throughput gain.
Post metadata (Post ID, creator ID, timestamp, title, media URL, etc.).	Wide column NoSQL (Cassandra)	Factoring traffic and storage estimates into account, Cassandra supports very high write throughput and natural sharding by user identifier. For chronological reads, clustering can be performed by timestamp. It supports high-performance range-based queries [2].
'Likes' and 'comments' counters	Redis with atomic INCR with periodic flush to Cassandra	Atomic increments in Redis avoid contention. Cassandra supports a durable copy of the data.

Data	Data store	Justification of the choice
Media content, i.e., actual binaries	Object store (AWS S3 or likewise with tiering plans)	Highly durable, can scale seamlessly, easy or native integration with a CDN, and comes with tiering plans to support cold storage

Table 10.2: Data classes and their chosen data stores

All image and video binaries can be stored in AWS S3 (object storage). Media access will be granted via a CDN that can efficiently handle regional read traffic. It also ensures global availability by suitable replication. An LFU (Least Frequently Used)-based eviction policy will be a good choice for keeping these assets in CDN. This is because hot assets (images/videos) tend to get accessed frequently for some time.

A basic domain entity model will look something like *Figure 10.1*:

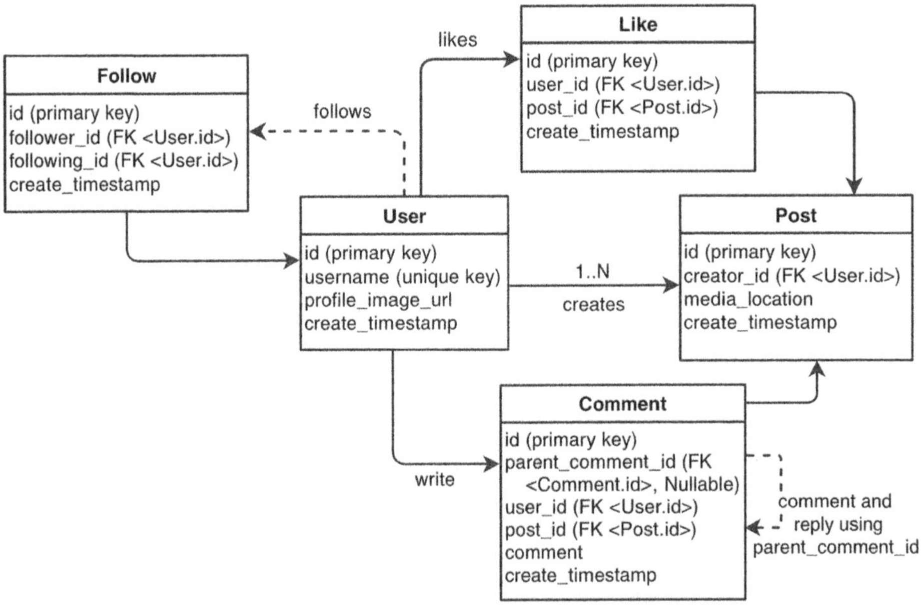

Figure 10.1: Core domain entity model for the social media system

System design

In this phase, we will, as usual, start with the high-level design where all the major components will be shown. We will develop a detailed understanding of the components shown to gain stakeholder buy-in. We will then move on to the detailed design. The detailed design will elaborate on the building blocks used in the high-level design with the help of a few journeys related to users. Let's start with the high-level design.

High-level design

The system is decomposed into services aligned with the different functional requirements, with each service capable of scaling independently, as shown in *Figure 10.2*. Cross-service interactions follow an event-driven architecture using Kafka. For example, when a 'post creation' event occurs, it is placed in a relevant topic for the feed service to fan out.

Media binaries (videos and photos) bypass the core application layers, providing an independent media storage path isolated from the application. During media upload, the application is responsible for generating a time-bound presigned URL [5]. We will discuss this in depth in the detailed design.

The uploaded media can then be passed on to the CDN for feed rendering.

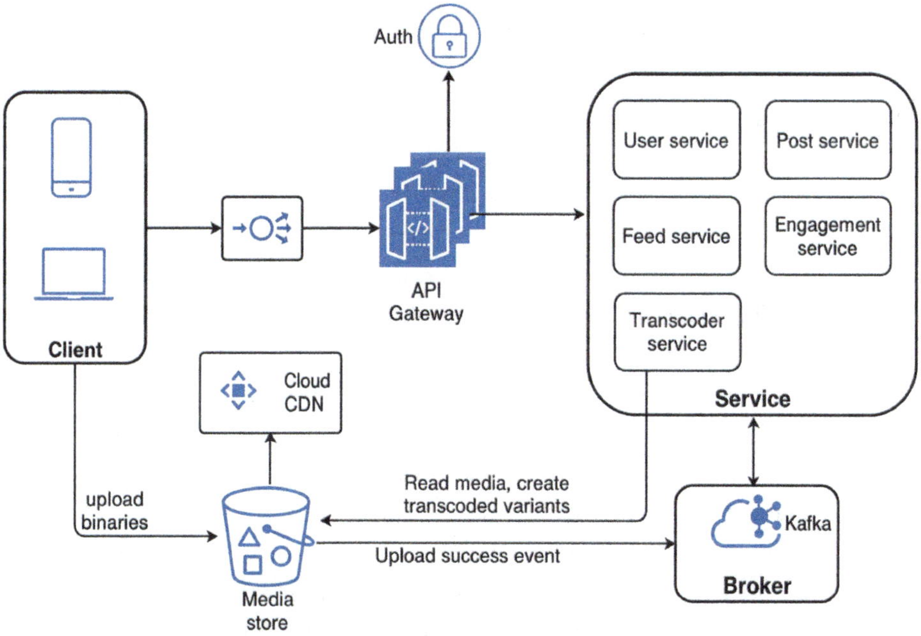

Figure 10.2: High-level design of an Instagram-like social media platform

Let us understand the purpose of different components as captured in *Figure 10.2* :

- **Client:** It can be any browser or app accessing the system.
- **Load balancer:** It is a layer 7 load balancer. It is mainly used as a pass-through layer for the API Gateway. It constantly performs gateway health checks and routes traffic to healthy nodes. In a multi-region configuration, the load balancer can be configured to route traffic to the nearest API Gateway component, depending upon the use case.
- **API Gateway**: This component is the single-entry point for any request getting into the system. It is fronted by a load balancer layer for traffic management. Rate limiting and other best practices are implemented at the gateway layer. This layer also ensures only valid and authenticated (as applicable) requests can access the system. After authentication is performed by the auth server, the API gateway is capable of validating the JWT token internally without making any database calls.
- **Auth**: An authentication system used by the API gateway to handle user login.
- **Service:** This layer represents a set of independent services to meet the system's requirements. These services and their function are:
  - **User service**: It deals with all user-related activities, including user creation during registration, followers and following graph management. It uses PostgreSQL for user records and Neo4j to maintain social graphs. User profile images can be stored in the media store.
  - **Post service**: It deals with all the posts and their metadata management, including media upload facilitation. Post metadata is stored in Cassandra for high write throughput and fast reads. [3]
  - **Feed service**: It generates personalized feeds for users. It also listens to events created by the post service to fan out when a new post is created. The fan-out requires careful consideration to avoid hotspot (celebrity) problems. The main storage system here is Redis to serve requests from cache for latency. It also uses Cassandra as a persistent backend store.
  - **Engagement service**: It facilitates functions such as likes, comments, etc. Likes and comments arrive at extreme volume during viral events. The design treats both as event streams. A 'like' is published as an event on Kafka. Consumers increment the per-post counter in Redis (atomic INCR) and asynchronously persist the like record to Cassandra.
  - **Transcoder service**: It is a special-purpose service that converts an uploaded media into multiple formats and resolutions compatible with different devices

where it can be seen. Any content safety or media scan actions are executed by this service.

- **Broker:** It is the Kafka-based implementation that enables services to communicate with each other, in near-real time.
- **Media store:** It is an object store that contains all the media files and their transcoded variations. Media placed in this store is constantly synced to CDN for client access. [4]
- **Cloud CDN:** It is a cloud-native CDN (content delivery network) implementation that caches media files recently added into the media store for quick access to viewers. An LFU (Least Frequently Used)-based cache eviction policy can be implemented to optimize media presence in the CDN.

Detailed design

The entry path is common to all journeys except for media upload. Every request, whether a read or a write, travels through the load balancer and API gateway, with the authentication server acting as the gatekeeper for all operations. This shared foundation ensures consistent security and traffic management across the entire system. We are now going to detail two main journeys associated with this system.

Write journey (posting media)

Now let's analyze the write journey for any post the user wants to post on Instagram. This journey consists of four main parts:

a. Media upload

b. Media optimization using the transcoder service

c. Post creation

d. Feed fan-out

We will explain the detailed steps of each part to understand the journey better.

Media upload and optimization

In this journey, a user will upload the media content to a designated content host. The content is then optimized internally to support different devices and quality during media display. Refer to *Figure 10.3* that depicts interactions during a media upload.

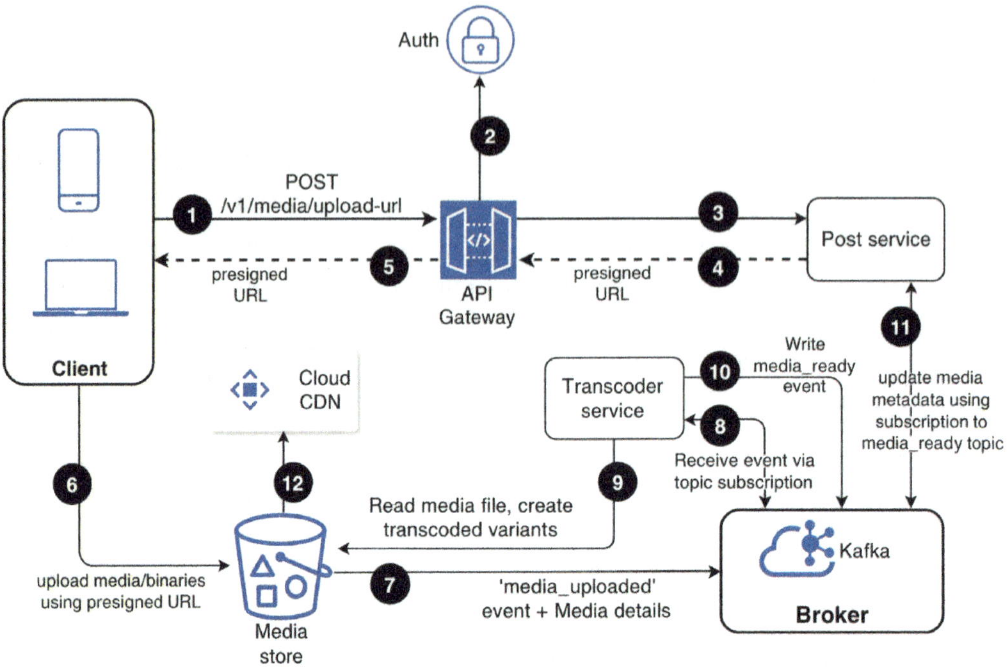

Figure 10.3: Media upload and transcode journey

From *Figure 10.3*, during a media upload, the following interactions and actions occur behind the scene:

1. User or client calls an endpoint to upload an image
2. User authentication is performed
3. After successful authentication, the request moves to the post service
4. The post service generates a presigned URL, ensuring its validity period from the time of issue and single-media use for a predetermined target store location. Here, we have used the post service to generate the presigned URL but this can be done independently by the API Gateway component as well.
5. The user receives a presigned URL without noticing it. The user then clicks the upload button.
6. The request connects to the media store using the presigned URL received from the post service. The media store can identify and validate the URL and allow the media to be uploaded.
7. Once the upload is complete, the media store generates an event and stores it in the `'media_uploaded'` topic within Kafka

8. The transcoder service is a subscriber to this topic. It activates on completion of step 7 above in an asynchronous way.
9. The transcoder service then connects to the media store to transcode the uploaded media file into multiple variants to support different needs. It stores all the variants in the same media store.
10. The transcoder service then creates a new event in the `'media_ready'` topic with the details of all the transcoded binaries it has created.
11. The post service reads all the media variants via its subscription to the relevant topics within the broker.
12. All the newly created media files are sent to the cloud CDN for downstream access.

Post creation

Once the media content is uploaded, creating a post is all about storing the metadata information. Here's the complete workflow:

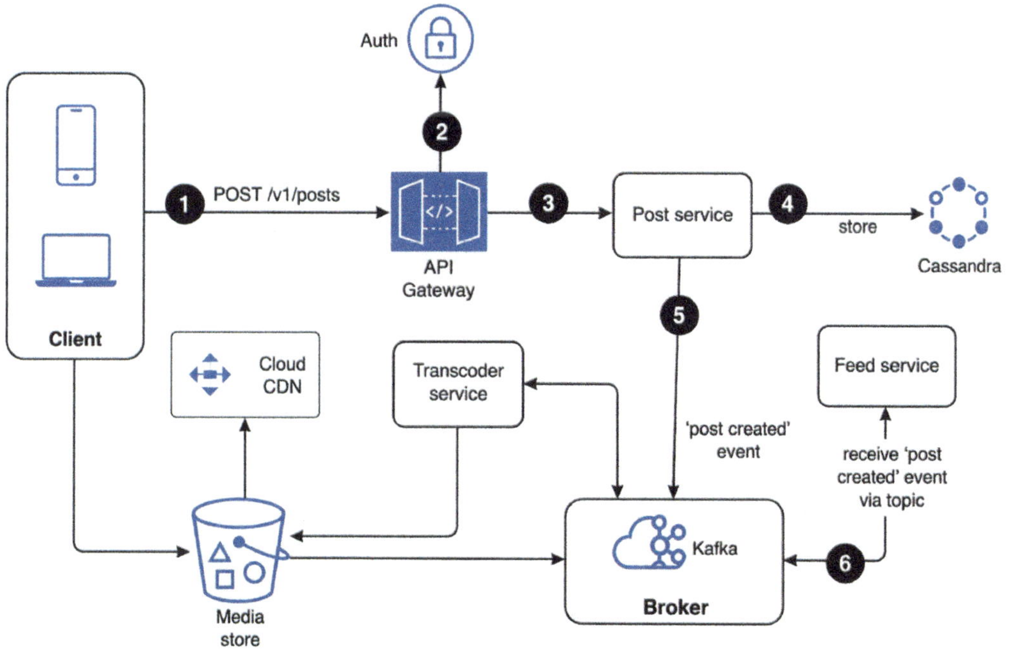

Figure 10.4: Create a post journey

As shown in *Figure 10.4*, the creation of a post involves several steps, as follows:

1. The client makes an API call to the post service via the API gateway. The call contains all the information regarding the post in its request body, including uploaded media references, caption, and text.
2. User authentication is verified. If needed, the user will be asked to re-authenticate
3. The gateway forwards the request to the backend post service
4. Post service stores the received information in its backend (Cassandra) store.
5. The service then writes a success event, 'post_created,' to the 'post' topic of the broker. The broker is updated after the post information is stored into the backend store successfully.
6. The feed service, which subscribes to the topic will asynchronously receive a new event in the 'post created' topic to act.
7. The client will receive post success confirmation (after step 5 above)

Feed fan-out

The fan-out approach highlighted for this journey occurs on post creation. *Figure 10.5* depicts the end-to-end journey.

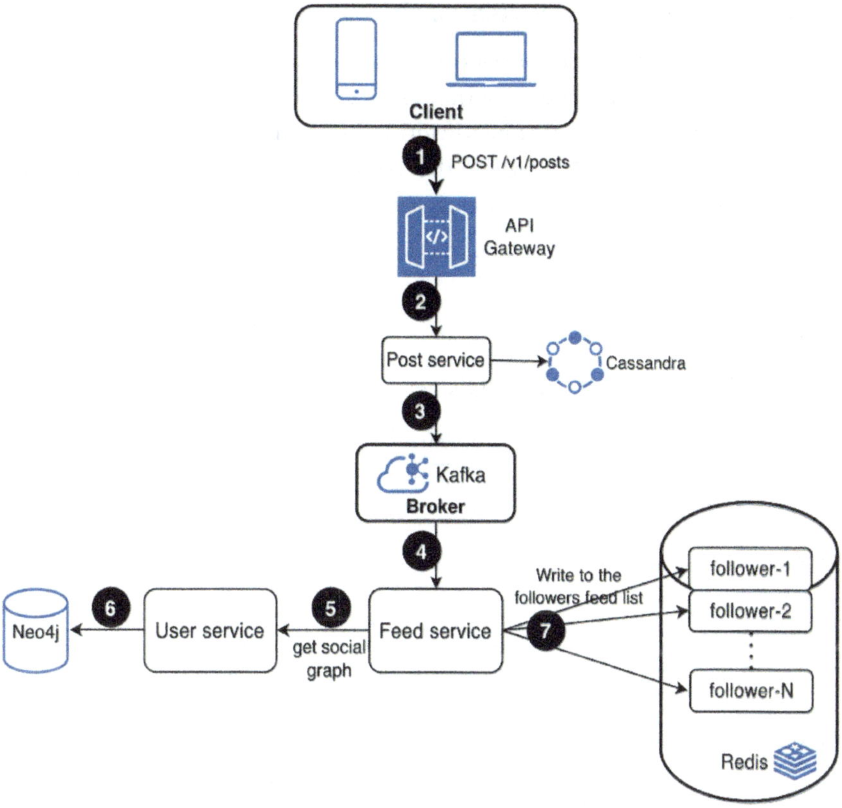

Figure 10.5: Feed fan-out on post creation

In the fan-out journey, on post creation, a corresponding event is captured in the broker. The feed service picks the event for fan-out action. The service first interacts with the user service to get the current snapshot of the user's social graph. For each of the 'followers' as returned in the graph, the service writes an entry into the follower cache. Here, the cache is the reference point used when a user receives her feed. The entire journey (step 4 and later in the figure) is performed in an asynchronous way during post creation and hence the user does not face any latency issues. The trade-off in this approach is, if a user has 1 million followers, then there will be an equal number of write operations as per step 7 in the figure. That means the write complexity of this approach is O(N). But during read, the complexity is O(1) making it an ideal approach for a read-heavy system with a strict p99 requirement.

Performance estimates - write path

As we have detailed, the write path consists of a combination of synchronous and asynchronous journeys. There are three synchronous journeys - presigned URL generation, media file upload (whose duration depends on network bandwidth), and post creation - and one asynchronous journey, transcoding. *Table 10.3* presents the performance estimates for the synchronous journeys, along with the assumptions made while estimating.

Assumptions: • Clients and servers are in the same geographical location • Hit ratio for both CDNs and Cache implementations are 95% • Cassandra is a 3-node configuration with read and write quorum of 2.	
Presigned URL generate	
Client to edge network round trip	60ms
Load balancer	3ms
API Gateway (JWT verification)	12ms
Gateway to post service round trip within data center	2ms
Post service generates presigned URL	5ms
Response generation	2ms
Presigned URL generation Total	**84ms**
Create post	
Client to edge network round trip	60ms
Load balancer	3ms
API Gateway (JWT verification)	12ms
Gateway to post service round trip within data center	2ms
Post service business logic and save to Cassandra	40ms
Create and store an event into Kafka topic	20ms

Response generation	2ms
Post creation Total	**139ms**
Media file upload: This is a direct upload to AWS S3 or likewise object store. Since it completely depends on the client's external network bandwidth, it does not contribute to application load.	
Total performance estimate for the write journey	**84 + 139 = 223ms**

Table 10.3: Performance estimates for creating a post

Read journey

With most of the complexity abstracted during the post creation journey, the read journey becomes slightly more straightforward. All the media content during read will be served using a CDN to gain the latency benefit of edge locations.

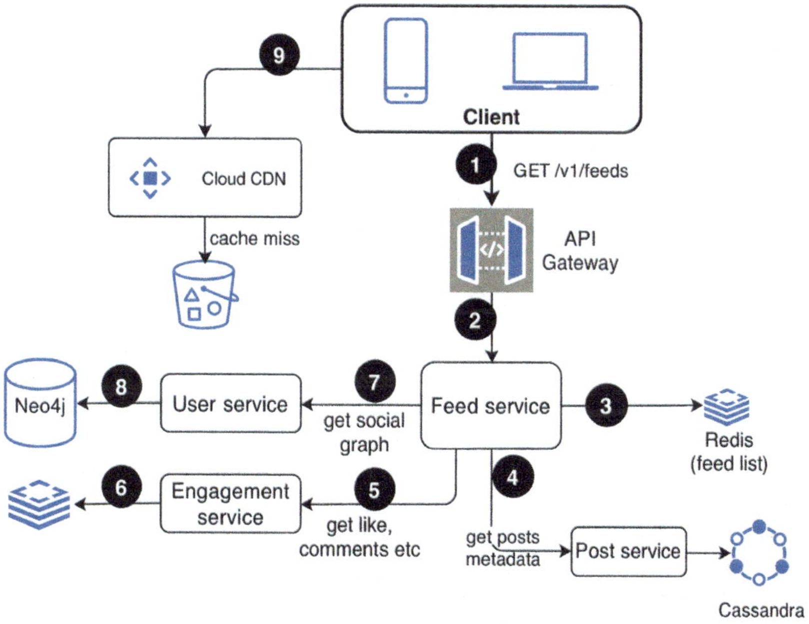

Figure 10.6: Feed generation and retrieval flow

The preceding journey considers the case when the logged-in user's social graph is not available in the feed service application-level cache or if the cache requires a refresh. *Table 10.4* presents the performance estimates for the read path, including the assumptions made for the purpose.

Performance estimates - the read path

Assumptions: • Clients and servers are in the same geographical location • Hit ratio for both CDNs and cache implementations are 95% • Cassandra is a 3-node configuration with read and write quorum of 2.	
Read feeds for the user	
Client to edge network round trip	60ms
Load balancer	3ms
API Gateway (JWT verification)	12ms
Gateway to feed service round trip within data center	2ms
Feed service to Redis feed list and feeds selection	10ms
Feed service to Post service (get post metadata)	20ms
Feed service to Engagement service (get likes, comments etc.)	20ms
Feed service to User service (get social graph)	20ms
Generate response	5ms
Feed read path total	**152ms**
Media first byte (cache hit scenario)	
DNS resolution	5ms
Client to same region CDN connect	40ms
Cache hit, media first byte access in CDN	50ms
Media first byte total	**95ms**

Table 10.4: Performance estimates for reading posts

The preceding estimates meet the requirements. In case of a cache miss during media first-byte rendering, the origin server will be consulted to load the media file(s) into the CDN, which will increase latency further. But as per our assumption of a 95% cache hit rate, such a scenario will occur only for the remaining 5% of cases. If this comes up during an interview, you can highlight it and agree on the next steps for improvement.

Engagement journey (like/comment)

The design treats *likes* and comments as event streams as they can be at massive volume for a trending post. These streams are handled via the Kafka broker to meet their final consistent state. For both of these events, a counter and a record are maintained. The counter is maintained in Redis for quick turnaround, and the record itself is maintained in underlying persistent storage (Cassandra) in this case. Data in Redis is flushed to the persistent store periodically to maintain consistency, compaction, and sync.

Failure handling

No system at Instagram's scale operates without failure. The choices made throughout this design are not just about performance under normal conditions but are about graceful degradation when things go wrong. Let's talk about a few of them specifically:

- **Load balancer:** It acts as the first line of defense. If one API gateway instance becomes unavailable, it is removed from the load balancer's healthy pool automatically. The request is automatically rerouted to healthy instances.
- **Media pipeline**: In the design, a failed media upload does not leave any record in the system. A routine backend job can be created to remove all orphan uploads where a corresponding metadata entry does not exist. Also, in case the user could not upload a media file within the time limit allocated in the presigned URL, the action will be nullified, and the user will be required to repeat the upload process. This is to enforce a level of security.
- **Fan-out during post creation**: It is possible that a post is created, but the feed service could not update followers' cache for some reason, for example, Redis is not available. A retry will be created for the feed service to replay any such events in the broker. The implementation will also include deduplication logic based on the post identifier before updating followers' cache.
- **Cache stores (Redis)**: It is used as a cache and hence should not be treated as the source of truth. It should be configured with replication across multiple nodes. In the event of a node failure, reads and writes can be served from replicas with minimal disruption.

Similarly, the media store benefits from redundant storage to prevent media loss in the event of hardware failure.

- **Cloud CDN:** It introduces a natural layer of resilience for read operations. Because media is cached and distributed across multiple edge locations globally, a failure in one region does not affect users being served from other locations.

Resolving bottlenecks

The design considers a fan-out approach for a post during its creation. It enables the system to demonstrate very fast reads, but write operations can create contention because of the celebrity problem. If a user has over a million followers, the approach will perform that many write operations during fan-out. A more practical approach could be to determine, while creating a post, the number of followers the user has. If that number can lead to the celebrity problem, then do not fan out on post creation. For such users, implement fan-out during the feed-read operation. The trade-off here is relatively slower read for some users, but the overall system performance will remain acceptable.

The post service first persists data into Cassandra and then stores a corresponding event into the Kafka topic. This can lead to the dual-write problem in distributed systems. To mitigate this issue, a transactional outbox pattern or CDC (Change Data Capture) approach can be implemented. In the outbox pattern, data and an outbox event are saved in the same local storage using a single atomic transaction. A background worker then reads the event and relays it to the broker.

Also, to further enhance the overall performance of feed service during post metadata lookup, Cassandra backend can be fronted by a distributed cache like Redis.

The design does not factor in any ranking-based feed recommendation. This can be achieved using a plug-in utility. The utility itself can have either a simple chronological or complex machine-learning logic for such recommendations.

Scaling considerations

The design is created with horizontal scalability in mind at every layer, allowing individual components to scale independently based on demand rather than requiring the entire system to scale as a single unit.

- The load balancer and API gateway layer can scale horizontally to handle spikes in traffic during peak usage hours, viral content events, or rapid user growth without any changes to the underlying service architecture.

- The feed service and post media service are stateless by design; meaning, additional instances can be spun up quickly during periods of high demand and scaled back down when traffic normalizes. This elasticity is particularly important for a platform where usage patterns vary significantly throughout the day.
- Neo4j, as the social graph database, requires careful scaling considerations given the complexity of graph traversal at large volumes. Read replicas can be introduced to distribute the query load as the user base grows, ensuring that feed generation remains fast even as the social graph becomes more densely connected.
- The metadata store should be designed with sharding in mind as data volume grows, partitioning records in a way that distributes read and write load evenly across nodes and avoids hotspots as certain users or content types generate disproportionate traffic.
- CDN scaling is largely handled by the CDN provider, but cache invalidation strategy becomes increasingly important at scale, ensuring that updated or deleted content is removed from edge caches promptly and consistently across all regions.

Summary

Designing an Instagram-like platform forces you to confront read-skew, fan-out, and media-pipeline complexity together. In this chapter, we covered the significance of a clear requirement boundary. We saw how estimation can help in making informed decisions early, e.g., the use of caches, CDNs, and object stores. The concept of a presigned URL was introduced in this chapter, and we explained how it can be used to upload media files directly to the final target without consuming application bandwidth. We also looked at an event-driven service decomposition over Kafka, which decoupled multiple functional building blocks and revealed a system built around the core principles: separation of read and write concerns, asynchronous processing for resilience under load, and CDN-based media delivery for speed at scale.

A well-designed system tells a story. Every component has a reason for being there, every connection has a purpose, and every trade-off has been made consciously. That is what this chapter was designed to show you, and it is exactly what your interviewer is listening for when they ask you to walk them through your design.

The same patterns - hybrid fan-out, polyglot persistence, event-driven inter-service communication, and CDN-first media delivery - reappear in TikTok, X (Twitter), YouTube, and Pinterest. Internalizing them through this case study transfers directly to a wide class of interview problems.

This chapter designed a system for humans consuming content. The next chapter designs a system where the content is produced by machines reasoning on your behalf. The shift is more than cosmetic - the components that made Instagram work (fan-out, caching, ordered storage) still apply, but the actors are now autonomous LLM-driven agents that collect market data, analyze signals, generate hypotheses, and compose reports. That change forces a new set of design questions: how do agents coordinate, how do we control their cost, and how do we trust an output no human wrote?

References

[1] Krikorian, R. "Timelines at Scale." Twitter engineering talk, QCon 2012. `https://www.infoq.com/presentations/Twitter-Timeline-Scalability/`

[2] Instagram Engineering Blog. "Sharding & IDs at Instagram." `https://instagram-engineering.com/sharding-ids-at-instagram-1cf5a71e5a5c`

[3] Lakshman, A., & Malik, P. "Cassandra: A Decentralized Structured Storage System." SIGOPS Operating Systems Review 44(2), 2010. `https://www.cs.cornell.edu/projects/ladis2009/papers/lakshman-ladis2009.pdf`

[4] AWS - Amazon CloudFront performance and cache behavior. `https://docs.aws.amazon.com/AmazonCloudFront/latest/DeveloperGuide/ConfiguringCaching.html`

[5] AWS - "Uploading objects with presigned URLs." `https://docs.aws.amazon.com/AmazonS3/latest/userguide/PresignedUrlUploadObject.html`

11

Designing an Agentic AI System for Investment Research

An investment research desk executes complex and sensitive activities that involve gathering data from the market, building models, and then deciding what goes into the portfolio. The work is intense, opinionated, and unforgiving. A missed earnings revision or an unread regulatory filing can move a fund's quarterly return by basis points (the term 'basis point' is a unit used in the finance sector to express small percentage changes. Traditionally, 1 basis point = 0.01%). Our task is to design an agentic AI system that augments an investment research desk with a fleet of autonomous AI agents.

What makes this an interesting system-design problem is not the LLM itself because that is a black-box dependency but the orchestration. We need many agents possibly running in parallel, sharing memory, calling external tools (market-data APIs, simulators, and databases), and converging on a single, auditable artifact. We therefore treat this as a distributed workflow problem with a probabilistic compute layer bolted on. The main difficulty lies in scheduling, observability, cost control, determinism, and the safety envelope around tool calls.

The terms *thesis*, *recommendation*, and *report* are used repeatedly in this chapter. They carry regulatory weight in the investment domain. It is worth detailing each one in simple terms before moving forward:

Thesis: It is a research-based written proposition about what to buy, sell, or hold about a security [1]. Most financial regulatory bodies suggest that a thesis should be prepared using reasonable evidence. The evidence should be well documented and if needed, the thesis can be reproduced using the supporting evidence.

Recommendation [2][5]: A recommendation is a decision with some associated specific actions e.g., buy security 'A' or sell security 'B'. For its chosen securities and associated action, a recommendation justifies both with supporting evidence that can be audited by regulators, and highlights any material risks that could invalidate the decision.

Report [5]: A report is a formal written document that packages the research elements from thesis and decisions from recommendation, discussed above, for consumption by portfolio managers or other stakeholders. Generally, a report contains an executive summary, ranked recommendations with target price and time horizon, evidence chains, associated disclaimers, etc.

> **Note**
>
> The chapter uses the term 'asset manager' and 'portfolio manager' interchangeably. In the real world the term may belong to separate entities depending on work focus, organization size, etc. In this chapter the term refers to the same entity.

In this chapter, we will cover the following:

- Understand the problem domain: investment research
- Core Agentic Concepts and Terminology
- Requirements, estimation, API design, and database design for investment research
- High-level system design
- Detailed system design
- Guardrails
- Resolving bottlenecks, and
- Testing and evaluation

Problem statement: Design an agentic AI system that continuously analyzes market data, generates and evaluates investment hypotheses, and produces a daily recommendation report that can be used by asset managers in making informed investment decisions.

Understand the problem domain: Investment research

Because the constraints of investment research shape almost every design decision that follows, let's begin by grounding the system in the domain it serves.

Investment research is the work of forming opinions about securities, i.e., equities, credit, commodities, currencies, etc., and turning those opinions into portfolio positions. It is done on both the sell side and the buy side. Sell-side research (at banks like Morgan Stanley or Goldman Sachs) publishes opinions for client consumption. Buy-side research (at asset managers, hedge funds, pension funds, and sovereign wealth funds) is the in-house engine that decides what the firm itself buys and sells. The system in the current chapter is built for the buy-side. The consumers are the firm's own portfolio managers (PMs), not external clients.

A typical buy-side research desk is organized by sector or strategy. One group gathers data and builds models. The other group produces written theses. Portfolio managers combine those theses with risk constraints to construct and rebalance portfolios. A separate trading desk implements the orders. Also, a compliance team polices what may be held and traded, and a risk team enforces exposure limits. An investment lifecycle is dependent on four questions:

1. What is the thesis (why does this trade have a positive expected return?)
2. What is the catalyst (what specifically will cause the market to agree with us, and when?)
3. What is the sizing (how much risk are we willing to take on this view, given the rest of the portfolio?)
4. What is the exit strategy (under what conditions do we cut losses or take profit?)

The agentic system in this chapter addresses the first three of these and leaves the fourth to humans.

To add some detailed insight around the data domain, there are three main areas of data that influence every research decision. They are:

- **Market data:** It consists of prices, volumes, derivatives implied volatility, order-book depth, etc. It mainly falls under the category of structured data and usually arrives in a high frequency.
- **Fundamental data:** It consists of financial statements, regulatory filings (e.g., 10-Ks, 10-Qs in the US and annual reports and half-yearly reports in the UK), transcripts of earnings calls, guidance, etc. It arrives in semi-structured format, low frequency because of its nature but in high volume as the data can be dense.
- **Alternative data:** Such data can arrive from multiple sources, usually unstructured. It can consist of information from newswires, broker reports, satellite imagery, credit card panels, supply-chain shipping records, social media sentiment, etc. For instance, images of crops can signal agricultural activity that may be central to a company's business. The data under this category is of very high volume. Analyzing such high-volume, unstructured data manually is a time-critical, complex, and exhausting activity. This is the area where an LLM-based agentic system can be leveraged to supplement human effort.

Asset managers operate under disclosure, custody, and conduct rules administered by national regulators, e.g., the Financial Conduct Authority (FCA) in the United Kingdom or Securities and

Exchange Commission (SEC) in the United States. There are three main areas of consideration for remaining compliant with such regulatory requirements:

1. **Record keeping:** The basic requirement here is to maintain a copy of recommendations and the material behind them in a non-rewritable, non-erasable format for a certain number of years [3]. Such a requirement leads to maintaining such data in a WORM (write once, read many) compatible archive.
2. **Regulation Fair Disclosure (Reg FD),** a US SEC rule used here as a representative example [4]**:** This is to guide and restrict how non-public information can flow. Any information about its origin or reliability that cannot be confidently determined must be documented and flagged.
3. **Managing conflicts of interest:** Recommendations should be made in the client's interest, and any conflict must be disclosed to and managed by compliance.

So, how can agentic AI help with this? The volume and variety of unstructured market-relevant data have outgrown what a team can manually read. LLMs (large language models) are increasingly capable of structured extraction, summarization, and explainable reasoning over text, while also expressing uncertainty when appropriately instructed and constrained. And cloud-native orchestration (durable workflows, vector stores, and observability) makes it feasible to wire a fleet of specialized agents together with the auditability that regulators and portfolio managers require.

Before getting into the system design for this problem, it is helpful to understand some core fundamentals associated with an agentic system.

Core Agentic Concepts and Terminology

Below we have explained some important concepts related to an agentic system that are used in this chapter extensively. A thorough knowledge of the concepts will help you better relate to the explanation during the system design phase.

Agent: An agent is a stateful loop around an LLM that (a) reads a task, (b) decides whether to call a tool [6], draft a sub-goal, or emit a final answer, and (c) updates its scratchpad/memory and continues. The loop terminates on a success criterion or a hop limit. Each of the agents that will be used while designing this problem - market-data, signal, hypothesis, simulation, reporter, evaluator, and compliance - is one such loop with a tailored system prompt and a restricted tool scope.

Tool: A tool is a typed function the agent can call, e.g., a REST endpoint, a SQL query, a vector search, or a backtest job. Tools are described to the agent through a schema (name, JSON-schema arguments, return type, and error semantics). The runtime intercepts the model's tool-call output [7], validates the arguments, executes the function, and returns the result as the next observation. Restricting which tools an agent may call is our primary safety boundary.

Orchestrator: It is also known as **the planner** [8][9]. It decides which agent runs in which order and what input each agent receives. Two common patterns are a 'graph orchestrator,' where edges are explicit, and a 'free-form supervisor,' where one LLM dispatches to others. This design picks the graph orchestrator for production work because it is replayable and easier to test. The supervisor is reserved for the interactive follow-up chat (covered in design).

Memory: Agents have three memory tiers: 'short-term scratchpad' inside one run, 'episodic memory' across runs (e.g., stores what happened yesterday or the last week), and 'semantic memory' for longer-term (e.g., a vector store of every document the agent has ever read). The component 'Memory' is the difference between a general chatbot and an agent that learns [12]. Human interaction with an agent contributes to its learning process as the agent maintains the context from previous interactions.

Evaluator: An evaluator is an agent (or a deterministic rule) that grades another agent's output. In this design an evaluator will be used to score hypotheses for novelty and evidential support before they enter the simulation queue. This is the safety net against the LLM fabricating or hallucinating earnings numbers.

Compliance Agent: A dedicated agent (or rule set) that checks a finished report against policy, regulatory, and disclosure rules before it can be released. It is the final gate before a recommendation is stored and shown to a human.

Requirements, estimation, API, and database design

With the agent vocabulary in place, we can point it at this specific build, and, as with any system, that starts by pinning down what it must actually do.

Requirement clarification

As explained earlier, an investment research system has a vast scope to accomplish using a single system. It is absolutely important to fully understand the extent of the problem you are expected to solve. At each logical stage you should keep validating your understanding with the business or interviewers. The following are some questions that should help:

Q: What is this system expected to do?

A: The system must ingest available information from the market (e.g., news headlines, press releases, regulatory filings, and social media sentiment) to produce recommendations.

Q: What is the main business objective of this system, and who will be the users?

A: The system is being built to facilitate buy-side research. It will be used by people like portfolio managers, analysts, and other team members to gather information in a timely manner from the market for making investment decisions. The main objective of this system is to reduce the research time by performing efficient information discovery and generating recommendations that can be used to improve quality and consistency during investment decision-making. Trade execution will be performed by the designated human counterpart.

Q: What is the expected data and user volume?

A: To start with, let's take a ballpark number of a million documents the system interacts with per day across all the sources. It will increase over time. There will be approximately 10,000 users made up of portfolio managers, analysts, researchers, etc.

Q: Do we have to maintain a record of the source and reference materials used to generate a recommendation?

A: Yes. It is a regulatory requirement to maintain such information. It should be maintained in a non-rewritable form for a minimum of 10 years. The records should be available for auditing and similar purposes during this period.

Q: Is this research report needed at a particular time of the day, or is it continuous near real-time?

A: A daily morning report must be available before trading starts. During the day, in case some new information is found with significant impact, a new analysis should be presented. The system should remain functional during core business hours with 99.9% availability. A slightly relaxed availability is fine outside this window.

Q: Should previous analyses have any influence on the future recommendations?

A: Yes. Also, any stale information should not be considered.

Q: How should the system align itself around the risk posture?

A: All recommendations must undergo an associated risk assessment and include the evaluation.

Q: What is desired in case of a conflict between agents and also during recommendations?

A: Any conflicts between agents before generating a recommendation should be handled by the system internally. All conflicting recommendations, along with the conflict details, should be presented to the human user to make a final decision.

Q: Would a chat-style detailed follow-up on the data, i.e., recommendations, be helpful?

A: Absolutely. It is something that is needed for people like portfolio managers to gather additional confidence in the recommendations.

Q: Are we building the system for web-based access or multiple-device support as well?

A: To keep it simple, we will only focus on web-client-based access for this task.

Requirement summary

Extracting the information from the conversation during the requirement clarification phase earlier, we can summarize the overall requirements as follows:

Functional requirements

- Ingest market data daily with frequent refresh. The data includes - news headlines, press releases, regulatory filings, pricing ticks, fundamentals, and social media sentiment - across an instrument list. The system covers an average of 10,000 publicly traded stocks (commonly called '*tickers*' within the industry).
- Convert raw inputs into structured features (earnings surprise, momentum, sentiment polarity, factor exposure, etc.).
- Generate investable theses with explicit evidence chains.
- Score each hypothesis against the current book for evaluating investment strategies and forecasting portfolio performance.
- Compose a recommendation report ranking the top hypotheses with confidence intervals, drawdown estimates, and human-readable rationale.
- Allow a portfolio manager (PM) to ask follow-up questions, request a deeper dive, or override an agent's conclusion. The system records every decision for audit.

Non-functional requirements

- Availability = 99.9% during trading hours
- **Reliability**: The system should have a built-in retry mechanism to overcome any temporary failure. The workflow should resume from the point at which it failed.
- **Consistency**: Strong consistency for recommendations. This is because a recommendation is the source of truth that triggers downstream reporting and investment-related processes. The information must be available to all the viewers in a consistent manner at any given point in time. The research documents/data can use eventual consistency because their main use case is further querying and auditing.
- **Scalability**: The system should be scalable to handle an increase in market data research document volume.
- **Durability**: Reference materials must be stored in a durable store for the defined period with the capability to be read on demand in a WORM (Write Once, Read Many) fashion.

Assumptions

Making the right set of assumptions while designing such a complex system involving agents is a must-have step. This step adds clarity to the underlying ambiguity that could be difficult for interviewers to relate to for a relatively new technology. We will elaborate on some of the assumptions during their usage with the detailed design.

- An average user makes 50 queries in a day.
- The average document size post-normalization is 5 KB.
- The average number of chunks per document used for embedding is 3.
- Embedding vector dimension is 1536 (an optimal dimension for research-related work). As the system matures, it can be updated. The given dimension uses 6 KB per chunk.
- The system users are aware of prompting best practices for querying. The average number of tokens consumed per query is 10,000 for input and 2,000 for output. This count is agnostic of the number of instruments. It will help during cost calculation.
- The prompt and response cache hit ratio is assumed to be 30%.
- The system will use a polyglot persistence model. Some of the data stores and their estimates can be included at a later stage to keep the focus on the mainstream requirement.
- LLM pricing can be determined depending on the enterprise pricing model and hence not included in the design for now.
- Users interacting with the system are authenticated.

> **Note**
>
> **Vector embedding:** It is a way to derive a numerical representation (a fixed-length list) of supplied data elements, e.g., text, images, and audio so that they can be compared numerically rather than the original content form. For a data element, a machine translates it into a list of coordinates called a vector. Data with similar meaning or intent end up placed near each other on the coordinate space. For instance, 'Football' and 'Hockey' will be placed close to each other in the coordinate space if you compare them with the placement of the word 'Food' in the same space.

> **Note**
>
> **Vector dimension**: A vector dimension is the total number of numerical values used in the fixed-length list mentioned in 'vector embedding' above. If you think of a 2D mathematical space, the dimension is 2 (x, y coordinate). For a 3D space it will be 3 (x, y, z coordinate). For an N-dimensional space, the dimension is N. That means a data element is represented in its 'N' mathematical dimensions. As we increase the number of dimensions, it improves the embedding accuracy but the trade-off is in the speed and storage space required. For research-related work, 1536 is presented here as a reasonable dimension.

Estimations

Estimation for an agentic system spans more areas than the other use cases we have covered so far. This is mainly driven by the fact that the agents can run autonomously and hence require their own execution space that will consume resources. An estimation for such resource utilization covering storage, compute, cost, etc. creates a better overall understanding of system usage for the stakeholders.

For estimation purposes, all calculations round 86,400 seconds in a day to 100,000 seconds and 365 days in a year to 400 days for ease of mental arithmetic.

Here are the workload model QPS estimates:

```
Daily active users (DAU) = 10,000
Queries per user per day = 50
Number of queries per day = 10000 x 50 = 500000 queries per day
Average QPS = 500000 / 100000 = 5 QPS
Average QPS for trading hours (assuming an 8-hour average) = queries per day /
8hrs = 500000 / (8 x 60 x 60) = 17
Peak QPS for trading hours (10x) = 17 x 10 = 170 QPS.
```

Given the sensitive nature of the business, some additional headroom is a better idea while designing such a system. Allowing a further 25% headroom on the peak QPS, the baseline **peak = 213 QPS.**

Storage estimates

There are different storage categories where estimates will be helpful. These include raw documents, embeddings, agent traces, hypothesis records, etc. More details about the storage are added in the relevant section to follow.

Raw Document Storage:

```
No. of documents x document size = 1000000 x 5KB = 1M x 5KB = 5GB
Assuming a 2% change in the document every day because of news refreshes, or
likewise = 5GB x 2% = 100 MB per day.
Annual growth = daily change scaled to a year = 100MB x 400 = 40GB/year
```

Embeddings storage:

```
No. of docs x no. of chunks x size per vector = 1000000 x 3 x 6KB = 18GB
Using 2% change as in the case of document storage above, daily growth = 18GB x 2%
= 360MB per day
Annual growth = 360 MB x 400 = 144 GB
```

Agent traces (per agent) storage:

```
Assuming each query to the agent generates 10 KB for tracing, observability
purposes
Daily traces = No. of queries/day x 10KB = 500000 x 10KB = 5GB
Annual storage = 5GB x 400 = 2TB
```

Hypothesis record storage:

```
Assuming 2KB is needed for a hypothesis
Storage requirement = 500000 x 2KB = 1GB/day = 400GB/year
```

LLM token consumption estimates

Token estimation is important in such problems because of its direct impact on budgeting. This is because the main contributor of LLM pricing is the number of tokens consumed. Hence, as token consumption increases, the overall cost increases.

```
Input: No. of queries x tokens per query = 500,000 x 10,000 = 5 billion/day
Output: No. of queries x tokens per query = 500,000 x 2,000 = 1 billion/day
Cache hit ratio = 30%
Net input tokens = 5B x 70% = 3.5 billion input tokens/day
Net output tokens = 1B x 70% = 0.7 billion output tokens/day
```

API Design

The system requires three main types of interactions:

1. Users interacting with the system, e.g., interactions by portfolio managers and analysts.
2. Agent interactions, and
3. Administrative access for management purposes.

For the API design work, we have considered only the first two interactions. The administrative access interaction requires some associated understanding of operations-side requirements and hence can be created at a later stage, outside the scope of this task.

The following API endpoints support the key research workflows, from initiating and retrieving reports to providing feedback and enabling conversational queries:

- `POST /v1/research/reports` - Triggers the research work for a list of sectors or tickers. It accepts input parameters in the request body. It can be executed on-demand or at a scheduled time. It fetches the recommendation reports. The default is datetime=current-time. This call stores supporting documents, e.g., PDF and JSON, used to formulate hypotheses. The API requires adequate authorization for the triggering entity.
- `GET /v1/research/reports` - Lists all the research executions. It will return the list depending on the underlying authorization model in line with the principle of least privilege.
- `GET /v1/research/reports/{id}` - Gets the research report by ID.
- `POST /v1/research/reports/{id}/feedback` - Allows portfolio managers to accept or reject a hypothesis. Once accepted, the report becomes immutable.
- `POST /v1/research/chat` - Conversational query leveraging LLM capabilities, performed by portfolio managers or similar users with adequate access.

Storage and database

We use polyglot persistence in this case because of the different access patterns. Time-series prices require column-oriented compression, documents require full-text and vector search, agent traces require append-only storage and structured querying, and recommendation reports require document-style versioning. Table 11.1 captures a view of the different types of storage needed for solving this problem along with their reasoning.

Data	Datastore	Reason for the choice
Raw news, filings, transcripts, normalized metadata	`PostgreSQL` and `S3`	`PostgreSQL` for strong consistency for canonical data. S3 as cold storage.
Document embeddings by chunk Vector store	`Pgvector`	Nearest-neighbor search for RAG
Knowledge graph	`Neo4j`	The system receives information from existing reliable sources as well as open information from the web. The information received from such sources is then converted into a knowledge graph. This is needed to plot relationships between entities, e.g., company 'A' acquired company 'B' in year 'Y'. This information can have an impact on recommendations for 'A' and 'B'.
Feature store for signals computed by the agent, e.g., momentum, surprise, sentiment	Feast (feature store) over Redis	Actual data resides in Parquet format. It is to support online lookups and offline backtest parity.
Logging/monitoring, traceability	`OpenSearch/ ELK`	To achieve free text search and aggregations for debugging. It will contain traces for every LLM call, agent-to-agent communication, etc.
Hypotheses	`PostgreSQL`	Stores generated theses and the portfolio manager's feedback on it.
Report archive	`S3/ Glacier`	For non-rewritable documents.

Table 11.1: Storage used to build an investment research system

System design

At a high level, designing an agentic AI system looks a lot like any other design problem. You still list the components, sketch how they integrate and talk to each other, and check that they meet the functional and non-functional requirements that are provided to you by the stakeholders. The difference shows up the moment you open up one of those components and look inside.

In a conventional design, a component is *deterministic* - the same input produces the same output, and the interesting questions are about throughput, latency, and consistency. In an agentic system, at least one component is an LLM-driven agent whose behavior is *probabilistic*, whose "code" is a prompt, whose failure modes include hallucination and prompt injection, and whose cost per invocation is measured not in CPU cycles but in tokens and dollars.

That one shift changes many things in your design. Interfaces between components become natural-language contracts rather than typed function calls. Observability has to capture the reasoning, not just the result. Testing becomes an evaluation problem rather than a unit-test problem. And safety stops being an add-on; rather, it becomes a first-class design constraint. The rest of this chapter walks through what those shifts actually look like in practice. We will look at how you decompose the workload into specialized agents, how you bound their behavior with tools and guardrails, and how you compose them so the whole thing is auditable, cost-predictable, and trustworthy enough to put in front of a portfolio manager.

High-level design

The requirements and estimates establish what to build and at what scale; the design now shows how the pieces fit together, starting with the high-level view.

The high-level design for the system is created using a well-structured layered architecture as shown in Figure 11.1. The web clients can interact with the downstream system via the exposed web module. The orchestration layer owns the DAG (Directed Acyclic Graph). The DAG dictates agents' execution order and criteria. The agent layer contains a set of independently executing modules with their execution order controlled by the DAG. Each agent runs in its defined boundary. Separating the overall research tasks using multiple agents makes the system modular, independently testable, and independently scalable, with clear and focused responsibilities. If there is a need to introduce a new agent or to update/remove an existing agent task, it can be done with minimal impact. Such separation creates an environment where agents can run in parallel. Also, based on the nature of the task associated with an agent, it is easier to choose an appropriate model. Not every agent will require the top-tier model for its function, for example, the hypothesis agent will use a top-tier model, but the market data agent need not.

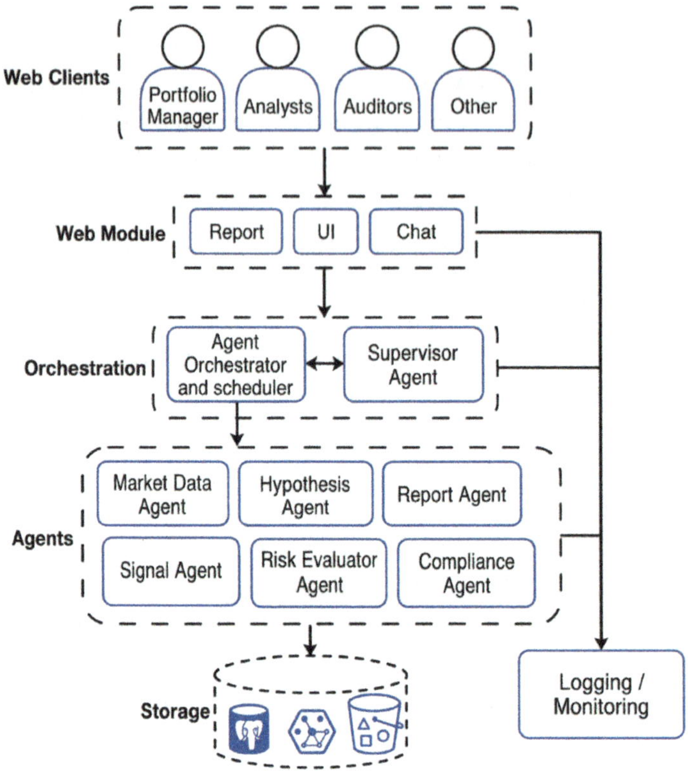

Figure 11.1: High-level design of an agentic AI investment research system

During its execution, agents store data into their connected backend store for persistence. Each layer in the preceding diagram generates traces that are shipped to the Logging/Monitoring module.

Detailed design

The high-level view in the previous section showed what the components are. Now we will go through the detailed design to follow a single run through those components. We will start from the trigger point that begins a journey and will take it through to the creation of a persisted, approved report. We will also take a look at the feedback loop where human-agent interactions are detailed.

The journey has two main trigger points:

1. Client-initiated journey and
2. Scheduler-initiated journey

The scheduler-based journey is responsible for ensuring time-bound report generation. A user- or client-initiated journey handles report approval, further queries, and human-initiated feedback for agent learning and maturity.

Below we have used the scheduler-initiated journey to explain the backend, agent-based interactions and processing. Agent interactions, as captured in *Figure 11.2*, are agnostic of the trigger route.

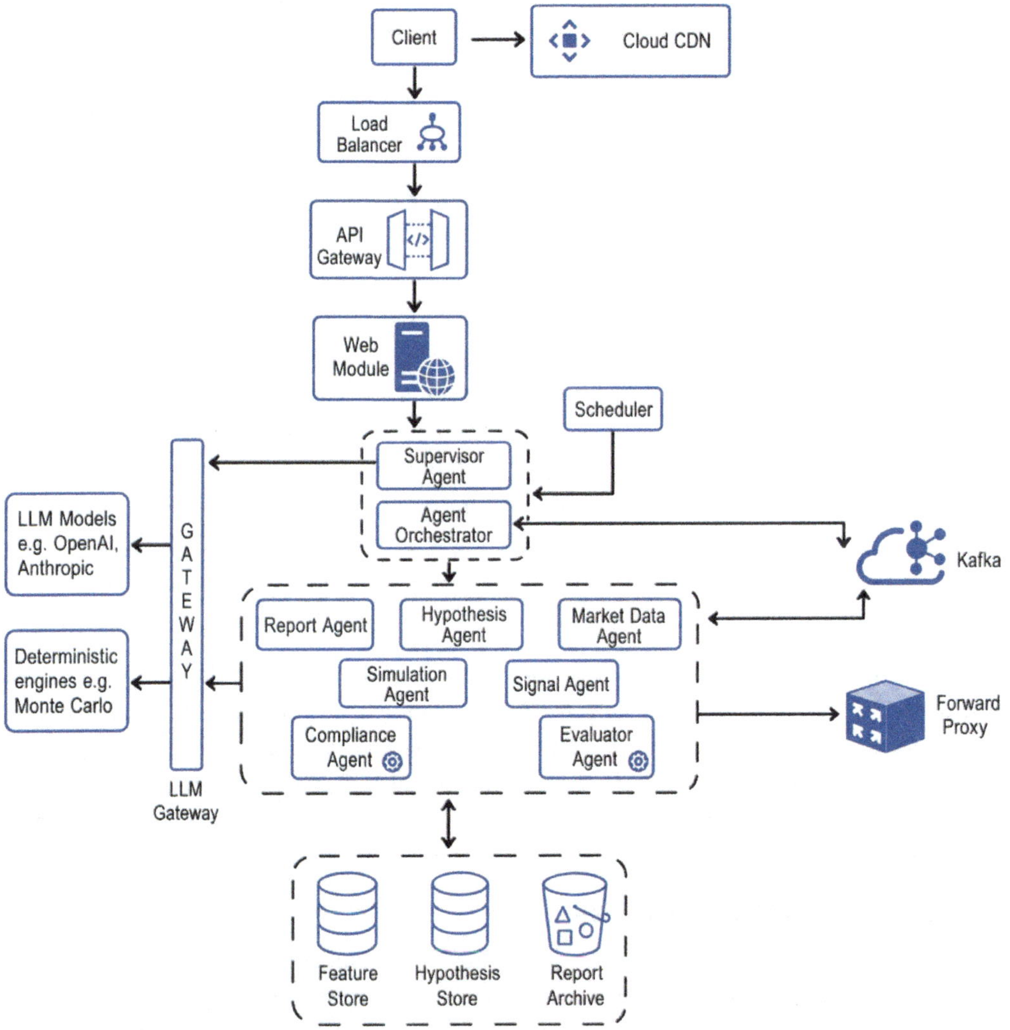

Figure 11.2: Detailed design for Agentic AI investment research

The workflow is triggered on a schedule or on user demand, and the request is routed by type. If the request is user-initiated, it will be first picked by the supervisor agent. If the request is to trigger the workflow, then the request will be passed to the agent orchestrator with the desired action.

The orchestrator is the service that owns the entire end-to-end agentic workflow. Services such as 'Temporal' can be a good fit for workflow management. One important rationale behind the choice is - its ability to run workflows with durable execution [10]. If a worker abruptly stops mid-run, it can use a different worker to resume the execution from the last confirmed checkpoint. The resilience matters here because gathering information from the web can be a time-consuming task (over an hour in the worst-case) and built-in recovery is far better than rebuilding it by hand.

Here, it is also important to understand that DAG management is separate from what a workflow manager, e.g., Temporal, manages. Such a workflow manager uses the DAG to execute the agents in the required order.

The forward proxy in the diagram enables external communication. It uses strict domain whitelisting (allow-list). It can be a NAT Gateway or a similar service component within AWS infrastructure. In this design, the Kafka broker is used for event backbone management between agents. Each agent has its dedicated inbound and outbound topic for reading and writing. Each workflow will be identified by its specific `execution_id`. The `execution_id` will remain immutable and will remain present in all interactions made by any agent. Some sample events that the agents can generate during the process of their execution are `market_data_ingest_start`, `ingest_complete`, `signal_complete`, `hypothesis_accept`, `hypothesis_scored`, `report_generated`. [11]

Interaction with LLM models and their providers is facilitated by the LLM Gateway component. The gateway component is responsible for implementing and enforcing security, including scanning for data flowing through a model for PII redaction, policy enforcement and prompt-injection checks [14][15]. The gateway also performs routing to the appropriate model and implements caching to render results for an identical call, reducing cost because of the reduction in model token spend.

Scheduler-initiated journey

This design uses multiple independent agents rather than a single monolith. Keeping multiple independent models adds flexibility and also supports cost optimization. For instance, not every agent requires the same level of model, compute, storage, and other resources. The type of model you use has a direct impact on cost. The most effective approach is to separate agents according to the nature of the tasks they are designed to perform.

Let's examine the complete agentic journey with the help of *Figure 11.3*. For each agent we have explained their purpose, roles and responsibilities, and data dependency. Arrows & annotations are used in the diagram to explain an ideal order of agents' execution during its first run. Additional execution routes may exist for specific scenarios. Execution of each agent is initiated and controlled by the agent orchestrator depending on the chosen DAG for that run.

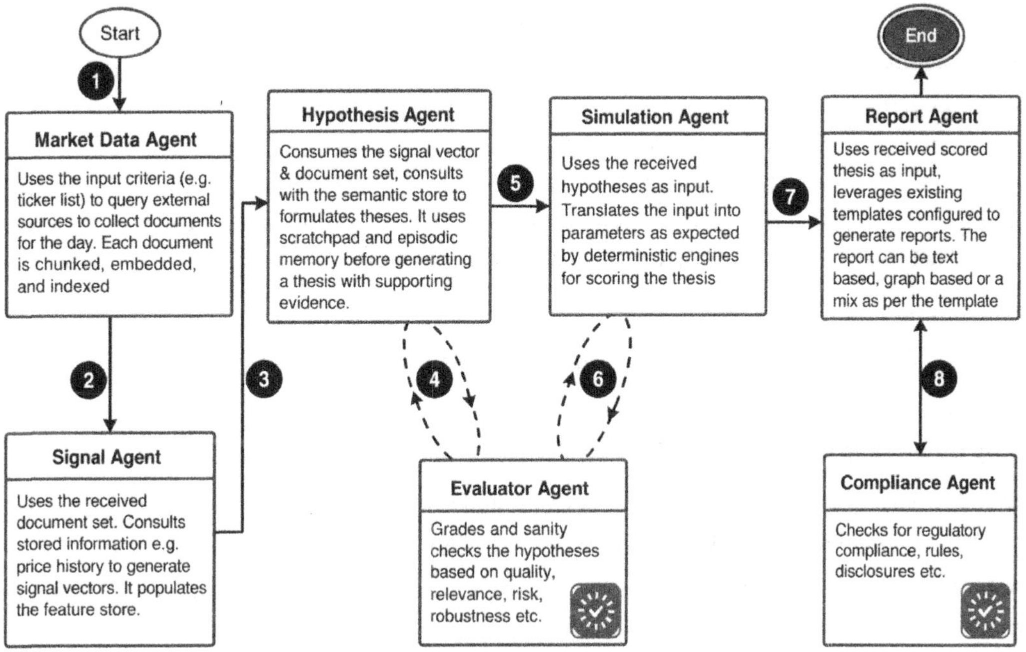

Figure 11.3: Multi-agent topology

The journey can be triggered either by a scheduler or an on-demand human user that invokes the workflow by calling the Orchestrator. The orchestrator service uses its configured DAG to initiate the agentic workflow (or simply agents). Below, we detail each agent as shown in *Figure 11.3*.

Market data agent

The execution starts by the invocation of the 'Market Data' agent. This agent is responsible for collecting documents, i.e., information from all the available sources, e.g., Bloomberg, S&P, and the open web. Separate dedicated connectors will be configured to ingest data from such sources, e.g., a sentiment connector will be configured to ingest licensed social feeds from media platforms. It then performs a level of scrubbing, e.g., deduplication of similar news, and persists the document. Each new document is chunked, embedded, and indexed into the pgvector store. If applicable from the data received, a knowledge graph (KG) will be prepared and stored in Neo4j, our chosen store. An example of candidate information for the KG store would be a company being acquired by another. A market data agent can benefit from the parallel execution to collate information from multiple origins. The role of the LLM in this case is mainly for tagging the received entities and summarizing the feeds, and hence this agent does not require a top-end model for its function. On completion of its tasks, the agent publishes its state event to the Kafka broker so that the orchestrator can execute the next planned action, i.e., run the next agent based on this event.

Signal agent

On completion of the market data agent's work, the 'Signal' agent is triggered. The agent looks at the newly ingested documents, including the KG store, and computes a structured feature vector per stock (ticker). This may include features like sentiment polarity, earnings surprises, momentum, etc. Such features are stored in the feature store for offline use. The agent updates the Kafka broker with its execution state on its task completion.

Hypothesis agent

The next agent to run is the Hypothesis agent, one of the most intensive stages. Its loop runs as follows:

Step 1: it picks up the signal vector and the document set.

Step 2: it retrieves prior learnings from episodic and semantic memory, then drafts theses, each carrying a reference to at least one supporting document.

Step 3: each thesis is sent to the Evaluator agent for grading. The agent grades it on multiple criteria such as evidence coverage and quality.

Step 4: if the evaluator rejects a thesis due to a conflict, the hypothesis agent regenerates and resubmits it for evaluation. This feedback loop repeats until the evaluation results in an acceptable grade, i.e., a thesis clears the grade threshold, or the configured number of attempts is exhausted without an acceptable one.

Step 5: the run state is then published to the broker.

Simulation agent and evaluator agent

When the hypothesis agent completes successfully, the next stage is to simulate the thesis to produce a more deterministic result. The orchestrator invokes the 'Simulation' agent for this task. It uses a lightweight LLM that can convert the hypotheses into consumable input parameters for the deterministic engines. The purpose of this step is to generate a numerical rating for the hypotheses that can be used for scoring. The simulator agent then interacts with the evaluator agent to perform the sanity check of the scored hypotheses. The sanity checks may include steps such as assumption consistency and validation. In this design we have used the evaluator agent to perform hypothesis evaluation as well as a sanity check of the simulator results. In a production environment a better approach would be to separate them. All hypotheses that do not pass this step will be dropped before the next stage. The system may maintain the list of such dropped hypotheses. On completion, the simulation agent will publish its state to the broker and finish its execution.

Report agent and compliance agent

Once the simulation agent completes its scoring task, the orchestrator invokes the 'Report' agent. The report agent ranks all the scored hypotheses. For ranking, the agent leverages the scoring performed by the simulation agent's deterministic engines, and hence there is no role of LLM in this activity. LLM is used to summarize the pros and cons associated with each ranked hypothesis. The agent uses ranking and a configured report template to generate the report. The templates are usually a mix of text and graphs. If more than one template is configured, the agent can choose the most suitable one for the report. Before the report can be considered complete, it is sent to a compliance agent to perform policy, regulatory, and other compliance checks. On compliance success, the report, along with its supporting evidence and traces are stored in the WORM S3 bucket. The report is also uploaded into the configured CDN so that all the authorized users can access it globally with speed. A human user, e.g., a portfolio manager, can then review, give feedback, and accept or reject the proposal. Once it is accepted by the human user, the report becomes a record.

Agents' activities are comprehensively logged and monitored. In case of any abnormality in execution, e.g., an evaluator rejecting a hypothesis with an unusual rate, the tokens spent by a model are much higher than anticipated; an automated process will be triggered to terminate the active process and notify the support representative for investigation. This approach also safeguards against token misuse by an agent, whether intentional or accidental.

The client-initiated (follow-up) journey

Alongside the scheduled run, a portfolio manager can work with a finished report interactively. This path is handled by the supervisor agent rather than the graph orchestrator, because the questions are open-ended and the order of steps cannot be fixed in advance. A typical follow-up runs as follows:

Step 1: The user opens a published report from the CDN and sends a request through the chat endpoint (POST /v1/research/chat), for example, approving a recommendation, asking why a thesis was ranked where it was, or requesting a deeper dive on one ticker.

Step 2: The supervisor agent authenticates and authorizes the user, loads the report context along with its stored evidence and traces, and decides what is needed to answer.

Step 3: For a simple explanation, it answers directly from the stored report, evidence, and semantic memory, with no new pipeline run. For a deeper request, it dispatches only the agent it needs, for example rerunning the hypothesis or simulation agent for a single ticker, and waits for the result.

Step 4: It composes the answer, keeping it grounded in the same evidence the report used, returns it to the user, and logs the exchange.

Step 5: If the user approves or rejects a recommendation, or leaves feedback (POST /v1/research/reports/{id}/feedback), that decision is recorded. Approval turns the report into an immutable record; feedback is written to episodic and semantic memory so later runs can learn from it.

Because a deeper dive by a user can trigger real compute, the same cost tracking, rate limits, and compliance checks that guard the scheduled run apply to this path too.

Next, we are going to discuss the end-to-end flow of one of the agents from the entire suite discussed above to help you better understand how different elements and components are joined together to make a fully functional agent. We are expanding on the 'Market data' agent, being the first one in the chain. But other agents more or less follow a similar path.

Figure 11.4 captures the agent's end-to-end flow, walked through step by step below.

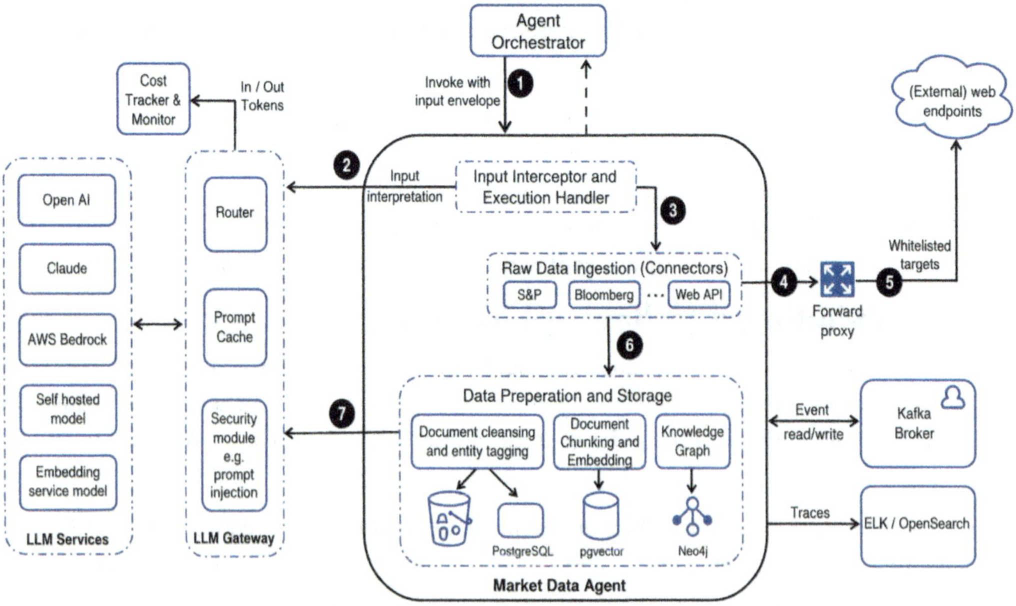

Figure 11.4: Market data agent detailed view

The steps mentioned below are executed regardless of whether the workflow is triggered by the scheduler or a human user.

Step 1: the orchestrator calls the agent with an input envelope containing `execution_id`, `ticker_list`, and `free_text_criteria`.

Step 2: The request is picked up by the input interceptor, which makes a lightweight LLM call through the gateway to determine the overall intent of the query and build a task list, e.g., of which connectors to invoke and which can run in parallel.

Step 3: Once the execution planning is done, the module uses connectors to make external calls for document gathering. Rate limits and circuit breakers are built in, so calls stay within agreed limits and any failure is handled gracefully.

Steps 4 and 5: connector traffic leaves through a forward proxy with strict domain whitelisting. The interceptor and execution handler neither read nor alter the data that comes back from external sources.

Step 6: The data received is handed to the data-preparation and storage module.

Step 7: At this stage, a series of functions are executed on the received data, including deduplication of information for a ticker, tagging of different entities, chunking and embedding, and population of the knowledge graph. Each function stores the metadata and associated data into its designated store for future use. Functions like entity tagging and embedding will require interactions with the LLM services module that is facilitated by the LLM gateway.

Step 8: The gateway component is also linked to the cost tracker and monitor module. The purpose of this module is to keep the overall cost factor associated with the agentic modules within limits. If the cost goes beyond the expected budget, an appropriate action can be triggered by this module depending on the business use case, e.g., send an alert when 80% of budget is consumed or stop any calls to LLM services if the cost is over 95% of the budget.

During its execution, the traces generated by each module within the agent are shipped to the ELK/OpenSearch implementation for comprehensive logging and monitoring.

When the execution of this agent is complete, it will write an `ingest_complete` event to its designated Kafka topic. The agent can write to the broker at different configured stages of work, e.g., at the start of the work, after completion of the planning phase, after receiving documents from external sites, and so on. Keeping track of each and every event can be useful if there are or can be some downstream business functions dependent on such events. The trade-off of maintaining all the events is space consumption.

All other agents used in this chapter can follow a similar approach, as shown in *Figure 11.4*. The differentiating component will be the one marked as 'Market Data Agent' in the diagram. This will change depending on the business function an agent is being built to deliver.

Any system design problems involving agents must explicitly talk about the different guardrails in place to deal with the edge cases or negative scenarios. It creates a great deal of confidence in the system where most of the heavy lifting work is handed over to agents. Below we have highlighted the guardrails used while designing the system.

Guardrails

In the system design phase, we have used these guardrails while discussing the system functionality. In this section we have captured them in a more explicit way.

For agents to perform their designated tasks, a toolset guardrail is used. The toolset enables an agent to pick tools that are just enough for its execution. For instance, a market-data agent can interact with the external web for data gathering but a report agent cannot. You can think of this guardrail as an agentic equivalent to the principle of least privilege in case of a human user. Also, all external interactions are guarded by a strict allow-list of URLs via a forward proxy where each URL access is strictly logged and monitored.

The system further talks about a cost and budget guardrail (refer to *Figure 11.4*) that is one of the most important aspects to consider. It keeps the overall agentic execution cost within limits. Depending on the desired outcome, the LLM Gateway can be configured to start notifying its stakeholders when an agent has consumed a defined threshold of its assigned tokens. Or it can block access to LLM services altogether if an agent has exhausted its token limit. The design additionally safeguards agentic process execution by constant monitoring using a backend monitoring process that can even terminate an agent process if the agent is confirmed to demonstrate abnormal behavior. The LLM Gateway component also ensures an overall robust security posture of the system while interacting with LLM services, including sensitive-data and PII redaction. The gateway also has a dedicated module to identify and neutralize prompt injection.

Rate-limiting and circuit breaker patterns are implemented to prevent agents from overwhelming the other systems they interact with, including the external web.

The evaluator and compliance agents help ensure a deterministic outcome from probabilistic background work. Also, each recommendation and thesis is supported by adequate evidence with complete traceability that creates a strong background for regulatory requirements.

The most important guardrail in place is human-in-the-loop. The agents only perform their background activities to produce an outcome for humans to assess and take some action. A human user can reject a recommendation, query further with follow-on questions, and provide feedback to the agents. All such information is collected by the agent to improve its behavior for its user base. Also, an agent cannot execute any action on tickers, e.g., buy or sell. Such actions are executed by a human user.

Resolving bottlenecks

Every agentic system inherits the same class of bottlenecks that any distributed system does: hotspots, single points of coordination, and cache-hit sensitivity, but a few of them appear in forms that are unique to this architecture. A few worth calling out for this chapter are as follows:

For the LLM Gateway, the ceiling is set by vendor rate limits, not by your servers. One way to improve this is by sending traffic across more than one vendor.

Use of pgvector to perform vector search might become a bottleneck after approximately 50 million chunks (platform limitation). The mentioned number might look large but with this type of data-intensive use case the limit can be exceeded easily. A purpose-built ANN (Approximate Nearest Neighbor) store can be implemented for this purpose, e.g., Milvus, Pinecone, Qdrant. [13]

The design measures overall cost in terms of tokens consumed. If overall execution cost is a bottleneck, then configuring a slightly higher cache-hit rate can provide substantial cost benefit because of the reduction in tokens consumed.

The design stores traces into a WORM store. The partitioning of such storage should be based on `execution_id` rather than per ticker. This is because a hot, famous ticker can overwhelm the storage partition if it is maintained based on ticker.

Testing and evaluation

Testing is where an agentic system goes beyond a conventional one. Because the components you care about are probabilistic, a pass or fail in a unit-test suite tells you very little. Testing of such a system should be done using a layered evaluation exercise.

The first step in such testing is to create golden datasets. A dataset can be small but reasonable for your use case. This can be achieved by growing your set steadily using realistic inputs such as actual news headlines, genuine company filings (some filing information is publicly available), research, and the kinds of actual questions a portfolio manager asks. Also gather grading information for different combinations of criteria from your golden datasets based on past evaluations by human analysts. Every agentic deployment, regardless of whether it involves a prompt change or a model change, must run against this golden dataset to return the expected output. Satisfactory test execution is the only path for getting the change deployed in production.

Regression evaluation is another area. A small change in prompt might improve output quality significantly but may end up consuming most of the allocated tokens for an agent. It should be treated as regression and not an improvement.

Some strict criteria should be outlined in your test scenario. For instance, a thesis must cite at least one source. Or no restricted ticker may appear anywhere (it could also be restricted because of your company policies).

Build and use negative scenario-based testing. For example, attempt prompt injection, supply sensitive/PII data, use a malformed URL, or randomly remove an allow-listed URL from the forward proxy to block external access. Such testing should run as a continuous background process to highlight any shortcoming.

For human sampling, a portfolio manager or an analyst can grade a subset of samples on a regular basis that can contribute to the evaluator agent's training. Such a step reduces the gap between the evaluator's grading in the production and test environments.

Summary

This chapter designed an agentic AI system for buy-side investment research, a problem whose difficulty lies less in the language model than in the orchestration around it. The system augments a research desk with a fleet of specialized agents that continuously read the market, turn raw information into structured signals, generate and score investment theses, and compose an auditable recommendation report for a portfolio manager to sign off on. Treating it as a distributed workflow problem with a probabilistic compute layer bolted on kept the focus on what actually makes it hard: scheduling, observability, cost control, determinism, and the safety envelope around every tool call.

We built up the core agentic vocabulary first, the agent loop, tools, the orchestrator, the three tiers of memory, and the evaluator, and then put it to work. Requirements were clarified with the business and split into functional and non-functional needs, assumptions were stated openly, and only then did we size the workload, storage, and token consumption. Those numbers informed a set of deliberate choices: a graph orchestrator running on a durable workflow engine such as Temporal, a Kafka event backbone with a dedicated topic per agent, an LLM gateway for routing, caching, PII redaction, and prompt-injection defense, and a polyglot persistence layer that matches each kind of data to the store that fits its access pattern.

The high-level design arranged these pieces into clean layers, and the detailed design followed a single run from the scheduler or a user request through to a persisted, compliance-checked report, tracing the handoffs between the market-data, signal, hypothesis, simulation, report, evaluator, and compliance agents. A closing deep dive into the market-data agent exposed the internal anatomy every agent shares: an interceptor that plans the work, connectors guarded by rate limits, circuit breakers, and a whitelisting proxy, a preparation stage that chunks, embeds, and populates the knowledge graph, and cost and trace instrumentation throughout. The throughline is that a dependable agentic system is built from familiar distributed-systems discipline applied around a probabilistic core that must be kept auditable, cost-bounded, and safe. Those instincts, not the model, are what an interviewer is listening for.

This brings us to the end of the system design part of the book. What you carry forward is not a set of blueprints to copy, but a way of thinking. You can sit in front of an interviewer, hear a problem you have never seen before, and start pulling on the right threads: what are the requirements, where does the state live, what does the read path look like at scale, which trade-off is the interviewer really testing? It is the same skill the strongest engineers use every day in production, not just in interview rooms. Do not be surprised if it feels a little awkward the first few times you try it in a real conversation. Fluency comes from practice. The vocabulary is yours now, and the confidence will follow every time you use it.

An interview is never just about the whiteboard. Even the strongest technical answer only reaches its target if the person across the table can follow you, trust you, and see themselves working with you. Companies do not hire the cleanest architecture; they hire the person they can rely to build alongside them, to disagree well, to lead without being watched, and to keep learning long after the interview loop ends. That is exactly what the next part of this book prepares you for.

References

Investment research and portfolio management

[1] Grinold, R. C., & Kahn, R. N. Active Portfolio Management: A Quantitative Approach for Producing Superior Returns and Controlling Risk. 2nd edition, McGraw-Hill, 1999. `https://books.google.com/books/about/Active_Portfolio_Management_A_Quantitati.html?id=a1yB8LTQnOEC`

Regulatory and compliance frameworks

[2] CFA Institute. Code of Ethics and Standards of Professional Conduct. `https://www.cfainstitute.org/standards/professionals/code-ethics-standards`

[3] U.S. Securities and Exchange Commission. Rule 17a-4: Records to Be Preserved by Certain Exchange Members, Brokers and Dealers. 17 CFR §240.17a-4. `https://www.sec.gov/rules-regulations`

[4] U.S. Securities and Exchange Commission. Regulation Fair Disclosure (Reg FD). 17 CFR §§243.100-243.103. `https://www.sec.gov/rules-regulations/2000/08/selective-disclosure-insider-trading`

[5] Financial Industry Regulatory Authority (FINRA). Rule 2241, Research Analysts and Research Reports. `https://www.finra.org/rules-guidance/rulebooks/finra-rules/2241`

Agent design and multi-agent orchestration

[6] Yao, S., Zhao, J., Yu, D., Du, N., Shafran, I., Narasimhan, K., Cao, Y. ReAct: Synergizing Reasoning and Acting in Language Models. ICLR 2023. https://doi.org/10.48550/arXiv.2210.03629

[7] Schick, T., Dwivedi-Yu, J., Dessí, R., et al. Toolformer: Language Models Can Teach Themselves to Use Tools. NeurIPS 2023. https://arxiv.org/abs/2302.04761

[8] Wu, Q., Bansal, G., Zhang, J., et al. AutoGen: Enabling Next-Gen LLM Applications via Multi-Agent Conversation. arXiv:2308.08155, 2023.

[9] LangChain. LangGraph: Stateful, Multi-Actor Applications with LLMs.

https://langchain-ai.github.io/langgraph/

Workflow orchestration and messaging infrastructure

[10] Temporal Technologies. Temporal Documentation - Durable Execution. https://docs.temporal.io/

[11] Kreps, J., Narkhede, N., Rao, J. Kafka: a Distributed Messaging System for Log Processing. Proceedings of the NetDB Workshop, 2011. https://notes.stephenholiday.com/Kafka.pdf

Retrieval, memory, and vector search

[12] Lewis, P., Perez, E., Piktus, A., et al. Retrieval-Augmented Generation for Knowledge-Intensive NLP Tasks. NeurIPS 2020. https://arxiv.org/abs/2005.11401

[13] Malkov, Y. A., & Yashunin, D. A. Efficient and Robust Approximate Nearest Neighbor Search Using Hierarchical Navigable Small World Graphs (HNSW). IEEE Transactions on Pattern Analysis and Machine Intelligence, 42(4), 2020. https://arxiv.org/abs/1603.09320

Safety, guardrails, and AI risk management

[14] Greshake, K., Abdelnabi, S., Mishra, S., et al. Not What You've Signed Up For: Compromising Real-World LLM-Integrated Applications with Indirect Prompt Injection. ACM AISec 2023. https://arxiv.org/abs/2302.12173

[15] NIST. AI Risk Management Framework (AI RMF 1.0). NIST AI 100-1, January 2023. https://www.nist.gov/itl/ai-risk-management-framework

Part 2

Behavioral Intelligence

Technical expertise may help you solve a problem, but how you approach that problem, work with others, make decisions, and respond to challenges tells a much broader story. This part explores behavioral intelligence and the signals your experiences provide about how you operate in real-world situations. You will learn how to recognize those signals, turn your experiences into compelling stories, and build a story bank that reflects your strengths and growth. Along the way, you will pick up practical frameworks you can apply directly to navigating conflict, reasoning about risk and trade-offs in decision-making, managing stakeholders with tools such as stakeholder mapping and the RACI matrix, structuring answers, and calibrating your stories to the seniority and role you are targeting. These chapters also explore core values and leadership principles commonly assessed by technology organizations. Finally, you will learn how to demonstrate behavioral intelligence clearly and authentically when your experiences are being evaluated.

This part of the book includes the following chapters:

- *Chapter 12, The Signal Beneath the Stories: What Behavioral Intelligence Is*
- *Chapter 13, The Power of Behavioral Intelligence at Work*
- *Chapter 14, From Experience to Signal: Frameworks and the Story Bank*
- *Chapter 15, Behind the Big Tech Bar: Core Values and Leadership Principles*
- *Chapter 16, Demonstration to Evaluation of Behavioral Intelligence*

12

The Signal Beneath the Stories: What Behavioral Intelligence Is

Careers in technology depend on two dimensions: what you can build and how you behave while building it. The first is technical intelligence, and Part 1 of this book was devoted to it. The second is behavioral intelligence, and it is the quieter of the two. Rarely named, rarely taught, yet weighed in every design review, every escalation, every promotion discussion, and every interview you will ever sit.

It is worth pausing on why this second dimension carries so much weight. Almost no technical work happens in isolation, and the hardest problems are rarely solved by the person who writes the most code. They are solved by the person who can align a team, raise a risk early, and hold the quality bar when the pressure is on. This is why careers seldom stall for technical reasons. Engineers are promoted for what they can build, then held back by how they work with others. As you move up, the skill gap between you and your peers narrows, and behavior becomes the deciding factor.

Artificial Intelligence widens this gap further. As tools take over more routine execution, such as writing boilerplate and generating tests, the technical baseline rises for everyone, and raw coding speed stops being the thing that sets people apart. What AI cannot do is decide which problem is worth solving, weigh the trade-offs behind a call, and get a team to trust that call enough to commit to it. That work is precisely the behavioral part, and it is becoming the clearer differentiator as the routine work is automated away.

This chapter defines that capability before anything else, i.e., what behavioral intelligence is, why it predicts success, the seven dimensions in which it shows, and how the bar rises with seniority. Only then do we turn to the place where it is most deliberately measured, the behavioral interview. Everything in this part of the book stands on these foundations.

By the end of this chapter, you will understand what behavioral intelligence is, the seven dimensions it shows up in, and how the bar rises with seniority. You will also see how it is measured in an interview, and where you stand today.

In this chapter, we will cover the following topics:

- What behavioral intelligence is: a definition and a three-part model
- Why behavioral intelligence predicts success, and the research behind it
- How the bar moves with seniority, from early career to executive
- The seven dimensions where behavioral intelligence shows up, and the AI questions that map onto them
- The measurement moment: behavioral interview formats, including panels, loops, and AI-led screening
- A self-assessment and scorecard approach to baseline where you stand today

What is behavioral intelligence?

We have been using the term, so before leaning on it any further, let us pin it down.

"Behavioral intelligence is the ability to read what a situation demands, to act in ways that visibly meet it, and to adapt as the situation changes, consistently enough that others trust you with greater responsibility."

That definition has three moving parts, and we will name them Decode, Demonstrate, and Adapt. They map directly onto the three phrases above.

Decode is reading the signals around you: what a company values, what a role expects, what a question is scoring, what the mood in a room is telling you. This is the "read what a situation demands" part.

Demonstrate is converting your experience and judgment into behavior others can observe: decisions made, stories told, commitments kept. Nobody can score your intentions; they score what they can see and hear. This is how you "act in ways that visibly meet it."

Adapt is adjusting in real time as new information arrives: a skeptical stakeholder, an unexpected follow-up question, a project that changes shape mid-flight. This is the "adapt as the situation changes" part.

Together, these three, Decode, Demonstrate, and Adapt, form the model we will use throughout. *Figure 12.1* shows how they fit together.

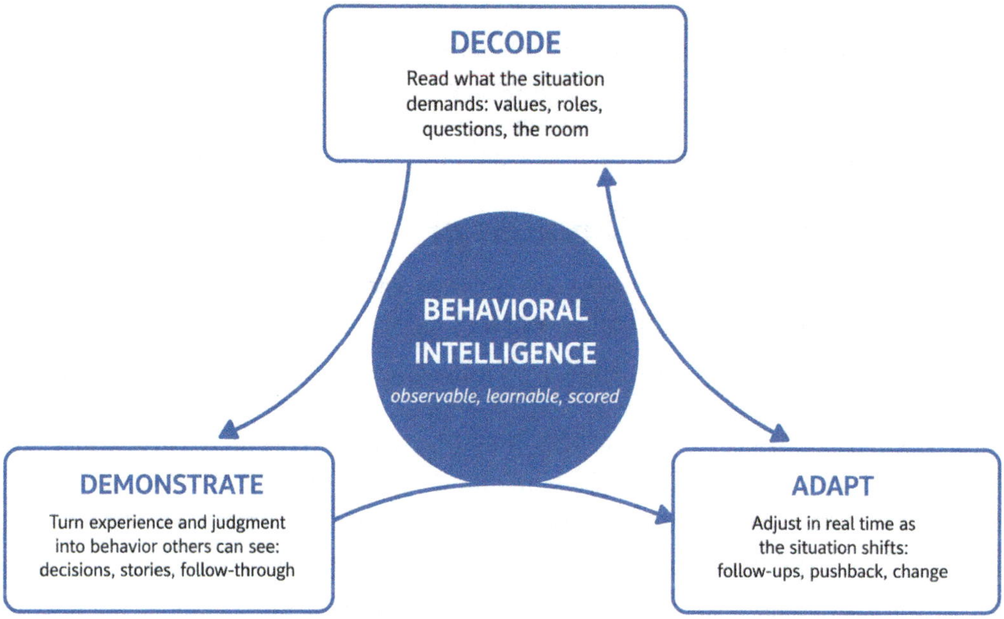

Figure 12.1: The three components of behavioral intelligence: decode, demonstrate, adapt

Now let's think about **what behavioral intelligence is *not*.** It is not IQ, which gets you into the conversation. And it is not the same as emotional intelligence, also known as emotional quotient (EQ), though the two overlap.

Emotional intelligence is a broad capacity like reading emotions, understanding what drives people, managing your own reactions, and handling relationships. Behavioral intelligence draws on much of this, but it focuses on a narrower and more visible slice - the observable choices and responses you make once you have read the situation.

That distinction matters because observable behavior is one of the primary things an organization can evaluate, reward, or promote. It is also why behavioral intelligence is learnable. It is not a personality trait; it is a discipline, built from paying attention, acting deliberately, and reviewing honestly.

As mentioned before, beyond a certain level, careers are decided behaviorally. Systems are designed by teams, defended in reviews, rescued in incidents, and funded in rooms where no code is visible.

The behavioral interview, which this part covers in depth, is the most concentrated hour of that reality - one hour designed to test how you decode, demonstrate, and adapt under pressure. Master the capability, and the interview becomes a place to show it, not something to survive. We understand that it is a large claim, so let us look at the evidence before going further.

Why behavioral intelligence predicts success?

Employers settled on behavioral interviews for a simple reason: everything else they tried, such as coding tests and technical assessments, predicted less. The case rests on four points.

Past behavior is a stable signal. Tools can be learned and skills can be taught. Patterns are harder to change: how you respond under pressure, make decisions with incomplete information, influence without authority, and recover when things go wrong. Under pressure people fall back on their habits, and habits change slowly; technical skills can be rebuilt in months, while the way you react to being wrong, blocked, or bored changes over years. An interviewer who samples those patterns is measuring something that will still be true of you next year.

The evidence is strong, and it points to one thing: structure. This is not a single study or one author's opinion. A century of selection research, pooled through meta-analyses across thousands of cases and many industries, keeps reaching the same conclusion. What gives an interview its predictive power is the discipline behind it: the same job-related questions for every candidate, scored against defined criteria. The most comprehensive recent review found that a structured interview predicts performance far better than a loose, unstructured conversation, 0.42 against 0.19, and ranked it at the top of all selection methods, ahead of job knowledge tests, work samples, and cognitive ability, once older statistical corrections are fixed [1].

The picture is easiest to see where the methods are lined up side by side. *Figure 12.2* shows how common selection methods compare on how well they predict job performance, drawn from the 2022 review. The structured interview leads, while a friendly, unstructured chat and raw years of experience predict the least.

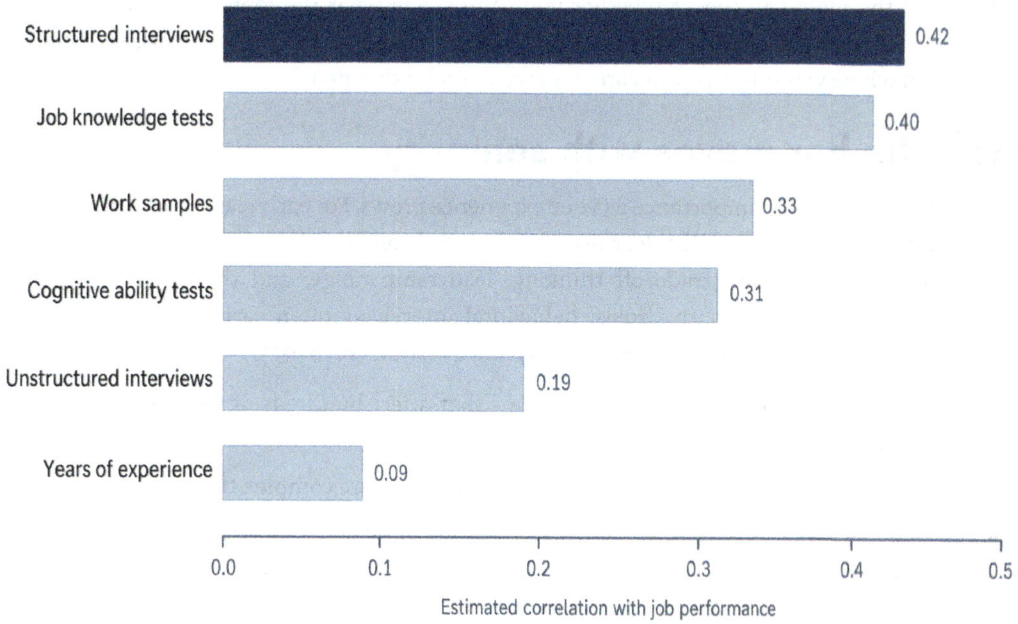

Figure 12.2: What best predicts job performance, from Sackett and colleagues' 2022 re-analysis of a century of selection research.

Google reached the same conclusion from its own data: unstructured interviews added little signal, so it rebuilt hiring on structured behavioral questions scored against rubrics [2].

The good news is that structure is exactly what you can prepare for, and it is the kind of interview this book gets you ready for.

Real stories are hard to fake. A specific story with real trade-offs and numbers survives probing and follow-ups; an invented one collapses at the second question. That is why trained interviewers probe rather than collect answers. AI has made this point sharper, not weaker: now that polished-sounding answers are cheap to produce, the follow-up is the one part of the interview no script survives, and companies lean on it harder than ever.

It protects both sides. For the employer, hiring is expensive and a poor match is more expensive still; how you collaborate, adapt, and communicate decides how far your technical skills travel, and the behavioral round is where all of that shows. A technical test proves you can code; a behavioral interview shows how you will handle deadlines, friction, and real work. For you, the same conversation reveals the culture you are about to join: your values against how the company actually operates, before you commit years to it.

Put simply: the interview checks whether you can decode what the room needs, demonstrate evidence on demand, and adapt when that evidence is questioned. How much of each is expected depends on where you stand in your career, so we calibrate that first.

How the bar moves with seniority

These interviews grow in importance as your experience grows. For early-career roles, they assess potential: curiosity, accountability, learning mindset, and collaboration. At senior levels the same questions assess judgment, trade-off thinking, leadership range, and the ability to operate through ambiguity. For executive roles, behavioral interviews often carry more weight than technical ones, because the interviewer is answering questions such as:

- Can I trust this person to make decisions that affect hundreds of people or millions of dollars?
- How do they behave when problems are unclear or more complex than usual?

The stakes rise with the level, and so does what the same question is scoring. Take one question through that lens: "Tell me about a challenging situation you faced." Depending on your experience, they are assessing different things:

- Early career (0 to 5 years of experience): Did you take ownership? Did you ask for help appropriately? Did you learn?
- Mid-level (5 to 10 years of experience): How did you balance delivery with quality? How did you influence peers and stakeholders?
- Senior (10+ years of experience): How did you frame the problem? Which constraints did you accept or challenge? What did you trade off, and why?

> **Note**
>
> Please note that the range of years above is only indicative and not rigid.

Every behavioral question surfaces one or more of three things:

- **Judgment**: how you choose between imperfect options
- **Impact**: the scope, scale, and durability of your outcomes
- **Self-awareness**: what you notice about your own behavior and improve over time

To see how this calibration works in practice, let's take one question through three career stages: *Tell me about a time you disagreed with a technical decision.*

Early career, strong answer: "My tech lead chose a library I thought would not scale. I benchmarked both options over a weekend, presented the numbers, and he kept his choice for reasons I had not seen: vendor support and team familiarity. I said so, committed to it, and learned to bring evidence early rather than opinions late." Scored: ownership, evidence, and the ability to lose gracefully. Nobody expects this candidate to have changed the decision.

Mid-level, strong answer: "Two teams had settled on an integration pattern that I believed would double our on-call load. Instead of arguing in the review, I built a thin prototype of the alternative, brought the on-call data from a sister team, and got the two leads to co-present the revised design. The decision changed." Scored: influence without authority, and knowing that who proposes matters as much as what is proposed.

Senior, strong answer: "I disagreed with a vice president's platform bet. I wrote a two-page dissent with the three conditions under which I would be wrong, put dates on them, and said I would commit fully either way. The bet went ahead. Two of my three conditions never triggered, so by my own criteria the VP was right, and because I had executed hard instead of hedging, the platform worked. I keep the memo; being wrong in writing is how my judgment improves." Scored: judgment, disagree-and-commit practiced for real, and self-awareness you can point to in writing.

Same question, three altitudes, and notice that nothing is replaced as you rise; things are added. Evidence, then influence, then stewardship of your own judgment. In the model's terms, the weights shift across a career. Early on, you are scored mostly on demonstrate: doing the thing well. The middle years add decode: reading the system the thing lives in. The senior and executive years are scored increasingly on adapt: steering yourself and others through change without losing the standard. All three are always present. The mix is what moves. The principle stays constant across career levels; only the depth changes.

The newest expectation that moves with every level is AI fluency. Early-career candidates may increasingly hear "*Tell me about a time you used AI in a recent project,*" and the interviewer is listening for verification, not enthusiasm: what you checked before trusting the output. Mid-level candidates are asked how they set AI practices for a team. Senior leaders are asked where they draw the line: what stays human, how AI output gets reviewed, and what happened the day it was wrong. The question is new; the scoring is not. It is judgment and adaptability in current clothing.

Later chapters cover how responses should evolve with seniority. For now, one more foundation that you will see through the behavioral section of this book is the dimensions in which behavioral intelligence shows up.

The seven dimensions of behavioral intelligence

Behavioral questions cluster into seven dimensions, and the clusters are old news; every interview book lists something like them. What matters is what the lists leave out. Interviewers do not score a dimension by its name; they score the behaviors underneath it, and every dimension has a *counterfeit*: a way of sounding strong that collapses under one good follow-up. For each dimension below, we name the real signal, the counterfeit, and what convinced us when we sat on the scoring side. As you read, notice that each one is simply decode, demonstrate, adapt applied to a different kind of pressure. The seven dimensions are shown together in *Figure 12.3*, and the sections that follow take each one in turn.

Figure 12.3: The seven dimensions at a glance.

Problem-solving and critical thinking

The secret of this dimension is that interviewers score the diagnosis, not the solution. Anyone can describe a fix that worked; the signal is the question you asked before you touched anything, the alternatives you rejected, and the moment your first theory turned out to be wrong. Most real problem-solving involves at least one wrong turn, and a story that includes one reads like honest diagnosis rather than a neat path you only see clearly in hindsight.

The counterfeit: the tidy narrative in which the first hypothesis was correct, the fix worked immediately, and nothing was learned because nothing went wrong. One probe ("what else did you consider?") and it folds.

What convinces: a candidate who keeps the wrong turn in the story. Picture the answer: *"Our nightly data job started overrunning by two hours. Everyone's instinct, mine included, was bad queries, and I spent a week optimizing them for a four percent gain. That failure made me actually measure, and the real cause was contention with a backup window someone had moved. Rescheduling fixed it in a day. I keep the week of wasted tuning in the story on purpose: it is why I now measure before I optimize."* The dead end is not a weakness in this answer; it is the evidence.

Leadership and initiative

Where problem-solving plays out mostly in your own head, leadership is about what happens when other people enter the picture. Strip the job titles away, and leadership questions ask one thing: what happens around you when nobody is obliged to follow? The strongest evidence in this dimension comes from moments when you held no authority at all, because influence without power is impossible to fake with an org chart. Interviewers also listen for durability: what did your team do differently after you left the room, the project, the company?

The counterfeit: the headcount story. "I led a team of twelve" describes your circumstances, not your behavior. The probe that kills it: "name a decision only you could have made, and what it cost you."

What convinces: a candidate who led with no authority to lean on. Picture the answer: *"At 2 a.m., two teams were pointing at each other over a payments outage, and I did not outrank anyone on the call. I opened a shared timeline doc, started logging what we knew, and proposed splitting the investigation by hypothesis instead of by team. Both leads adopted it because it was useful, not because I had standing. That doc became the incident template we still use."* Decode the vacuum, demonstrate by filling it, and let others adopt what works.

Teamwork and collaboration

If leadership is influence over people who do not report to you, teamwork is the everyday version: producing alongside people you did not choose. Interviewers in this dimension are listening for how honestly you separate your individual contribution from the team's. It is not about how often you say "we." it is whether your "I" and "we" are placed honestly: "I" for decisions and mistakes, "we" for outcomes, and naming colleagues when acknowledging their contributions. Candidates who credit specific people with specific contributions read as safe to work with, because gratitude with detail cannot be faked on the spot. The dimension is not about liking people; it is about producing with people you did not choose.

The counterfeit: Harmony theater. "We never really had conflicts" signals either low exposure or low honesty, and both score the same. Friction is assumed; the question is what you built with it.

What convinces: a candidate who turned friction into something the team kept. Picture the answer: *"A new senior engineer kept rewriting my merged code overnight. I was furious for a week, and then asked to pair with him instead of escalating. Two days in, it was obvious we were carrying different style assumptions from different companies, so we drafted the team style guide that did not exist. The rewrites stopped, and the guide outlived both of us on that team. He is the person I would call first today."* Notice what carried the answer: a named person, a swallowed ego, and an artifact.

Adaptability and flexibility

Teamwork assumes the plan holds; adaptability is about the moment it does not. The scored moment in this dimension is the beat after you learn you were wrong. How long did you defend the dying plan? What did updating cost you publicly, and did you pay it? Strong candidates also know the boundary that keeps this dimension honest: you adapt plans, not standards. Bending the roadmap to reality is flexibility; bending the quality bar to the deadline is erosion, and senior interviewers listen for whether you know the difference.

The counterfeit: change tourism: reciting the reorgs, migrations, and pivots you have lived through. Surviving change is attendance. The probe: "what did you change about your own behavior, and when?"

What convinces: a candidate who killed their own plan the moment it was wrong. Picture the answer: *"Six weeks before launch, the platform we had bet on was deprecated. The design was mine, and I had argued for it hard, so the fastest thing I could do was kill it myself before anyone had to convince me. We reused my own evaluation matrix to pick the replacement in three days, and I made sure the engineer who had originally opposed my choice ran the selection, publicly. We shipped two weeks late instead of two months."* Adapting fastest to being wrong is the whole dimension in one move.

Time management and prioritization

If adaptability is changing course when reality shifts, prioritization is the quieter, daily form of the same discipline. A priority list without a casualty list is a wish list. That sentence is the entire dimension. Interviewers are not asking how you fit everything in; they are asking what you deliberately dropped, who you told, and how early. Deliberate, broadcast dropping is senior behavior; heroic silent absorption is the junior pattern that burns people out and surprises stakeholders. The follow-ups here are predictable because there is only one: what did it cost?

The counterfeit: the busyness epic: all-nighters, weekend pushes, forty Jira tickets. Volume is not signal. At senior levels a story about working harder is scored as a story about triaging worse.

What convinces: a candidate who dropped something on purpose and said so early. Picture the answer: *"Three stakeholders each declared their item the top priority, which means nothing was. I wrote a one-page cost of each pairing, forced a ranking in a thirty-minute meeting, and we shipped two and killed one. The owner of the killed item was unhappy, but she heard it from me in week one instead of discovering it in week six, and she asked for me by name on her next project. Early bad news is a prioritization skill."* The signal is the item named and dropped out loud, not the two that shipped.

Communication and interpersonal skills

Deciding what matters is only half the job; the other half is making other people understand it. The skill being scored here is altitude control: the same fact rendered for an engineer, a product manager, and an executive without losing its truth at any height. This matters even more at *packet-driven companies*, where the interviewers' written write-ups are collected into a single "packet," and a committee makes the decision from that packet rather than from meeting you. Your answer gets retold in writing by someone else, so the real test is whether your point still holds up in those few written lines. Listening is scored more directly than candidates expect: what you repeat back before answering, and whether your answer is to the question asked or to the question you rehearsed.

The counterfeit: Eloquence without transfer: the polished monologue that leaves the listener no wiser about what to do next. Interviewers score whether they could act on what you said, not whether they enjoyed it.

What convinces: a candidate who pitched one truth at three altitudes. Picture the answer: *"During a checkout outage I wrote three messages in twenty minutes: the executive one led with customer impact, revenue at risk, and the single decision we needed from them; the team one led with our two live hypotheses and who owned each; the customer one was four plain sentences with no internals. Three audiences, three altitudes, one truth."* The candidate who explains why the messages differ has already passed the dimension.

Achievement and motivation

Communication faces the audience in front of you; achievement turns inward, to the standard you hold when no one is watching. This dimension hunts for your internal metric: what "done well" means to you when nobody is checking. Interviewers listen for the standard behind the achievement, whether your drive survives unglamorous work, and what you did the week after the win, because raising your own bar after success is rarer than clearing one someone else set. Sustained pace convinces more than a single spike; anyone can sprint once.

The counterfeit: borrowed impact, for example - quoting the organization's outcome as your own. "We grew revenue forty percent" is a company fact until you can trace the line from your own work to the number, and the follow-up will ask for exactly that.

What convinces: a candidate whose standard held when nobody was watching. Picture the answer: *"The launch went fine, but the achievement I actually rate is the two weeks afterward, which nobody asked for: I wrote the runbook and walked the on-call rotation through it. The next incident was resolved in twenty minutes by an engineer who had never touched the system, using that doc. My internal metric is whether things work when I am not in the room."* That last sentence is the dimension, stated by someone who owns it.

The AI question. One question family is now becoming increasingly common in loops, i.e., "Tell me about a time you used AI in a recent project." "Tell me about a time an AI tool got it wrong, and how you caught it." "How do you decide what not to hand to AI?" These are not an eighth dimension; they are the existing ones in new clothing. The first is problem-solving and achievement: what changed, by how much, and what you verified before trusting the output.

The second is judgment and adaptability: how you caught the error, and what guardrail followed. The third is decision-making maturity. Treat them like any other story, but also explain how you checked your own judgment.

The candidates who fail these questions are not the ones who used AI too little; they are the ones who cannot show where their judgment entered.

What all seven dimensions have in common is that you cannot prepare for them overnight, and a weak or rehearsed answer usually falls apart under the first follow-up question. The dimensions stay stable across companies and decades, and the previous section showed how the bar for each rises with seniority. What remains is the room where all of it gets measured.

The measurement moment: behavioral interviews

The capability we have defined gets measured most deliberately in one setting - the behavioral interview. Part 2's remaining chapters live there, so let us look at the measurement itself.

A behavioral interview is a structured approach to evaluating how a candidate thinks, acts, and leads in real situations. It is a conversation in which the interviewer explores real past experiences to understand how you make decisions, collaborate, and learn. Unlike technical or hypothetical questions, these interviews reveal patterns of behavior and judgment that are hard to teach and harder to fake.

> **Task:**
>
> Think about all the different types of interviews you have done in the past and note them down. Once you finish the next section, place each one under one of the categories.

Types of behavioral interviews

Here is something nobody tells you when you are preparing for interviews - the format matters as much as what you say.

You might have the perfect example ready, but if you deliver it in a panel interview the same way you would in a relaxed one-on-one, you will struggle. We have seen exceptionally talented people fail interviews, not because they were unqualified, but because they did not adjust to the room they were in. To avoid that, let's start by learning the formats you are likely to face. Reading the format is the decode step aimed at the room itself, and it is the easiest preparation in this entire book. *Figure 12.4* maps out the main formats you are likely to face.

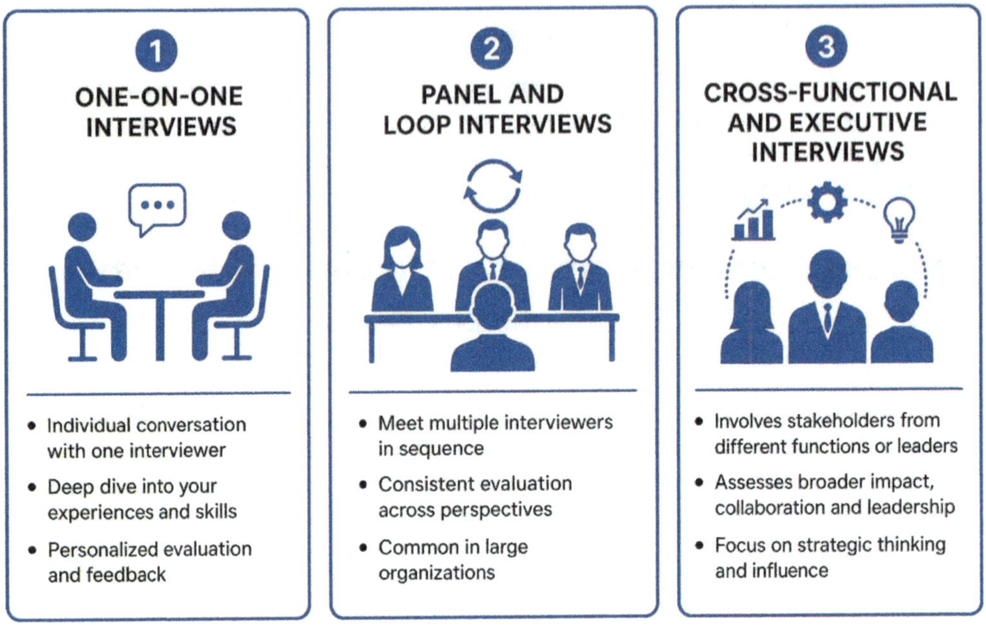

Figure 12.4: Types of behavioral interviews

We will explore each type of the behavioral interview in the following sections.

One-on-one interviews

Most people find this format the most comfortable. It involves you and one other person for 45 minutes to an hour, and it can be your screening call, your hiring manager's first assessment, or the final decision-making round. The conversation feels natural, which is both helpful and dangerous.

When you are describing a tough project and your interviewer nods knowingly, you are resonating. If they ask follow-up questions, lean in. There is room to breathe here. One-on-one conversations may drift from the point, and good interviewers know how to steer you back on track.

Consider who is interviewing you. An engineering manager will focus on how you mentor junior developers and make technical decisions under pressure. A product manager will care about how you handle ambiguity and prioritize features. Your experiences stay the same; your emphasis should not.

One recent development deserves attention here: your first one-on-one may not involve a person at all. AI-led screening interviews, whether one-way recorded video on platforms such as HireVue or a live conversation with an AI voice interviewer, have moved from novelty to mainstream. In a 2025 survey of more than 4,100 job seekers, recruiters, and hiring managers, 54 percent of US job seekers said they had already encountered an AI-led interview [3].

Treat these screens with the same discipline as any other interview format. Since there is no interviewer to read, your structure has to carry the answer by clearly explaining the situation, your actions, and the result while staying within the time limit. Resist the temptation to have an AI assistant feed you answers from a second screen as the same report found 39 percent of hiring managers adding more in-person rounds precisely to verify authenticity. What gets you through an AI screen is what gets you through a human one, i.e., a clear story, told in your own words.

Panel and loop interviews

These formats separate candidates who are ready from those who are hoping for the best. Both involve several interviewers, but the difference is simple: in a panel, you face them all at once; in a loop, you face them one at a time. Let's look at each in more detail.

The panel: managing multiple attention spans

A panel interview puts several interviewers in the room with you together, usually two to five, for a single session of about an hour to ninety minutes. You answer to the group, and they often build on one another's questions. If that prospect makes you nervous, you are not alone.

Panels are efficient for the company; they evaluate you without burning everyone's time separately, and they can be assembled to ensure inclusion or to cover several assessment areas in one sitting. For you, it is a conversation played on several boards at once.

You are no longer just answering questions. You are managing eye contact across multiple people, reading different body-language cues, and working out who cares about what. The senior engineer in the corner might look bored during your explanation of stakeholder management but light up when you mention technical architecture. The product manager might act the opposite.

The tactical part: when someone asks a question, acknowledge them, but do not lock eyes with them for your entire answer. Glance around the table and bring everyone along. If someone looks confused, pause and check in - "Does that make sense, or should I clarify?" If someone is already taking notes, you have probably said something that matters.

The mental game differs too. In a one-on-one, failing to click with your interviewer is bad news. In a panel, it is survivable, because each person may be evaluating something specific rather than forming a single overall impression.

Expect interruptions. Someone will jump in before you finish an answer. Someone may challenge a decision or ask you to defend your reasoning. Do not read that as hostility; it is usually a signal of engagement. They are testing how you think under pressure and whether you become defensive or thoughtful when challenged. A panel interview is not only about what you know. It is about how you operate in a room full of competing perspectives.

The loop: the endurance test

A loop breaks the day into four to six back-to-back interviews, each with a different person or pair, over half a day or a full day. Amazon is well known for this format, mapping each interview to one of its Leadership Principles (Source: "Your complete guide to the Amazon interview process," Amazon News, aboutamazon.com, 2026). Microsoft does it. Google does it. So do many startups beyond the initial stage of their selection process.

Loops are demanding in a different way from panels. The challenge is not managing several people at once; it is staying sharp across several hours.

> **Note**
>
> **Story of an Amazonian:**
>
> I can still recall how exhausted I felt during my Amazon loop round in 2025. I started my interviews around 10 am and went until 4 pm. Each interview was intense, ran 45 minutes to an hour, with a 10-to-15-minute break in between. By the third round of the interview, I was mentally drained. And in the fifth one, I was running on empty.

This experience points to the trap in every loop, and it catches most people off guard. The person interviewing you in slot five has not sat through your day. In fact, to them, you are fresh. They expect the same energy and clarity you had that morning.

Fair? No.

Reality? Yes.

The biggest mistake people make in loops is repetition. You should limit the use of the same conflict-resolution story to three different interviewers, unless it demonstrates different competencies and your story bank has enough breadth. Interviewers compare notes afterwards, and if everyone heard the same example, it looks like the only situation you have ever navigated. To avoid that, you need a well-crafted story bank mapped to interview types, which we cover in upcoming chapters. Preparing for a loop is different because you are not rehearsing a few good stories, you are building a repertoire.

Energy management is real. Use the breaks between interviews properly. Get water. Step outside for two minutes. Shake out your hands. Take a few deep breaths. These are not luxuries; they are part of your performance strategy. Your brain needs those micro-resets to stay effective. And if it is at all possible, request two half-days for a loop round instead of having everything scheduled on one day.

Panels and loops describe how an interview is arranged, but format is only half of it. The other half is who is sitting across from you, because a peer, a partner from another function, and a senior executive are each assessing something different. The next two formats are defined by exactly that.

Cross-functional Interviews

Most roles today require working with people who do different jobs. Engineers clarify requirements with business analysts. Product managers negotiate with legal and finance. This is why modern interview processes include cross-functional conversations as they assess whether a candidate will fit the working environment as a whole or is limited to a core skill.

These conversations are not about whether you know your job. They are about whether you can work with people who think differently from you, because that is where most workplace friction lives - not in incompetence, but in competing priorities and the failure to bridge them.

Your job is to demonstrate that you understand this. The best examples for cross-functional interviews are the messy ones. Times you aligned people who did not report to you. Situations where you built consensus across teams with competing goals. Moments you chose collaboration over being right.

Executive interviews

You have survived multiple rounds. Now you are sitting with someone whose title contains "Chief" or "Head of". This is often the final conversation before an offer decision.

First thing to know is that executives rarely have time for elaborate stories. They have seen hundreds of candidates over the years, and they can tell within a few minutes whether you think strategically or merely execute tasks someone else defined.

They care less about what you did and more about why it mattered. How did your work move the business forward? What did you learn that you will apply next? Can you connect your day-to-day decisions to bigger outcomes?

Most executive interviews run about thirty minutes. Start with impact, not process. Talk about results. Frame your experience in terms of business value, organizational change, or market position. Whatever you say, be crisp.

Executives also ask uncomfortable questions. Tell me about your biggest failure. Describe a time you were entirely wrong. What is the most controversial decision you have made? They are not trying to catch you out. They are testing whether you are self-aware, whether you learn from mistakes, and whether you can own your decisions even when they did not work out.

Answers to signals: Why this matters

For most hiring managers, hiring is a tough job, and assessing whether the right person gets the role is even harder.

Same person, same background, same qualifications: put them in different interview formats and you get entirely different results. Some people are excellent in one-on-ones but freeze in front of a panel. Others ace a loop yet come across as over-rehearsed when talking to an executive. That does not mean they are not good enough. It means they have not adapted to the situation and *demonstrated* without *decoding*.

Depending on the role, organization, culture, interview format, and interviewer, you must adapt and prepare accordingly. The rest of this book builds the frameworks and techniques to succeed across all of these formats - how to structure your stories, how to prepare effectively, and how to stay sharp when the pressure is on. But it starts with one foundational step. Know what kind of interview you are walking into. It is a simple step, and yet so many candidates either hesitate to ask or never do.

Ask your recruiter. Get specifics. Then adjust your approach. The story you tell matters. How you tell it, and who you are telling it to, matters just as much.

You now know what behavioral intelligence is, what it predicts, where it shows, and how it is measured. One question remains - how much of it do you have today?

Where do you stand? (a self-assessment)

Before moving on, take a baseline. In *Table 12.1*, score each statement from 1 (rarely true of me) to 4 (consistently true of me), honestly rather than aspirationally. Nobody sees this but you, and an inflated score only cheats your own preparation.

Statement	Component	Score (1–4)
Before a meeting or interview, I can name what the other side actually cares about.	Decode	
I notice when the mood in a room shifts, and I can usually say why.	Decode	
I read job descriptions and project briefs for the expectations behind the words.	Decode	
For each major claim I make about myself, I can tell a specific story with numbers in it.	Demonstrate	
When I describe past work, I separate what I did from what the team did.	Demonstrate	
Colleagues would say my behavior under pressure matches how I describe it.	Demonstrate	
When challenged or probed, I get more specific rather than more general.	Adapt	
I change how I communicate based on who is in the room, without changing the facts.	Adapt	
After a setback, I can state what I changed as a result, not just what I learned.	Adapt	
I regularly collect feedback and can name a behavior I changed in the last six months.	All three	

Table 12.1: The behavioral intelligence self-assessment.

Please note that some of the above statements' outcomes may not be measurable with a score and if you find it hard to score them, you can consider using specific evidence or relevant metrics instead of numbers.

Reading your score: If you scored 34 to 40, your foundation is strong. Your main work now is calibration, making sure the intelligence you already have lands at the right level for your seniority and holds up under a trained interviewer. If you scored 25 to 33, you are solid but have a visible gap. Find the component that scored lowest, whether decode, demonstrate, or adapt, and focus your reading and practice there. If you scored 10 to 24, this part of the book was built for you. Work through it in order and do the tasks rather than reading past them.

Score yourself again when you finish Part 2. When these numbers move, this part of the book is doing its job, and the retest shows you where to focus next.

One more thing before you turn the page, and it matters more than any number you just wrote down. Behavioral intelligence is not charisma, and it is not performance. Some of the best engineers we know spent years believing they were bad at interviews, when the truth was simpler and kinder - nobody had ever shown them what the room was measuring. If your score today is lower than you hoped, you are not behind; nobody ever showed you what the room measures, and that is easy to fix. The gap between how good you are and how good you come across is the easiest gap in your career to close, and the rest of this part exists to close it.

Summary

Part 1 of this book was about what you can build. Part 2 is about how you behave while building it, and this chapter made the case that the second decides your career as surely as the first. Behavioral intelligence is not a soft or vague quality. It is a definable capability, reading what a situation demands, acting in a way others can see, and adjusting as things change, and a century of hiring research shows it predicts performance better than almost anything else an employer can measure. What looks like a fixed trait is really a set of behaviors that grow more demanding as you rise, surface across seven recognizable dimensions, and get tested most deliberately in the behavioral interview. That is the hopeful part: because it is behavior and not personality, it can be learned, which makes it the most reliable advantage available to you.

The next chapter moves from definition to practice, into the workplace situations where behavioral intelligence is built and shown long before any interview, talking about conflict, risk, performance, productivity, and influence without authority.

References

[1] Sackett, Zhang, Berry, and Lievens, "Journal of Applied Psychology, 2022. https://filiplievens.squarespace.com/s/APL-2022-4078_R3.pdf

[2] Google re:Work Editorial Team, "A Guide to Structured Interviewing for Better Hiring Practices," Google re:Work, updated Mar. 2026. https://rework.withgoogle.com/intl/en/guides/a-guide-to-structured-interviewing-for-better-hiring-practices

[3] Greenhouse, "2025 AI in Hiring Report," November 2025. https://www.greenhouse.com/uk/newsroom/an-ai-trust-crisis-70-of-hiring-managers-trust-ai-to-make-faster-and-better-hiring-decisions-only-8-of-job-seekers-call-it-fair

13

The Power of Behavioral Intelligence at Work

What senior people do when there is no playbook: conflict, risk, performance, productivity, and stakeholders.

Behavioral Intelligence is easiest to see in the situations that have no script: a conflict between two strong engineers, a risk nobody owns, an underperformer everyone likes, a stakeholder with power but no time. Structured situations make competence easier to demonstrate. What separates senior people is how they act once the playbook runs out. Across every one of those moments: read what is actually going on, choose a deliberate response instead of a reflex, and fold what you learn back into how you work. That is behavioral intelligence at work, and it is the central theme of this chapter.

The frameworks that follow, the categories of conflict, the risk strategies, the 9-Box Matrix, the delivery metrics, and the stakeholder models, are the shared vocabulary for that judgment. They give language to good instincts and structure to hard calls, but they are tools, not a substitute for the judgment itself. Anyone can describe what they did in a difficult situation; far fewer can explain why they made the choices they did, which tools or models informed their thinking, and what they carried forward. The same clarity that makes you effective at work is what later makes your interview answers stand out. (We will return to the answer frameworks themselves in *Chapter 14*).

To keep these ideas concrete, we will be using one running example across all sections. Picture a team migrating a legacy subscription-billing platform onto a new service, with a hard regulatory cutover date and renewals that cannot be allowed to fail. We will call it the 'billing migration project' and return to it in each section, because every kind of unscripted moment shows up somewhere in a project like this.

In this chapter, we will cover the following topics:

- Managing conflicts and disagreements: three categories of conflict and the 4-D Model
- Risks and trade-offs in decision-making: risk strategies, the risk heatmap, and weaving risk into your answers
- Performance and talent management: the 9-Box Matrix and what your answers say about your leadership
- Measuring productivity: DORA, flow, and quality metrics
- Stakeholder management and working without authority: RACI, Mendelow's Matrix, and the Salience Model

Across all five areas, the move is the same: act with judgment first at work, and the language to talk about it, including in an interview, follows on its own. We will start with the theme that surfaces most often without being directly named.

Managing conflicts and disagreements

Conflict is inevitable in any workplace, so the question about how you manage it is always a possibility. This theme surfaces more often than you think, sometimes wrapped inside a question about stakeholders, teamwork, or decision-making. It is also the first unscripted moment the billing migration runs into.

> **Note**
>
> **On the billing migration**: Imagine two senior engineers, Lena and Dev, creating a deadlock. Lena wants a clean rebuild; Dev wants a strangler pattern that swaps the old system out piece by piece. Both are right about something, the meeting is going in circles, and the deadline is not moving. Same facts, two strong opinions. Before choosing a strategy, the team lead has to decode what kind of conflict this actually is.

Three categories of conflict

Before jumping into strategies, understand what kind of conflict you are actually dealing with. Conflicts usually reduce to three categories:

- **People:** conflicts arising from personalities, relationships, and interpersonal dynamics (team member disagreements, difficult stakeholders, disputes between colleagues).

- **Approach:** conflicts rooted in differing solutions, proposals, or technical judgments (disputed defects, rejected proposals, process decisions).
- **Values:** conflicts where someone's behavior or views clash with organizational or ethical principles.

Strategies for each category

> *The quality of our lives depends not on whether or not we have conflicts, but on how we respond to them.*
>
> *–Thomas Crum*

Different conflicts call for different responses. What works for a technical disagreement will not necessarily work when someone's values are misaligned. Naming the gap and matching a response to it is what turns a heated exchange into a workable decision; it reflects strategic alignment, decision clarity, integrity, and negotiation skill. Once you have named that gap clearly, you are in a far better position to apply the relevant strategy discussed below. One principle, however, runs through every strategy, which is to **separate the person from the problem**. Focus on the gap between two opinions, ideas, or approaches, not on the individuals involved.

For ownership-related conflicts, the RACI (Responsible, Accountable, Consulted, or Informed) matrix (explained in detail, later in this chapter) is a remarkably effective tool. When people are unclear about RACI, friction is almost unavoidable. Bringing clarity to roles removes the ambiguity that fuels these disputes in the first place.

For technical conflicts, lead with evidence rather than opinion. Opinions are easy to dismiss; facts are harder to argue with. Bring objectivity to the conversation and keep returning to the shared goal: quality, delivery, customer value, or the best long-term outcome. Framing the discussion around what both sides are trying to achieve shifts it from a debate into a collaboration.

For misunderstandings between people, the most powerful thing you can do is slow down and listen. Paraphrase what you have heard, check that you understood correctly, and invite the other person to confirm. It sounds simple, but this alone can defuse tension quickly, and it signals that you value their perspective. Similarly, for conflicts with stakeholders, present multiple options with their pros and cons, and invite shared decision-making. This respects the stakeholder's position while keeping the conversation rational and forward-moving.

Note

On the billing migration: Lena and Dev's deadlock is an Approach conflict: a disagreement about the right technical solution, not a personality clash. The first move is to take the two people out of it and compare only the two options, a clean rebuild versus a strangler pattern. Because it is a technical question, the team lead settles it with evidence, not seniority. The team builds a small prototype of each and tests both against the two things that cannot move: the fixed regulatory date and the renewals that must keep working. That makes the difference clear. A clean rebuild switches every customer over on a single day, so if anything fails on that date, it fails for everyone at once, with no easy way back. The strangler pattern moves customers a slice at a time, so a problem hits only a small group and each step can be undone. Against a hard deadline, the safer and reversible option is the stronger one, and that, not who argued hardest, is what settles it. What began as Lena versus Dev becomes one decision the whole team stands behind.

Figure 13.1 shows how the type of conflict points to the right response, with values-based conflict handed off to the 4-D Model.

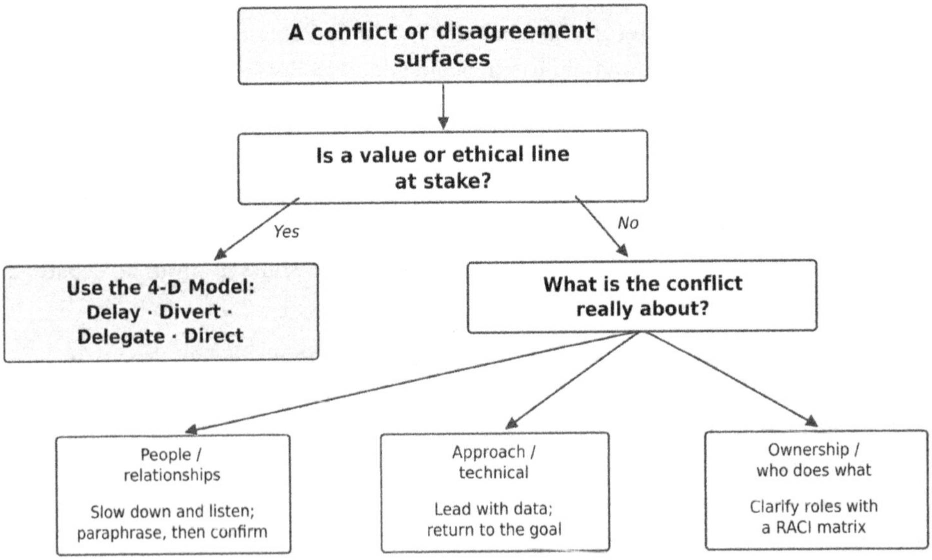

Figure 13.1: Choosing a conflict strategy by conflict type.

The 4-D model: When values are at stake

Conflicts involving values or seniority require a more careful touch. These are situations where a direct, immediate confrontation can do more harm than good. This is where the 4-D Model becomes useful. It is not a rigid sequence of steps but a decision framework. The appropriate response depends on the nature of the conflict, its urgency, and the potential impact of delaying action. Experienced leaders use judgment to decide which approach best fits the situation.

Delay: Sometimes the wisest move is to wait. If emotions are running high, engaging too soon risks making things worse. Delay the conversation until the person is in a more neutral, receptive state and open to hearing a different perspective rather than defending their own. However, use this approach with judgment. Delaying a conversation that is causing ongoing harm to the team, project, or customer can allow the conflict to intensify. Delay should improve the quality of the discussion, not postpone necessary action.

Divert: If a conversation is heading in a direction that will only deepen the divide, redirect it. Steering away from the friction point is not avoidance; it buys the space needed to approach things more thoughtfully. The key is to make the diversion explicit by agreeing to revisit the issue at an appropriate time. Without that commitment, diversion can easily become avoidance, leaving the underlying conflict unresolved.

Delegate: Sometimes you are not the right person to have the conversation. Delegating to someone with the right relationship, seniority, or credibility can achieve far more than a direct exchange. Knowing when to step back is a sign of maturity, not weakness.

Direct: When the other approaches have been tried, are unlikely to help, or the situation demands immediate action, speak plainly. Keep the conversation focused on what is misaligned: not the person, not emotions, but the gap between their behavior or viewpoint and what the situation calls for. The aim is clarity and resolution, not confrontation. Some situations require direct action from the outset. Where safety, ethics, compliance, or serious policy violations are involved, delaying or diverting the conversation may increase risk or allow further harm. In these cases, address the issue promptly, respectfully, and in line with organizational policies.

Note

On the billing migration: settling the deadlock did not remove the deadline sitting underneath it. Agreeing on the strangler pattern decided how the system would be moved, but not whether the move itself would go cleanly. That put the next problem in front of them, one no one had owned yet: the cutover risk, the point where the old billing system is switched off and the new one takes over live customers. Managing the conflict cleared the air. Managing the risk is what keeps the delivery honest.

Risks and trade-offs in decision-making

Risk management is expected at every level, but senior engineers are increasingly judged by their ability to anticipate risks early, evaluate trade-offs, and make decisions that prevent issues from emerging.

It is not a textbook exercise; it is the difference between a delivery that absorbs surprises and one that is derailed by them. The habit that matters is carrying a risk mindset into how you work by default, spotting and shaping uncertainty rather than reacting to problems once they land. That habit is also exactly what senior interviewers listen for.

Note

On the billing migration: The regulatory cutover date is fixed, and the legacy system is barely documented. No one can say for certain how many edge-case subscriptions will break on switchover. That uncertainty is not an issue yet; it is a risk, and the team's job is to name it, size it, and decide what to do about it before it becomes a 2 a.m. incident.

Most experienced professionals already practice risk management in some form; they just do not always name it explicitly. The opportunity is not simply to use the right terminology, but to articulate the thinking behind the decisions you made. At senior levels, interviewers are looking for evidence that you can identify risks early, evaluate trade-offs, take appropriate action, and influence outcomes. Using the right terminology helps you communicate that thinking clearly and show how effectively you applied the framework in real situations.

The following are the foundations worth knowing:

- **Risk vs. issue:** this distinction alone can set you apart. A risk is an uncertainty, something that might happen. An issue is something that has happened. When you can show that your early identification of a risk prevented it from becoming an issue, you are demonstrating proactive thinking in its clearest form. That is half the battle won before you have described your solution.
- **Probability vs. impact**: the risk heatmap. Not all risks can be treated equally, and your response to risks should reflect that. In reality, you should assess each risk on two dimensions: how likely it was to occur, and how significant the impact would be, measured not just for the end user but also for the organization's reputation and delivery commitments.

Plotting risks across these two axes creates a risk heatmap, and the ones demanding immediate attention sit in the red zone: high probability, high impact (shown in *Figure 13.2*). Referencing this framework shows structured thinking and prioritization, both of which matter enormously to a hiring manager and in the workplace as well.

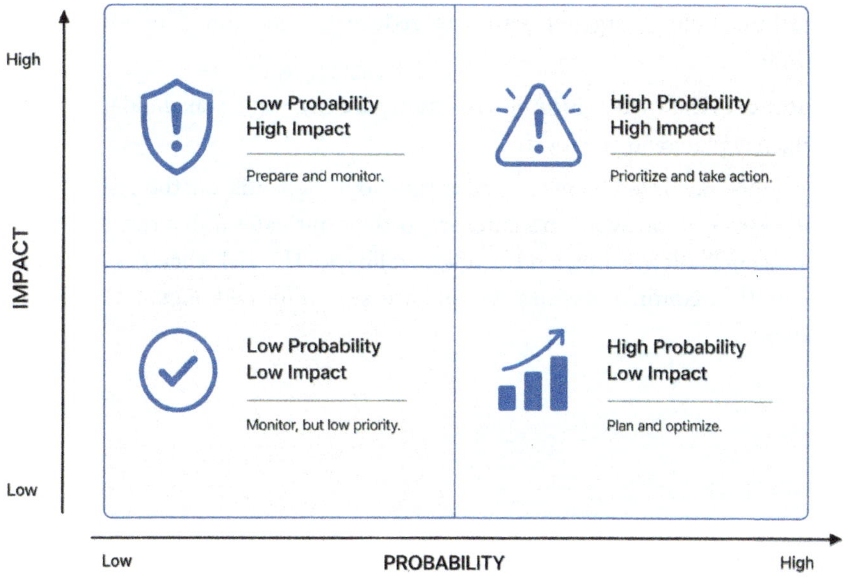

Figure 13.2: The risk heatmap (probability vs. impact)

For unknown risks, acknowledge that not every uncertainty can be predicted during the planning phase. While maintaining appropriate buffers and learning from data points from similar projects can help, strong risk management also includes building resilience into the execution plan. This may involve designing rollback strategies, defining contingency options, creating recovery paths, and ensuring the system or process can adapt when unexpected situations arise. Clear acceptance criteria further reduce the gap between expectations and delivery, mitigating one of the most common and costly risks of all: missed requirements.

Ownership of risk, versus the blame game, is one of the clearest signals of leadership, at work and in any later conversation about it. Whatever the outcome, close by naming the lessons learned and the practices you put in place if a risk did convert into an issue.

Risk strategies

There are four strategies you can apply while dealing with a risk:

- **Avoidance:** Changing the situation so the risk cannot materialize in the first place.
- **Transfer:** Shifting the impact or ownership of the risk to another party, internal or external, while keeping the accountability.
- **Mitigation:** Taking targeted action to reduce the likelihood or impact of the risk occurring.
- **Acceptance:** Acknowledging the risk transparently with stakeholders and keeping a contingency plan ready if it occurs.

These strategies are not interchangeable; the right one depends on the risk. On the billing migration, the team cannot avoid the cutover, so they mitigate: a dry run against a copy of production, a reconciliation script, and a tested rollback. The risk they cannot remove, they accept openly, with a contingency and Compliance kept informed. *Figure 13.3* shows how to choose a risk plan:

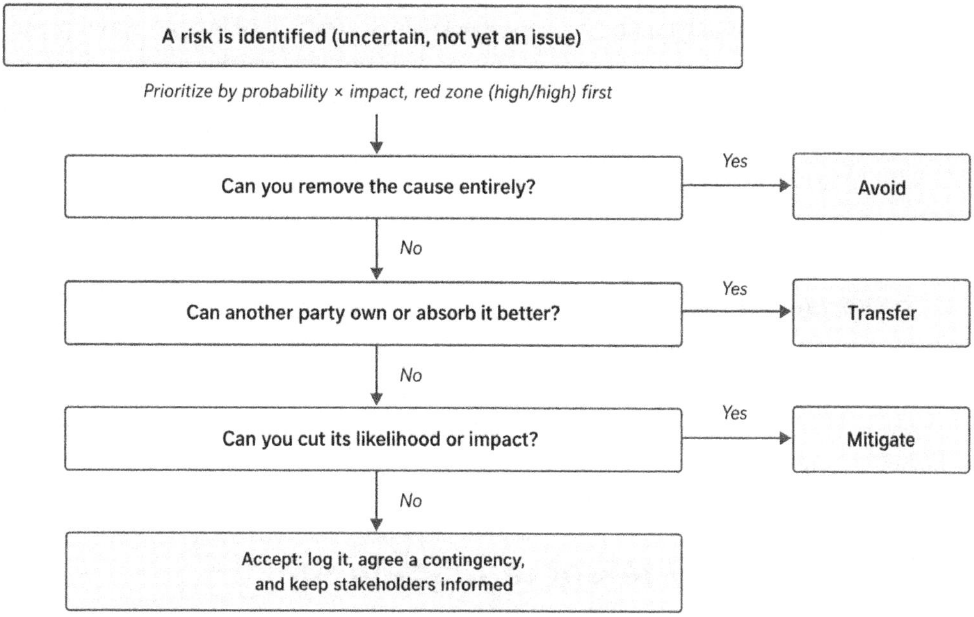

Figure 13.3: Choosing a risk response

Knowing the frameworks is one thing; weaving them naturally into how you work, and into how you talk about it in a review, a retro, or an interview, is another. The rest of this section will help you do exactly that.

Bringing risk into practice

When working on a project or talking about your experience, you should set the context by establishing risk awareness as part of your thinking from the beginning, not as something you reacted to later. Let's see how you cover these dimensions:

- ***Risk identification and monitoring:*** Call out the early identification of risks and track them continuously through the project lifecycle, rather than flagging them once and forgetting them. This alone signals a proactive mindset.
- ***Choosing the right strategy:*** Be specific about which risk strategy you applied and why, driven by assessing probability against impact. Reference the risk heatmap as the tool that helped you prioritize, with particular focus on anything in the red zone.
- ***Stakeholder transparency:*** Mention how stakeholders were involved from the start, kept informed at every stage, and included in agreeing on the approach. This reflects transparency, integrity, and collaborative decision-making, which matter as much as the technical strategy itself.

- ***Risk tracking:*** Risks are not a one-off conversation. They should be reviewed continuously through regular delivery checkpoints, governance forums, sprint planning, retrospectives, and other relevant review mechanisms. Referencing a risk register or risk dashboard, capturing each risk's summary, owner, expected closure date, status, and mitigation actions, demonstrates that risks were actively monitored, managed, and driven to closure over time.
- ***Planning for the unknown:*** Show how you handled the risks you could not foresee, using the buffers and acceptance criteria described above.
- ***Ownership over blame:*** Interviewers pay close attention here. As noted earlier, taking ownership when an outcome was imperfect signals leadership far more than pointing at circumstances or other people.

A plan can account for every technical risk and still fail, because plans are carried out by people. On the billing migration, the risk register was solid, but two people on the team were about to test a different kind of judgment: the human one.

Performance and talent management

As professionals gain experience, they reach a critical juncture: remain an individual contributor or expand the technical role into managing people. If the role requires people management, Behavioral Intelligence shows up as your ability to manage team performance, deliver difficult messages with empathy when the organization makes hard decisions, and keep team members motivated and secure, all alongside your technical skills.

> **Note**
>
> **On the billing migration:** As the pressure builds, two people stand out for opposite reasons. Sam, a mid-level engineer, has gone quiet and is missing commitments; the work is slipping and no one is sure why. Danny is shipping fast and unblocking others, but skipping reviews and leaving risk in his wake. One needs support; the other needs a boundary. Neither is a performance-review-season problem; both are leadership moments that require action now. Waiting until the next review cycle would allow Sam's disengagement to deepen and Danny's risky habits to become normalized.

Strategic tools for performance and talent management

In most organizations, performance is evaluated alongside future potential, and one such framework worth referencing is the 9-Box Matrix: a 3-by-3 grid. It provides a structured approach to identifying and categorizing development needs, making talent decisions more objective and consistent rather than relying purely on instinct. When discussing real situations from your experience, augment them with relevant strategic tools and frameworks.

Table 13.1 lays out the nine boxes, plotting current performance against future potential.

	Low performance	Medium performance	High performance
High potential	Skill or will issue?	Assign stretch goals	Should be given next-level goals
Medium potential	Inconsistent; needs regular coaching	Core player	Key performer; needs bigger challenges to reach potential
Low potential	Underperformer	Needs motivation to progress in career	Trusted team member; look out for development needs

Table 13.1: The 9-Box Matrix

On the grid, Sam looks like a capable contributor stuck in a bad patch, not a low-potential underperformer, which points to support and a clear, time-bound plan rather than a warning. Danny is a high performer whose behavior, not his output, is the problem, which calls for direct feedback that protects the team's standards without losing his contribution.

Management in practice

Do you focus solely on deliveries and outcomes, or do you bring your team along, investing in their growth and converting underperformers into contributors through coaching and mentorship? How you handle people like Sam and Danny speaks to the culture you build around you and whether people would want to be led by you. The measure of a leader here is depth, not breadth: not how many people you managed, but whether you changed the trajectory of one. That is what your team feels day to day, and it is what a thoughtful interviewer will probe for.

The key dimensions worth covering:

- **Goal setting:** Anchor individual goals to the broader strategic themes or Objectives and Key Results (OKRs) of the portfolio. Frame them as SMART objectives: Specific, Measurable, Achievable, Relevant, and Time-bound. This shows your team's work is deliberately connected to organizational priorities, not happening in isolation.
- **Continuous feedback:** Move away from feedback as an annual exercise. Talk about sharing structured feedback on a frequent cadence and in a timely manner, always supported by facts and data.
- **Personal development:** Show real interest in your team members as individuals. Talk about how you engage with their development plans, understand their aspirations, and actively support their goals. This signals that your leadership extends beyond task delivery.
- **Growth mindset over performance management:** The most forward-thinking leaders shift the conversation from managing performance to building capability. Talk about encouraging your team to develop future skills through stretch assignments that push them beyond their comfort zone, or opportunities that let them explore cross-functional initiatives that align with their interests and broader organizational needs. This reflects a culture of growth rather than compliance.
- **Keywords worth weaving in:** Certain terms signal strategic awareness. Where relevant and natural, incorporate language such as: data-driven decisions, continuous feedback, succession planning, psychological safety, performance calibration, future skills and learning, motivation and engagement.

Performance or people management is judged by your team every day, and by an interviewer in an hour, on the same thing: how you show up for your people, how you create opportunities for others to thrive, and whether the culture you build is one worth being part of.

In our case study, steadying Sam and setting a boundary with Danny bought the team back its focus. But focus is a feeling, and leadership eventually has to answer a harder question with evidence: is the team actually getting better? For that you need numbers, and the next section focuses on exactly that.

Measuring productivity

As organizations push for faster delivery cycles with AI tools, productivity and efficiency have moved from background metrics to front-and-center leadership conversations. Whether you are an individual contributor, architect, or engineering leader, the ability to understand what to measure and how to interpret those signals is becoming a critical skill.

It helps you identify bottlenecks before they become blockers, uncover root causes behind failures, and contribute to continuous improvement in how systems and teams operate. While measuring productivity, you should reflect on three things: how you measure productivity and success, how you diagnose when things are not working, and how you drive improvement in a structured, sustainable way.

> Note
>
> **On the billing migration**: Three months in, senior leadership asks a fair question. The team adopted AI coding tools and swears it is faster, but the migration is still behind. Are they genuinely more productive, or just busier? Feeling fast and being fast are not the same thing, and the only honest way to tell them apart is to measure.

Metrics worth knowing

The following are three categories that reflect productivity, flow, and quality, each signaling a different dimension of engineering and delivery maturity. As a leader, depending on the situation, you should be able to identify which metrics are most relevant to your actions.

Productivity metrics: The DORA Metrics

DevOps Research and Assessment (**DORA**) is a research initiative that studied how engineering teams deliver software effectively and reliably. Based on extensive research (part of Google Cloud), it introduced four key metrics that organizations use to assess software delivery performance, operational stability, and engineering effectiveness.

DORA metrics are widely recognized as an industry standard for measuring software delivery performance.

Reference these when discussing delivery speed, deployment health, and system resilience.

- **Lead time for changes:** The time from an idea being raised to it reaching production. A shorter lead time reflects a mature, efficient delivery pipeline.
- **Deployment frequency:** How often the team releases changes to production. Frequent, smaller iterative deliveries and a possible Minimum Viable Product (MVP) approach are indicators of a high-performing team.
- **Change failure rate:** How often a change causes a failure or needs to be rolled back. Go beyond the number: talk about what you learned and what you put in place, such as additional regression scenarios, stronger peer review practices, or business sign-off before user-facing releases.
- **Mean Time to Restore (MTTR):** How quickly the team recovers when something goes wrong. This speaks directly to system resilience and the importance of a well-defined backout approach ready before any release.

Figure 13.4 brings the four DORA metrics together in a single view.

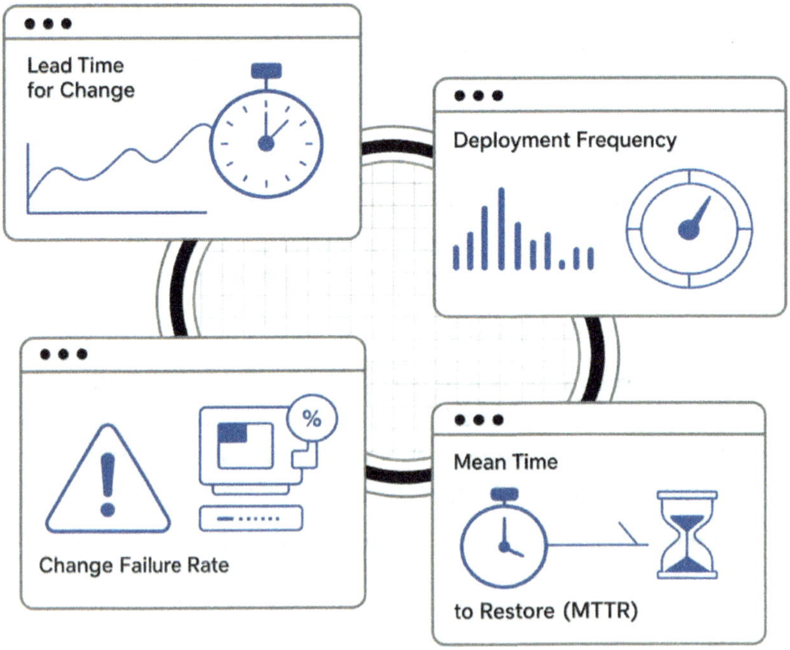

Figure 13.4: The four DORA metrics

If you lead a team that uses AI coding tools, you should watch closely what those tools do to your metrics. DORA's 2025 report found AI adoption among software professionals reaching 90 percent and now correlating with higher delivery throughput, while still correlating with worse delivery stability where validation practices lag [1].

> **Note**
>
> **On the billing migration**: The team ran into exactly this trap. After adopting AI tools, they were deploying more often and shipping more changes, but the change failure rate and MTTR were going up too. They were doing more work, but breaking more along with it. So before treating the speed as a win, they added more testing and validation to catch the failures. Faster only counts if quality holds, and being able to show that you kept quality steady while moving faster is what stands out at work and, later, in an interview.

Flow metrics

Where DORA measures delivery outcomes, flow metrics look at how work moves through your system, helping identify where delays, dependencies, and inefficiencies are hiding.

- **Lead time:** The total time for a task to move from creation to completion. A high lead time often points to toil in the system: wait time, handoffs, or dependent teams creating friction.
- **Cycle time:** The time from when a task is actively worked on to when it is completed. A useful complement to lead time, isolating active work from waiting.
- **Flow velocity:** How much a team delivers within a sprint, often managed through a Work-in-Progress (WIP) limit. Controlled WIP prevents overloading the team and improves throughput.
- **Flow predictability:** How consistently a team delivers against committed timelines. High predictability builds trust with stakeholders and reflects disciplined planning.
- **Flow efficiency:** The proportion of total time where work is actively progressing versus sitting idle. The tool most commonly used to surface this is Value Stream Mapping (VSM), which visualizes every step in the delivery process and highlights bottlenecks in the form of wait time and handoffs. When referencing this, talk about the steps you took to remove those bottlenecks and improve flow.

Note

On the billing migration: flow metrics answered the rest of the question. The team felt fast, but the total lead time had barely changed. The reason was that most of the delay came from work waiting on handoffs between teams, not from the coding itself. AI had made the coding quicker, but coding was never the slow part. Once the flow efficiency numbers made this clear, the team focused on cutting the wait time and handoffs, and that is what actually sped up delivery.

Quality metrics

Delivery speed means little without quality. Quality metrics demonstrate that your team is not just moving fast, but moving in a controlled and sustainable way.

- **Defect density:** The concentration of defects within a module or area of the codebase. Useful for identifying where quality investment is most needed.
- **Defect leakage:** Defects that escape into production. A critical metric reflecting the effectiveness of your testing strategy.
- **Code coverage:** Measures the percentage of code executed by automated tests. While good coverage helps identify gaps in testing, it does not guarantee effective defect detection; test quality and meaningful test scenarios matter more. Many teams use practices such as Test-Driven Development (TDD) to encourage stronger test discipline.
- **Automation coverage:** The proportion of testing that is automated, directly reducing manual effort and accelerating the test cycle for faster, more reliable deliveries.
- **Vulnerability management: H**ow secure the system is, measured by identifying and prioritizing code vulnerabilities by criticality. Referencing this signals awareness beyond functional quality into security and risk.
- **Accessibility coverage: O**rganizations increasingly measure how well their systems meet accessibility standards. The benchmark most commonly referenced is the Web Content Accessibility Guidelines (WCAG), reflecting a commitment to inclusive design.

Quality metrics tell you whether the work is sound; they do not move the people around the work. On the billing migration the team could finally prove it was improving, but proof means little to a Finance director who was never consulted, or a Compliance lead who hears the cutover date too late. The widest unscripted arena is the one full of other people.

Stakeholder management and working without authority

One of the most critical and underestimated aspects of successful delivery is stakeholder management. Many professionals, when asked about their stakeholders, default to customers or the business, unknowingly leaving out some of the most influential voices in the room.

Stakeholders extend far beyond the end user. Anyone who touches the delivery or operational flow, internal teams, dependent teams, platform owners, support functions, and the users of the application themselves, is a stakeholder. Missing this broader picture in an interview response signals a narrow view of delivery; demonstrating it signals someone who understands how work actually gets done in complex organizations.

> **Note**
>
> **On the billing migration**: The stakeholder list is longer than the engineering team. Finance owns the revenue the system collects. Compliance owns the deadline. Security signs off on how customer payment data is handled. The platform team owns the new service the migration depends on. Customer Support will absorb the fallout if renewals break. An executive sponsor is watching the date, and the customers themselves never see any of it, until something goes wrong. Not all of them need the same thing, and treating them as if they do is how good deliveries still fail.

Start with stakeholder mapping

Before any delivery begins, identifying your stakeholders and what they need from you is one of the key early delivery activities. Two kinds of tools help with that: the RACI matrix for role clarity and stakeholder prioritization frameworks, because not all stakeholders carry the same weight, and treating them as if they do is a common mistake.

Mendelow's Matrix

Once your stakeholders are identified, the next step is understanding how to engage each of them meaningfully. Mendelow's Matrix plots every stakeholder against two dimensions: their power (or influence) over the outcome, and their interest in it.

Figure 13.5 illustrates Mendelow's Matrix:

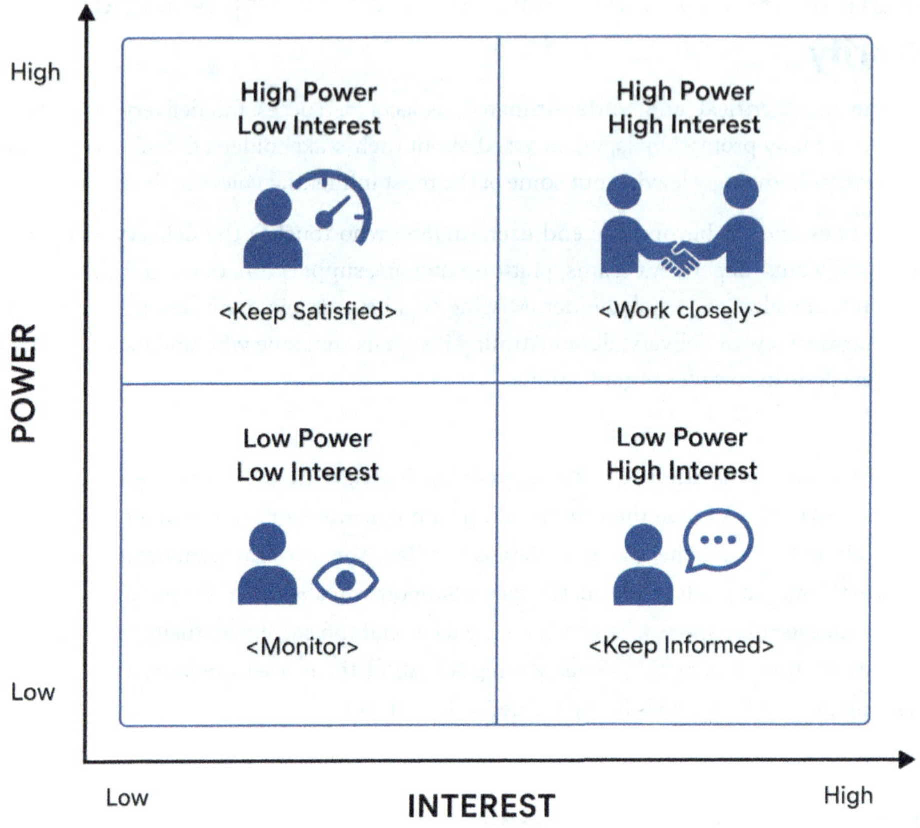

Figure 13.5: Mendelow's Matrix

Each quadrant calls for a different communication approach: high power and high interest, work closely; high power and low interest, keep satisfied; low power and high interest, keep informed; low power and low interest, monitor.

Using the matrix well means more than naming it. Mapping your stakeholders tells you whose communication style to tailor, how often to engage each one, and where to spend energy that is always limited. When you later describe this in an interview, the same detail—how you used it rather than simply knowing it—is what signals deliberate rather than reactive engagement.

Figure 13.6 maps the billing migration's stakeholders onto the grid, and the placement drives the plan: the executive sponsor, Compliance, and the platform team are managed closely; Finance and Security are kept satisfied; Customer Support and the end customers are kept well informed.

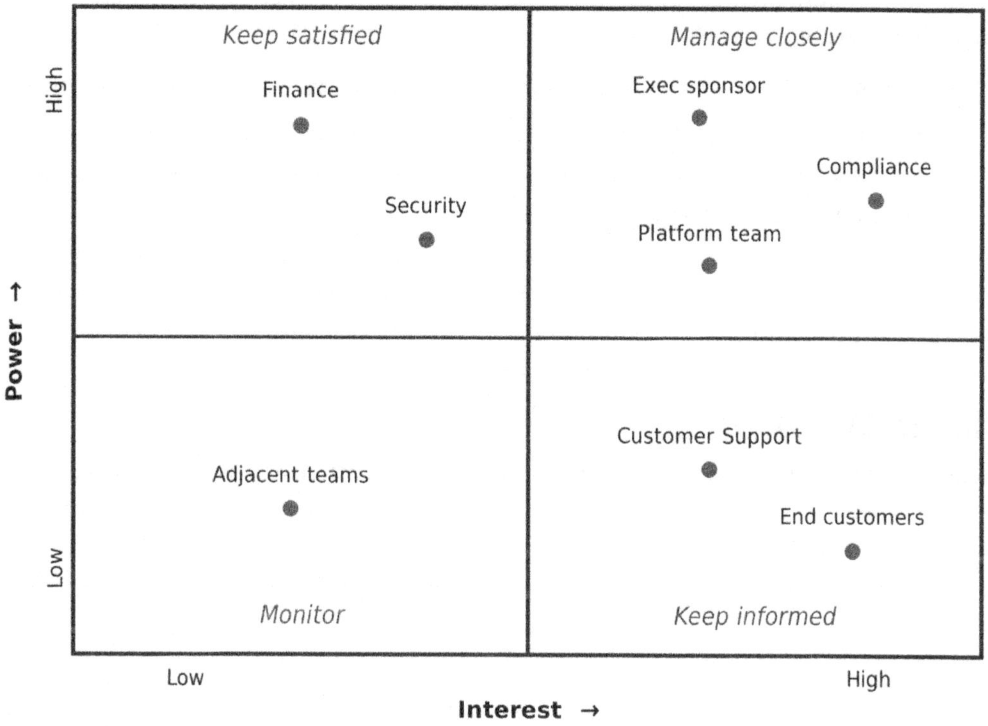

Figure 13.6: The billing migration's stakeholders on Mendelow's Matrix

Task:

Plot some of your own stakeholders on this matrix. It will help you identify how communication should differ between them.

The Salience Model

Mendelow's Matrix works well in most situations, but complex deliveries often involve stakeholders whose priority shifts with circumstances. The Salience Model addresses this by evaluating stakeholders across three attributes:

- **Power:** the degree of influence a stakeholder holds over project decisions and outcomes.
- **Legitimacy:** how appropriate or valid their involvement is in a given situation.
- **Urgency:** the extent to which a stakeholder requires immediate attention based on the criticality of their needs at a point in time.

The real strength of this model is its dynamic nature. Unlike a static grid, the Salience Model acknowledges that stakeholder priority is not fixed; someone with high urgency at one stage of delivery may become less critical at another. Referencing it demonstrates that your stakeholder management is fluid and context-aware, not a one-time exercise.

The RACI Matrix

Alongside prioritization, the RACI matrix is one of the most effective tools for resolving conflict when it arises. By listing every key deliverable and assigning the roles of Responsible, Accountable, Consulted, or Informed to each stakeholder or team, it creates shared clarity on who owns what. *Figure 13.7* shows a sample RACI grid, with each deliverable as a row and each role marked R, A, C, or I.

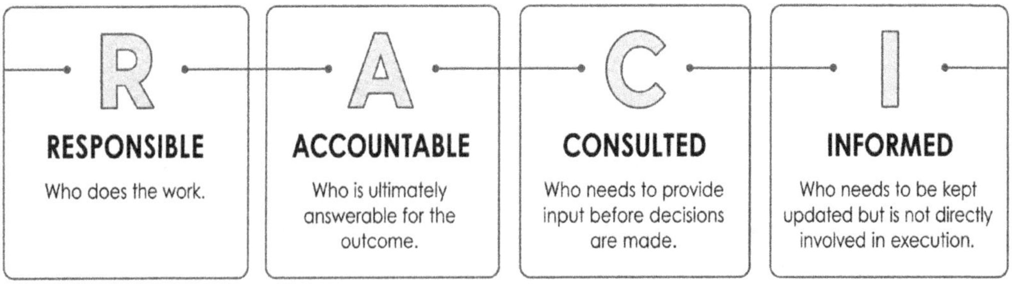

Figure 13.7: A RACI matrix

Used in practice, the RACI matrix prevents role clarity from being left to assumption; it forces the question of who owns what before mid-delivery friction forces it for you. Described later in an interview, that same upfront alignment signals maturity: you invest in clarity early and prevent the duplication and conflict that surface when expectations are not set.

Table 13.2 shows a slice of the billing migration's own RACI: one Accountable owner per deliverable, and no gaps left to assumption.

Deliverable	Engineering Lead	Platform	Compliance	Finance	Support
Data migration and cutover	A	R	C	I	I
Regulatory sign-off	C	I	A	C	I
Rollback plan	A	R	I	I	C
Customer communications	C	I	C	I	A

Table 13.2: A worked RACI for the billing migration (A = Accountable, R = Responsible, C = Consulted, I = Informed).

Stakeholder management principles

Frameworks and matrices are only as effective as the behaviors behind them. Successful stakeholder management ultimately comes down to a few principles no tool can replace:

- **Transparency over comfort:** share the right information, even when it is difficult. Hiding facts may feel protective in the short term but erodes trust far faster than a difficult conversation ever would.
- **Facts and data over opinion:** ground your decisions and communications in evidence. This removes ambiguity and gives stakeholders confidence that you operate with clarity and objectivity.
- **Structured and consistent communication:** establish a regular cadence. Stakeholders should never have to chase you for an update.
- **Clear acceptance criteria:** define scope and timelines explicitly from the outset, so there is shared understanding of what success looks like before work begins.

- **Early escalation over late surprises:** raise risks and blockers as soon as they are identified, along with the impact, mitigation options, and decisions needed. The cost of a late surprise is almost always higher than the discomfort of an early conversation.
- **Trust through consistency:** trust is not built by a single difficult conversation. It is earned over time by consistently delivering on commitments, communicating honestly, and following through on agreed actions.

In the billing migration case study used throughout the chapter, none of these tools shipped a single line of code. They are what kept the people around the code aligned long enough for the code to matter.

Summary

The moments in this chapter share one thing: each one arrives without a script. A deadlock with no obvious right answer, a risk no one has named, a person who needs either support or a boundary, a claim of progress that has to be proven, and a room full of stakeholders who each want something different. Behavioral Intelligence at work is what you do in those moments. On the billing migration that meant settling an approach conflict with data, mitigating a cutover risk instead of hoping, supporting Sam while holding Danny to a standard, measuring whether the team was truly faster, and aligning stakeholders who never touched the code.

The frameworks, the three categories of conflict and the 4-D Model, the risk strategies and the risk heatmap, the 9-Box Matrix, the DORA, flow, and quality metrics, and Mendelow's Matrix, the Salience Model, and RACI, are the shared vocabulary for that judgment, not a substitute for it. They are thinking tools, and what makes any of them land is the self-awareness and honesty you bring when you use them. That is also why these moments carry so well into an interview: they are where the difference between a good leader and a great one becomes visible.

The next chapter turns from the work itself to the interview room: the answer frameworks, from STAR and its Reflection extension to CAR and SOAR, and the story bank that turns your experience into ready evidence.

References

[1] Google Cloud, DORA State of AI-assisted Software Development Report, 2025. `https://cloud.google.com/resources/content/2025-dora-ai-assisted-software-development-report`

14

From Experience to Signal: Frameworks and the Story Bank

> *"I am convinced that life is 10% what happens to me and 90% of how I react to it."*
>
> *—Charles Swindoll*

Knowing the behavioral intelligence dimensions, and seeing how they play out in real work, gets you only so far. The harder part is turning your own experience into evidence someone can act on. Strong behavioral answers are built, not improvised, and this chapter is where you build them. You will work with the answer frameworks that shape raw experience into a clear response, the story bank that keeps those responses ready, and the calibration that makes the same story land at the right level for your seniority. *Chapter 12* gave you the seven dimensions your stories need to cover. Here you put them to work and start writing your own. Keep a notebook nearby as you work through the chapter.

The chapter then moves into the preparation behind those stories. You will learn how to understand a company and what it values, read a job description beyond the list of requirements, and get a clearer picture of the role you are actually stepping into. We will also look at how to approach your preparation when your career path has not been a straight line. When you prepare well, the rest becomes easier, from choosing the right stories to asking thoughtful questions.

By the end of this chapter, you will have a working method and the start of a story bank you can actually draw on: structured, well-chosen stories matched to the right level, and the habits to walk into any behavioral assessment prepared.

This chapter will cover the following topics:

- Behavioral answer frameworks: STAR and STAR+R in depth
- Choosing the right framework: CAR, CARL, SOAR, and PAR compared
- Crafting your story bank and mapping them using STAMP framework
- Level calibration through a seniority lens, with role-play examples
- Common failure modes at senior levels
- Understanding the company and defining the role beyond the job description, including the common mistakes that weaken strong answers
- Adapting the method when your career path is not a straight line

Let's start with the industry-wide frameworks, and how they turn your experience into something you can use throughout your career.

Behavioral answer frameworks

Before the frameworks, consider what their absence looks like from the other side of the table.

> **Note**
>
> **From the debrief room—here is a candidate's response with no framework:**
>
> *"We migrated the service to microservices."*
>
> *"I worked closely with the team to deliver the project."*
>
> *"We had some performance issues, but we fixed them."*
>
> On paper, those sound like solid answers. In an assessment, these statements tell almost nothing.
>
> In this scenario, a hiring manager was on the other side of the table, interviewing a senior engineering candidate. The expectation was to hear about the decisions the candidate had made, the trade-offs considered, the challenges they faced, and the impact they had.
>
> Instead, every answer stayed at 30,000 feet.
>
> After fifteen minutes, it became clear that the candidate probably had the experience. The problem wasn't a lack of technical depth; it was an inability to communicate it.

> The hiring manager had to do most of the heavy lifting, asking probing questions after every answer to understand what the candidate had actually contributed.
>
> *"What was your role?"*
>
> *"Why did you choose that approach?"*
>
> *"What alternatives did you consider?"*
>
> *"What was the outcome?"*
>
> An interview shouldn't feel like an investigation. Your interviewer shouldn't have to dig for evidence of your impact. Your answers should bring it to the surface, in most cases.

Without structure, even the strongest professionals come across as unprepared, unclear, or uninspiring, exactly the outcome you want to avoid. That is the problem structured frameworks exist to solve. They give you a method to tell your story clearly, highlight impact, and demonstrate leadership, so that every answer reflects not just what you have done but who you are.

A clear way to structure your answers makes a substantial difference. Over time, industry experts have created plenty of frameworks for this, such as STAR, STAR+R, CAR, CARL, SOAR, and PAR (the next section and Table 14.1 describe them), along with a few others. Each has a slightly different twist, but they share the same core goal: helping you tell your story in a way that highlights the situation, what you did, and the impact you made.

The differences between them are fairly subtle. Some frameworks emphasize the challenges you faced, others highlight the goals you aimed for, and some include a reflection or learning component.

We will zero in on STAR and STAR+R, the two most widely recognized and practical frameworks. They are straightforward, easy to apply, and effective, especially in senior-level interviews where clarity and structure matter most. Once you have mastered STAR, you will find it simple to adapt the same principles to CAR, CARL, SOAR, or PAR, depending on the situation and the story you want to tell.

> **Note**
>
> You can jump directly to the section *Extending STAR: The Second R of Reflection (STAR+R)* if you already know the STAR framework.

The STAR Framework: Your guide to structuring responses

One of the most effective ways to navigate conversations, especially in behavioral interviews is the STAR method. This structured approach helps you give clear, complete answers that cover every essential aspect of your experience. STAR stands for:

- **Situation (S):** Start by setting the context. Describe the scenario you were in, where this happened and why it mattered. Example: "*In my previous role as a software developer at XYZ Company, we were working on a major update for our flagship product.*"
- **Task (T):** Explain your responsibility in the situation and the challenge you faced. What was expected of you? Example: "*I was tasked with leading the upgrade of the existing payment gateway platform, focusing on reducing latency. The objective was to improve transaction efficiency and deliver a more reliable payment experience for end users.*"
- **Action (A):** Detail the specific steps you took. Focus on what *you* did, clearly distinguishing your own contributions while acknowledging relevant team effort. Example: "*I began by researching payment gateways to find one that met our technical requirements. After selecting the most suitable option, I coordinated with the design and backend teams to implement the integration, and I developed a testing protocol to ensure the new system worked seamlessly.*"
- **Result (R):** Share the outcome of your actions, with quantifiable metrics wherever possible. Example: "*Transaction speeds increased by 25%, user satisfaction scores rose 15%, and payment-related support tickets fell by 30%.*"

Figure 14.1 lays out the STAR framework:

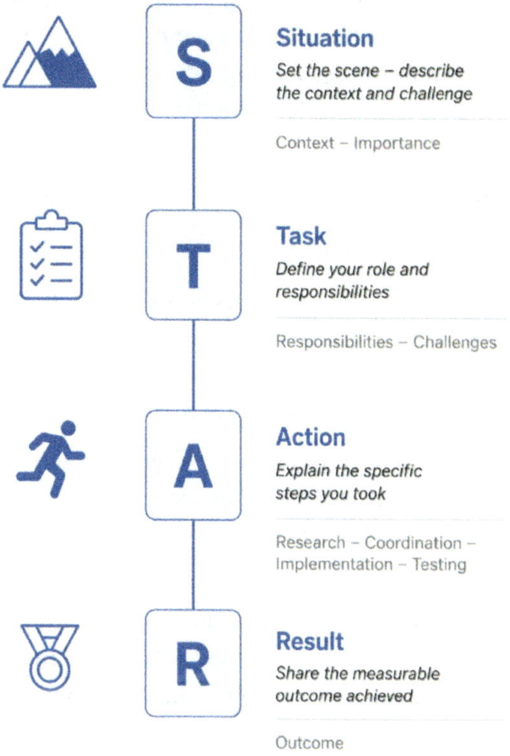

Figure 14.1: The STAR framework

It is easy to nod along to a framework and still freeze when the question lands. Imagine two engineers are asked the same thing, "*Tell me about a time you improved a system's performance,*" and both reach for the same payment gateway upgrade described above. Only one of them makes it land.

The first candidate starts in the middle. "*So, we had this payment system, and there were a lot of issues, latency mostly, and we looked at a few options, and eventually things got better and the team was happy.*" None of it is untrue, but the interviewer is now doing the work by figuring out what was this person's actual role, what did they do, and how much better is *better*? The story stayed a fog, and the follow-up questions had to pull it into focus.

The second candidate tells the same story very differently. "*Last year, one of our flagship products was losing transactions because the payment gateway was introducing too much latency. I was responsible for leading the gateway upgrade, so my first step was to evaluate a few alternatives against our performance, reliability, and integration requirements. Once we selected the best option, I coordinated with the backend and frontend teams on the rollout, built a testing strategy to validate the migration, and monitored the release closely. In the end, transaction latency dropped by 25%, customer satisfaction improved by 15%, and payment-related support tickets fell by nearly 30%. The biggest lesson for me was that choosing the right technology was only half the job. Planning, testing, and coordination were just as important to delivering a successful outcome."*

The difference was not the work; both had done the same job. It was how they presented their case. That approach, and how to make it work for you, is what the rest of this section is about.

How the STAR method improves your answer

Clarity: It provides a structure that makes your answers easy to follow. Under pressure, it is easy to leap straight to the outcome or wander through backstory; the frame gives the listener a familiar path, context, your task, what you did, and what happened, so they spend their attention on your judgment rather than on reconstructing the order of events.

Completeness: It ensures you cover every necessary aspect of your experience. Each letter is a prompt that stops you leaving out the part that matters. Many answers stall because the candidate sets up the situation and jumps to the result, skipping the action, which is the part an assessor most wants to hear.

Relevance: It keeps you focused on the question without getting lost in unnecessary detail. Think of the framework as a filter. If a detail does not help explain the situation, task, action, or result, leave it out. This keeps a two-minute story from turning into a five-minute tangent and shows that you can separate what matters from what does not.

Impact: It highlights the outcomes of your actions, showcasing your effectiveness. Ending on the result closes the loop between what you did and what changed because of it. It is the difference between saying you led a migration and showing that the migration cut deployment time by a third, which is the detail that stays with a decision maker after you have left the room.

Tips for using the STAR framework

Prepare in advance: Think of several experiences from past roles that showcase different skills and qualities, and practice structuring them with STAR. Aim for a small, versatile set of stories that cover conflict, failure, delivery, teamwork, and leadership dimensions so you are recombining prepared material rather than inventing under pressure. Rehearse them out loud rather than only in your head; the gap between a story you have thought about and one you have said aloud can be wider than it looks.

Be specific: Avoid vague statements. Provide enough detail to make your story compelling and believable. Name the system, the constraint, the roles of people involved, and what was at stake without sharing any confidential details. Specifics are what make a story sound lived rather than rehearsed, and they give the assessor concrete threads to pull on, which is usually a sign your answer is landing.

Focus on your role: Even if you were part of a team, emphasize your personal contribution. Decision makers are leveling you, not your team, so be precise about the decisions and actions that were yours. Use *I* for what you did and save *we* for work that was shared; a story told entirely in *we* leaves the evaluator unsure what you brought to it.

Quantify results: Numbers provide concrete evidence of your achievements. Percentages, time saved, revenue, incidents avoided, and users affected can turn your example into evidence. When you do not have a precise metric, reach for a defensible proxy or a before-and-after comparison rather than dropping the result altogether.

Stay relevant: Tailor your stories to the job you are applying for. Read the role and its level, then lead with the stories that speak to what it actually rewards; an answer that impresses for a hands-on engineering role can be the wrong pick for a position that is about influence and scope. Well-prepared candidates choose the story to fit the question, not the other way around.

Extending STAR: The second R of Reflection (STAR+R)

Many companies, particularly at mid-to-senior levels, want to know more than *what you did.* They want to know *what you learned.* This is where STAR extends with a second R, for Reflection (STAR+R). You may also see this extension called STAR+L, for Learning; however, we will use STAR+R throughout this book.

Reflection (R): The Reflection step is your opportunity to explain the insights you gained and how they influenced your future approach, decision-making, or leadership style. It answers the interviewer's unspoken question: *How did this experience make you better?* This final step is particularly valuable because it demonstrates qualities that organizations look for in senior professionals. It shows that you actively reflect on your experiences rather than simply moving on to the next challenge.

- It signals reflection, a growth mindset, and evolving judgment
- It shows your ability to adapt and improve processes
- It highlights maturity and leadership thinking

> **Note**
>
> **Example (STAR+R)**
>
> **Question**: *Tell me about a time you managed conflicting priorities.*
>
> **Situation**: During the final month before launching a new payment platform, my team was simultaneously handling critical production defects, regulatory compliance changes, and several high-priority customer feature requests.
>
> **Task**: As the engineering lead, I had to ensure the regulatory deadline was met without compromising production stability or delaying key customer commitments.
>
> **Action**: I worked with product, compliance, and engineering teams to prioritize work using an impact-versus-urgency matrix. We deferred two low-value features, reassigned engineers to the compliance workstream, and scheduled daily risk reviews to track dependencies and unblock issues quickly.
>
> **Result**: The platform launched on schedule, all regulatory requirements were met, production incidents remained at zero during the release, and the deferred features were delivered in the following sprint with minimal customer impact.
>
> **Reflection**: This experience taught me that conflicting priorities are rarely solved by working harder. Rather, they are solved by making transparent trade-offs. Since then, I have introduced a lightweight prioritization framework that helps teams align on decisions earlier, reducing conflict and improving delivery predictability.

Introducing STAR+R here sets the stage for the role-play examples in the section *A Framework for finding the right story*, where senior-level answers include reflection to distinguish them from mid-level and early-career responses.

> **Task**:
>
> Think about both frameworks above and the stories from your own career that align with them, and map them out in a notebook or electronically.

Reflect on challenges (not just wins)

Reflect on moments when you overcame obstacles like tight deadlines, unclear requirements, tricky stakeholders, failed ideas, and how you got past them, focusing on your problem-solving and resilience. Consider experiences that led to personal or professional growth as well. These stories can be especially compelling because they demonstrate your ability to learn and improve.

Growth stories do not need to be huge; however, they need to be honest and show a constructive mindset.

Choosing the right framework: CAR, CARL, SOAR, PAR

Each framework offers a slightly different lens. All of them aim to highlight context, action, and impact; the nuances in focus, whether emphasizing challenges, objectives, or reflection, make some better suited to certain situations or seniority levels. STAR and STAR+R provide a balanced structure that works across most interviews, with STAR+R adding a reflective dimension for senior individual contributors (ICs) and leaders. CAR and CARL suit problem-focused or leadership storytelling, particularly when overcoming obstacles is central. SOAR emphasizes goal alignment, which makes it effective for strategic discussions, while PAR offers a concise, result-driven option for high-level or time-constrained settings. All these frameworks are listed in *Table 14.1*. Keep one thing in mind—many companies now tell you in advance the format they expect your answer in. If they do, answer accordingly.

Framework	Components	Focus/strength	Best For
STAR	Situation, Task, Action, Result	Balanced story structure	All levels
STAR+R	STAR + Reflection	Adds learning, self-awareness	Senior ICs, managers, directors
CAR	Challenge/Context, Action, Result	Problem-focused, dynamic storytelling	Leadership, problem-solving
CARL	CAR + Learning	Shows reflection after challenges	Senior leadership, executive interviews
SOAR	Situation, Objective, Action, Result	Emphasizes alignment with goals	Strategic/leadership interviews
PAR	Problem, Action, Result	Short, result-focused	Quick answers or high-level impact stories

Table 14.1: Commonly used storytelling frameworks

Understanding these differences helps you choose the framework that communicates your experience most effectively, so your answers resonate with the evaluators and highlight the qualities being evaluated. *Figure 14.2* helps you understand the framework selection quickly.

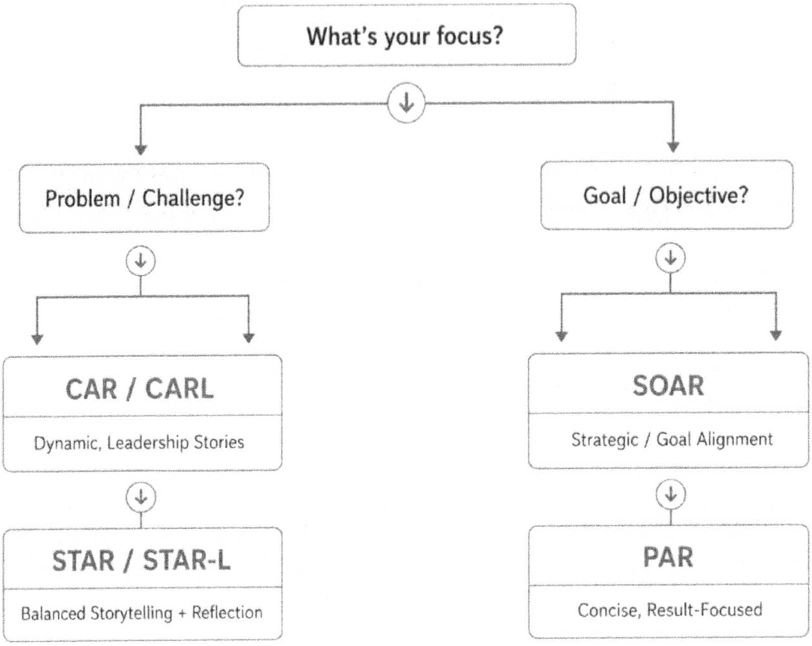

Figure 14.2: Choosing the right behavioral framework

With these frameworks in your toolkit, you are ready to move from concept to practice.

Crafting and maintaining your story bank

Let us accept this: writing is hard. Expressing an idea clearly is often harder than having the idea itself. Most of us know what we want to say, but putting it into words that are clear, concise, and engaging takes effort. Good writing rarely happens in the first draft. It comes from rewriting, refining, enhancing, and simplifying until your message says exactly what you intended.

> *"If you find that writing is hard, it's because it is hard."*
>
> — *William Zinsser*

It is also the highest-leverage preparation habit we know, an Engineering Manager at Google, shared with us how he has kept his story bank for almost two decades.

> **Note**
>
> **Anecdote from an Engineering Manager at Google**
>
> I may surprise you by sharing this, but I started writing my stories back in 2007, when I first began attending job interviews in the IT industry. I captured them in handwritten notes, carefully logging each one. After every conversation about interviews, every session with HR, and every discussion about my experiences, I made it a habit to write it all down. My notes were not limited to behavioral questions. They included every piece of conversation, the responses I gave to the best of my memory, and the improved versions I would use if I met those questions again.
>
> Over time, this practice became the foundation of my story bank. Fast-forward to 2025: when Google called me for their interview process and the recruiter said, "*You will need to prepare a lot of stories for your interviews*," my story bank was already there. All I had to do was map it to the Leadership Principles that would be covered in the interviews.

What you build, note by note, is a story bank—a curated collection of examples that demonstrate your impact, leadership, and problem-solving. At senior and leadership levels, relying on memory alone is often not enough; structured preparation ensures your stories are ready, relevant, and compelling for any scenario. It is also about knowing your history well enough, aligned with the job you have understood and defined, to talk about it confidently. Building such a story bank takes four steps.

Step 1: Identify core competencies

Start by listing the key skills, behaviors, and leadership qualities decision makers typically assess at your level. Examples include:

- Strategic thinking and decision-making
- Leading cross-functional teams
- Driving complex projects to success
- Managing conflict or change
- Mentorship and team development

This becomes the blueprint for the types of stories you need to capture. Please refer to *Chapter 12* for further guidance on leadership dimensions.

Step 2: Collect your stories

For each competency, recall past experiences that clearly illustrate your contribution and impact and develop concise, clear stories. Focus on stories that have:

- **Context:** what was the situation or challenge?
- **Action:** what specific steps did you take?
- **Impact:** what was the measurable result or outcome?

If you struggle to recall such an instance, look for small wins, as even they can become compelling stories if framed correctly around leadership, problem-solving, or learning.

This step can be done independently as well initially. However, once you have gathered the stories, you need to align them with the competencies as discussed in *Step 1* and ensure you have enough for each one of them.

Step 3: Structure using a framework

Once you collect experiences, organize each story using a framework such as STAR. This ensures consistency and clarity, and makes it easier to adapt stories to different questions without rewriting them entirely. You should also anticipate probing on your stories, so be prepared for follow-up questions that dig deeper. Think about what additional details might be requested, especially the reflection points someone may want to explore. Capture those details as well.

Step 4: Review and Refresh Regularly

A story bank is a living document. After every assessment, reflection session, or major project, update it:

- Add new stories that showcase growth and recent impact
- Refine old stories based on lessons learned
- Practice delivery to keep your examples crisp and confident

AI assistants such as ChatGPT, Claude, or Gemini can be useful when building and refining your story bank. Use them to draft, review, and stress-test your stories, but treat them as an editor rather than an author. Your experiences, reflections, and outcomes should remain your own. Their live voice modes can take this a step further by acting as a conversational partner. Give the model your target role, selected stories, and instructions to challenge you with follow-up questions.

Map your stories to the dimensions

Use *Table 14.2* to turn your experiences into a searchable bank. Read down the keywords under each dimension, then write the numbers of the stories that fit in the last column. Most strong stories map to more than one dimension, so the same number will often appear in several rows. Fill it in once and you can find the right story in seconds during an interview.

Dimension	Related keywords	Your stories
Leadership	Mentorship / leadership Influence others Take a stand Convincing Conflict resolution	
Adaptability	Flexibility Adjust to a colleague's style Handling a crisis An unexpected situation Turning a challenge into opportunity	
Communication	Convincing Negotiation A coworker's view of you Influence others Handling negative feedback	

Dimension	Related keywords	Your stories
Problem-Solving	Creativity Deciding with limited data A challenging situation Turning a challenge into opportunity Handling a crisis	
Achievement	Your strengths Your weaknesses Handling failure Handling negative feedback Working with a deadline	
Time-Management	Working with a deadline Competing team priorities An unexpected situation A challenging situation Deciding with limited data	
Teamwork	Conflict resolution Working with difficult people Compromise to achieve a goal Negotiation A coworker's view of you	

Table 14.2: Map your stories to the seven behavioral dimensions

Task:

Now it is time to build your own story bank around the seven dimensions discussed in *Chapter 12* and map your stories to them.

A framework for finding the right story

Many candidates lose a behavioral question in the first few seconds despite having a great story bank. They hear the question, pick the first story that comes to mind, and start speaking before thinking about what the interviewer is really trying to assess. The answer can quickly become unfocused, making even a strong candidate sound uncertain.

Here we are providing a framework, a repeatable way to map the question to the right story in your story bank. We call it **STAMP**, a five-step approach that helps you make those decisions calmly and quickly.

Start by studying the question. Look beyond the wording and identify the behavior being tested. If an interviewer asks you to describe a time when you influenced a decision you did not own, they are not just interested in the decision itself. They want to understand how you influence people who do not report to you. Identify that before you start answering.

Next, tag the dimension. Ask yourself what the question is really testing. Is it leadership, communication, teamwork, time management, or something else? Once you identify the dimension (discussed in *Chapter 12*), you have a clearer idea of what your answer needs to demonstrate.

Then, associate your stories. Look through your story bank and identify the stories that fit the dimension. Create a small shortlist of your options.

Now, mark the best one. Choose the story that answers the question most directly and, where possible, one you have not already used in the interview. One strong, relevant story is better than several that only partly fit.

Finally, present it using STAR+R. Structure the story around Situation, Task, Action, Result, and Reflection. This gives the interviewer both the evidence and what you learned from the experience.

Figure 14.3 provides a visual of the STAMP method to help you remember this framework.

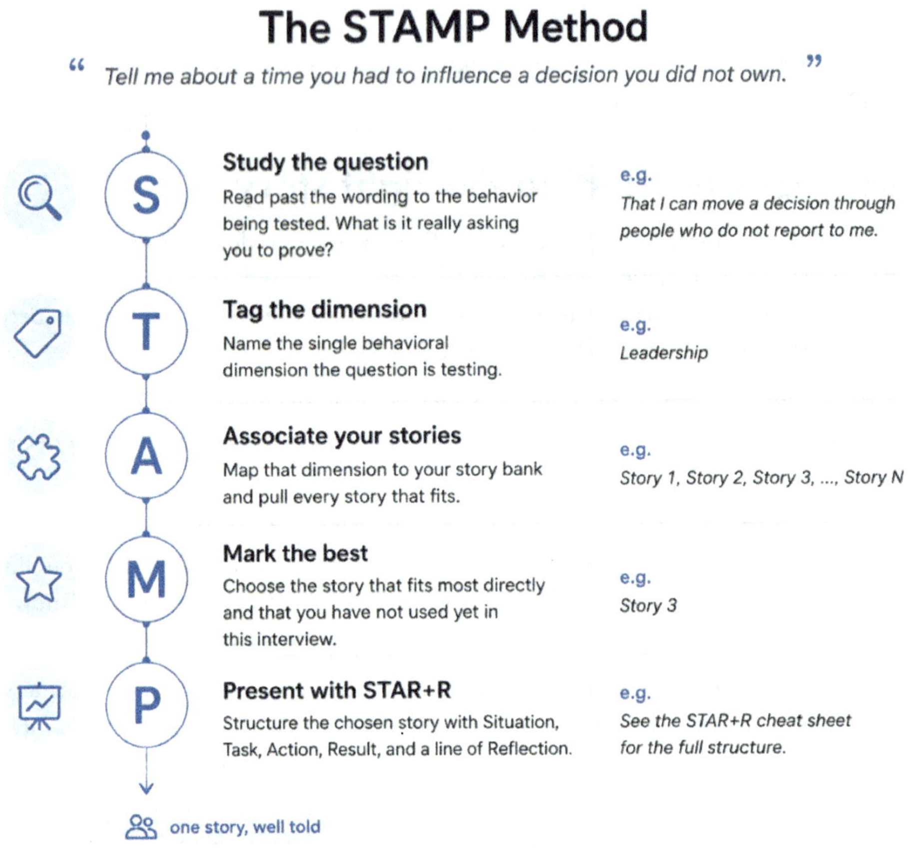

Figure 14.3: Framework for answering a behavioral question

Once STAMP becomes a habit, the whole process can take only a few seconds. It builds on the work you have already done by learning to recognize behavioral dimensions and building a strong story bank. With practice, an unexpected question becomes less intimidating because you are no longer trying to remember a prepared answer. Instead, you have a method for finding the right answer.

Now let's put these ideas into the perspective of seniority. Strong, calibrated stories still have to be aimed. The same example lands differently from one company to the next, so the rest of the chapter turns from shaping your stories for your experience level to researching the company and role you will tell them to.

Level calibration: Through a seniority lens

Two engineers can describe the same project and walk out with different levels. Not because one did more, but because one told the story from a higher altitude, reflecting the broader scope, complexity, and impact expected at their level of seniority. Many behavioral discussions quietly convert your experience into a level. That level is shaped by the scope, complexity, autonomy, and influence of your work. Your story should be told from the right altitude so those qualities become visible to the assessor. Senior candidates are often leveled down not because they lack the experience, but because they tell a story from a narrow perspective, leaving their judgment and impact hidden.

This matters because the same question is doing different work depending on who answers it. Ask a mid-level engineer and a director to tell you about a poorly defined problem, and you are testing two different things: can the engineer create clarity for themselves, and can the director create clarity for an organization. The words are identical; the bar behind them is not. Calibration is the skill of hearing which bar a question is really setting, and answering to it.

> Note
>
> **From the debrief room**
>
> Two candidates were asked about a launch that slipped.
>
> The first walked through everything they had personally shipped: the tickets they closed, the bug they chased at midnight, the weekend they gave up. It was honest and hard-working, and it was entirely about effort.
>
> The second spent one sentence on the fix and the rest on the call: which part of the scope they chose to cut, who they told first, and what they deliberately left unprotected to save the date. Same event, same slipped launch.
>
> In the debrief, the first was leveled as a solid senior engineer, the second as a lead. Neither had done more work. One had simply told the story from where the decisions were made.

The three altitudes: Execute, decide, shape

It helps to think in three altitudes. At the lowest, you *execute*: you own a task and deliver it, and the assessor wants to know you can be trusted to finish what you start. One level up, you *decide*: you make a defensible call under uncertainty, and now the interesting part of the story is the trade-off, not the task. At the top, you *shape*: you change the conditions rather than just the outcome, reframing the problem, aligning people who do not report to you, and setting what will and will not be solved.

Most stories can be told at any of the three. The question is which altitude the role is hiring for, and whether your telling reaches it. The following table shows the different altitudes and related questions you should think about.

Altitude	What the assessment is really asking	What a strong answer foregrounds	The signs you're thinking one level too low
Execute	Can you own a task and deliver it?	What you did, how you unblocked yourself, the result you shipped	The story is all activity: steps taken, hours worked, tickets closed
Decide	Can you make a good call under uncertainty?	The trade-off you weighed, the option you rejected, and why	You narrate what happened but never the decision inside it
Shape	Can you change the conditions, not just the outcome?	How you reframed the problem, aligned others, and named what would not be solved yet	You fix the problem in front of you but never touch the system that produced it

Table 14.3: The three altitudes, and what each one asks of your story

Raising the altitude of a story

For senior candidates, the shortage is rarely altitude in the work. It is altitude in the telling. You made the call; you just narrated the task. Raising a story is not exaggeration, and it is not swapping "I" for grander verbs. It is a few deliberate moves. Lead with the decision rather than the activity, opening on the choice you faced instead of the ticket you picked up.

Make the trade-off explicit, including the option you turned down and what it cost, because the most meaningful decisions usually involve rejecting a viable alternative. Show the counterfactual, i.e., what would have happened had you not stepped in. Reach for the second-order effect, the thing that changed after the immediate fix, whether a process, a norm, or how the next team approached the problem. And own the imperfect outcome plainly. Few things signal seniority faster than someone who can describe a reasonable decision that did not fully work and explain why they would still make it.

Common failure modes at senior levels

The failure modes at senior levels are rarely about a lack of experience; they are more often communication gaps that prevent strong experience from being recognized. They are altitude leaks, small habits that pull a strong story back down. The most common is over-claiming through the collective "we." It feels gracious, but in a leveling conversation it erases the one thing they are trying to find, which is your specific decision. Be precise about your own part first, then be generous about the team. Its mirror image is false humility, deflecting ownership so hard that no decision seems to have been yours at all, which reads not as modesty but as absence.

Then there is outcome obsession, leading with the result and skipping the reasoning, which works against you at senior levels because the reasoning is the product; a clean outcome with no visible judgment behind it sounds like luck. There is context dumping, the long runway of background before anything happens, which buries your decision under setup and makes the assessors dig for it. And there is the quiet one, overplaying successes and hiding failures; senior assessors are not collecting wins, they are testing how you think when things are uncertain, and a candidate who has never made a hard call with an imperfect result is either early in their career or not being candid.

Calibration is not about inflating your stories; it is about telling the truest version of them at the right altitude. As you build your story bank, tag each story with the highest altitude it can honestly support, the moments where you decided or shaped rather than only executed, and lead with those when the level you are interviewing for calls for them. Matching the altitude of the story to the altitude of the role is one of the key habits that separates candidates who are simply experienced from those who are clearly ready for the next one.

This section helped you calibrate the stories at the right level. Now, these stories still have to fit the company asking for them and the role you are targeting, and that fit begins well before the discussions.

Understand the company and define the role

Preparation for any behavioral conversation comes down to two moves. One, research the company you hope to join, then two, define the role you are actually stepping into. Do both well and the rest, from the stories you choose to the questions you ask, falls into place.

Understand the company

Start with the company, because your answers only land if they fit the place you are describing them to. The goal is not to memorize facts; it is to understand what the company values and how it operates, so you can recognize those signals in the room and speak to them. It also helps you judge whether the place is right for you.

A few sources give you most of what you need:

- The company's own site and blog are where it states what it believes. Browse the About, Mission, and Careers pages for its values and the qualities it praises in its people; when a phrase or value shows up more than once, treat it as a priority worth echoing in your stories.
- Employee reviews on Glassdoor and Indeed give an unfiltered read on management, work-life balance, and the day-to-day culture. Look for repeated themes rather than the extremes, and if you are senior, read the interview reviews too, since they reveal what the company screens for.
- Leadership talks, podcasts, and social channels show the company off-script. A short discussion with a founder or executive often tells you more about the culture, and the words leaders keep returning to, than an hour on the corporate site.
- A brief chat with a current or former employee is the fastest way to learn the unwritten rules. LinkedIn makes this easy through first- and second-degree connections, and firsthand accounts of team dynamics, project scope, and daily work rarely surface in public sources.

You do not need to master everything. However, you need enough to tell which of your experiences will resonate and to ask questions that show you did the work. The deep-research modes in AI assistants can compile a first draft of this brief in minutes, but read the tone of reviews and leadership talks yourself, because that judgment is part of the value.

Define the role beyond the job description

A job description (JD) is *not* a checklist. It is a signal. Defining the role is about understanding what the job is asking for—not just the bullet points on the posting, but the skills, behaviors, and expectations behind them. The clearer you are on the role, the easier it becomes to pick the right stories and show why you fit.

Here are three questions that turn the job posting into a clear target:

- What problem is this role really meant to solve, and why is the company hiring for it now? The verbs in the responsibilities tell you the altitude: support and coordinate mean contributing within a structure, while own, drive, and shape mean accountability for outcomes.
- What would strong performance look like in the first six months, and what scope of ownership does that imply? The required skills set the baseline expected from day one, while the nice-to-haves quietly reveal where the team is heading next.
- Which of my experiences map most closely to that work? Match by impact rather than job title, and scan similar roles elsewhere, since the same title can carry very different responsibility from one company to the next.

Answering these turns a generic posting into a clear target, so you can choose examples that prove you already operate at the level the role needs, and that clarity shows the moment you start speaking. Tools such as ApplyArc can support this process by analyzing a JD and generating role-specific questions, talking points, and areas to prepare, rather than relying on generic behavioral questions. As AI-assisted tools continue to evolve, use them to make your preparation more specific to the role, not to replace your own thinking and reflection.

Common mistakes to avoid

Keep your stories natural and grounded. Even with excellent preparation, people slip into a few patterns that weaken their answers. Be vigilant for the ones shown in *Table 14.4*:

The mistake	How it shows in the room	The fix, and the step that prevents it
Stories that do not match the role	A good story proving a skill the role does not need, or proving it at the wrong level	Match every story to the competencies and seniority you identified. Define.
Shallow company research	Generic answers to values questions; closing questions the careers page already answers	Even one focused hour can materially improve the quality of preparation. Understand.
Forgetting the interviewer	The same story told the same way to an engineer and a hiring manager	Five minutes on their profile helps you know who may want depth and who wants outcomes. Understand.
Over-rehearsing	Scripted tone; the first follow-up that breaks the script breaks you with it	Practice ideas, not sentences. If you can tell a story three ways, you own it. Reflect.
Never practicing out loud	The first spoken telling is twice as long and half as clear, and it happens in the discussion	The first three tellings are rehearsal; do them before the day. Reflect.
Skipping the hard parts	A frictionless story that reads as luck or fiction	Keep the wrong first attempt and the disagreement in; that is where judgment shows. Reflect.
Only preparing wins	Nothing to say when the question asks about failure, conflict, or pressure	Prepare setbacks with the same care; they carry your best reflection lines. Reflect.

The mistake	How it shows in the room	The fix, and the step that prevents it
Tasks instead of impact	"I was responsible for the migration," with no number and no consequence	Every story ends with the impact, quantified where possible and described qualitatively when necessary. Define and Reflect.

Table 14.4: Eight common mistakes and how to prevent them

Notice the pattern in the right-hand column: every common mistake is a skipped step. If your preparation followed understand, define, and reflect honestly, you have already avoided them. This table is your final check, not a new list to memorize.

Remember, your goal is not to give perfect answers. It is to sound like the person who understands the company, knows the role, and has real experience to back it up.

When your path is not a straight line

Understanding a company and defining a role are useful for every candidate. But when your career has not followed a straight line, both can feel a little harder.

Careers rarely unfold exactly as planned. You may have moved across industries, changed roles, or taken an unexpected turn along the way. Your resume may look less linear than someone else's, but that does not make your experience less valuable. In fact, a non-linear career can give you a broader perspective and richer experiences. The challenge is making that story clear to the assessor and showing what you learned, how you grew, and how those experiences connect to where you are going next. The preparation is the same at its core; what changes is how you frame your journey. Let's look at some of the most common situations and how to approach them.

Employment gaps and layoffs: It is becoming increasingly common to have career gaps. If you have one, acknowledge it calmly and without apology or over-explaining. Then focus on how you used that time productively, whether through courses, projects, freelance work, caregiving, or other experiences that helped you build useful skills. Many professionals understand that layoffs are business-driven and not verdicts on you. The key is to explain calmly without being defensive about it.

Non-native English speakers: Clarity generally matters more than vocabulary in conversations. A well-structured STAR+R answer in simple language is often more effective than a fluent but unfocused response. Slow down when needed, and practice your stories out loud to ensure the phrasing is yours. Your accent is not something to apologize for as it reflects the different cultures and teams you may have worked with across the globe. Confidence matters, but it should make your message clearer, not harder to understand. Tools such as Gemini's voice mode can help you practice by identifying places where you speak too quickly or could communicate more clearly.

Introverts: Behavioral discussions reward substance over charisma, which makes them the format where preparation pays well. Your prepared specificity, real numbers, and honest reflection are usually more valuable than improvised charm alone, because scorecards record evidence, not just energy. Manage the parts that drain you; for example, request breaks in loops and use the energy strategies from *Chapter 12*, and remember that a thoughtful pause reads as judgment, not hesitation.

Career changers :Your stories can transfer even when your job titles do not, because behavioral questions assess how you handled situations, not just the industry you worked in. A project manager who resolved a conflict between competing stakeholders, for example, already has a story about influence and negotiation, even if the new role is in a different industry. Use the understand step to learn the target industry's language, then retell your existing stories in that context—that is, the same experience with translated vocabulary. Additionally, do not overlook the career change itself. Choosing to switch, planning the transition, and closing the skill gap can become a strong story about adaptability and learning.

Neurodivergent candidates: You may request accommodations, such as questions in writing, extra time, camera-off screens, or a quieter setting, and in many places, employers are required to provide reasonable ones. Asking is normal, and disclosure is yours to time and to word. Scripts and structure help: the story bank and the rehearsal tools in this chapter turn an unpredictable conversation into a largely prepared one. If eye contact or small talk costs you effort, spend your energy on the answers; that is what the scorecard records.

One reminder ties all of these together: the scorecard does not score your path; it scores your behavior. These preparation steps work identically whatever route you took to the room, and the bends in that route are usually where your strongest stories live.

Summary

Turning experience into signal is a skill you can practice, and this chapter gave you the tools. You have the answer frameworks that shape raw memories into clear responses, STAR and STAR+R at the core, with CAR, CARL, SOAR, and PAR to reach for when a story calls for a different frame. You learned to build a story bank and map each story to the behavioral dimensions, so the right example is ready before the question arrives, and to calibrate that story to your level, telling it at the altitude of execution, decision, or shaping depending on the role. STAMP tied these together into a repeatable way to move from any question to the strongest story you have.

The chapter then turned outward. You saw how to research a company and read a role beyond its job description, how to sidestep the common mistakes that weaken otherwise strong answers, and how to adapt the whole method when your path has not been a straight line.

Prepared this way, you walk in with framed, calibrated, well-aimed stories rather than hoping the right memory surfaces under pressure. The next chapter goes inside Big Tech behavioral interviews, showing how companies like Meta, Amazon, Apple, Netflix, and Google anchor their questions to their values and principles, the questions they actually ask, and how to craft responses that meet each bar.

15

Behind the Big Tech Bar: Core Values and Leadership Principles

Candidates think they are answering questions

Interviewers think they are collecting evidence.

That difference explains why technically brilliant people still fail behavioral interviews at Big Tech companies like Meta, Amazon, Apple, Netflix, Google, OpenAI, Anthropic, and SpaceX. These companies operate at the pinnacle of the tech industry, and their behavioral interviews reflect the exceptionally high standards they maintain.

This chapter takes you inside that system. It explains why these companies interview the way they do, what happens after you leave the room, how the scorecards are filled, who actually makes the hiring decision, and why the strongest answer is rarely the longest one.

Two things matter before we begin. First, Big Tech interview processes are among the most structured and studied in the industry, making them an excellent reference model even if you never interview at one of these companies. Second, every idea in this chapter builds on the same Behavioral Intelligence frameworks introduced in *Chapter 14, From Experience to Signal: Frameworks and the Story Bank.*

This chapter covers the following topics:

- The hidden drivers of high-stakes interviews
- Core values, leadership principles, and cultural signals at Big Tech companies
- How Big Tech interviewers are trained, who actually decides, and what they write down, and the anatomy of the loop end to end

- One story told five ways, and how to craft responses
- Pro-level strategies: curveball questions, stress management, tailoring responses, and lasting impressions

> **Note**
>
> **A note on the acronym**
>
> Jim Cramer coined FANG in 2013 to spotlight high-growth tech stocks (Facebook, Amazon, Netflix, Google). Apple's inclusion made it FAANG, and the 'M' arrived when Facebook became Meta, changing the acronym to MAANG. In the context, Microsoft was originally left out as a mature, slower-growth company. By mid-2026 the financial press had begun replacing FAANG/MAANG with MANGO (or MANGOS) — Meta, Anthropic, Nvidia, Google, OpenAI, and SpaceX. [1] [2]
>
> For hiring purposes, the ticker debate matters less than the underlying trend: the set of companies running deliberate, principle-anchored behavioral interviews is growing, not shrinking. We use Big Tech throughout this chapter, but the techniques apply equally to these companies and many others following a similar standard for hiring.

Let's start by looking at some of the key drivers of these interviews. These might not be explicitly discussed or stated, but they are essential to know. Understanding them will make your interview journey more predictable and help you prepare with greater confidence.

The hidden drivers of high-stakes interviews

These companies seek candidates who demonstrate a balance of top technical talent and alignment with their cultures and values. Here is why behavioral interviews are a staple in their hiring:

Emphasis on leadership and innovation: Big Tech companies thrive on innovation and leadership. Behavioral questions identify people who can contribute by leading projects, thinking creatively, and driving change.

Team collaboration: These companies work on large, collaborative projects. Understanding how you work within a team, handle conflicts, and contribute to group goals is crucial.

Adaptability: The tech industry is fast-paced and ever-changing. Big Tech values employees who adapt to new challenges, learn quickly, and pivot when necessary.

Customer-centric approach: Understanding customer needs and striving to exceed them is fundamental. Behavioral interviews assess your ability to prioritize and deliver customer satisfaction.

Cultural fit: Each Big Tech company emphasizes distinct core values. Google emphasizes creativity and openness, while Amazon focuses on customer obsession and operational excellence. Behavioral interviews help ensure candidates will thrive in these environments.

Culture fit is an important aspect of the overall process and deserves a closer look. Along with that, the next section explores the core values of Big Tech companies and how they influence their hiring decisions. It also provides an overview of each company's interview focus and explains who typically makes the final hiring decision.

Core values, leadership principles, and cultural signals

Before diving into the details, it is important to understand the core values and interview focus of these companies. *Table 15.1* summarizes key cultural values of Big Tech and provides an overview of the areas they emphasize during the interview process, based on information published on their respective websites.

Company	Core values	Interview focus
Meta (Facebook) (`metacareers.com/culture`)	Openness, boldness, and building community. Meta values people who take initiative, think creatively, and collaborate effectively	Expect questions about how you handle challenges, work in teams, and contribute to a mission-driven environment.
Amazon (`amazon.jobs/en/principles`)	Customer obsession, ownership, and a focus on results. Amazon emphasizes Leadership Principles such as delivering results, thinking big, and bias for action.	Prepare for questions that probe your ability to take ownership of projects, make data-driven decisions, and prioritize customer needs.
Apple (`apple.com/careers/us/shared-values.html`)	Innovation, simplicity, and attention to detail. Apple looks for people who are passionate about their work, notice the details, and can innovate.	Expect questions that explore your passion for technology, your ability to innovate, and how you maintain high standards in your work.

Company	Core values	Interview focus
Netflix (`jobs.netflix.com/culture`)	Freedom, responsibility, and a focus on results. Netflix values independence and accountability, and a commitment to high-quality work.	Be prepared to discuss how you manage responsibilities, work independently, and contribute to a high-performance culture.
Google (`about.google/commitments`)	Innovation, transparency, and a focus on user experience. Google values creativity, collaboration, and a commitment to positive impact.	Expect questions that assess your problem-solving abilities, creativity, and how you contribute to a collaborative environment.

Table 15.1: The loops at a glance.

As shown in *Table 15.1*, each company has its own values and priorities, so your responses should demonstrate alignment with the qualities and behaviors it values most. However, this does not mean changing your experiences to fit a company's values. Instead, the goal is to understand what the company looks for and identify the parts of your own experiences that best demonstrate those qualities.

Table 15.2 provides additional context on each company's culture focus, along with common pitfalls to avoid during the interview. Use these insights to shape and strengthen your stories so they clearly demonstrate alignment with the core values of your target company. The same experience can often highlight different qualities depending on how you frame it. For example, a story about resolving a production issue could demonstrate customer focus, ownership, technical judgment, or collaboration. The key is to choose the dimension that is most relevant to the company and role you are targeting.

Company	Cultural anchor	Who decides	Fastest way to fail
Meta	Openness, boldness, impact at scale	Written packet reviewed beyond the loop	Impact you cannot quantify
Amazon	16 Leadership Principles	Debrief led by a Bar Raiser with veto power	"We" stories with no "I" in them

Company	Cultural anchor	Who decides	Fastest way to fail
Apple	Craft, simplicity, attention to detail	The team and hiring manager, same-day debrief	Indifference to the product
Netflix	Freedom and responsibility	Hiring manager, against the keeper test bar	Waiting for permission and process
Google	Innovation, collaboration, Googleyness	Hiring committee that never met you	Rehearsed answers that collapse under follow-up
OpenAI	Safe AGI mission, intensity	Team loop plus senior leadership behavioral rounds	Corporate-safe answers about the mission
Anthropic	AI safety, honest skepticism	Loop plus a standalone value round	Enthusiasm without a defensible position
SpaceX	Mission obsession, first principles	Hiring manager and management chain	Waiting for someone else to own it

Table 15.2: Companies, core values, assessor, and common mistakes to avoid

The AI-era loops: OpenAI, Anthropic, SpaceX

OpenAI, Anthropic, and SpaceX run processes similar to the MAANG companies, with one clear difference: mission alignment is a formal, scored part of the interview. At Anthropic and OpenAI it is often the deciding round.

OpenAI (openai.com/interview-guide)

OpenAI publishes its own interview guide and runs a multi-stage loop that candidates consistently report. It consists of recruiter screen, technical screen, a take-home work trial (likely), onsite rounds, and two to three behavioral conversations, at least one with a senior leader from the hiring team (*Source: OpenAI, Interview Guide, openai.com; process details: IGotAnOffer, accessed July 2026*). The behavioral expectations are different here. Rehearsed or overly polished answers about AGI (Artificial General Intelligence) and safety can work against you. Interviewers may challenge your views to see whether you can explain and defend them, adapt your thinking, or admit when you are wrong. Go in with your own views on where the technology is heading, but be open to changing your mind when presented with a stronger argument.

Anthropic (https://www.anthropic.com/careers)

Anthropic's loop includes a standalone values and culture conversation, separate from the technical rounds, and candidate reports consistently name it as the stage that decides more outcomes than any other; post-onsite rejections cite it more often than technical performance (Source: *IGotAnOffer, Anthropic Interview Process, accessed July 2026*). The round rewards honest skepticism over enthusiasm, i.e. it does not test whether you hold approved opinions about AI, but whether you hold your own under pressure. Here, the decode step matters more than usual. You should read what the company publishes and form your own view on it, rather than plainly quoting it back. Anthropic also publishes explicit guidance on how candidates may use AI during its process (`anthropic.com/candidate-ai-guidance`).

SpaceX (spacex.com/careers)

SpaceX's loop is less standardized than the MAANG processes but consistently probes four traits: mission obsession, ownership under pressure, first-principles judgment, and speed of iteration, with a large share of onsite time spent on behavioral ground despite the company's technical reputation (Source: `techinterview.org` and public interview reports, accessed July 2026; third-party accounts). In SpaceX, expect the personal version of the mission question, i.e., not whether making life multiplanetary matters, but why it matters to you. One structural note for planning here - SpaceX roles generally require US citizenship or permanent residency, so check eligibility before investing in the process.

At all three companies, prepare your answer to "why do you want to work here" with the same care as any story in your bank.

The preceding discussion has considered the interview process at length, and the ways in which a candidate can structure their preparation for it. Now let's shift the focus to the other participants in the process - the interviewers.

Interviewing has two dimensions. The first is the **structured dimension**, which includes the defined evaluation criteria and assessment process. The second is the **human dimension**, which involves personal judgment and is influenced by factors such as discipline, first impressions, and interpersonal skills. With deliberate practice, candidates can become better at navigating this human dimension.

The following section focuses on the structured dimension and provides general guidance to help you understand the interviewer's assessment lens.

Inside big tech interviewing

What most candidates never think about is that the person sitting across from them in an interview has been trained to do this. Not casually, not through a quick onboarding module, but through a **structured**, deliberate process designed to ensure that every interviewer at every level evaluates candidates against their corporate criteria, in a consistent way, every single time.

That changes everything about how you should prepare.

In interviews at companies where such structure is missing, the human dimension takes over the structured dimension to a great extent. You are largely at the mercy of whoever happens to be in the room. Some interviewers are experienced and well-calibrated. Others are less consistent in their approach. The questions vary, the scoring is inconsistent, and whether you get the job often depends more on interviewer's personal judgment than on any structured assessment of your skills.

Before an employee at these companies is allowed to interview candidates, they go through interviewer training. At Google, this includes practice interviews, calibration sessions, and feedback from experienced interviewers before someone is cleared to interview independently. At Amazon, interviewers are trained specifically on the Leadership Principles and how to score answers against them using a structured rubric. At Meta, interviewers learn how to probe for impact at scale and how to distinguish strong signal from a candidate who is just good at telling stories.

The result is a more structured, consistent, learnable, and predictable hiring process than most candidates realize.

The decision machinery

To complete the full cycle, it is also important to understand "How a decision is made". From the moment you leave the room until an outcome is communicated, a series of activities take place behind the scenes. Below we have highlighted the machinery that works during your interview and behind the scenes to reach an outcome. It differs at each company but the key is "Your answers enable them to create your report card".

Amazon: the Bar Raiser. Every Amazon loop includes a Bar Raiser, an intensively trained interviewer from outside the hiring team who serves as an objective third party, leads the debrief, and can veto a hire that everyone else wants, including the hiring manager. Bar Raisers are calibrated across hundreds of interviews, and their mandate is to ensure each hire raises the company's standard, judged against the **Leadership Principles** rather than the team's short-term staffing needs [4]. For you this means consistency matters. The Bar Raiser compares notes across the whole loop, so a story that changes shape between interviews reads as a signal problem [6].

Google - The hiring committee: At Google, the people who interviewed you do not make the decision. Each interviewer files structured written feedback, and a hiring committee of Googlers who never met you reviews the packet, weighing four dimensions: role-related knowledge, general cognitive ability, leadership, and Googleyness [7]. Your answers have to survive being retold in writing by someone else. Give your interviewer quotable numbers and crisp decision logic; you are writing their notes for them.

Meta - The packet: Meta interviewers are trained to collect signal and submit written feedback with a hire or no-hire recommendation before they can see anyone else's, and the assembled packet is then reviewed beyond the loop itself [8]. The practical consequence matches Google's approach - the specific, quantified, durable parts of your answers are what travel.

Netflix - The keeper test: Netflix publishes its standard directly in the culture memo: managers apply the keeper test, asking whether they would fight to keep a person who was thinking of leaving [9]. Interviews are run against that bar, and decision authority sits with the hiring manager rather than a committee. Expect questions that probe judgment, candor, and whether you operate on context instead of control.

Apple - The team decides: Apple is the outlier here. No central committee and no company-wide rubric. Each team runs its own process, your interviewers are your prospective colleagues, they typically debrief the same day, and the hiring manager makes the call [10]. Chemistry, product passion, and pride in craft carry more weight in the room precisely because the room is where the decision happens.

This leads to two preparation strategies. At Google and Meta, where decisions are made by a committee, focus on what gets documented: numbers, decision-making, and consistency. At Apple and Netflix, where the interviewers have more influence on the decision, focus on the people in the room, their product, expectations, and questions. Amazon sits between the two, with the 'Bar Raiser' as the written record's enforcer.

The anatomy of the loop, end to end

Candidates prepare hard for the interviews and rarely for the process around them, and that gap can cost an offer. The full pipeline looks as shown in *Figure 15.1*:

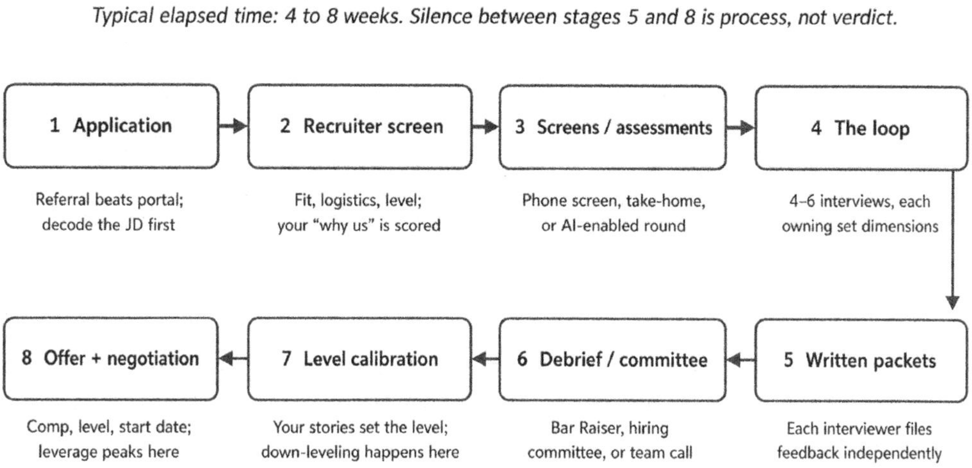

Figure 15.1: The hiring loop end to end

The stages that are hard to reach, five through seven, are where the decision actually happens. Three parts of this pipeline deserve more attention than they get.

First, the debrief gap after your final interview is often part of the process, not a reflection of your performance. Interview feedback is usually collected within a day or two, while debriefs and hiring committees may meet on a fixed schedule. So, if you do not hear back for two weeks, it may simply mean your feedback is waiting for the next meeting, not that you have failed. Ask your recruiter for the decision timeline on the day of your loop. It is a normal question, and it saves you two weeks of unnecessary worry.

Second, level calibration is a real stage, not a formality. The same evidence that gets you hired also sets the level you are hired at, and the committee calibrates level from your stories' scope, not from your years of experience. This is where the calibration lens from *Chapter 14* stops being theory.

> **Note**
>
> **The down-level offer (a composite; details changed)**
>
> Someone interviewed for a senior role, and every answer was real, specific, and quantified. But every story was execution inside someone else's frame: the goal arrived, and she delivered it impressively. Nobody in the loop heard her set direction, eliminate an option, or carry a decision she could have escalated. The committee approved the hire, one level down. She took the offer, and spent the next eighteen months earning, with visibility, the level her stories could have earned in an afternoon.
>
> Level calibration is a story problem before it is a talent problem, and it is exactly what the calibration guidance in *Chapter 14* is for.

Third, the offer stage is part of the interview although it is not about your assessment anymore. You are through with the assessment phase. Negotiation behavior is remembered by the people you will work with, which is an argument for negotiating professionally, not for skipping it.

This pipeline, built from the steps we discussed, runs four to eight weeks at most of these companies, and knowing its shape makes the waiting far easier to manage.

What interviewers are actually writing down

Here is the part that matters most for your preparation. Interviewers are not sitting there deciding whether they liked your answer. They are filling out a scorecard either in real time, or immediately after the interview. They evaluate your responses against a defined set of behavioral signals, aligned to their corporate core values even when the specific language varies. What they listen for falls into the dimensions we mapped in *Chapter 12*.

Figure 15.2 is an illustration created for readers to relate to the 'scorecard' we discussed earlier. Actual scorecards are company specific and not available for general access.

Figure 15.2: An illustrative behavioral interview scorecard

You have learned about different Big Tech companies' core values, who makes the decision, and how decisions are made. If you refer back to the topic 'The decision machinery', your answers should create enough evidence for your interviewer to present your case for a decision. And hence, crafting your response to align with the specific company's core values and other related criteria is not an option. The next section turns that knowledge into answers.

Crafting responses that survive the room

We start with one story told five different ways, because tailoring is easier to see than to describe, and then cover the principles for crafting responses. The full set of company-by-company sample questions and answers sits in the appendix at the end of this chapter. The formats vary on purpose, from full stories to answer skeletons, probe chains, and interviewer notes, so you learn to recognize a strong answer in every form it takes.

One story, five companies

You do not need five sets of stories for five companies; you need one true story and five tellings. The tellings are needed to keep your story aligned to the target company's core values. Take a single project you have worked on. For example, you led the migration of a checkout service to a new payment provider. Midway, load testing revealed a 300-millisecond latency regression, the deadline was fixed by a contract expiry, and you shipped on time after coordinating three teams.

Note that we have deliberately skipped the STAR format here while creating the story tellings. That is an exercise for you.

Observe how the emphasis shifts in *Table 15.3*.

The Amazon telling *"I owned the migration end to end. When load testing showed* a 300-millisecond regression, *I pulled the latency traces myself and found that our retry logic, not the provider, was the bottleneck. We fixed the issue and shipped on time. The payment failures dropped 18 percent. Looking back, I would have load tested in week one; I have done it that way ever since."* Emphasis: ownership, diving deep, and a metric the Bar Raiser can quote.
The Meta telling *"The checkout path carried about 40 million transactions a month, so a 300-millisecond regression was a seven-figure risk. I shipped the fix behind a flag to 5 percent of traffic, measured, then rolled it to 100. Failures dropped 18 percent at full scale."* Emphasis: scale, speed, and measured iteration.
The Apple telling *"The easy call was to ship with the regression;* A 300-millisecond regression is below what most dashboards flag. *But you can feel 300 milliseconds at checkout. We held the line, fixed the retry logic, and shipped an experience we were proud of, on time.* It also helped reduce payment failure incidents by 18 percent." Emphasis: the user's experience and refusal to lower the bar.

The Netflix telling *"The team consensus was to delay the launch and renegotiate the contract. I disagreed: the data pointed to our retry logic, not the provider. I made the case candidly, took the judgment call, and it held. We shipped on time* with an 18 percent drop in payment failure incidents." Emphasis: independent judgment, candor, and results without hand-holding.
The Google telling *"I framed it as three options: ship with the regression, delay, or fix the retry logic within the window, each with explicit trade-offs. I aligned the payments, platform, and mobile teams on the third option, and we validated with a staged rollout. My hypothesis about the retry logic held at every stage.* We delivered on time with an overall 18 percent reduction in payment failure incidents" Emphasis: structured thinking, collaboration, and hypothesis-driven delivery.

Table 15.3:Tailoring your story for the audience

Same facts, five tellings, each aligned to its target audience. Tailoring in practice here means not inventing new experiences, but knowing which dimension of a real one each scorecard is built to reward.

Approach to crafting responses

We have covered this in the previous chapter, but it is worth the reminder when crafting your responses:

- **Align with company values:** tailor your responses to reflect the values and priorities of the company. Use language that resonates with their mission and culture.
- **Use the STAR method:** structure your answers with Situation, Task, Action, Result for clear, easy-to-follow responses.
- **Be specific:** provide concrete examples from your past. Avoid vague or general statements.
- **Quantify results:** include measurable outcomes wherever possible to show the impact of your actions.
- **Practice and prepare:** rehearse responses to common questions in advance so you deliver them confidently and naturally.

Let us additionally look at some "Do" and "Don't" statements with the help of *Table 15.4*:

Company	Language that lands	Language that backfires
Amazon	"I owned...", "the data showed...", "I disagreed and committed"	"We did..." with no "I", scale left vague, blame shifted elsewhere
Meta	"shipped to 40 million users", "behind a flag", "measured, then scaled"	Impact without numbers, "I waited for direction"
Apple	"the user feels...", "we refused to ship at that quality"	"Good enough", "we cut corners to make the date"
Netflix	"it was my judgment call", "I gave the feedback directly"	"I escalated for approval", "the process required it"
Google	"my hypothesis was...", "the trade-off we weighed..."	Buzzwords without mechanism, answers that cannot survive "why?"

Table 15.4: Language that lands, company by company.

Before your next behavioral interview, run each of your prepared stories through this checklist:

- Is it clear what I personally did, separate from what the team did?
- Does it include at least one real metric or number that shows scale or outcome?
- Does it show how I made a decision, not just what the decision was?
- If it is a failure story, does it show a real change in behavior afterward, not just a lesson learned?
- Can I answer a follow-up question about any part of it without scrambling?

If the answer to all five questions is 'Yes', you have an answer that is ready for Big Tech's scorecard. If any of them is a 'No', that is your preparation agenda, and it is far more useful than running through fifty more practice questions.

Pro-level strategies

Behavioral interviews often demand that you respond to challenging questions, especially for senior positions or top-tier tech companies. This section covers advanced strategies for the unexpected like handling curveball questions, managing stress during the interview, tailoring your responses, and leaving a lasting impression. In the model's terms, this section is about adapting and staying effective when the interview stops going to plan. *Figure 15.3* shows the strategies at a glance that we will describe one by one.

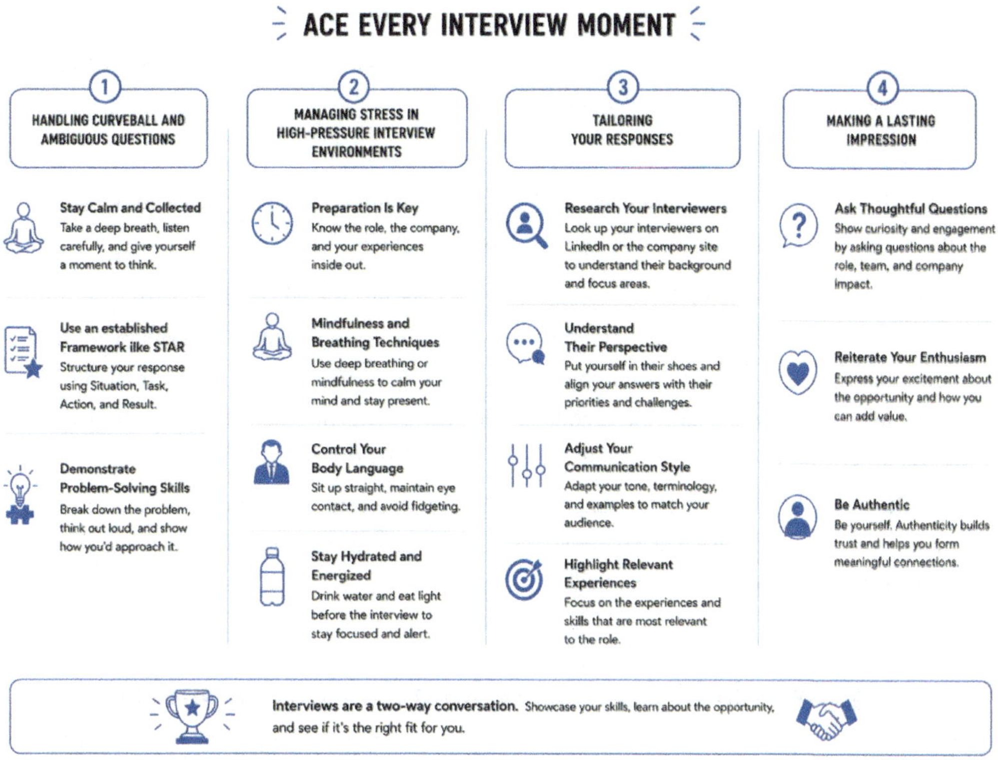

Figure 15.3: Pro-level strategies at a glance: curveballs, stress, tailoring, and lasting impression.

Handling curveball and ambiguous questions

By dictionary definition, curveball means "*something such as a question or event that is surprising or unexpected, and therefore difficult to deal with*" [3]. Even with thorough preparation, some questions can catch you off guard. They are designed to test your ability to think on your feet and adapt.

Curveball questions test how you think without a script. Take the pause; five seconds of silence before answering such a question reads as composure, not confusion, and a clarifying question shows the interviewer how you think. Then look for the familiar shape underneath, because most unexpected questions are a prepared story in disguise: identify the skill being probed, and adapt your nearest story to fit it.

When no experience fits, say so and reason forward: "*I have not faced exactly that, so here is how I would approach it,*" followed by your method, then a bridge back to the closest thing you have done. In these moments, showing your reasoning matters more than reaching a polished conclusion.

Note

Q: "If you were suddenly tasked with leading a project in an unfamiliar area along with a deadline, how would you approach it?"

Sample Response

Situation: "In a previous role, I was asked to lead a project involving a technology I wasn't initially familiar with, and delivery was due in three months."

Task: "My task was to get up to speed quickly and keep the project on track."

Action: "I researched the technology thoroughly and reached out to colleagues with more experience in the area, attending relevant training sessions to build my knowledge. I leveraged the expertise of team members who knew the technology, coordinated their efforts, and aligned people and resources against the tasks due in the window."

Result: "Despite the initial challenge, the project was completed successfully, and I gained valuable expertise in a new area. It taught me the importance of being adaptable and resourceful in unfamiliar territory."

Managing stress in high-pressure interview environments

Stress is a natural part of the interview process, especially for high-stakes positions at top companies. Managing it effectively makes a measurable difference in performance.

Stress management in an interview is not a wellness topic; it is what keeps your ability to adapt working. Under stress you stop reading the room, reach for memorized lines, and freeze on follow-ups. The protections are practical: mock interviews that make the pressure familiar in advance, a slow breath before each answer, water within reach, and enough sleep to think clearly.

In the room, two habits help. **First**, focus only on the question in front of you; replaying your last answer is how the next one gets lost. **Second**, remember that interviewers expect nerves and discount them; what they score is how you recover. A visible pause followed by a clear answer is a stronger signal than a rushed, unfocused one.

Tailoring your responses

You may meet multiple interviewers, each with their own perspective and priorities. Tailoring your responses to each one builds a stronger connection and leaves a better impression.

Research your interviewers

LinkedIn profiles: Look up your interviewers to learn their background, role, and expertise. It hints at what they will focus on.

Company bio: If available, review the interviewer's bio on the company website for additional context on their responsibilities.

Understand their perspective

Technical vs. non-technical interviewers: A technical interviewer cares about your problem-solving process and technical depth; a non-technical interviewer focuses on teamwork and communication.

Hiring managers: Emphasize how your skills and experience align with the specific needs of their team.

Adjust your communication style

Formal vs. casual: if possible, match the interviewer's tone and adjust your style accordingly. But make sure to maintain your depth and authenticity. This is a useful trait, since matching the tone makes a conversation smoother.

Detail vs. big picture: Technical interviewers appreciate detailed explanations; senior managers want the big picture and overall impact.

Highlight relevant experiences

Tailored examples: Choose examples most relevant to the interviewer's role or department. It shows you understand their priorities.

Specific achievements: If an interviewer values certain skills, you can highlight achievements that demonstrate exactly those qualities.

> **Note**
>
> **Scenario**:
>
> you are interviewing with a technical lead and a hiring manager in the same loop. Here is the same project, told for each room:
>
> **Same project, two rooms**
>
> **To the technical lead**: "The feature had a performance bottleneck: page loads over three seconds at p95. I profiled the codebase, found the hot path in two unindexed queries and a chatty API, added targeted caching with staleness bounds, and cut p95 by 30 percent. Happy to go into the cache invalidation trade-offs."
>
> **To the hiring manager**: "I led the delivery of a feature that was at risk of missing its date. I kept three teams aligned through a weekly decision log, made the call to defer two nice-to-haves, and we shipped on schedule; engagement rose 20 percent in the first month. The deferred items shipped a sprint later."
>
> Same project, same person, both versions true. Only the level of detail changed for the audience, and that is what honest tailoring means.

Making a lasting impression

Leaving a strong impression is about more than answering questions well. It is also about demonstrating enthusiasm for the role, alignment with the company's values, and the contribution you will make to the team.

During the interview, the last 10-15 minutes are for you to ask questions. This is another crucial opportunity for you to make a lasting impression. You can ask about the future you would be joining, not facts the website already answers.

Some examples are: "Can you tell me more about the team I would be working with, and how this role fits the overall structure?", "What are the biggest challenges the team is facing, and how could I contribute to solving them?", "How do you see this role evolving over the next few years?" Questions like these show that you are reading the organization as carefully as it is reading you.

Then close warmly and specifically, i.e., one sentence on why this role, one on what you would contribute first, both in your own words. Authenticity beats polish here for a structural reason you now understand: the interviewer is about to write your packet, and a specific, sincere closing hands them quotable material. Performed enthusiasm gives them nothing to write down.

Summary

Big Tech behavioral interviews are not necessarily difficult because the questions are harder. They are difficult because the evaluation is more deliberate and structured. Understanding that alone puts you ahead of many candidates. This chapter took you beneath the surface of high-stakes interviews to the hidden drivers behind them, why core values and leadership principles are the actual scoring criteria rather than company branding, and how trained interviewers fill out scorecards while you are still mid-sentence, and who actually makes the final call after you leave the room.

OpenAI, Anthropic, and SpaceX now run similar processes with mission alignment scored formally, and you saw the hiring process end to end, including the level calibration that sets your offer. The goal was never a perfect answer; it was the right answer for this role, this company, and this moment in the conversation.

In the next chapter, we will widen the lens beyond any single interview. We will learn how to turn every interview, whatever its outcome, into career capital through different strategies and be on the other side of the table once the right opportunity presents itself.

References

[1] Wikipedia. "Big Tech." Wikipedia, The Free Encyclopedia. `https://en.wikipedia.org/wiki/Big_Tech`

[2] Axios. "MANGO is the new FAANG" October 15, 2025. `https://www.axios.com/2025/10/15/mango-faang-ai-tech-companies`

[3] Cambridge Dictionary. "Curveball." Cambridge University Press. `https://dictionary.cambridge.org/dictionary/english/curveball`

[4] Amazon. "About Amazon — Our Leadership Principles." `https://www.aboutamazon.com/about-us/leadership-principles`

[5] Google. "How We Hire." Google Careers. `https://www.google.com/about/careers/applications/how-we-hire/`

[6] IGotAnOffer. "Facebook (Meta) Interview Process: A Comprehensive Guide." https://igotanoffer.com/blogs/tech/facebook-interview-process

[7] Netflix. "Netflix Culture — Freedom & Responsibility." https://jobs.netflix.com/netflix-culture.pdf

[8] Interviewing.io. "Apple Interview Process: What to Expect and How to Prepare." https://interviewing.io/guides/hiring-process/apple

16

Demonstration to Evaluation of Behavioral Intelligence

Going through the interview process is not just hard; it sometimes shakes your confidence too. So much so that you doubt yourself, your credibility, the knowledge you built over days and late nights, and the experience you gained over years. We have seen this happen to people at every level, from young graduates walking into their first interview to seasoned professionals with 20, 30, or 35 years behind them. Self-doubt does not discriminate by title or tenure and finds everyone eventually, and underneath the nerves runs the same quiet question, i.e., am I actually good enough for this? The answer, almost always, is yes, as interview outcomes rarely provide a complete measure of a candidate's ability or potential.

This is the last chapter of the book, and it is about everything that happens once the interview itself is over. First, what to do the moment you walk out, whatever the result, from reflecting while it is fresh to following up well and asking for feedback. Then how those habits compound. Every process you run leaves you with sharper stories, a clearer read of the market, relationships worth keeping, and real leverage for the next negotiation. We will look at how to handle rejection, juggle several processes at once, weigh competing offers, and step into a new role with a strong first ninety days.

Then the chapter turns around. Once you are inside a company, sooner or later you will be asked to interview other people, and being good at it is part of being senior. We show you how to run a strong behavioral interview, the mistakes new interviewers make, and the part that surprises everyone.

Nothing sharpens your own answers faster than sitting on the other side of the table and scoring someone else's. That is where the two halves of this book meet. The behavioral intelligence you built to get hired is the same intelligence you use to hire well, and to keep growing long after the offer.

In this chapter, we will cover the following topics:

- A real candidate, real situation: what a rejection sometimes actually means
- Post-interview strategies: following up with intent, reflecting on your performance, seeking and using feedback, and strategizing your next opportunity
- Dealing with rejection, strategic networking, tracking multiple processes, and handling multiple offers
- Career capital: stories, market intelligence, relationships, and leverage
- Preparing for a strong onboarding with the L.E.A.D. framework
- Sitting on the other side: running interviews, with the common mistakes to avoid
- What scoring other candidates teaches you about your own answers

Let's start with a candidate's story to understand how every conversation can turn into a career asset even before you realize it.

Real candidate, real situation: A story worth sharing

Things do not always go as planned, and a career can take an unexpected turn. Sometimes you are sure you are ready for a promotion, and it does not come. Sometimes you have earned a raise or a bonus after a strong year, and it never shows up. And sometimes you walk out of an interview thinking you certainly did well, only to get a rejection.

This story shows how to respond when a situation does not go your way, and how to structure and adapt your behavior when things turn unpleasant. It begins right after Claire (a pseudonym), a software development manager (SDM), left Amazon.

> **Note**
>
> After moving on from Amazon in December 2025, Claire was certain that she would take only an executive role next. She was highly selective about the companies she wanted to work for, their tech stacks, and the scope of the work. Just before leaving Amazon, she interviewed for a role that felt exactly right. One after another, she did six interviews for the role, including with people in the C-suite. As the process wrapped up, she followed some practices she had set for herself, which you will read about later in this chapter.
>
> A few weeks later, HR called to offer her a different role, which she turned down; it was not what she wanted. She found it hard to believe that she had not been selected for the

> role she applied for. Within a minute of that call, she was disappointed. How could that be? As per her understanding, she was a perfect fit. As many candidates feel, she also thought that every conversation had ended with positive signals, clear synergies, and a strong desire to bring her on board. So, what went wrong? HR kept insisting that she accept the other role, and when she refused firmly, HR suggested at least a conversation to give it a chance, but Claire was clearly not interested.
>
> Six months later her phone buzzed with a message from a name she thought she recognized – it was the hiring manager for the position she had interviewed for. It had been almost six months since they last spoke, and she had moved on, accepting that she was probably not ready for that role and someone must have done better to get the position. The message, however, changed her perception forever.
>
> Claire had been selected. Her interviewers spoke highly of her and had wanted to hire her as soon as possible. She was not rejected. The role could not be offered to her because an internal candidate moved into it, for reasons that will surprise no one. The other role had been offered precisely because they wanted her inside the organization one way or another. Her decision to turn it down had been respected and understood, and now they had created another role like the one she originally wanted, and they were asking her to consider it.

There are many such stories we hear from candidates about rejection turning into another opportunity. Another one below from Jill shows the same:

In another instance, Jill Wilson applied for a Delivery Manager role at a startup and received a rejection within a few days. But immediately after, a direct email from HR asked whether she would be interested in a more senior position better suited to her profile.

Read this twice, if necessary, because it is the lesson we are trying to hand you with all the force we can:

> **Tip**
>
> Every time you didn't get a call from a company, every interview you did and did not hear back from, and every rejection you received may not be because you are less capable. Hiring decisions are influenced by many factors, and sometimes the outcome is shaped by circumstances outside your control.

We share these experiences because the outcome of your interviews is not always a simple boolean of selection or rejection. There is always a possibility that you will be matched with another suitable role. And having sat on the hiring side for years, we can confirm that hiring managers can also be disappointed when they cannot move forward with a strong candidate. Strong candidates are often remembered, and when the time comes, they get reconsidered for future roles. It also saves hiring managers from reviewing a fresh pile of resumes and investing more time, provided the candidate is still willing and available.

> *"It is not whether you get knocked down. It is whether you get up."*
>
> *—Vince Lombardi*

Post-interview strategies

The hiring process does not end exactly when you walk out of the room. How you handle it afterwards can strengthen your overall experience and keep the door open for future opportunities as depicted through the stories shared in the first section of this chapter. This section covers the strategies to use after the interview to leave a lasting positive impression, learn from the experience, and prepare for future opportunities. *Figure 16.1* brings these strategies together in one view. Each step, from your first debrief to weighing a final offer, is a way to keep the door open, learn from the experience, and prepare for what comes next.

Figure 16.1: Post-interview strategies

In the coming sections, we will look at each of these strategies in more detail.

Reflecting systematically on your performance

An interview can feel different once you walk away from it. You may remember the questions, what exactly you said, where you hesitated, or which answer led to an unexpected follow-up. This is why it is important to take a few minutes soon after the interview to write down what happened while the details are still fresh. Here are a few questions in *Table 16.1* that you can ask yourself and use as a template for an interview debrief:

Question	Your notes
What questions were asked?	
Which answers worked well? Did I choose the right example?	
Where did I struggle?	
Which follow-up questions surprised me?	
Did I give enough detail?	
Did I spend too much time anywhere?	
Which story should I improve?	
What would I answer differently next time?	
What should I add to my Story Bank?	
What will I do differently in my next interview?	

Table 16.1: Debrief Questions

Tip

Add your own questions to this as you go through the process. This is only a template to help you begin with.

Then ask yourself one simple question - if I answered this again tomorrow, what would I change? That answer usually teaches you more than guessing whether the interview went well or badly. The goal is to capture the learning while the experience is fresh and carry it into the next interview. Over time, these small debriefs become one of the best ways to strengthen your stories, sharpen your answers, and grow your comfort with questions you did not see coming.

Reflection on your performance lets you assess what went well, what could have been better, and how to prepare more effectively next time. It is a critical part of the learning process and of your growth as a professional. Once you are done with this, it leads to another important step specifically related to your story bank.

Refresh your story bank

Every assessment you go through is an opportunity to look back at the discussion you had and update two things from there. First, identify what helped you from the story bank and ensure you weigh those stories higher on your list. Second, add new stories for questions you did not already have covered in your story bank. This exercise helps you evaluate the completeness of your story bank and gives you an opportunity to add any new ideas from the latest hiring process.

This does not apply only to the behavioral stories but also applies to technical assessments such as coding interviews or a system design round. If there are problems you have not solved before, look for the solutions afterward and update your notes accordingly. Look closely at your stories as well. Did you choose the right example? Did you explain your own role clearly? Did the story show the scope and impact the role calls for? Were you able to reflect on what you learned, or did you stay too focused on what happened?

> **Note**
>
> As the Engineering Manager at Google shared in *Chapter 14*, he has maintained his story bank since 2007 and also explained how he recorded feedback from his conversations and about his skills. He started by capturing his notes on paper and later moved to digital formats. Today, he uses AI tools such as Google's NotebookLM to review his notes, identify recurring patterns, and surface areas for improvement. Over time, this practice of journaling has helped him recognize areas for growth and work on them gradually.

While your notes are still fresh, turn outward as well. The simplest way to stay in touch is to follow up.

Following up with intent

The simplest way to stay in touch, keep communication open, show appreciation, and reinforce your interest is a thank-you note to the respective people. It is a professional courtesy that can set you apart.

You can keep the note concise, sincere, and personalized by including:

- **Express gratitude:** thank the interviewer for their time. "Thank you for taking the time to meet with me today. I appreciate the opportunity to discuss how I can contribute to your team."
- **Highlight key points:** mention something specific from the interview that resonated with you. "I particularly enjoyed our discussion about the challenges your team faces with scaling the new product. I'm excited about the possibility of contributing my experience in [specific skill] to help address those challenges."

- **Reaffirm your interest:** close by restating your enthusiasm for the role. "I'm very enthusiastic about the prospect of joining [Company Name] and applying my skills to help your team achieve its goals."
- **Keep it short:** no more than four or five lines. The goal is to remind the interviewer of your strengths and stay top of mind.

Send the note within a day or two of your interview while it is still fresh in their minds. It signals promptness and thoughtfulness, and it keeps the positive impression fresh. Furthermore, if you have not heard back after a week or two, a polite follow-up email is fine.

Silence often means delay, not rejection. Express continued interest and ask about next steps. For example: "*Dear Sharon, I hope you're doing well. I wanted to follow up on my recent interview for the Engineering Manager position. I remain very interested in the opportunity to join Amazon and contribute to your team. I would appreciate any updates you can provide regarding the next steps in the process. Thank you again for your time and consideration. Best regards, Ann.*"

Seeking and using feedback

So, why does feedback matter? Asking for feedback after an interview, regardless of the outcome, is a valuable way to learn and improve. Constructive feedback can give you insight into how you were perceived, what worked well, and where you could improve. Keep in mind, though, that some companies may choose not to provide feedback. Here's how you can ask for feedback:

- **Express gratitude:** "Thank you once again for the opportunity to interview for the software engineering position."
- **Request feedback:** "I'm always looking to improve, and I would appreciate any feedback you could provide about my interview performance."
- **Be open-minded:** "I'm very open to constructive feedback as I continue to refine my skills and approach."
- **Handling negative feedback:** it can be tough to receive, but it is an invaluable tool for growth.
- **Stay constructive:** the purpose of feedback is to help you get better. Do not take it personally; treat it as an opportunity to learn.
- **Analyze and apply:** consider how to apply it to future interviews. If the feedback says you struggled with a specific type of problem, dedicate more practice time there.
- **Follow up:** if appropriate, send a brief note thanking the interviewer for the feedback and sharing how you plan to address it. It shows you are proactive and committed to improvement, and it can open doors at the firm later.

Strategizing your next opportunity

Treat every interview as a learning experience. Whether you succeed or not, each one is a stepping stone to strengthen your skills, refine your approach, and prepare better for the next opportunity.

Based on your reflections and feedback, update your plan. Prioritize the growth areas where you struggled; if dynamic programming tripped you up, allocate more practice there. But revisit your strong areas too, so you keep your edge. The balance builds a comprehensive skill set.

Set up mock interviews by:

- **Finding a partner:** a friend, mentor, or coach who will give honest, constructive feedback.
- **Simulating the environment:** treat the mock as the real thing. Dress appropriately, set up a quiet space, time your responses.
- **Recording and reviewing:** if possible, record your mocks. Reviewing the recording helps you spot issues in delivery, body language, and clarity.

You can also use **AI-powered practice tools** to simulate interviews and get immediate feedback on your responses. Current options include `Remasto`, which offers role-specific AI mock interviews with dynamic follow-up questions, and the live voice modes of general assistants such as `ChatGPT` or `Gemini`, which can role-play an interviewer using any question set you provide.

One word of caution here. AI can generate impressive-sounding language but you should try to resist it. Clear, simple, well-structured answers always outperform complex, over-engineered ones.

> Note
>
> **A simple AI test:**
>
> If you removed AI from the process entirely, could you still explain your decisions clearly, adapt your answers to different questions, and go deeper when challenged? If not, you are relying on AI too much. Your experiences, your critical thinking, and your creativity are what make you stand out. Use AI to prepare harder, and show up as yourself.

Not every process ends well, so you must be ready to deal with rejection as well.

Dealing with rejection

Rejection is a natural part of the search, and how you handle it matters. Accepting it gracefully demonstrates professionalism and resilience. A rejection is not a reflection of your worth; it is part of the journey toward the right fit, as you learned from Claire's story shared at the beginning of this chapter. Each rejection is an opportunity to grow. Reflect on what might have gone wrong and consider asking the interviewer for feedback.

Do not dwell. Update your resume, refine your skills, and keep applying for roles that excite you. The right opportunity will come, and you will be more prepared when it does.

Strategic networking post-interview

Even if you do not get the job, the people you met during the process may be worth staying connected to. If company policies allow it, connect with relevant people and keep the relationship genuine rather than reaching out only when you need something. Engage with their posts occasionally, share something relevant to their work, or reach out for advice when you have a genuine reason to do so. Over time, these small interactions can help build relationships and keep you on their radar for future opportunities.

Do not overlook alumni networks either. If a previous company has an active alumni community, join it and take part in events, discussions, and knowledge sharing. Alumni networks can lead to useful connections, advice, and job opportunities, but they are most valuable when you contribute to the community rather than simply looking for what you can get from it.

Tracking multiple interview processes

Keeping track of your applications keeps you organized and ensures timely follow-ups, so no opportunity slips through. A spreadsheet or dedicated app with columns for company, position, application date, interview dates, contacts, and follow-up status can help you monitor progress and stay on top of the search.

Dedicate some time to analyze trends: review the tracker periodically for patterns. If you keep reaching final rounds without offers, that points to your closing strategy, or to the questions you ask about the role and company.

Negotiation and offers

When you receive an offer, you should look beyond the salary. Consider the scope of the role, total compensation, benefits, work-life balance, company culture, travel requirements, and long-term growth opportunities. A simple pros-and-cons comparison can help you weigh the immediate benefits against your longer-term career goals. Choose the role that best aligns with your skills, values, and aspirations. If you decide to decline other offers, let those companies know promptly, thank them for their time, and leave the door open for future opportunities.

Negotiation is a normal part of the hiring process. Make your case professionally and support it with data. For example: "*Based on my research and experience, I believe a salary in the range of [amount] would be more aligned with the market. I'm excited about the opportunity to contribute to [Company Name] and would be happy to discuss how we can bridge the gap.*"

When it comes to negotiation, many candidates focus only on base salary. In reality, particularly at larger companies, base salary may be one of the least flexible components because it is often tied to internal pay bands. Other elements of an offer may have more room for negotiation. AI tools can also help you identify which components are worth targeting based on your situation. *Table 16.2* outlines the main components you can negotiate, the typical flexibility employers may have, and approaches you can use when negotiating each one.

Component	Flexibility	What to say
Base salary	Moderate: constrained by pay bands at larger companies	Anchor to market data. Cite Levels.fyi or Glassdoor explicitly. Ask for a specific number, not a range.
Signing bonus	High: a one-time cost that sidesteps pay band constraints	Ask for a signing bonus to bridge the gap if base cannot move. Frame it as offsetting what you are leaving behind.
Equity/RSUs (Restricted Stock Units)	Moderate to high, especially at startups and growth-stage companies	Ask for accelerated vesting, additional grant size, or a better strike price. Research the company's equity history first.
Start date	High: companies rarely have fixed start dates	Request a later start if you need it. Most companies would rather wait two weeks than lose a candidate they have chosen.
Remote/hybrid Work	High at most companies post-2024	Ask directly, clearly, and early in the negotiation. It is part of total compensation and should be treated as such.
Title/level	Low to moderate, often tied to band and headcount approval	Pursue only with a strong case. Leveling up at the start affects your trajectory, bonus targets, and equity grants long-term.

Table 16.2: What to negotiate and how

A successful negotiation can improve both your compensation and your satisfaction with the role. However, there is no guarantee that every negotiation will lead to a better offer, so approach it thoughtfully and know what matters most to you.

More importantly, the value of an interview process does not end when you accept or decline an offer. Each process can leave you with feedback, new relationships, a stronger reputation, and greater leverage for the opportunities that follow.

Career capital: Stories, market intelligence, relationships, leverage

Whatever the outcome of an interview, you can walk away with something that lasts beyond the result. Think of it as career capital. Over time, each interview can add to four things: your stories, your understanding of the market, your relationships, and your leverage.

The first is your story bank. Real interviews, follow-up questions, and even unexpected silences test your stories in ways that solo practice cannot. If a story falls flat in the third round, you know what needs fixing before the next conversation. The second is market intelligence. After going through a few interview processes, you start to see what skills companies are looking for, how they define levels, and what they are willing to pay. That is useful firsthand information.

The third is relationships. An interviewer or recruiter may not be able to offer you a role today, but a good conversation can still leave an impression. You may cross paths again months or even years later. The fourth is leverage. Keeping track of feedback and having other opportunities gives you more confidence and options when it is time to negotiate.

None of this happens automatically. The reflection and tracking habits from the previous section are what turn each interview into something you can use later. Claire's call six months later was a good example. The interview had not resulted in an offer, but the connection had stayed with her. That is the point - even when an interview ends in rejection, the experience does not have to end there.

Not every process ends in a no. When one ends in the offer you wanted, the work shifts from winning the role to starting it well. Preparing for a strong onboarding is that next step.

Prepare for a strong onboarding

This is where the excitement begins. Once you have accepted an offer, preparing for onboarding is the next step, i.e., familiarizing yourself with the company's tools, culture, and expectations before day one.

A useful way to approach onboarding is to think beyond simply completing a 30-60-90 day plan. Your first few months are about learning the environment, building relationships, aligning expectations, and then delivering meaningful value. The L.E.A.D. framework provides a simple way to structure this transition: Learn, Establish, Align, and Deliver.

Note

The L.E.A.D. framework

L – Learn before you change

Understand the business, product, customers, architecture, team, metrics, and existing priorities. Ask questions before forming strong opinions.

E – Establish relationships

Map the people you need to work with and build relationships early. This includes your manager, peers, team members, technical partners, and key business stakeholders.

A – Align on expectations

Draft provisional goals before joining, then discuss them with your manager after you understand the team's actual priorities. Agree on what success looks like at 30, 60, and 90 days.

D – Deliver early value

Look for one or two meaningful areas where you can contribute early. Avoid trying to change everything at once. A small, visible improvement can help establish credibility while you continue learning.

Once you are inside and settled, the tables turn. You are no longer the candidate being assessed. You are now ready to be part of the team making those assessments.

Sit on the other side: Interviewing as a skill

Chapter 15 showed you how deliberately the Big Tech companies train interviewers, calibrate them, and structure their decisions. All of that machinery runs on eligible and trained volunteers like engineers, managers, and specialists who interview on top of their day jobs. If you join one of these companies, or any company that takes hiring seriously, the invitation is coming, and how you respond shapes more than your calendar.

First, hiring is one of the most important responsibilities professionals may take on. The right hire can contribute to a team for years, while a poor hiring decision can affect the team and business long after the interview is over. Second, interviewing is a decoding practice of the purest kind.

You learn what a scorecard rewards by filling one in, and after a dozen interviews you can no longer be surprised by one, because you know the machinery from inside. Third, it can help build your reputation within the organization. Experienced interviewers become trusted by recruiting and leadership, and opportunities such as Amazon's Bar Raiser program can give you visibility beyond your day-to-day role.

When you start interviewing for the first time, ask to shadow two or three interviews before you run one, take whatever training your company offers, and treat your first solo loops as a skill you are learning rather than a chore you are absorbing. The candidate opposite you is having one of the more consequential hours of their year and they deserve an interviewer who has prepared.

> *"I am convinced that nothing we do is more important than hiring and developing people. At the end of the day you bet on people, not on strategies."*
>
> *—Lawrence Bossidy, Execution (2002)*

Running a strong behavioral interview

The case for structure is not just a matter of preference. Decades of research have shown that structured interviews are better at predicting job performance than informal, unstructured conversations. A widely cited 1998 study found that structured interviews were significantly more reliable predictors of job performance than unstructured ones [1].

The reason is fairly simple. A structured interview forces you to weigh evidence against defined criteria rather than leaving the decision to gut feeling. This is why companies that hire at scale, including Google, use defined questions, scoring guides, and interviewer calibration instead of leaving the conversation entirely to individual judgment [2]. Everything below shows how to put that structure into practice.

Before the room. Strong interviews are designed, not improvised, and the design starts with your assignment. In a structured loop you own specific dimensions, perhaps ownership and conflict, while colleagues cover the rest; freelancing across all of them produces a shallow packet and duplicated questions. Choose two primary questions with probe chains behind them rather than a list of ten, because two stories examined deeply yield more signal than five summaries.

Spend ten minutes with the resume and write two probes only this candidate could answer. And know what good looks like at the target level before you start. An answer that would impress you from a graduate should not clear the bar for a senior hire, which is the calibration lens from *Chapter 14* pointed the other way.

> **Note**
>
> **Before you walk in**
>
> The dimensions you own, in writing. Two primary questions, with three probes behind each. Two resume-specific probes. The level bar, agreed with the hiring manager or rubric. A clock you can see.

In the room. The ratio to hold is eighty-twenty, which means that the candidate talks, you steer. Open with one broad question, then probe downward - what did you do, as distinct from the team; what alternatives did you weigh; what would the other person in that story say. Take notes on what the candidate actually said and did, rather than your own impressions. You do not need to capture their exact words; summarize the response accurately and record the specific evidence behind your assessment.

Watch the clock on the candidate's behalf. Going deep on two stories beats skimming five, and the last five minutes belong to their questions. Remember that you are the company for this hour. Candidates retell their interviews for years, and previous chapters argued that every interview builds the candidate's network and market intelligence; you are now the other side of that ledger.

The write-up. Write your feedback the same day, while the quotes are alive. Lead with evidence, then judgment - the quote, the behavior it shows, the score it earns against your assigned dimension. Vote independently before reading anyone else's feedback, exactly as the packet-based companies in the previous chapter require, because the value of your signal is its independence. The standard worth holding is this - a stranger reading your write-up should be able to re-derive your vote without meeting the candidate. That is what hiring committees do, and write-ups that meet the bar are what make them work.

Figure 16.2 places the three phases side by side; the shift from designing, to steering, to deciding is the whole method in one view. You saw this scorecard from the candidate's side in *Chapter 15* and now you are the one filling it in.

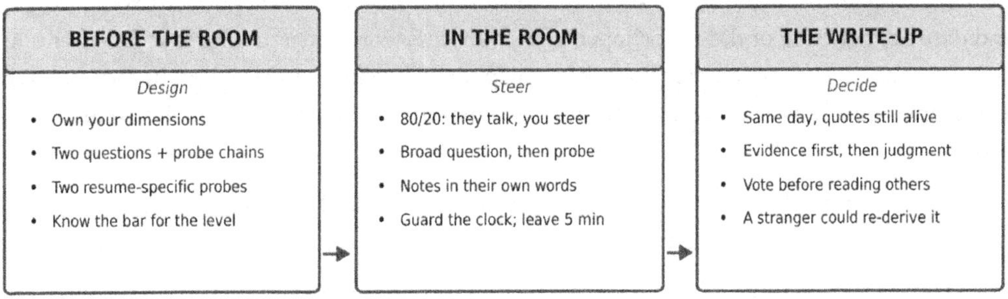

Figure 16.2: Anatomy of a strong behavioral interview.

The mistakes new interviewers make

Many experienced interviewers make a few mistakes, especially early on. The key is to recognize them and reduce them with practice. Before we get into the details, let's look at a few research findings that reveal how these biases can show up.

> **Note**
>
> In 1920 the psychologist Edward Thorndike found that officers rating their soldiers let one general impression influence every specific trait, and gave the effect its name (Source: Thorndike, Journal of Applied Psychology, 1920).
>
> Nearly a century later, the same pattern was still evident in hiring. In 2015, Laszlo Bock, who built Google's hiring practices, observed that "*the interviewer spends the first ten seconds forming an impression and then spends the rest of the interview confirming it*" [3].

Different settings, same human tendency: once we form an early impression, we naturally look for evidence that supports it. It is easy to form an opinion about someone early in an interview and then see everything else through that lens. We may naturally feel more comfortable with people who remind us of ourselves, or let one particularly strong or weak answer influence our view of the rest of the conversation. Sometimes the decision is almost made in the first few minutes, and the rest of the interview becomes a search for evidence to support it. A better approach is to keep an open mind and assess each area on what the candidate actually demonstrates.

The way we conduct the conversation matters just as much. Leading questions can tell candidates what answer we are looking for, while an overly aggressive approach can make even a capable candidate nervous and less able to show what they can do. Ask clear, open questions and give the candidate time to think.

The same applies to vague ideas such as "culture fit." If you cannot point to something the candidate actually said or did that shaped your view, it is worth questioning that judgment. And when someone has changed careers, taken a gap, or followed an unusual path, focus on what they learned and how they worked rather than making assumptions from the shape of their resume.

These common mistakes happen often enough to recognize and watch for. *Table 16.3* lists each one, along with what to look for and how to correct it.

Mistake	How it shows in the room	The fix
Mini-me bias	You warm to the candidate who resembles you and read familiarity as competence	Score against the dimension, not your own reflection
First-five-minutes verdict	You decide early, then spend the hour confirming it	Hold the vote open; the late-blooming answer is the signal early verdicts destroy
Halo and horns	One brilliant or weak answer floods every other dimension	Score each dimension on its own evidence
Leading the witness	Long setups telegraph the answer and produce a performance	Ask short, open questions and let silence work
Interrogation mode	Pressure makes an anxious candidate produce less evidence	Keep it a conversation the candidate feels safe inside
The vibe vote	A culture-fit verdict with no evidence behind it	If you cannot quote the moment, score against defined values instead
Grilling the bend in the path	You treat a gap or a career change with suspicion	Probe the behavior inside the story, not the shape of the resume

Table 16.3: Interviewer mistakes at a glance

Here is the payoff this chapter promised. The moment you start evaluating candidates, you also start evaluating your own habits through a completely different lens.

What the other side teaches you about your own answers

After ten interviews as the scorer, you hear the failure patterns everywhere - the "we" that never resolves into an "I," the impact that never gets a number, the story that ends at the result with no reflection behind it. Hearing them in others is the fastest cure for producing them yourself, and interviewers routinely report that their own answers sharpened more from scoring candidates than from any preparation book, including this one.

You also stop fearing probes, because you now write them. You learn from the inside that the interviewers want candidates to provide enough evidence and hope they succeed. Furthermore, feedback writing turns out to be story bank editing in disguise. Every time you reduce an hour of conversation to evidence, behavior, and judgment, you are rehearsing exactly the compression your own stories need.

You can use a practical cadence by volunteering for two interviews a month, shadowing a stronger interviewer each quarter, and spending five minutes after each session scoring yourself - what would you have rated your own questions, your notes, your write-up? That habit is behavioral intelligence practiced at its source, and it compounds on both sides of the table.

Summary

Most people treat the interview as the finish line. We want you to see it as a turning point instead. Whether you get the offer or not, what you do next is what compounds. In this chapter you built a system for exactly that, reflecting while the details are fresh, following up with intent, asking for feedback, and folding all of it back into your story bank so every process leaves you sharper than the last.

We looked at how that work accumulates into real career capital, stronger stories, a clearer read of the market, relationships worth keeping, and the leverage to negotiate from strength. We also covered how to handle rejection without reading it as a verdict, how to manage several processes and competing offers at once, and how to step into a new role with a focused first ninety days.

Then the table turned. Once you are inside a company, you become the one asking the questions, and we showed you how to run a structured interview, how to catch the biases that trip up new interviewers, and why scoring someone else is the fastest way to sharpen your own answers. That is the quiet theme of this whole book. The behavioral intelligence you built to get hired is the same intelligence that helps you hire well, work with people, and keep growing long after the offer is signed. Careers are long, and the people who go furthest are not the ones who never get knocked back. They are the ones who treat every conversation, the good ones and the hard ones, as something to learn from and carry forward.

References

[1] Schmidt, F. L., & Hunter, J. E. (1998). "The Validity and Utility of Selection Methods in Personnel Psychology: Practical and Theoretical Implications of 85 Years of Research Findings." Psychological Bulletin, 124(2), 262–274.

[2] Google re:Work Editorial Team, "A Guide to Structured Interviewing for Better Hiring Practices," Google re:Work, updated Mar. 2026. https://rework.withgoogle.com/intl/en/guides/a-guide-to-structured-interviewing-for-better-hiring-practices

[3] Bock, L. (2015). Work Rules!: Insights from Inside Google That Will Transform How You Live and Lead. https://www.goodreads.com/book/show/22875447-work-rules

17

Unlock Your Exclusive Benefits

Your copy of this book includes the following exclusive benefits:

Complete Code Bundle

Download the full source code for this book's examples and projects.

DRM-Free PDF Version

Download DRM-free PDF and ePub copies of this book.

7-Day Packt Library Access

Get 7-day unlimited access to 8,000+ books and videos. No credit card required.

Available for first-time Packt+ trial users only.

Next-Gen Reader Access

Read this book on Packt Reader with progress sync, dark mode and note-taking.

Follow the guide below to unlock them. The process takes only a few minutes and needs to be completed once.

Unlock this Book's Free Benefits in 3 Easy Steps

Step 1

Keep your purchase invoice ready for *Step 3*. If you have a physical copy, scan it using your phone and save it as a PDF, JPG, or PNG.

For more help on finding your invoice, visit `https://www.packtpub.com/en-us/unlock?step=1`.

> **Note**
>
> If you bought this book directly from Packt, no invoice is required. After *Step 2*, you can access your exclusive content right away.

Step 2

Scan the QR code or go to `packtpub.com/unlock`.

On the page that opens (similar to *Figure 17.1* on desktop), search for this book by name and select the correct edition.

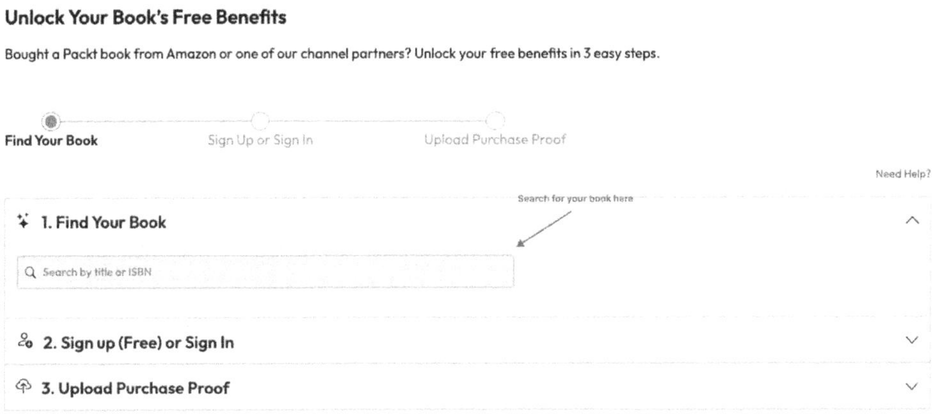

Figure 17.1 – Packt unlock landing page on desktop

Step 3

After selecting your book, sign in to your Packt account or create one for free. Then upload your invoice (PDF, PNG, or JPG, up to 10 MB). Follow the on-screen instructions to finish the process.

Need Help

If you get stuck and need help, visit `https://www.packtpub.com/unlock-benefits/help` for a detailed FAQ on how to find your invoices and more. This QR code will take you to the help page.

Note

If you are still facing issues, reach out to `customercare@packt.com`.

Appendix

Quiz answers

Chapter 1: The Art and Science of System Design

Q1: B, system design ensures scalability, reliability, and performance at scale.

Q2: C, debugging syntax errors is a coding concern, not a system-design goal.

Q3: B, microservices are independent services that communicate over APIs.

Q4: D, a distributed system lets multiple independent machines work together as one.

Q5: B, a cluster of web servers behind a load balancer spans multiple machines.

Q6: B, event-driven components react to events and communicate via message passing.

Q7: C, event-driven systems give a high degree of decoupling and real-time responsiveness.

Chapter 2: Concepts Refresher: Knowledge Bites

Q1: B, HTTP/3 runs over QUIC (which itself runs over UDP).

Q2: B, QUIC establishes connections faster, often in 0-RTT or 1-RTT, and reduces latency.

Q3: A, QUIC multiplexes streams without head-of-line blocking, unlike TCP.

Q4: B, throughput is measured in operations or bits per second.

Q5: B, vertical scaling adds CPU/RAM to a single machine (scaling up).

Q6: C, latency is the delay before a response is received.

Q7: B, high throughput with high latency means many requests are handled but each one takes longer.

Q8: B, failover is the automatic switch to a standby system when the primary fails.

Q9: D, check first whether the load balancer is distributing requests evenly.

Q10: C, resources are within limits and users are spread across regions, so network latency from geographic distance is the likely cause (a CDN or edge presence is the fix).

Q11: A, in a stateless system each request carries all the information needed to process it.

Chapter 3: Distributed Systems: Algorithms, Techniques, and Patterns

Q1: B, Snowflake generates globally unique, time-ordered IDs across distributed nodes.

Q2: A, B, and C, a Snowflake ID encodes a timestamp, a machine/worker ID, and a sequence number (not a database ID).

Q3: D, Raft roles are Follower, Candidate, and Leader; there is no Coordinator role.

Q4: B, Raft elects a leader and reaches consensus on a replicated log.

Q5: B, horizontal scaling adds more nodes to share the load (scaling out).

Q6: B, in a token bucket, a request that arrives with no available token is rejected/dropped.

Q7: B, the maximum burst equals the bucket size, which is 10.

Q8: D, the sliding window avoids the sharp boundary spikes of fixed-window counters and is smoother.

Q9: A and B, a queue or a sorted list of timestamps is typically used (a plain list also works; a fixed array is least suitable).

Q10: C, a Snowflake generator produces globally unique, time-ordered IDs at scale.

Q11: B, the worker-ID field is 5 bits, giving 32 machines per data center (with another 5 bits for the data center, 1,024 machines in total).

Q12: B, nodes are kept sorted on the ring, so a binary search locates the node in O(log N).

Q13: B, on a node crash or removal consistent hashing remaps only a fraction of keys, unlike modulo-based partitioning.

Q14: A, you traverse the ring clockwise to the next node.

Q15: B, consistent hashing minimizes remapping, and therefore cache misses, when nodes are added or removed.

Chapter 4: The Building Blocks of System Design

Q1: B, virtual nodes spread each physical node across many ring positions, reducing hotspots and balancing load.

Q2: B, least connections routes to the server with the fewest active connections.

Q3: B, synchronous replication gives strong consistency but can reduce availability, since a write waits for replicas.

Q4: D, replication improves availability and fault tolerance.

Q5: A, weighted round robin sends more traffic to higher-capacity servers.

Q6: C, session management is an application concern; persistence, query support, and indexing are database traits.

Q7: D, Oracle is relational; MongoDB, Cassandra, and Redis are NoSQL.

Q8: C, MongoDB is a document store.

Q9: B, a graph database fits social-network graphs.

Q10: D, document databases store XML or JSON-like structures.

Q11: C, under a partition, CAP forces a trade-off between consistency and availability.

Q12: B, PACELC adds the else case: it distinguishes the trade-off during a partition from the one in normal operation.

Q13: B, with no partition, PACELC weighs latency against consistency.

Q14: B, a relational (ACID) database suits financial transactions.

Q15: B, a graph database suits a recommendation engine built on relationships.

Q16: D, MongoDB's flexible schema fits a catalog whose fields vary by product type.

Q17: B, Neo4j (a graph DB) efficiently traverses friends-of-friends relationships.

Q18: A, MongoDB gives quick access to JSON-like user documents.

Q19: A, a relational, ACID-compliant DB keeps inventory counts correct under concurrent updates.

Q20: B, rejected (rate-limited) requests return HTTP 429 Too Many Requests.

Q21: C, during rate-limiting, the service reports remaining quota information to clients through HTTP response headers.

Q22: A, the first bit is the sign (signed) bit, kept 0 so the ID stays positive (Refer to chapter-3 for details).

Q23: C, the 10-bit machine identifier combines a data center id with a machine id (5 bits each). (Refer to chapter-3 for details)

Q24: A, True; in a point-to-point queue each message is consumed by exactly one consumer.

Q25: B, a point-to-point queue delivers each message to one consumer, while pub-sub can deliver to many subscribers.

Chapter 5: Cross-Cutting Concerns: Security and Observability

Q1: B, without proper signing/verification an attacker can tamper with the claims inside the token.

Q2: B, the access token is for authorization (what you can access); the ID token is for authentication (who you are).

Q3: B, JWT access tokens are short-lived and self-contained; refresh tokens are long-lived and used only to obtain new access tokens.

Q4: C, the resource server serves protected resources and validates access tokens.

Q5: B, the authorization server issues the access token.

Q6: A and B, rate limiting rejects requests past a threshold, while throttling queues or delays them instead of rejecting outright.

Q7: B, publish-subscribe fans a stream out to many consumers, which suits logging and monitoring pipelines.

Q8: A for dropped, B for delayed; dropping the extra requests is rate limiting, delaying them is throttling.

Q9: B, the four golden signals are latency, traffic, errors, and saturation.

Q10: C, 99.99% over a 30-day month leaves 0.01% of (30 x 24 x 60) minutes; which is about 4.3 minutes.

Chapter 6: Elements and the Method to Design a System

Q1: B, availability and consistency trade off under a network partition (CAP).

Q2: B, durability guarantees patient data survives failures and is never lost.

Q3: C, throughput is the requests per second a system can sustain (a performance measure).

Q4: B, scalability lets the system absorb sudden growth in traffic.

Q5: A, latency is the delay before a new post appears in the feed.

Q6: C, durability prevents permanent loss of user-generated content.

Q7: B, seeing stale likes and comments is a consistency problem.

Build Your Story Bank: Behavioral Intelligence

Chapter 12: The Signal Beneath the Stories

Drawing on the seven behavioral dimensions and the decode, demonstrate, adapt model.

1. Problem-solving. Tell me about the toughest, most unclear problem you have owned, where the right answer was hard to see. How did you approach it?

2. Leadership without authority. Tell me about a decision you led across functional teams you did not manage. What did you do when a more senior person pushed back?

3. Teamwork. Tell me about working closely with a peer you did not naturally get along with. How did you deal with the friction and still deliver the work?

4. Adaptability (AI). Tell me about a time a change in your field, such as new AI tools, forced you to drop a plan you were working on. How did you decide what to keep and what to let go?

5. Time management (AI). Tell me about a time you chose to drop or delay something important on purpose. How did you decide, and where did AI or automation help you save time if it did?

6. Achievement. Tell me about a standard uplift you did when no one was watching or measuring it. Why did it matter, and what was the outcome?

7. Communication. Tell me about a time you had to explain the same complex idea to an engineer, an executive, and a customer. How did you change it for each without losing the point?

8. Reading the real need (AI). Tell me about a time what the business asked for was different from what it actually needed. How did you spot the difference, and where did data or AI help or mislead you, if it did?

Chapter 13: The Power of Behavioral Intelligence at Work

Drawing on conflict and the 4-D model, risk and the risk heatmap, the 9-Box, DORA metrics, and stakeholder management.

9. Conflict. Tell me about a conflict rooted in values between two strong people, where there was no clean compromise. How did you resolve it, and what did it cost the relationship?

10. Risk and trade-offs. Tell me about a big decision you made when the outcome was uncertain. How did you weigh the likelihood of the risk against its potential impact? What risk did you knowingly accept, and how did you explain it to leadership?

11. Performance and talent. Tell me about managing a strong performer who had become a problem for the team or a senior person who was struggling. How did you decide what to do?

12. Measuring productivity (AI). Tell me about a time you had to prove your team's productivity or the value of a new tool, such as AI coding assistants. How did you measure it honestly, and what did the numbers actually show?

13. Stakeholder management. Tell me about a complex project with many stakeholders pulling in different directions. How did you work out who mattered most, and how did you handle a powerful one with a hidden agenda?

14. Influence without authority. Tell me about a cross-team effort that stalled because no one clearly owned it. How did you create clarity and get it moving again?

Chapter 14: From Experience to Signal: Frameworks and the Story Bank

Drawing on STAR, STAR+R, CAR, CARL, SOAR, PAR, level calibration, and the STAMP method.

15. Reflection. Tell me about a decision you would make differently today. What exactly did you learn, and where have you used that lesson since?

16. Learning from failure. Tell me about a failure that changed how you work and the deeper lesson it taught you.

17. Impact. Tell me about a level above work you did and are most proud of, its size, the trade-offs, and its lasting result.

18. Working at a higher level. Tell me about a time you shaped the problem itself rather than carrying out a plan someone else set, changing the direction of a system, a team, or a strategy. How did you work at that level?

19. A non-linear path. Tell me about a big change in your career, moving industry or role, or a gap, and how your skills carried over. How do you present that change as a strength?

20. Working with AI (AI). Tell me about a time you used AI to improve how you worked. What did you delegate to AI, what did you handle yourself, and how did you validate its output?

Chapter 15: Behind the Big Tech Bar: Core Values and Leadership Principles

Drawing on the core values and leadership principles used across Big Tech companies.

21. Ownership. Tell me about something you owned from start to finish that was outside your formal role, and how did you balance it with your direct role?

22. Customer focus. Tell me about a time you stood up for the customer against internal pressure, cost, or a deadline. What did you give up, and what happened?

23. Bias for action. Tell me about an important call you made quickly with incomplete information. How did you keep it possible to undo if you were wrong, and what happened?

24. Delivering under constraint. Tell me about delivering an important result after your resources, team size, or timeline were cut.

25. Disagree and commit. Tell me about a time you disagreed with a senior leader's direction, said so clearly, and then committed. How did you handle being overruled?

26. Earning trust. Tell me about a time you had to give hard news to leadership or a customer or own a serious mistake in the open.

27. Raising the standard (AI). Tell me about a time you raised the quality standard on your team, in hiring, in code, or in how work gets done. How are you thinking about keeping that standard high as AI-generated work becomes common?

Chapter 16: Demonstration to Evaluation of Behavioral Intelligence

Drawing on post-interview reflection, career capital, negotiation, onboarding, and interviewing others.

28. Bouncing back. Tell me about a big career setback, a rejection or a missed promotion, and what you did in the months after.

29. The first ninety days. Tell me how you settled in and earned credibility when stepping into a new senior role or team before. What did you choose to do in the first few days?

30. Interviewing others (AI). Tell me about a hiring decision you influenced as an interviewer or hiring manager. How did you tell a genuinely strong answer from a polished one that might have been AI-assisted?

31. Coaching people (AI). Tell me about a time you coached someone to grow, including helping them use AI well without leaning on it too much.

Other Books You May Enjoy

If you enjoyed this book, you may be interested in these other books by Packt:

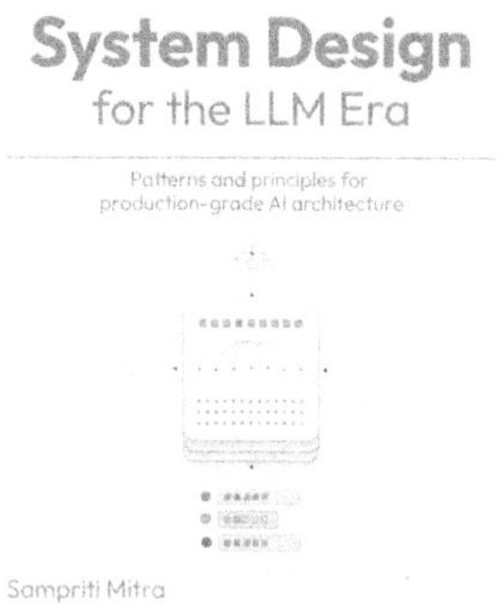

System Design for the LLM Era

Sampriti Mitra

ISBN: 978-1-80778-993-0

- Architect a complete, production-grade AI-powered system from scratch
- Design and mitigate the unique challenges of LLM APIs, like high latency and cost
- Implement key software engineering patterns like circuit breakers and rate limiting for AI systems
- Choose the right databases and data models for AI applications, including vector search engines
- Build a scalable and resilient system that can handle high load and ensure user privacy

The Generative AI Career Masterplan

Dr. Ali Arsanjani, Sadid Hasan, Maxime Labonne, Andreas Horn, Leonid Kuligin

ISBN: 978-1-80669-145-6

- Understand the global impact of Generative and Agentic AI on jobs and industries
- Master key GenAI Agentic AI concepts for any professional background
- Identify your best-fit AI career path and transferable skills
- Build familiarity with LlamaIndex, Haystack, Hugging Face, and core RAG workflows
- Build an AI-enhanced personal brand using the 5-Layer LinkedIn Strategy and Portfolio Showcase Framework
- Apply ethical and responsible AI principles and governance in real-world practice
- Create a lifelong learning and upskilling roadmap for sustained growth

Packt is searching for authors like you

If you're interested in becoming an author for Packt, please visit authors.packt.com and apply today. We have worked with thousands of developers and tech professionals, just like you, to help them share their insight with the global tech community. You can make a general application, apply for a specific hot topic that we are recruiting an author for, or submit your own idea.

Share your thoughts

Once you've read *System Design and Behavioral Intelligence*, we'd love to hear your thoughts! Scan the QR code below to go straight to the Amazon review page for this book and share your feedback.

https://packt.link/r/1808344057

Your review is important to us and the tech community and will help us make sure we're delivering excellent quality content.

Index

C

D

E

F

G

H

I

J

K

L

T

U

V

W

Made in the USA
Monee, IL
08 November 2026

68142657R00282